TROTTER AIR GETS YOU THERE

PARRY

Rodney Charlton Trotter (DIC)
Head of computer section

Parry Printing, Peckham, London

БРУТ ИМПЗРИДП

MONT CHERNOBYL
CHAMPAGNE

MC 744043

1995

12 X 1 Litre

FROM THE VINYARDS
OF THE UKRAINE

Last Will &
Testament of

Albert Gladstone

Trotter

PECKHAM
Spring Water

1 litre ℮

BOTTLED AT
SOURCE

STILL
From an Ancient Natural Source

SOUTH LONDON & LOCAL, VOCAL WEEKLY

Peckham Echo

Thursday July 5 2000

DELIVERED
TO YOUR DOOR
Telephone:
0207 946 0005

PUBLIC OUTRAGE AT PLANS FOR WASTE SITE

Plans to create a cemetery at the old amenity tip

Real life Lassie

BBC Books, an imprint of
Ebury Publishing
20 Vauxhall Bridge Road,
London SW1V 2SA

BBC Books is part of the Penguin Random House
group of companies whose addresses can be found
at global.penguinrandomhouse.com

Penguin
Random House
UK

First published by BBC Books in 2021
www.penguin.co.uk

This book is published to accompany the
television series entitled *Only Fools and Horses*
first broadcast on BBC One in 1981.

A CIP catalogue record for this book is available
from the British Library
ISBN 9781785947537
Deluxe Edition ISBN: 9781785947759

Commissioning Editor: Yvonne Jacob
Editors: Joanna Stenlake and Bethany Wright
Designer: Mike Jones

Printed and bound in Italy by Printer Trento

The authorised representative in the EEA is Penguin
Random House Ireland, Morrison Chambers, 32
Nassau Street, Dublin D02 YH68

Penguin Random House is committed to a
sustainable future for our business, our readers
and our planet. This book is made from Forest
Stewardship Council® certified paper.

MIX
Paper from
responsible sources
FSC® C018179

ACKNOWLEDGMENTS:

This book wouldn't have been possible without the
contribution of Perry Aghajanoff and the *Only Fools
and Horses* Appreciation Society's collection.

John Sullivan interviews originally conducted for
The *Only Fools and Horses* DVD collection.

BBC Studios, Jill Baker, Susan Belbin, Vas Blackwood,
Ray Blake, John Challis, Peter Clayton,
Michelle Dewar, Andy Dewar, Kerrie
Doogan, Tony Dow, Sarah Duncan,
Caroline Ellis, Antoni Corone, Treva
Etienne, Michael Fenton Stevens,
Mandie Fletcher, Jillianne Foot, Chris
Fry, Marcus Hearn, Tim Hines,
David Hitchcock, Joan Hodges,
Sue Holderness, Olivia Hubbard,
Graham Jarvis, Heather Jones,
Alistair McGown, Rosalind Lloyd,
Graham Lough, Alex McIntyre,
Chris McNeill, Patrick Murray,
Sheree Murphy, Ian Napier,
Rachael Oakley, Tessa Peake-
Jones, Adrian Pegg, Dawn
Perllman, John Pierce Jones, Jae
Pickles, Andrew Pixley, Nayef
Rashed, Mic Rolph, Jill Shardlow,
Paul Simpson, Stuart Snaith,
Jeff Stevenson, Nick Stringer,
Gwyneth Strong, William
Thomas, James Tizzard,
Chris Wadsworth, Josephine
Welcome, Richard Webber.

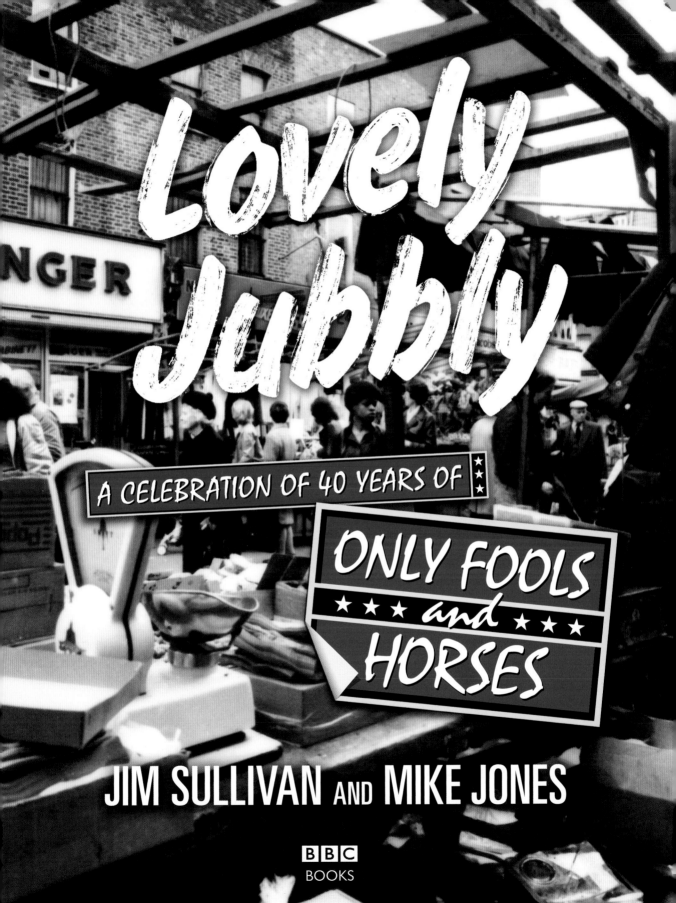

Lovely Jubbly

A CELEBRATION OF 40 YEARS OF

ONLY FOOLS *and* HORSES

JIM SULLIVAN AND MIKE JONES

BBC BOOKS

CONTENTS

INTRODUCTION ★★★

Au revoir. Derek Trotter here, bidding you a warm and cushty welcome to this official celebration marking 40 years of the life and times of the Trotters of Peckham. Now if that ain't bonnet de douche, I don't know what is!

A lot has changed since Trotters Independent Traders first set out on the road to fame and fortune.

At the time we were just a small family firm with big dreams. The matriarch of the family, my dear Mum, Joan, had long since departed (she died) and the last time I'd seen my old man, Reg, was on a wanted poster printed in 1965.

Anyway, back to the firm:

There was me, the ambitious and good-looking chairman of the board, you know, charm like laser beams, winning smile, own teeth and all that game. I was the founder and driving force behind the whole enterprise. On top of that, I was (and still am) the external optimist, and I knew deep down in my heart of hearts that no matter what life threw at us, one day we'd make it and become millionaires.

Then there was Rodney, my moist-behind-the-ears and suspiciously tall and dippy younger brother.

Also known, among other things, as 'Peckham's conscience', he was very much a diamond in the rough that required frequent polishing, so much so that to this day I'm still not quite sure what his role in the firm was. Over the years he had more titles than Waterstones, everything from Financial Advisor to Director of Sales and Commercial Development to Chief Car Cleaner. Nothing ever really stuck. He did have two GCEs, one in maths and one in art, but the only time they came in handy was when I asked him to count some tins of paint.

There was also Grandad, our old and frequently comatose... well, Grandad. Every now and then he'd prise himself out of his armchair and do what he could to help, usually when the telly was at the menders or his Nobby Stiles were

playing up. When we lost Grandad (we didn't actually lose him, he died) our great uncle Albert joined the team. And whilst his long and winding tales of a life spent mostly on (and under) the ocean waves proved a great incentive when you just wanted to zone out and give the old filbert a break, it's fair to say his contribution to the business side of things was lacking somewhat. Then again, he would lug a box or two around if you blackmailed him with enough brandy. There's not a day goes by I don't miss the old sods. God rest their souls.

Now, in order for you to fully grasp what lies ahead (or behind... whichever way you look at it I s'pose), I first need to transpose you back in time to where it all started. It was the beginning of a new era: an imperfect time, granted, but there were still reasons to be cheerful. The seventies had just ended and we were enjoying the fruits of the common market, which – as a man who's always been partial to a bit of the par les vous the old Francais – was right up my street! In many ways everything felt right with the world. Hot summers were still just hot summers, Tizer still tasted like Tizer, and breaking news was still breaking. Oh, and everyone tolerated gluten (seriously, back then I'd never even heard of celeriacs, let alone met one!).

Yes, you could say that overall it was a more innocent and straightforward time and that people in general were a lot less frail and... well, to put it politely – dippy! Of course, there was none of this social-media lark: no 'smart' devices, no Zoom sessions and no apps to download (back then 'Angry Birds' had an entirely different meaning). This was a time when there were actual communities and people actually went outside and looked at each other when they talked. Don't get me wrong, there were still plenty of dipsticks about, it's just that without the internet there was no way for them to consolidate and inflict their dipstickishness on everyone else. We only had four television channels and two of them were usually on the blink, so when pandemics came along people

6

either didn't get the memo or they just put their heads down and ploughed on (I don't know about anyone else, but I always found a tub of Vicks and a twice-weekly mutton vindaloo was more than enough protection). There was none of this 'new normal' or 'freedom passport' cobblers – we'd only some thirty-odd years earlier given the Third Reich a good clump, so that sort of thing just wouldn't wash. Yeah, back then the only people who wore masks were bank robbers, and the only time I recall Rodney and I ever 'self-isolating' was that afternoon Grandad dropped a particularly violent one on us, the dirty old goat. In many ways these were the halogen days, a time when you could pop out for a pint of milk and a packet of Castellas and come back again without once being picked up by a camera. Nowadays it's pretty much impossible to stand on a street corner and attempt to flog a consignment of fire-damaged Cabbage Patch dolls without being recorded by some invisible twonk. Take it from me, I've tried it. Twice.

Another major difference was football, which was all about mullets, broken noses and beer guts (and that was just the WAGS!).

Oh yes, back then professional footballers were full-sized adults whose main focus was on playing football. They had names like Trevor, Norman, Razor and Psycho. This was when men were men, you see, long before the advent of skinny jeans, shoes made out of pineapple and the ever-pressing need

to 'create awareness'. They just missed their penalties, advertised pizza and moved on. You couldn't help but feel a sense of pride!

That reminds me, I've still got a crate load of personally signed Gareth Southgate football boots in the garage. Not one of my best investments, granted, but we all really did think football was coming home. Let that be a lesson for you: never use permanent ink.

Where was I? Oh yeah, the most important thing to know is that it was the perfect time for us Trotters to spread our wings, and for me to put TITCo firmly on the map. With ground-breaking ideas as my tinder and unstoppable enthusiasm as my flint, I set out to light the world on fire. And while you could argue that I didn't quite pull it off (the closest I got was a coach), I still like to think that we left a dent. Now, do us both a favour and pour yourself a Singapore Sling, maybe a Lilt and Pernod (or even a non-alcoholic lager-top, if that's the way you roll), lean back in the old chaise-lounge and come along as we take a blow-by-blow account of the saga that is our dent. With insightful commentary from those who lived it (including a few recently unearthed notes from Grandad and Albert) and a load of others who both witnessed events and played their own part. I guarantee that you're already onto a winner!

Cotes du Rhône.

DT

7

Chandelier-smashing, bar-falling and countless days on the market ducking 'n' diving – for 40 years, the priceless exploits of the Trotters have been a source of belly-laughs and quotable catch phrases which have brought together generations of television viewers. Looking back now it is almost unthinkable to imagine that it all came from the pen of one man, John Sullivan.

Born in Balham, south London, in 1946, Sullivan grew up in a tough working-class community, populated by colourful, strong-willed characters living off their wits in the wake of the Second World War. Money was tight, and tempers often frayed, but in close-nit communities there was fierce loyalty and a constant supply of humour.

For Sullivan, school was something to be tolerated, and hopes were not high. However, in the English classroom Sullivan was introduced to the works of Charles Dickens. Thanks to a teacher who drew out Dickens' vibrant characters and richly painted situations, Sullivan soon recognised a London he knew and the community he lived in. Inspired by what could be done on the printed page, Sullivan put pen to paper and began to craft characters and stories of his own.

Leaving school in 1961, aged 15 and with no qualifications to speak of, Sullivan began working a succession of jobs, selling at markets, plumbing and even working in a brewery. He spent the next 17 years grafting a living in a range of trades, continuing to write and create characters in his free time.

The year after Sullivan left school, Galton and Simpson's comedy *Steptoe and Son* first aired on BBC 1. With its well-observed mixture of humour

and pathos, and massive laughs woven into realistically drawn situations, Sullivan saw what could be done with television comedy and realised that this was what he wanted to do.

Now writing with a focus, Sullivan began developing new material, and, throughout the late sixties and seventies, sent countless scripts to the BBC, only to be met by a steady stream of rejection letters. By 1974, he finally decided that his best chance of fulfilling his dreams would be from within the organisation.

Enquiring for job vacancies, Sullivan was duly employed behind the scenes at Television Centre within the scenic department. Beginning in props, he soon moved onto set dressing, famously preparing the studio waterproofing and kerb stones for the Morecambe and Wise 'Singing in the Rain' sketch. The job gave him invaluable insight into the making of programmes, including the presentation and lay out of scripts.

It was whilst working on the set of the sitcom *Porridge* that Sullivan met its star, Ronnie Barker, who kindly agreed to look at some of Sullivan's

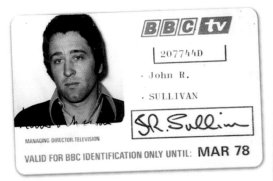

sketches. Barker was impressed by the quality of the writing and arranged for Sullivan to be put on contract as a writer for his popular Saturday evening sketch show, *The Two Ronnies*.

His confidence boosted, Sullivan seized the opportunity to approach comedy producer Dennis Main Wilson in the BBC bar, handing him a brand new script for an original series. The producer admired this determined and tenacious scene shifter and agreed to read the script, titled *Citizen Smith*.

Set in Tooting and telling the story of the likeable but hapless urban guerrilla Wolfie Smith (self-appointed leader of the Tooting Popular Front), Wilson was impressed and passed the script to the head of comedy, Jimmy Gilbert, who, equally taken, commissioned a pilot episode. John Sullivan's first television sitcom went into production.

Broadcast as part of the BBC's 'comedy special' (a strand to showcase new talent), on 12 April 1977, the

pilot's positive audience response lead to a full series following later that year.

Cast as Wolfie Smith was actor Robert Lindsay in his TV breakthrough. Lindsay carried off Sullivan's playful premise perfectly, shifting instantly between his earnest determination to change the world to an average easy-going London lad. One of the main strengths of *Citizen Smith* was that it mixed suburban authenticity with playful comedic scenarios.

Lindsay was joined by an ensemble cast that included Mike Grady as Ken Mills, George Sweeney as Speed, Tony Millan as Tucker, and Cheryl Hall as Shirley Johnson – Wolfie's girlfriend. Hall only appeared in the first two series, but Sullivan cleverly worked out how to keep her character alive within the world of the series.

Initially produced by Dennis Main Wilson, by the second series Wilson was joined by another producer and director, Ray Butt, whose own working class routes were similar to Sullivan's.

The series was mostly studio based, but enjoyed a healthy location budget. *The Glorious Day* episode memorably saw the cast ride a Scorpion Tank to Westminster. For the 1980 Christmas

Above top left: John Sullivan's BBC ID card.

Above top right: BBC comedy producer Dennis Main Wilson holds court at the BBC bar.

Above: Robert Lindsay as Wolfie Smith in *Citizen Smith*.

Left: A script to one of Sullivan's 'George and Sid' sketches, and how the scene appeared on screen, in the opening episode of *The Two Ronnies*' seventh series in 1978.

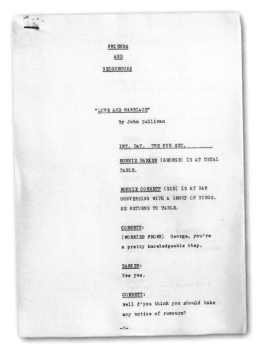

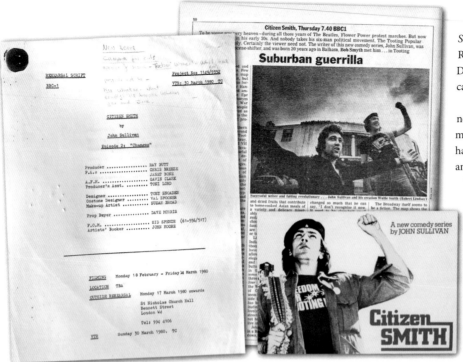

Citizen Smith, Thursday 7.40 BBC1

Suburban guerrilla

A new comedy series by JOHN SULLIVAN

Citizen SMITH

Successful writer and failing revolutionary... John Sullivan and his creation Wolfie Smith (Robert Lindsay)

Seconds Out, ironically staring Robert Lindsay as boxer Pete Dodds. The BBC had decided to cancel *Over the Moon*.

Incredibly disappointed by the news, and worried what it could mean for his young family, Sullivan had to go back to the drawing board and come up with another idea.

To discuss future plans, he met producer Ray Butt for a drink and they talked about the various jobs the both of them had done before working in television. As fellow working class Londoners they had both worked in markets and realised this was a world that had never been explored in comedy in a satisfying way.

Sullivan immediately hit upon the idea of a market fly-pitcher – a hard-working salesman who is part stand-up comedian and part crafty entrepreneur. Having seen such characters on the market, the writer often wondered where they went when the day was over. Were they that loud and funny at home with their family?

On developing the idea further, Sullivan thought of the fly-pitcher's assistant; surely no one would do that just for the money, they must be related? So the writer added this to his idea, and expanded it further by adding an older man, resulting in a family of three, each a generation apart from one another – surely fertile ground for tension and comedy.

Above: The rehearsal script for the *Citizen Smith* episode *Changes*.

Above right: The *Radio Times* feature to launch the first series of *Citizen Smith* in November 1977.

Above middle: An audience ticket stub for a recording of an episode of *Citizen Smith*.

Below right: Actor Brian Wilde (pictured here as Mr Barrowclough in *Porridge*) was cast in John Sullivan's *Over the Moon*.

special the cast and crew visited Portmeirion in North Wales as a stand in for Italy.

After four successful series, in 1980 both Lindsay and Sullivan were ready to move on to different projects and decided that *Citizen Smith* had run its course.

Sullivan had been developing an idea for a new sitcom entitled *You'll Never Walk Alone*, set in the fictional northern town of Hoddensey, which followed the exploits of an optimistic football manager, Ron Wilson, and his underachieving club Hoddensey Athletic. The stories followed their progress as well as Wilson's dealings with his unforgiving landlady, Mrs Allardyce.

Jimmy Gilbert was very interested, and a pilot episode, now retitled *Over the Moon,* went into production under Ray Butt's direction. The star of this new series was to be Brian Wilde, the genial actor most known for playing Mr Barrowclough in *Porridge* and Foggy in *Last of the Summer Wine*. After reviewing the pilot episode positively, the BBC asked Sullivan to write a full series.

Sullivan was midway through writing the fourth episode when he received a call from Ray Butt. The controller of BBC 1, Bill Cotton, had serious concerns about the series, as the channel was already committed to another sporting-themed comedy to air in January 1981,

Due to tragic circumstances, this family – the Trotters of Peckham – were without a mother and father. In fact, a sense of something always being missing in their lives became a key motif in Sullivan's mind, and even their chosen mode of transport was missing a wheel.

Wishing to write about the gritty, modern and multi-cultural city that he knew, Sullivan pulled no punches in framing the situation of his new comedy and its portrayal of 1980's London. The home of the Trotters would be a grim-looking tower block, a smoky pub was the centre of the characters' universe and take-aways their regular cuisine. Their lives would revolve around buying and selling, and they would only ever deal with cash on the hip. Never cheques. Always in 'readies'. Littering each page with visual gags and witty lines, and all threaded with a tightly plotted story, he sketched a family who were frequently short-tempered and dismissive of one another, yet just beneath the surface ran genuine love and affection.

A draft script, under the working title of *Readies*, was promptly given to Jimmy Gilbert, who was instantly taken by what he read. An admirer of Sullivan's work since *Citizen Smith*, *Readies* was just what he had been looking for.

Since October 1979 ITV had enjoyed success with their post-watershed comedy drama series, *Minder*, which was set in a gritty London and featured some charming yet unsavoury characters. Gilbert and the incoming head of comedy, John Howard Davis, were both aware they were missing a trick, and Sullivan's *Readies* could very well be the answer. With its accessible family set-up, it also had the potential for even greater appeal.

In an unusual move, Gilbert bypassed the pilot episode stage and instantly gave Sullivan the green light to write a full series of six episodes.

For Sullivan, however, *Readies* was only ever a working title. *Big Brother* was the first title he submitted, but with the year 1984 approaching, Gilbert was concerned about viewers tuning in expecting some George Orwell-inspired series.

Sullivan hit upon a longer and more memorable title for his new series. It was a title he had used for an episode in the last series of *Citizen Smith*. Putting forward his suggestion, Gilbert and Davis were unsure. A tactical Ray Butt suggested to Sullivan that he let them have a go at choosing a title – knowing full well that they wouldn't ever reach a decision and would fall back to the writer's offering. Duly, Sullivan got his way and his new series was to be named after the old saying "only fools and horses work for a living" – *Only Fools and Horses* was born.

Left: Robert Lindsay leads the cast in the 1980 *Citizen Smith* episode *Only Fools and Horses*.

Above: John Sullivan with his son Jim, on holiday in Cornwall in 1979.

Below: John Sullivan pictured in 1981 to promote his new comedy series, *Only Fools and Horses*.

Above: The BBC rehearsal rooms in Acton.

Above top right: Marking out a set in one of the rehearsal rooms' 18 spaces.

Above middle: St Nicholas Church Hall in Chiswick, another popular BBC rehearsal space, as seen here in *Homesick*, doubling as the Peckham community hall.

Below: Television Centre's TC3 with producers' gallery visible. *Only Fools* would be recorded across several Television Centre studios over its run.

Below middle: The corridor sign for TC6, the studio where *Big Brother* was recorded on Sunday 7 June 1981.

Below right: A young Ray Butt manning the vision mixer next to producer Mary Evans in 1960.

THE BBC SITCOM

The BBC sitcom had become one of the mainstays of the corporation's entertainment output since the early 1960s, transmitted in a series of six or seven 30-minute episodes and screened in weekly instalments.

Similarly, whilst in production, sitcoms were made on a weekly turnaround, with the cast receiving a completed script on a Tuesday, beginning a week of rehearsals. The production would usually only get access to the sets and studio on the Saturday for an on-set rehearsal and camera rehearsals in advance of the audience recording on the Sunday evening. Whilst the cast would usually have a day off on a Monday, the director and a VT editor would spend that day editing the previous evening's recording.

With Television Centre always in use, the BBC had a purpose-built block in Acton. The BBC rehearsal rooms had five floors of rehearsal spaces where dummy sets would be mapped out with tape on the floor. Poles were used to indicate where doorways and walls would be. For *Citizen Smith* and the early episodes of *Only Fools*, however, producer Ray Butt preferred to take his rehearsals into St Nicholas Church Hall in Chiswick whenever possible.

In addition to studio recordings, sitcoms were allocated an average of one hour of location filming for each series. This would be utilised per the writer's discretion, but was usually spread over the series' run. This footage would be filmed and edited on 16mm film, prepared in advance of an audience recording.

During the Sunday evening recordings, filmed segments were played back in sequence amongst the live studio portions of an episode. This meant the audience were presented with a seamless version of the story. Since their live laughter was recorded and added to the final mix of the televised episode, this was essential.

During recording, up in the gallery, the director and producer would work with the vision mixer to piece together the episode live – although carefully prepared camera scripts and camera rehearsals had helped to plan shots and cuts in advance.

"Technically in those days it was far more basic. But it really had an air of electric excitement," remembers director Tony Dow. "We didn't isolate any cameras, so that was when the vision mixer came in. It was frightening, you were actually cutting the show live, you could do odd cutaways and things to get you out of trouble afterwards. But what was going through the machine *was it*."

To add even more urgency, BBC studio recordings worked to a strict time-scale, usually requiring all recording to be completed by a 10.30pm curfew.

CASTING

At the heart of John Sullivan's original idea for *Only Fools* were a trio of characters, Del Boy, Rodney and Grandad. The success of the series would greatly depend on getting the right actors to play them.

The casting for the series' youngest character was the easiest.

"John Howard Davis, told me he wanted to bring in Nicholas Lyndhurst," remembered John Sullivan, "I thought it was a wonderful suggestion because I had seen Nick in the Ronnie Barker series *Going Straight* and he was terrific. He played a great cockney and a great character."

Lyndhurst was also well known at the time for starring in the BBC comedy *Butterflies*, written by Carla Lane. In this series the actor played a suburban middle-class kid, but showed he had the skills to convey a young man's petulance and attitude perfectly.

For the role of Grandad, Sullivan was immediately convinced by actor Lennard Pearce with his gentle, lackadaisical cockney delivery. During recent years Pearce had mostly worked in the theatre, but he had also built up a list of small screen credits in the likes of *Dixon of Dock Green* in 1965 and *Softly Softly: Task Force* in 1972. His most recent role, however, was as a court clerk in the Arthur Lowe sitcom, *Bless Me Father* in 1981.

Finding someone to play the lead role would prove to be more difficult. Future Oscar-winning actor Jim Broadbent was the initial choice put forward by John Howard Davis, but the actor turned down the role when he realised it would conflict with his theatre work.

The part was also offered to Scottish actor Enn Reitel (best known today for his voice over work), but he was committed to another project.

It was whilst watching a Sunday evening repeat of an episode of *Open All Hours* that Ray Butt saw Del Boy for the first time. To begin with, Sullivan had concerns that the series' co-star, David Jason, might not have a sharp enough edge to play Del. As well as soppy Granville in *Open all Hours*, Jason had previously starred in ITV sitcoms *Lucky Fella* and *A Sharp In Take of Breath*, all in which he had portrayed playful innocents, a far cry from the tough and streetwise fly-pitcher.

Hearing Sullivan's doubts, Butt assured the writer that he knew Jason had the range and could be a perfect Del. Duly the three actors were assembled to see if they had the required chemistry.

"If you're casting a three-hander, you're casting them one at a time, but before you book 'em you've got to see them together," remembered Ray Butt.

When the trio came together it was immediately clear that this was going to be the Trotter family. The physical differences between the tall and slim Lyndhurst and Jason's shorter, stockier build was the perfect improbable balance the series needed for its unlikely siblings. With the addition of the retiring older figure, the picture was complete. This was the cast.

"It was inspired putting David and Nicholas together," remembers director Mandie Fletcher, "they're really different as actors. Nick sort of came with the performance, so it always looked quite easy for him, whereas David finds the character and performance. They came at it differently but were brilliant together."

Above left: Ronnie Barker, Lynda Baron and David Jason in *Open all Hours* (1973, 1976-1985).

Above: Andrew Hall, Geoffrey Palmer, Wendy Craig and Nicholas Lyndhurst in *Butterflies* (1978-83).

Below: A signed publicity shot of a young Lennard Pearce.

ONLY FOOLS AND HORSES - PILOT
DEL

rich leather casual jkt

beer belly

flashy jewellery watches, neck chains etc

his right here and here

hair carefully blow dried over ears and dyed

suspicious of built-up insoles — otherwise feet seem in proportion to build up above, and footwear

tall, dingy and droopy

palestine liberation scarf

shapeless vest nice sack + t shirt, or limp black v-neck (acrylic)

horrible ancient moorland sheepskin black/brown stained and ripped

bronzed buckle on belt

wranglers

trainers

long stringy hair or mutton chops

GRANDAD

hat never removed

muffler and the rim

cardigan worn over pyjama top

indeterminate grey trousers

incongruous new pirelli slippers

COSTUME DESIGN

The Trotters' wardrobe in the first series of *Only Fools* was carefully researched and assembled by BBC Costume designer Phoebe De Gaye, in her first professional job in costume design.

The whole look of the series had to fit the brief of the contemporary gritty London John Sullivan was writing about, away from the caricatured TV image of what a cockney was seen to be. The look of *Citizen Smith* and ITV's *Minder* had shown how a realistic London could be brought to screen successfully. And the hope was for *Only Fools* to take this further, as if the studio doors had opened and half of Shepherds Bush street market had walked in.

To inform her work, De Gaye explored the streets and markets of London, capturing dozens of research photos to inspire her designs and the costumes she would buy.

In this pre-production period a collection of clothes for Del were assembled from warehouses and boutiques dotted around the capital. From these trips, gaudy coloured shirts, leather jackets and a certain sheepskin coat (which would become synonymous with the series) would emerge.

De Gaye soon realised that jewellery was a central part of the culture of people working on

Above left to right: Phoebe De Gaye's concept sketches of Del Boy, Rodney and Grandad.

Right: The original "D" medallion worn by Del in the early years of the series.

Below: Reccie photos taken by De Gaye to inform her costume designs.

Bottom right: An alternate Del Boy concept sketch by De Gaye.

Opposite page top left: Nicholas Lyndhurst and David Jason in a publicity photo taken at Islington's Chapel Market.

Opposite page top right: Jason as seen in an outtake from the series' original title sequence shoot.

Opposite page Bottom: A shot of both Jason and Lyndhurst together taken at the same time as the title sequence photography.

dyed hair

neck jewellery

pneumatic grey sheepskin car coat or full length coat

wrist jewellery flashy watch etc

flashy rings

trousers tight over bum — beer belly problems in future

unpleasant colour combinations

teeny fashion conscious feet - lattice work etc BUILT UP HEELS

GETTING THE TROTTER STYLE

As much as fashion changes, true style remains eternal. Not a lot of people know this, but when it comes to dress sense, God is my inspiration. After all, it was the Good Book itself (Matthew 3:4) that said 'John's clothes were made of camel's hair, and he had a leather belt around his waist. His food was locusts and wild honey.' I first heard that in Sunday school when I was a nipper and it stayed with me ever since. Decades later it struck me just how similar John and I are in our fashion outlook: I've always been a big fan of camel hair and most of my belts are made of leather – genuine synthetic leather that is, none of that stimulated rubbish. Mind you, I've never been one for honey or locusts. A plate of egg and chips or a mutton madras is more my thing. You know, sometimes, when I'm really bored, I like to imagine I'm back in biblical times with John, out in the wilderness, going around spreading the good word and dunking people's heads in ponds. I reckon I could have flogged him a decent pair of desert boots. Lovely jubbly!

Del Boy

the market, garish gold chains and rings were an important part of many traders' looks, geared to inspire confidence and show their wealth. Identity was also key and monogrammed clothes and jewellery were popular.

For Rodney, one of De Gaye's research photos would directly inspire the character's first series ensemble of weather-beaten black leather jacket and moth-eaten scarf, whilst a faded 'Dan Dare: Pilot of the Future' T shirt and painfully-fitted light gray suit would complete the character's early wardrobe.

Tellingly, De Gaye's concept sketch for her Grandad costume has the character sitting in his arm chair. The lovable old-timer's limited wardrobe of striped shirts and muted cardigans helped to quickly establish the character, along with the long overcoat and Trilby Hat which would complete his basic look.

"Lennard made a lovely costume statement with his pyjama top," remembered John Sullivan. "Even when Grandad was going out, under his mac he'd still be wearing it. So he was always ready for bed."

Although De Gaye would only contribute ideas for the first series of *Only Fools* (before embarking on an award-winning career in costume design), her work in 1981 would set the tone and still be felt decades later.

1981

1982

1983

1985

1986

1987

Above: With the two armchairs, the curtains and the kitchen units being the only constants, the Trotters' flat changed a lot over the first seven years. The print of David Shepherd's painting *Wise Old Elephant* was first seen in 1983, the same year the first of four different cocktail bars was introduced. The distinctive bamboo wallpaper didn't make its debut till series five (in 1986).

THE FLAT

In the script of *Only Fools'* first episode, *Big Brother*, John Sullivan wrote a detailed description of how he wanted the lounge of the Trotters' flat to look:

The room should reflect their style of business. Nothing is permanent. The settee and two armchairs are from three separate suites as the other pieces were used as make-weights in various other swaps. There are three TV sets; one colour, one black and white, and one with its back off awaiting repair. There are a couple of stereo music centers standing one on top of the other. Various video games, talking chess games, etc, litter the room. Their phone is one of the ornate 1920s type with separate ear-piece on an alabaster base. The decor is clean but gaudy. Dozens of clashing patterns. It should look like the start of a bad trip.

Throughout the years, this would essentially remain the design brief for the many production designers who would contribute to the series.

1989

PLAZA DE TOROS MONUMENTAL

EXTRAORDINARIA
CORRIDA

DOMINGO
TARDE A LAS 5

6 BRAVOS TOROS 6

D. PEDRO SALAS GARAU

"EL DEL"

JUAN ANTONIO RUIZ "ESPARTACO"

Nothing was permanent and everything was for sale... although the flat's orange-patented curtains would remain in place throughout.

"We used to change the table that they'd sit at every week," remembered producer Ray Butt. "One week it would be a bit of teak, the next week an old garden table, just a throughway gag to keep on the continuity of what they were doing. They were wheelers and dealers."

Amongst the gaudy decor and revolving door of furniture, the Trotters managed to relax after a hard day on the market's streets.

Yet, ironically, for millions of viewers, instead of looking 'like the start of a bad trip' as Sullivan intended, the uncoordinated mass of mismatched colours (not to mention the tacky tropical trappings of the cocktail bar) would become a comfortable sight. The combination of the exciting panoramic view of London outside the balcony window, and the constantly changing stock, hints at all the adventures Del and Rodney must have had trying to flog it all on Hooky Street.

Above left: The set as it appeared in series six, featuring the "El Del"poster on the kitchen door (Above).

Bottom: The width of the set was significantly extended in 1990 to better fit the larger cast.

Below inset: In 2001, the set of the flat was reduced to be closer to its original proportions.

2001

1990

Above: A shot of the original A-reg van as seen in *The Russians are Coming*.

Above middle: Pushing Grandad into the van in *A Touch of Glass*.

Above right: Del dives into the D-reg van for a quick getaway in *Healthy Competition*.

Below: The Reliant Regal Supervan in full Trotter regalia.

THE VAN

Trotters Independent Traders' yellow Reliant Regal Supervan would serve Del Boy and Rodney throughout their many years on Hooky Street. Within the world of the television series this smoky 'old banger' would be a figure of fun, but for millions of viewers it would become a national icon.

John Sullivan chose the Trotters' vehicle very carefully: "In *Big Brother*, Rodney says that everywhere they look there is something missing in their lives; they're motherless and fatherless and even their van is lacking something – a wheel. Another reason for picking a three-wheel van was because in those days you only needed a motor cycle licence to drive one. So, as Del Boy was a Mod and rode a scooter, this would have been the only type of car he could have driven. And I asked for the Reliant Regal just because it was so gaudy!"

Manufactured from 1969 to 1973, the Reliant Regal Supervans featured in *Only Fools* were just over a decade old when they first appeared in the series, but thanks to their three-wheeled design they already looked every bit the dated product of a bygone age.

Throughout the 22 years of *Only Fools'* production, several Supervans were sourced for the series and given full Trotter livery to be used on screen.

As was the practice with a BBC comedy production at the time, vehicles would be hired from specialist car hire companies on a short-term basis for the required shoot of a series. In the case of the Trotters' van, the film and TV hire company Action Cars were tasked with providing vehicles for the early years of the series. When the van was returned to Action Cars after the location filming of a series, the company would remove the distinctive side panels and rear door, before scrapping the rest of the vehicle, finding it more cost effective to purchase a new model for each series and reattach those elements.

Because of this, the precise number of vehicles used is a matter of much discussion and conjecture. Cosmetic changes and subtle differences within the Trotters'

handwritten signage illustrate several variations however.

The first van used in the series (seen in the title sequence and throughout series one and two) was a 1969 model with registration APL 911H. This vehicle featured a distinctive off-white section on the bonnet and a range of travel stickers on the rear door. The inside colour of this van was red, suggesting that it started its life completely red.

1982's Christmas Special *Diamonds are for Heather* introduced the first major variation in the van, with a model taken from the end of the Reliant Regal Supervan production in 1972. This vehicle featured the fictional number plate which would remain for the rest of its life onscreen: DHV 938D. This van and all subsequent vehicles would dispense with the travel stickers seen on the back window, and the handwritten signage on the side panels is noticeably different.

As the series moved into the sixth series (preceded by the 1988 Christmas Special *Dates*), two new vans were purchased by hire company

Telefilm Cars for the production team to use on location in Bristol. A green 1973 Supervan was painted yellow for general filming, whilst another red van was painted yellow for the famed stunt jump scene. Duplicate DHV 938D plates were applied to both models and copies of the Trotter side panels were made.

By the time series seven went into production in 1990, MGM Cars in Elstree were supplying vehicles for the series. MGM decided it was worth having one good-quality functioning van which could be kept in full Trotter regalia and used whenever the BBC required it for a new episode. This van would be used for the rest of the series.

Above left: Slightly different writing appears on the van's side panel, as seen in *Happy Returns*.

Above: John Sullivan's children, Dan, Jim and Amy on location with the Trotter Van as seen on Buster Hill in 1986's *Tea for Three*.

Left: A stunt van was used for the jump scene in *Dates*.

Below left: A Reliant Regal Supervan brochure from 1969.

Below: The final van, pictured ready for location filming for the 1996 Christmas Trilogy.

Supervan III is a restyled, advanced version of the toughest, most economical multi-purpose vehicle in its class. Reliant have combined in Supervan III the materials of the future and expert design with more than 30 years' experience of commercial vehicle production.

Apart from the 'accountable' saving of 30 shillings a week the Supervan III owner also benefits from lower insurance rates, less costly servicing and spares, and the fact that the vehicle can be left out of doors at all times. And a Reliant three-wheeler can be driven on either a car or motor cycle licence.

SUPERVAN III
–versatile, reliable, economical

Above: Two alternate sequences of David Jason in character as Del were considered in 1981 but not used. The leather jacket sequence would be revisited in 1985.

Below: Alternate cropped stills from the 1981 cast title sequence.

THE TROTTER TRIO

With his quick-witted charm and smooth-talking ways, Del Boy is a natural market trader. Providing for his family since his father, Reg, walked out on his 16th Birthday, Del's intuitive knack for wheelin' and dealin' had managed to keep his family above water for decades. In that time, he also managed to keep his promise to his late mother, Joan, in raising and looking after his kid brother, Rodney (despite the way he went through shoes).

"My main inspiration for Del Boy came from the guys in the used car trade," remembered John Sullivan. "Everything about these traders would say 'look at me, I'm successful and doing well'. Even though mostly it wasn't real and maybe a lot of it was on borrowed money, but it didn't matter. These guys had to keep this image up, just like Del Boy."

It was also important for Sullivan to show that Del wasn't purely a streetwise rough diamond and that there was also a sensitive side to him: "He's the kind of man who I believe, secretly, would cry quite easily, particularly over his mother. I think he was always worried about Rodney, trying to replace that woman who had been so important in their lives."

Rodney is the conscience of Peckham, with a diamond where his heart should be. The proud achiever of two GCE certificates (one in maths, one in art), Rodney was also, according to Del, the winner of several "ugly bird contests". Not as streetwise as his older brother, but nowhere near as much of a plonker as he suggests, Rodney is Trotters Independent Traders' executive look out, resident art lover and moral compass.

"There's a lot of me in Rodney," remembered Sullivan. "When I was younger I was a little naive and a bit of a dreamer. I also had a few friends growing up who were like Rodney – they were never quite growing up fast enough. Rodney was very well protected by Del, so that was probably why he had this early naivety to him."

Whilst it is true that Rodney never smoked Astroturf, he was expelled from Basingstoke art college, where he was caught smoking a Moroccan woodbine with a Chinese girl.

Since living in Nelson Mandela House, Grandad has been patiently waiting for colour TV to be invented. Absent-minded and a truly terrible cook, Grandad has a firm sense of justice and is fiercely loyal to his grandchildren.

Sullivan based Grandad on his mother's father. "When I wrote the scripts, I'd described Grandad as being quite a lazy man who didn't do anything, because as a kid that's how I perceived my own grandfather. But in fact, he'd been gassed during the First World War and he'd also worked as a coal man. As a result, he suffered terribly from emphysema, which is why he wasn't very mobile. When Lennard Pearce first came to read for the part I immediately knew he was the right man. He had that lovely gravelly voice, which was an echo of my own grandfather – whose voice had been like that because of his condition."

LOGO AND TITLE SEQUENCE

On John Sullivan's first *Only Fools* script, he wrote a description of how he saw the series' titles:

We see various stills: Del Boy selling from a suitcase on the corner of Oxford Street – with Rodney acting as lookout, Bartering with a market trader, bidding at a second-hand car auction, drinking in pubs and discos. (In each of the stills, Del is wearing a different set of wide awake clothes. Rodney appears to be wearing the same clothes throughout.)

We see the South London council estate where they live. Parked there is their three-wheeler van. A Sign upon the side of which reads, 'Trotters Independent Trading Co' 'New York, Paris, Peckham'. We pan up to a window on the fourth storey of a tower block then zoom in.

Above: Shots from the original *Only Fools* title sequnce photograpphed by John Jefford. The smartly suited Del was chosen in favour of the duffel coat and leather jacket shoots.

Below left: Nicholas Lyndhurst in costume as Rodney in an outtake from the shoot.

Below right: It was decided that Grandad should be seated in his sequence and eating a hamburger, In reference to his dialoguen in *Big Brother*.

Above: Peter Clayton's original on-screen logo used from the beginning of the series to 1985's *Strained Relations...* followed by the slightly amended logo used from *Hole in One* to 1996's *Time on our Hands*. An horizontally scaled version of this title card was used for the final trilogy of episodes from 2001–2003.

Below right: Opening title photography by John Jefford, featuring Islington's Chapel Market and the Alma pub.

Below: Clayton roughly based his logo and peeling sticket design on Woodbine and Gold Flake cigarette boxes from the 1930s.

BBC graphic designer Peter Clayton was tasked with interpreting Sullivan's outline and developing it into a full sequence:

"Ray Butt called me up to his office and said, 'We've got this new show coming up, it's got a strange title, *Only Fools and Horses*' and he said it was about London boys who were market traders who do all these dodgy deals, but don't seem to ever hold on to any money."

Clayton had designed many pioneering animated sequences for various light entertainment series in the late seventies and early eighties, including *The Paul Daniels Magic Show* (1979) and *Mike Yarwod in Persons* (1981). For *Only Fools*, Clayton purposely stepped away from his established slick and modern approach in favour of something more down to earth and authentic to the series.

"When I sat down and thought about it, I thought that they have money, but it sort of blows away in the wind all the time and they keep losing it. That was roughly the original concept. It was also important in the titles to get the cast involved and establish the main characters, so Del had money and was flicking though his notes, and Rodney never had money, with his empty pockets."

Clayton hit upon the memorable device of an animated peeling note to house the series logo.

"I storyboarded the rough idea and took it up to Ray, and he just said 'go ahead mate', that was it. First of all I needed to get the three actors into a photographic studio and did a sequence of stills of them doing their actions, and then it was a process of getting all the prints made. It was a rostrum photo-shoot, all filmed on 35mm. We then needed to get a kind of 'page turn' feel, so we spoke to an animator, Brian Stevens, who animated all the mattes and masters for the flicking away of the notes."

For the logo itself, Clayton had originally considered using a bank note featuring Del Boy

instead of the Queen, before realising the issues of replicating a bank note on screen. For the logo Clayton eventually settled on, the designer was inspired by several 1930s cigarette boxes that he used to collect, and decided to use the casual-scripted Mistal typeface as it suitably fitted into the theme.

Taking the lead from Sullivan's original suggestions, Clayton and photographer John Jefford went on a journey around North London to assemble a group of shots: "We needed some stills to put behind the moving stickers, so we went out to some typical places that Del Boy would find himself in." Their travels took in Islington's Chapel Market, a car lot in Brentford and a bustling Holborn,

before ending at the north Acton tower block which doubled as Nelson Mandela House. On this final frame of the sequence, the Ford Cortina from the episode *Go West Young Man* can just be glimpsed parked outside the flat on the far left of the frame.

Alternative shots of the final frame of the sequence show a "Del – Pauline" window sticker on the Trotter van, revealing an out-take from the episode *The Second Time Around*. John Sullivan would reuse this gag to great effect in the 1982 episode *Diamonds Are For Heather*.

The resulting 40 second clip would be used throughout the entire run of the series, with the only changes being made to the cast stickers in 1985 and 2001.

Below first two rows: Shots of the inside of the car lot in Brentford were considered for the sequence but not used. Outside the car lot, Clayton is pictured by a sports car. The exterior of the car lot would be closely cropped in the final sequence.

Below bottom two rows: A shot of Eden's restaurant and wine bar – next to Holborn tube station – was featured in the final sequence, but these other West End street views were left on the cutting room floor.

Below: Clayton's final cast notes as they appear on screen, with animation by Brian Stevens.

Right: The penultimate shot of the opening sequence showing a panoramic shot of Nelson Mandela House; in reality the shot shows Corfe Tower and Harlech Tower, Park Road East, Acton.

Below: Designer Peter Clayton leans on the original Trotter Van, outside Beaumaris Tower, Park Road East, Acton.

Above and right: The first shots taken of the Trotters' van outside Harlech Tower, feature an unused gag from *The Second Time Around* a "Del Pauline" window sticker on the windscreen. As it wouldn't be right to tie the sequence to one episode, this sticker was duly removed and rephotographed for the shot which ended up in the final sequence.

The original closing credits for series one used the same animated stickers as the opening titles, but with the cast and crew credits listed on each and with the stickers on a black background. Too time consuming and expensive to do every week, a traditional roller caption was employed for the second series.

As assistant floor manager, one of Tony Dow's early duties on the series was to record these captions. "It was a bit rock and roll in those days," says Dow. "I remember the final credits were on a roller and we'd have to put them in a machine on the studio floor, and at the end of recording you'd film all those credits turning in the machine."

For the third series, graphic designer Mic Rolph was tasked with adding a little additional 'Trotter texture' to the end roller captions: "The brief I was given from Ray Butt was that the credits were meant to look like something the Trotters could have done themselves, as they were street traders and they didn't want it posh, they wanted it to look rough – so they got the ideal person to do it!" Mic's hand drawn credits featured various market stall doodles, drinks and stars, which although they only appeared in seven episodes, became synonymous with the series. From series four onwards the end credits would all be rendered within a computer in a range of styles.

MUSIC

John Sullivan's original brief for the music of *Only Fools* was for a 'honky tonk, Chas & Dave London sound' to reflect the gritty streets from which the Trotters flogged their wares.

Ronnie Hazlehurst was the BBC's Light Entertainment musical director, and had been composing the music for the majority of the corporation's comedy shows for the previous twenty years (including the theme tunes to *Some Mother's Do Have 'Em* and *Last of the Summer Wine*). Hazlehurst had also collaborated with Sullivan on *Citizen Smith*'s closing theme song 'The Glorious Day', sung by that series' star Robert Lindsay.

When approached to write the *Only Fools* signature tune in the summer of 1981, Hazlehurst composed a light jazzy brass instrumental. A solid enough piece for a variety comedy series, it didn't really reflect the authentic city where *Only Fools* was set.

For *Only Fools*' second series, John Sullivan decided to change things up and wrote and recorded his own opening theme. In part, the resulting song explains the programme's unusual title, but its lyrics also give a brief summary of the series' ethos and some of the slang the characters use.

Sullivan also gave the series its closing theme song, 'Hooky Street'. Taking the form of an almost spoken-word rap, the lyrics of this piece also gave details of the series' central characters and their attitude to life

Only Fools and Horses

Stick a pony in me pocket
I'll fetch the suitcase from the van
Cause if you want the best 'uns
And you don't ask questions
Then brother I'm your man

Where it all comes from
Is a mystery
It's like the changing of the seasons
And the tides of the sea
But heres the one thats driving me berserk
Why do only fools and horses work
La la lala - la la la la la

Hooky Street

We've got some half priced cracked ice
And miles and miles of carpet tiles
TVs, deep freeze and David Bowie LPs
Pool games, gold chains, wosnames
And at a push
Some Trevor Francis track-suites
From a mush in Shepherds Bush, Bush, Bush,
Bush, Bush, Bush, Bush, Bush

No income tax, no VAT
No money back, no guarantee
Black or white, rich or broke
We'll cut prices at a stroke

God bless Hooky Street
Viva Hooky Street
Long live Hooky Street
C'est magnifique Hooky Street
Magnifique Hooky Street

and business, via a catchy list of goods they have to offer.

Sullivan's original idea was for Chas & Dave themselves to sing and perform both of these themes, and the duo were on board right up until touring commitments made it an impossibility. With time running out, and after several pints of Dutch courage, Sullivan decided to sing them himself. The writer, already passionate about music and songwriting, possessed a natural laid-back rock voice, perfect for bringing the themes to life. Accompanying Sullivan, Hazlehurst arranged and conducted a bass-heavy rhythm section which instantly sounded much more appropriate.

Above left: Composer Ronnie Hazlehurst in the studio.

Above box: Some of Mic Rolph's distinctive doodles seen on the end credits of series three.

Right: Mic Rolph's end credit roll created for *Friday the 14th*.

Left: An example of the closing credits as seen in the first series (left) and how they appeared in 1985 (right).

SERIES ONE

★ ★

A lot of people said I was a right dipstick to make Rodney a partner in the firm. And within a fortnight of doing just that he'd proved them all correct. A new decade of golden opportunities lie before us. There I stood, at the helm of the good-ship Trotter, scouring the horizon for business opportunaire, ready to pounce at a moment's notice, and determined, one way or another, to make Trotters Independent Traders a success! Meanwhile that lazy little twonk was sitting on his brains doing the company accounts! Fair enough, I did tell him he could be the firm's accountant, but I never thought he'd actually do it! I had a right mind to make him walk the plank there and then, but he's family and I'd never have heard the last of it. Of course, there was also Grandad. He did what he could, bless him, but at the end of the day he was about as helpful as a wetsuit in a bath. All that said, the life of the general trader was the only life for me. It was exciting and unpredictable. I imagine the way I felt back then, when I loaded the van up of a morning before setting off for market, was how Coloumbo must have felt when he set sail to discover the new world. And despite everything, I wasn't too worried. With my charm, foresight, cool head and business acumen, I knew there'd be no stopping us. In fact, I think I can recall saying at the time, with some confidence: "This time next year, we'll be millionaires!"

★ ★

BIG BROTHER

8 SEPTEMBER 1981

We were definitely onto a potential winner with this one. Twenty-five executive briefcases of exceptional quality: old English vinyl, dinky little handles, combination locks, the full monty! Oh yes my son, Samsonite himself would've been proud! Only a wally of the highest order would have swerved such an opportunity, which is why it didn't at all surprise me when Rodney turned his nose up. I wouldn't have minded, but then he stuck that nose into the negotiation process and forced me to pay top whack for 'em! Anyway, it was a couple of hours later when we discovered that the combination codes for the locks were inside the briefcases, meaning I'd just coughed up two-hundred notes for twenty-five executive briefcases that no sod could open! Rodney and I then got into a right old barney about his 'role' in the firm. He saw himself as a 'financial advisor' (of all things!) whereas I saw him as.... well, as a Rodney. If that weren't grim enough, Grandad then threw his pennies worth in and started banging on about how much he hated cheeseburgers. Carte Noir! I knew they'd said never to work with family, but this was taking the piss!

Del

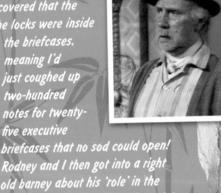

As the camera pans across the Trotters' Nelson Mandela House flat for the first time, *Big Brother* instantly draws us into the family's world. From Grandad's doddering cinematic confusion, Rodney's distracted nonchalance and Del Boy's playful vanity ("What an enigma. I get better looking every day. I can't wait for tomorrow") the scene and characterisation is perfectly set.

In the space of five minutes, John Sullivan establishes the family dynamic and Trotters Independent Traders' raison d'être. Del Boy almost pre-empts the series end theme song when he counts on his fingers all the things the brothers do and don't do: "we don't pay VAT, we don't pay income tax."

Location filming for the entirety of *Only Fools and Horses'* first series took place from 6 to 23 May 1981 (with an additional day for pick-up shots on 15 June). It was during this location filming period – a night shoot for *A Slow Bus to Chingford* in Stamford Hill – that producer and director Ray Butt suddenly suffered a serious back injury. That evening, fellow BBC director Martin Shardlow was quickly appointed and rushed down to take the reins and oversee the rest of the location filming and the studio recordings a few weeks later, with Butt staying on as Producer.

Despite being (quite literally) an eleventh-hour replacement, Shardlow was more than up to the task, having cut his teeth on *Last of the Summer Wine*, he would soon help to introduce *Blackadder* to viewers.

The main studio recordings for the first four episodes took place on consecutive Sundays from 7 June, with the last two episodes recorded on Saturday evenings (4 and 11 July).

As well as establishing the Trotter Family, *Big Brother* also introduced to the world another, soon to be iconic, comedy character: Trigger (effortlessly brought to life by actor Roger Lloyd Pack). Cast by Ray Butt, after having seen him in Stanley Price's play *Moving*, Lloyd Pack had enjoyed a host of impressive guest spots on British television over the last decade, from *Dixon of Dock Green* to *The Professionals*.

Originally introduced in the script as being '*a local part-time villain*' whose '*colour is of no importance*', Lloyd Pack's immaculate performances are seamless from the starting gun, and when the actor utters his first "Dave" – a bit of TV history is made.

Appropriately, it is Trigger who sets the plot in motion as he sells Del some hooky briefcases, which turn out to be useless since the combination codes are locked inside the cases! The montage of Del Boy attempting to sell his consignment of reject suitcases sees him wandering around Chapel Market in Islington, along some of the same streets featured in the series' opening titles. The 'Costumier and

Furrier shop' we see Del enter is situated on the nearby White Conduit Street, a popular curiosity shop which remains largely unchanged to this day.

Interestingly, this sequence is the only place to still hear Ronnie Hazlehurst's original *Only Fools and Horses* signature tune. All repeat screenings and home video releases of series one episodes have had the opening and closing titles edited to feature the more well-known themes introduced in series two.

The opening episode of any television series has a lot of work to do, but *Big Brother* does it brilliantly and succinctly by establishing a world and situation right off the bat. Whilst being jam-packed with wit and laughter, the tension of the situation and the sense of the characters being trapped by their circumstances is palpable.

Opposite page top right: Grandad enjoys a film in stereo.

Top left: Joyce the Nags Head's barmaid (Peta Bernard).

Top right: Trigger (Roger Lloyd Pack) has some briefcases to sell...

Left and above: On location in Islington's Chapel Market.

Below left: "illegal move!" Grandad is outwitted by a talking chess game!

Below: A happy ending after Rodney's homecoming.

In 1980, Ray Butt was looking for an actor to play a bent Chief Inspector for the *Citizen Smith* episode *Letter of the Law*. Eventually, John Challis was cast in the role, transforming himself into an uncompromising Londoner with a distinctive drawl. Challis recalls the moment well: "After the recording of the episode, John Sullivan very kindly came up to me and said, 'I really like what you did to that character, I'm going to try and use it again one day'. And I thought that's very nice, thank you very much, but years as a jobbing actor taught me not to think any more of it really."

A year later as Butt and Sullivan were preparing *Go West Young Man,* they remembered Challis' Inspector and realised they had the perfect man to play the part of their used car dealer. When Challis arrived at the Kingsbury Road location doubling as Boycie's forecourt on a May morning, little did he know what was just beginning: "It was a great scene and a nice little character, and I just put the same inflection I had given the Inspector in *Citizen Smith*, which was actually based on

someone in my local pub who had that way of talking."

In his first brief scene as Boycie, Challis instantly brings forth a fully formed creation: "I put it all down to the writing, which gives you the opportunity to say those words and flesh out that character. I had no idea that the character was going to become a regular, I just enjoyed doing that one episode and then went back to the National Theatre."

Aside from introducing a soon-to-be comedy icon, *Only Fools'* second episode manages to pack a lot of plot into its half hour, with Del Boy taking Trotters Independent Traders into the second-hand car trade and a memorable trip up west.

Guest starring in the episode as the Australian who buys the Ford Cortina from Del was actor Nick Stringer. Stringer recalls producer Ray Butt being genuinely convinced he was Australian, despite heralding from Devon. No stranger to sitcom, Stringer had recently acted alongside both David Jason and Nicholas Lyndhurst in *Open All Hours* and *Butterflies*. Required for *Go West Young Man*'s night shoot, Stringer would never forget the date: "We filmed in Chiswick on the night of the FA Cup Final replay between Spurs and Man City (Thursday

Above: "This is where our future lies Rodney, second hand motors" – Del consults a car price guide.

Above right: Boycie (John Challis) has a favor to ask of Del...

Below: An Australian car buyer (Nick Stringer).

Below right: At a nightclub, Rodney and Del meet Nicki (JoAnne Good) and Michelle (Caroline Ellis).

Opposite page top left: "Drink up Rodney, we're leaving!"

GO WEST YOUNG MAN

15 SEPTEMBER 1981

The moment I agreed to go up West with Rodney, I knew I'd end up regretting it. He kicked the evening off by taking us to a club called 'The Pink Panther', a dingy little gaff that was so dimly lit I almost went arse-over-tit twice just trying to get in. I dunno, either they were well behind on the electricity bills or they were holding a dummy run for a coal miners' convention. The staff were no better either. I mean, what kind of waiter hasn't heard of a Caribbean Stallion? Then, just as my eyes began to adjust to the gloom, Rodney confessed to me, in a gentle and round-about way, that he is in fact a warped, corrupted, twisted pervo. He followed that up by convincing me to pull a couple of birds who turned out to be a pair of dockers in drag! Just when I thought the evening couldn't possibly get any worse, he goes and gets Boycie's E-type Jaguar rear-ended. Stone me! I only went along cos he was hard-up for a bit of company.

Del

14 May 1981) and I remember the sparks and the chippies, all rooting for the London team, standing around a TV they had purposely rigged up to watch the game... Spurs won!"

Cast as the two girls who Del and Rodney chat up in the night club were actresses JoAnne Good (as Nicki) and Caroline Ellis (as Michelle). "When we started rehearsals, the series hadn't been seen by anyone, but even then, the cast and crew found it very difficult not to laugh," Caroline Ellis recalls. "We all quickly realised that the script was first class and that we could be on to something special."

And first class it certainly was, from the Ford Cortina's dodgy brakes and the transvestite reveal in the night club, to Rodney admitting that he has yet to smoke AstroTurf. *Go West Young Man* is a bit of an early *Only Fools and Horses* classic, packed to the brim with memorable moments.

Additional location filming for the episode saw Pitshanger Lane in Ealing used for the scene when Del and Rodney drive away from the night club in Boycie's E-type Jag. For this shot, the art department added a "Camberwell / Peckham" road sign to maintain the illusion of the series' setting. This episode would also mark the first episodic appearance of the North Acton estate, used as the location of the Trotters' home seen in the title sequence.

Behind the scenes, the opening shot of the episode would hold a special place for videotape editor Chris Wadsworth: "The first thing I ever did for *Only Fools* was to edit the *Open University* programme which Grandad was watching on his two TVs. I had to prepare this before the studio recording, as Ray Butt wanted the audience to react to the little bits of sound coming from the telly." Wadsworth would gradually move up the ladder to become the series' only editor and went on to work on dozens of other much loved TV shows.

SERIES 1 EPISODE 3

CASH AND CURRY

22 SEPTEMBER 1981

I've always had an eye for a bit of sculpture, fine porcelain and the like, so when I got caught up between Vimmal and Ram - two business associates involved in a centuries old barney over the statuette of some ancient Indian God or another - I was only too happy to act as the middle-man. I didn't reckon much of the statuette when Vimmal showed it to me, grubby looking little thing it was, but then I've always been more of a Ming man myself. That said, Ram was ready to pay £4,000 for it! The only problem was that he wouldn't cough up a single penny until he had the statuette safely in his hands. And that's when I seized the opportunity to tell Vimmal that the offer was £2,000. He knew it made sense and accepted, but only on the condition that he had the money safely in his hands before handing the statuette over. That's when I seized another opportunity (I had them coming out of my lug'oles back then). If Rodney and I could raise two grand, we could pay Vimmal and then nip the statuette over to Ram and pick up the four grand. That way, Vimmal would get two lovely grand, Ram would get his precious statuette and Rodney and I would double our money - everyone's a winner, apres moi la deluge! It weren't easy raising the dosh, though. We had to get shot of Rodney's leather coat, all my jewellery and Grandad's telly, but we finally managed it. We whipped round to Vimmmal, handed it over and then shot the statuette straight round to Ram, only to discover that the bloke we knew as Ram didn't actually exist, and that the statuette we'd just paid £2,000 for was selling in the market for 17 nicker. Needless to say, we then discovered that Vimmal had done a complete vanishing act. As Macbeth said to Hamlet in A Midsummer's Night Dream, "We'd been done up like a pair of kippers."

Del

Like many long-running television series, early episodes can often illuminate roads not taken and show the early development of soon to be familiar characters. Out of all the episodes of *Only Fools'* first series, *Cash and Curry,* is the prime example of a story which shows a series still establishing its direction.

After the titles, the story opens with a slightly mysterious piece of incidental music as Rodney parks the Trotter Van next to a 1964 Vauxhall Velox (which we later find out belongs to Del) and we see two shadowy figures look on. As the music shimmers to a crescendo, Rodney meets a slightly drunken Del in a grand foyer. The brothers are about to get caught between the heads of two rival Indian families, Mr Ram and Mr Malik, each of whom make a claim to an ancient statue which is in the possession of one family, but desired by the other. With the families unwilling to deal directly with each other, Del steps forward to serve as a 'go between'...

Cash and Curry is a story-led caper, with the Trotters woven into the plot from the opening moments. Tellingly we don't see the inside of the Trotter flat in this episode, and whilst he is mentioned several times, Grandad doesn't feature in the story.

Cast as Mr Ram, Renu Setna had just a few months previously appeared with David Jason in *the Open all Hours* episode *Laundry Blues.* Joining Setna as Vimmal Malik was actor Ahmed Khalil, who had notably appeared in the *Minder* episode *The Bengal Tiger* in 1979.

With its rhyming potential, a Vauxhall Velox is a perfect car for Del Trotter to drive (and dating from the early sixties it is tempting to suggest it came from Alberto's Autos as seen in *Rock & Chips*); however, in a minor way it undermines Sullivan's neat idea that the Trotters had something missing from every aspect of their lives – hence the three-wheeled van. Perhaps because of this,

the Velox is only ever seen and mentioned in this episode, and the writer would wait another ten years before making the Trotters a two-car family again.

Similarly, this would be the only time in the series that we hear some of Ronnie Hazlehurst's distinctive incidental music. This flute-led piece was specially recorded for *Cash and Curry*, and whilst Hazlehurst's light entertainment polish might feel at home during an episode of *To The Manor Born*, in the Trotters' gritty London, it just feels out of place.

Elsewhere in this episode, we see a photo montage sequence of Del and Rodders selling their wares to make the £2,000 needed to buy the statue. Much like the opening titles, this sequence was photographed by BBC stills photographer John Jefford. In this sequence we are treated to a literal snapshot in to the Trotters' world, as they sell the Velox to an unnamed second-hand car salesman, offload jewellery at a pawn shop, and meet another trader clad in a sheepskin

jacket. Location wise, this sequence was photographed in and around the north Acton estate near Harlech Tower and Chapel market in Islington. The car forecourt was the same Kingsbury lot used in *Go West Young Man*. Originally sound-tracked by Pink Floyd's classic 'Money', sadly for home video this is replaced by a brassy piece of stock music.

For live action location filming, West London's Hanwell Community Centre was used as the location for the Chamber of Trade Dinner Dance, and Vimmal Malik's Hotel was filmed on Somerset Road in Ealing.

In hindsight, *Cash and Curry* is a slightly unusual *Only Fools* instalment; but that certainly doesn't make it a bad one. With a script full of brilliant one-liners and great observations, it is no wonder that eight years later, John Sullivan would revisit the con-man caper on a grander scale in series six's *Chain Gang*, in a scheme with a much better outcome for the Trotters.

Opposite page top right: Rodney parks the van next to Del's Vauxhall Velox.

Above left: The Trotters and Vimmal Malik (Ahmed Khalil).

Left: Mr Ram (Renu Setna) and his bodyguard (Roy Questel)

Below: After selling all they have, the Trotters get the £2000 required... For the worthless statue!

Below: "We'll be rich my friend, very rich!" – Mr Ram and Vimmal Malik head north, ready to try their con again.

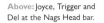

Above: Joyce, Trigger and Del at the Nags Head bar.

Above right: Del's old flame Pauline (Jill Baker) works her magic on Del...

Right: ... before making herself at home in the flat.

Below right: The Trotters visit their 'auntie' Rose (Beryl Cooke).

Opposite page above right: Director Martin Shardlow directs the cast in the scene where the Trotters return home to find Pauline gone... and the phone off the hook!

With the opening three episodes establishing the Trotter family and their way of life, the fourth episode of *Only Fools* was an opportunity for John Sullivan to throw a spanner into the Reliant Regal: "I'd read a letter on the agony page of one of my wife's magazines, about someone meeting an ex-partner and still being in love with them. I wondered what would happen if one of Del's old flames came back, and how it would affect the family."

Del's long lost love, Pauline Harris, was brought to life by actress Jill Baker: "The cast were all lovely and very in tune with it all as they'd all been doing it for a little while," Baker remembers. "John Sullivan was around quite a bit and I have worked with David Jason a few times and he is always so professional and delightful."

Baker would later appear in a string of feature films, most notably 1998's Oscar-winning feature *Shakespeare in Love*, a far cry from the multi camera studio set-up with a eagerly watching audience a few metres away. "The recording in front of the live audience at Television Centre was very scary and I was never quite sure whether to play to the camera or to the audience, but the audience were incredibly responsive which helped a lot."

The manipulative Pauline was a true 'femme fatale' with razor-sharp dialogue, a part which Baker revelled in playing. "The episode I was in was brilliantly written, which made it much easier to learn and work with as it flowed so well. I loved playing Pauline, but what an evil bitch! Poor Del Boy!"

THE SECOND TIME AROUND

29 SEPTEMBER 1981

All work and no play makes Del a very dull boy. That's why I always made sure to find time for the finer things in life, you know, a weekly visit to The Star of Bengal, the occasional liver-sausage sandwich washed down with a Pina colada or four. Lovely jubbly! And of course, there was always the birds. This time it was Pauline Harris, an old flame from back when I was a mod. Pauline had always had a touch of the old fem-fatal about her, especially when it came to winding me up with other blokes (I got into more fights than John Wayne), but when I caught glimpse of her again across the way in the Nags Head, I could feel my heart already beginning to fall. For some reason, Rodney and Grandad had never really taken to Pauline, so they copped the right needle when two days later we got engaged and I agreed to let her move into the flat with us. It was rough going at first and we had a few minor issues over corned beef, Grandad's teeth and Rodney calling her 'mein kommandant' and saluting her every time she walked into the room. But other than that, we were making it work. Rodney and Grandad thought she had me under her thumb, but it weren't like that at all. It may have looked like it, but the fact was I knew exactly what I was doing and I had her right where she wanted me. Anyway, I was just about to order a new engagement ring from my old mate Abdul, when I received the disturbing news that not only was Pauline a serial killer, but that I was next on her hit list. I won't lie, it did put a bit of a downer on the whole thing. Just as I was digesting this news, Rodney and Grandad informed me that they'd had enough and were buggering off to stay with Auntie Rose in Clacton. I didn't even know we had an Auntie Rose in Clacton, but after a quick weighing up of my options, I decided it was about time I also paid her a visit.

Del

When Pauline moves into Nelson Mandela House, she gradually makes Rodney and Grandad feel unwelcome in their own home, so much so that they decide to move.

Sullivan loosely based Pauline on a family friend who had met a twice married widow where both husbands had died: "She got the insurance money on both of them and it just seemed such an unusual story. Then I came up with the line, 'one more and she gets the match ball'. So, in the episode we get the idea that Pauline's not a safe option for Del."

Duly, the Trotters escape to the safety of Aunt Rose's in Clacton. This scene was filmed at Lowfield Road in Acton, ironically just down the road from the north Acton estate standing in for Peckham.

The Aunt Rose element of the story came from a trip to Ireland Sullivan went on to visit an elderly uncle: "While I was chatting to him, I realised he thought I was my dad. And I thought it would be funny if the Trotters went away to see someone they *think* they know, and the woman's moved on. But she's the right age, the right style and she's from London – so for the Trotters, she'll do!"

'Aunt' Rose was played by Beryl Cooke. Elsewhere, Peta Bernard reprises her role from the series' opening episode, as the Nags Head's barmaid, Joyce, her final appearance in the series.

A SLOW BUS TO CHINGFORD

6 OCTOBER 1981

Trotters Ethnic Tours really was the Capo Del Monte of ideas. You see, I'd been mulling over the fact that the tourist trade had never been so high, but at the same time the coach party trade was circling the proverbial Kermit. The reason being, I surmised, was that the average tourist was fed up with seeing the same old places. It struck me that the time was right for a new and dynamic approach, the kind that only me, Rodney and Grandad could provide. Oh yes, for the unbeatable price of seventeen quid, we were gonna show the tourists the hidden gems of London: the majesty of Lower Edmonton at dusk; a walk-about in Croydon; a guided tour of the kitchen of the Star of Bengal (with a complimentary souvenir onion bahji thrown in for good measure). It was perfect. We had the loan of a double decker bus, a driver (Rodney), and I'd even knocked up a load of advertising fliers written in all sorts of languages. You see, it had suddenly occurred to me that the vast majority of foreigners come from abroad, and so they don't speak proper English like what you and I do. All we had to do then was get the fliers out and wait for the punters to stream in. The one and only flaw in my planning was that I trusted Grandad to hand the fliers out, so you can imagine how I felt when I later discovered the lazy old goat had dumped them in the bin and buggered off down the Legion club. "It weren't me," he said, "It was my brain!" Sometimes I really did wonder why I bothered.

TROTTERS ETHNIC TOURS

Derek Trotter: .... Courier
Rodney Trotter: ... Coach Driver
Edward Trotter: ... Distribution
Director: .... John Sullivan

Explore Ethnic London in all its grandeur. This incredible value London bus tour grants you the freedom and convenience to explore the city in depth.

This tour encompasses world renowned attractions such as the Lower Edmonton at dusk, a walk around Croydon, and of course, the inimitable Buckingham Palace.

You will also see the most eminent regions of London, such as the distinguished Elephant and Castle, and world celebrated Lea Valley Viaduct.

This cultural Extravaganza doesn't stop there my friend, you will also see where Sherlock Holmes was born, and to North London where Jack the Ripper was buried.

As viewers would go on to discover, there is much more to Derek Trotter than simply fly-pitching in the market to make a pony or two. He is a bold dreamer with an idealised vision of becoming a millionaire the old fashion way: by building an empire! *A Slow Bus to Chingford* would mark the first instance where we see Del put his heart on his sleeve with a bold idea to make those dreams come true.

It also shows just how conniving Del Boy can be, as he sets up Trotter Watch (duly recruiting Rodney in his scheme by dressing him in a Traffic Warden's uniform) as he goes about setting up his latest venture: Trotters Ethnic Tours. John Sullivan's idea of a tour company exploring 'ethnic' London was inspired and so funny when rendered in Del's voice.

The opening of the episode sees Rodney enjoying a 'cultural encounter' in the flat with a female guest, Janice. Played by actress Gaynor Ward, a notable teen actor who had appeared in *The Tomorrow People* and *Grange Hill*, Janice would be one of Ward's final screen roles.

The studio scenes of this episode are a wonderful highlight with subtle touches, such as the sound effect of a dislodged record player needle as Del clumsily turns it off. The chemistry between David Jason and Nicholas Lyndhurst is already very much in place as Del talks Rodney into his scheme and Janice out of the flat.

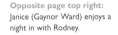

TROTTERS ETHNIC TOURS

Departure point

TROTTERS ETHNIC TOURS Departure point

Working throughout the first series of *Only Fools* as Assistant Floor Manager was Mandie Fletcher was Mandie Fletcher, who remembers first-hand the series' early development: "I was there at the very beginning when they were still trying to think of a name for it."

From her position on the studio floor, Fletcher saw the first few weeks of rehearsals, whilst Sullivan tinkered and honed his early scripts and Martin Shardlow tried out different things on set. "I was in a lowly position and was able to just observe. It was a funny old thing really, the characters were so brilliant , and I think when the audience came in for the first recording, they realised they had something really special."

A 1956 Leyland Bus (KCH 106) was hired from Grey-Green coaches for use in the episode; the company's Stamford Hill Coach Station was also used in the episode for Rodney's stint as a night watchman. The Trotters Ethnic Tours Departure Point was filmed at Ridley Avenue in Northfields, just down from the familiar north Acton estate.

With a coach lying empty and hope for the venture crushed (thanks to Grandad's very poor leaflet distribution) a dishevelled Del reveals his ultimate dream: owning a huge skyscraper on the South Bank with the initials of Trotters Independent Traders above it in 50-foot-high neon lettering.

"I hadn't really planned for the initials to spell something, it was an accident," remembered John Sullivan. "I'd just imagined Del coming up with a grand name. After a while, I noticed the initials spelt 'tit'. But Del hadn't realised – and nor had I!"

When Rodney points out what the initials spell, Del decides to retreat from the entrepreneurial battlefield for the day. But thankfully, this was just the beginning of his bold dreaming.

Opposite page top right: Janice (Gaynor Ward) enjoys a night in with Rodney.

Opposite page middle: One of the Trotters Ethnic Tours flyers destined for the rubbish chute – thanks to Grandad!

Above left: An exhausted Rodney (after his Trotter Watch night shift) is not impressed by Del's grand designs.

Below: The Trotters Ethnic Tours excursion bus.

Del Boy has bought a pile of bricks from the site of a recently demolished factory, but it's the boxes of lead beneath the pile that have really caught his interest. Rodney investigates the contents and discovers paperwork which reveals that the boxes of lead actually form the parts to build a do-it-yourself nuclear fallout shelter.

With its topical leanings, *The Russians are Coming* has all the hallmarks of something written for the unmade fifth series of *Citizen Smith*. However, unlike Wolfie Smith and his gang of loveable revolutionaries, the Trotters' approach to the situation is a lot more earnest. The episode is notable for its stage-play like structure and setting, and particularly for Grandad's expressing harrowed memories of the First World War, something John Sullivan would never have written for his earlier series.

"Every so often I would dip my toe in the water to see how far we could push the more serious issues," Sullivan recounted. "Grandad's heartfelt speech about the treatment of young men in the First World

War came from my own grandfather. He was in WWI and he saw terrible things that he never really spoke about. I remember my grandfather – one night after a few drinks – exploding and saying 'we didn't know what happened' and he just started telling this terrible tale. I can't remember exactly what he said, but I'd read enough and knew enough about these experiences to write about it."

For the episode's location filming, the series returned to the north Acton estate to see Del and Rodney hilariously bundle Grandad into the van and speed away. The Trotter family's 'four-minute warning drive' was filmed in the Northfields area, culminating in Cranmer Avenue where Eric the policeman stops them for a chinwag.

Actor Derek Newark was cast as Eric. Newark was a popular television guest artist, memorably appearing in the likes of *Doctor Who* and *Rising Damp*. Ray Butt would soon cast him as Eddie Brown, the menacing boss of Vince in Sullivan's *Just Good Friends*. Newark is joined in his police car by actor Kelly Garfield as the siren-happy Wayne.

The Russians are Coming would close the first series and mark Martin

Shardlow's final directorial contribution to *Only Fools*. Reflecting on his brief tenure, his wife Jill looks back fondly: "Martin loved it. The overall memory I have is one of a very happy team who seemed to get on well with each other and enjoy themselves – I know Martin was sad to hand the series back to Ray when he recovered!"

Elsewhere on the credits, the name 'Anthony Dow' appears for the first time, listed as Assistant Floor Manager. After many years working in the theatre, Dow was at the start of a three-month course working across the BBC light Entertainment Department when *Only Fools* went into production: "I remember on the first day I went on to *Blue Peter* to trail on the studio floor, and then on the second day, I went to look at my chart and it said *'Only Fools and Horses'*, and I didn't know what that was – I had assumed it was a pet show!" Joining the series mid-way through its first production block, Dow trailed fellow assistant floor manager Mandie Fletcher, helping to set-up props and gradually getting a feel for the production and the cast. "I assume they gave me a credit on the last show because I had been there sometimes," Dow remembers. "It was great, because it was something I understood. It was actors. And that is when I first met Ray Butt and John Sullivan."

The unusual closing shot of the episode (which the end credits would appear on) sees the Trotters' fully built fallout shelter on the roof of Harlech Tower, in a slow zoom-out filmed from the top of the nearby Beaumaris tower.

Broadcast on consecutive Tuesday evenings at 8.30pm on BBC 1 from 8 September, the first series of *Only Fools* would pull in an average of 7.67 million viewers for each episode. Whilst these numbers were not seen as amazing, the corporation was in the good habit of giving a new series a chance to grow...

THE RUSSIANS ARE COMING

13 OCTOBER 1981

A lot of people thought Del and Rodney had lost the plot when they decided to build a nuclear fall-out shelter on the roof of Nelson Mandela House. The council weren't very happy about it either when they found out. But as Del explained to them, we were having a dummy run for nuclear war: it was all done in the name of science and, apart from that pigeon that kept trying to nest in our air tube, no one was harmed. We had originally planned to build it on my allotment, but what with the four-minute warning there was no way we could get there on time. The sad fact of the matter is that you never know when those missiles will start flying, and it's always better to be safe than sorry. As far as I could tell the main issue was the lead walls. They played havoc with the signal on the portable telly, and I ended up missing the season finale of The Chinese Detective. Other than that, it was all quite cozy.

Grandad

CHRISTMAS CRACKERS

28 DECEMBER 1981

'Twas the season to be bored and depressed. Rodney was moping about reading dirty books. Grandad was in the kitchen melting utensils, and I just wanted to get through it and out the other end. It sounds pessimistic, I know, but Christmas had just never been the same since we lost Mum. Of course, that morning I'd popped down to see her at the cemetery, placed a few daffodils and told her all about the year gone and my plans for the one ahead, before nipping in at the Nags Head for a little pre-luncheon aperitif. I was was actually feeling quite chipper when I got back to the flat. Things took a very sudden nosedive the minute we sat down to tuck into Grandad's Christmas dinner. It was turkey again, although you wouldn't necessarily have known that to look at it. Being the caring and selfless bloke that I am, I made sure to serve Rodney and Grandad the good breast meat, leaving myself with the neck and and a bit of belly button. After a few initial and very tentative bites, it suddenly dawned on us all that Grandad had left the sodding giblets in, plastic bag and all! On closer inspection, it also became clear that this turkey was so underdone, a decent surgeon could have revived it (during the panic that ensued I could've sworn I saw it trying to crawl off the table!). Gordon Bennett, it was like staring into the jaws of hell! But what could I say to Grandad? Cooking the Christmas dinner was one of the few things left in life that filled him with a sense of purpose. Anyway, after dinner Grandad went for a kip and I was quite happy just to sit there in the armchair and pass the rest of the day away with a bowl of nuts and a glass or two of Bailey's and cherryade. And that's what I was doing, right up till Rodney went all dippy and started banging on about circuses and lemmings, and how we should go out, find a disco and pull a couple of sorts. I very gently explained to him that to leave Grandad by himself on Christmas Day would be nothing short of committing an immortal sin, but not even that would shut him up. Just when I was giving serious thought to giving him a clump, Grandad came in, announced that he was popping over to the old folks do at the community hall, and bid us a fair bonsoir. The saucy git! An hour later and Rodney and I arrived at the Monte Carlo club, and what an evening that turned out to be! Picture the scene: there we were, done up in our finest, me looking like a cross between Gordon Gekko and George Clooney, Rodney looking like a cross between Gordon the Gopher and George from Rainbow! I'd have had more joy going on the pull with Chewbacca!

Del

Behind the scenes, the hastily commissioned *Christmas Crackers* started life without either a producer or director. By December 1981, both Martin Shardlow and the now fully recovered Ray Butt were engaged elsewhere. On Ray Butt's suggestion, the Christmas special was produced and directed by Bernard Thompson in his sole contribution to the series. Thompson was a BBC comedy veteran, having worked on the likes of *Are You Being Served* and *Last of the Summer Wine*.

As a subject for his last minute commission, John Sullivan decided to tackle the boredom of Christmas: "Back then, Christmas could be particularly boring. There were circus shows on each TV channel, and everything was closed – shops, the pubs, everything... I purposely had Grandad doing the cooking to show how the loss of the mother affected the day. If there had been a woman there, it would have been different. But three men trapped in a flat at Christmas with nothing open in the whole of London, that's a dangerous situation!"

To Del and Rodney's distress, Grandad has managed to both undercook the turkey and leave the plastic bag of giblets inside. Later that evening Rodney suggests to Del they should go out to a club he knows that is open, but Del

reminds him they can't leave Grandad all alone on Christmas Night. Grandad, on the other hand, has no qualms about leaving Del and Rodney alone, and announces that he is going out to a party! In his absence the two brothers decide to head out to a night club in New Cross in an attempt to pull a couple of birds.

As the story moves on to the Monte Carlo Club, Desmond McNamara joins the cast as Del Boy's slow-witted friend Earl, said to also be a regular at the Nags Head but only seen in this episode. In many ways Earl seems to be *Christmas Crackers'* surrogate Trigger, suggesting that perhaps Roger Lloyd Pack wasn't available for the recording, necessitating his lines being given to a new character.

As Del and Rodney spot two girls, the two brothers debate a plan of attack. At the beginning of the episode Sullivan had Rodney reading a book: *Body Language – The Lost Art*. Now in the night club, the writer pays off the gag: "I thought it would be funny to see him staggering around trying to impress some girls when he's just looking ridiculous. I wrote the line about walking like an exaggerated John Wayne in the stage directions, and Nick was clever enough and a good enough actor to pull it off."

Christmas Crackers went before studio cameras on Wednesday 23 December and transmitted the following Monday. The more elastic nature of the

Christmas schedules meant that the episode was comfortably allowed to break the 30-minute transmission slot, with a viewing time of 34 minutes. However, if ever there was an episode which didn't need extra running time – it was this one.

There is no getting away from the fact that *Christmas Crackers* suffered by being made in a rush, with all the hallmarks of a tight production turnaround. The bar and costumes from *Go West Young Man* were dusted down again, and the studio-bound episode only featured two sets. But despite this, the episode contains some memorable visual gags and clever lines, including Del's plugless electric carving knife and his likening Rodney's image to a winkle barge sinking off the end of Southend pier.

With its simple premise and claustrophobic studio setting, and given what would happen over the next two decades, it now seems ironic that the Trotters' festive exploits began in such a humble and small-scale way.

Opposite page: Christmas 1981 in the Trotter household, a turkey with giblets and a burnt pudding and falling asleep in front of the telly!

Above and left: Earl (Desmond McNamara) meets the Trotters in the nightclub.

Below: Rodney's *Body Language – The Lost Art* Book.

Below left: Del finally gets talking to a couple of girls: "Excuse me, ladies. It's getting rather late and my brother and I were wondering if you were thinking of going home yet? ... Good, we'll have your chairs then!"

SERIES TWO

★ ★

When this time the previous year I'd said that by the same time the following year, we'd be millionaires, I realise now that my calculations may have been ever so slightly off. Just a smidge. Mistakes were made, but I held my hands up and was man enough to accept full responsibility, even though it was all Rodney's fault. But pas de basque (as they say in the Algiers), the thing to remember is that us captains of industry are natural-born risk-takers. Oh yes, there's nothing we like more than wading into unchartered jungle territory, fighting off gangs of blood-thirsty baboons as we hack through the undergrowth in search of mythical cities of gold... or something along those lines. The fact is you've gotta expect the occasional poison dart or two. So I pulled my socks up and recalled what my dear old Mum used to say: "The most important thing is that you learn from your mistakes." Well, with the amount of mistakes we were making I reckoned I was bound to learn something at some point. So yeah, we may still have been some way off from being millionaires, but I had a funny feeling in my gut that this year was gonna be the year. He who dares, wins. He who hesitates... don't.

THE LONG LEGS OF THE LAW

21 OCTOBER 1982

When Rodney confessed to me that he had a liking for women in uniforms, I hardly flinched. After all, what red-blooded bloke doesn't appreciate a smart and well turned out woman? When he told me that he had a preference for policewomen, I not only flinched, I brought up a bit of bile. And when we'd just polished off a full English at Sid's cafe and he told me that he'd just started dating a policewoman, I went into a state of shock and had to rush home and crack open the Andrews Liver Salts! Come the evening of the date, Grandad and I did our best to talk some last minute sense into him, but he paid no attention, he was too busy dousing himself in Brut and humming the theme tune to Juliet Bravo. In the end he went off on one of his great 'independence' speeches and stormed out the flat like a plonker on a promise, leaving me and Grandad to suck it all up.

"The world's a strange place, innit Grandad?" I said. "One minute you're walking along quite nicely, and the next minute, whack, life jumps out and gives you sobering thoughts."

"Oh I've had a lot of sobering thoughts in my time, Del Boy," he said. "It were them that started me drinking." But what could I have done? The boy was growing into a man. I didn't feel as needed as I used to be. But the most sobering thought of all was that one wrong word from that dipstick and I'd have ended up doing five years!

Del

To open the second series of *Only Fools*, John Sullivan looked to his family for inspiration: "My niece got a job as a policewoman and it basically came as a huge shock to all the family at the time, especially to my father. He just didn't like it because where we came from, you didn't join the police force. And because it was such a big culture shock to us, I thought I have got to write an episode about this, and how it affects the Trotters."

To begin with, however, Sullivan had a very different idea in mind for the episode: "The original plan was for Rodney to apply to become a policeman. Imagine what storms that would have caused in the Trotter household!"

But before Sullivan got around to writing the script, he found out that the BBC had a new comedy series in the works called *The Front Line* (which would star a young Paul Barber) about two West Indian brothers living in Brixton and one of the brothers becomes a policeman.

"So I had to change my script, and I thought 'what would be the second worst thing that could happen' as far as Del's concerned?' And, of course, it would be his future sister-in-law being a policewoman. It seemed the perfect episode to write because everything in the flat would have to be cleared out, and we already established in *Go West Young Man* that Rodney had a penchant for women in uniform, so it all fell into place very neatly from there."

With Ray Butt now firmly back in the director's chair, his overseeing presence seems to add a greater consistency to the series from the opening moments of *The Long Legs of the Law*. Similarly, the cast also seem more settled into their characters' skins.

Location filming for series two took place from 19 April to 7 May 1982, with studio recordings for

the seven episodes carried out on six consecutive Sundays from 23 May.

The Long Legs of the Law would be a studio-bound story, other than a brief establishing shot of the Old Oak Café, filmed at St Johns Parade in Ealing, where a certain greasy spoon proprietor would be introduced.

Despite only deciding to become an actor relatively late in life, by the time he came to the attention of Ray Butt as a contender to play the world weary Sid, Roy Heather had collected quite an acting CV both on stage and television. Heather's wonderful performance as every health inspector's nightmare won him a regular role on *Only Fools* for the

next two decades. With his hilarious disregard for hygiene, the character made for a great addition to the Peckham gang.

Another character making his 'debut' in this story is Del's long-running business associate, Monkey Harris. Whilst never seen on screen, Harris' name would crop up throughout the rest of the series as a (usually) dependable source of stock and wares.

Cast as the young policewoman, Sandra, who captures Rodney's affection, was actress Kate Saunders. More well-known now for her journalism and award winning fiction, Saunders delivers an absolutely cracking performance with just the right amount of deadpan delivery and, when called for, brief moments of sensitivity.

Perhaps it is not a complete surprise that when John Sullivan eventually creates the character who would become Rodney's wife, she has more than a few of the same qualities of Sandra, and of course a very similar name.

Above left: The Trotters pop along to the Old Oak Cafe and catch up with Sid (Roy Heather).

Above: Several memorable publicity shots for the second series were taken on the cafe set of *The Long Legs of the Law*.

Below left: Rodney's romance with Sandra (Kate Saunders) leads to the Trotters having to completely clear out the flat!

Above: The Trotters hear Trigger's sad news about his Gran.

Above top right: Trigger's Gran's sitting room... a place Grandad knows very well.

Right: "You're coming through louder than a CB, Rubber Duck...Is it forgiveness that you seek, Trotter?" – Del winds up Grandad.

Below: The urns featured in the story were a widely available design.

Below right: The Trotters attempt to dispose of the ashes in the Thames and at a bowls club.

Opposite page: Del talks to the road-sweeper (Terry Duggan) who sucked up the urn.

Trigger's gran, Alice, has passed on. Tasked with selling off the contents of her house on behalf of Trig, Del focuses on two valuable urns. Later at the Trotter flat, Grandad discovers that one of the urns contains the ashes of Trigger's grandad, Arthur!

"Following a family bereavement, we had the very difficult decision of what to do with the ashes," remembered John Sullivan. "It was simply a case of not knowing the best place to lay them and feeling very responsible. I thought 'how would Del look at this?' He'd be the kind of man who'd want to do the right thing. He's very respectful and wouldn't just throw these ashes away, even though there's a couple of times in the episode where he almost does!"

Adding to the complication of having to dispose of the ashes in a suitable way, we learn that Grandad had an affair with Trigger's Gran. Upon finding out, her husband swore to Grandad that he would one day come back and haunt him. This sets up one of the highlights of *Ashes to Ashes*: the scene in which Grandad talks to Arthur's urn, attempting to make amends for his past dalliances.

Lennard Pearce's gentle delivery is magnificent, with the actor keenly aware of how unimaginable it is that the old timer could have once enjoyed a steamy affair. When Del starts answering back with his traffic cone 'megaphone' it is simply an inspired addition, creating a cracking comedy moment.

ASHES TO ASHES

28 OCTOBER 1982

My grandad Arthur was a smashing man. He took care of me after my mum went. My dad died a couple of years before I was born, so I never got to know him. From what I could gather, my mum didn't know him that well either, so there's not much I can say about it. Not that it mattered, as I had Arthur and he was always there for me in times of trouble. Like the time after I left school and no matter how hard I tried I couldn't get any work. I lost count of the amount of interviews I had, which I never really understood, cos even though job satisfaction and a career path were important to me, I weren't all that fussy. I tried for a job as a milkman, a lollipop man and a grave digger, but they all turned me down. I even applied to become a traffic warden, but they said I was overqualified. Just when I'd given up hope and was about to my post my application form for the police force, Arthur stepped in and said he'd have a word down at the council depot. A week later I went down to the depot, was handed a broom and a dustcart and sent out onto the streets. And that was that. I haven't looked back since. I also got on alright with my Gran, and, even though she could be a right miserable cow at times, I was gutted when she died. It was a depressing time in general really, but Gran had left me a few bob so I decided to get away for a while and live it up a bit, you know, discos, nightclubs, golden beaches and blue skies. Unfortunately from the moment I touched down in Ireland to the moment I left, it was overcast. The discos weren't up to much either. At the end of the day it was a lot of fun, but I didn't enjoy it.

Trigger

Many years later in the *Rock & Chips* episode *The Frog and the Pussycat*, we learn from Grandad's estranged wife, Violet, that it was her finding out about his affair with Alice that originally led to Grandad living with his son, Reg, and the rest of the family.

The Script for *Ashes to Ashes* required the crew to take the Trotters and their Grecian urn on a trek around London as they attempt to dispose of the ashes in a fitting way. Their journey starts off at Acton bowls club before moving on to a rowing boat on the River Thames (off the shore of Bermondsey) and ending with an encounter with a road-sweeping van on the streets of Southall.

Ashes to Ashes would be the first episode to show Trigger as a road sweeper, a job for which his grandad Arthur taught him the ropes, and that he would remain working at for the rest of the series. Of course, in 1996's *Heroes and Villains* it is revealed that Trig has been using the 'same' broom for 20 years (albeit with 17 new heads and 14 new handles), suggesting that he has been sweeping for the council since at least 1976.

With a visit to Trigger's Gran's house and a plot revolving around his family, this would be the closest *Only Fools* gets to an episode directly about the Nags Head regular. "We never went to Trigger's flat," Sullivan would later recall, "We thought about it, but we could never really get into his head."

It seems that Sullivan realised that to put any more focus on Trigger would only take something away from the character and that it would be far funnier to keep him as an occasional presence – both physically and mentally.

A LOSING STREAK

4 NOVEMBER 1982

As good as Del is at hiding it when he's feeling the strain, I can always notice the little telltale signs. And knowing him as well as I do, the root of the problem is usually either a woman or money. This time it's money, and more's the point that he's been pissing it all away on poker games. Well, I've seen too many good men finish up in the gutter chasing 'easy' money. The thing is, most of the money Del's lost has been to that mate of his, Boycie, the second-hand car dealer from Lewisham. But I get the sense there's more to this than just cards. It's almost like there's some personal vendetta going on between them. From what I've heard about that Boycie fella, it wouldn't surprise me if he was using a marked deck, which is something you've always gotta look out for when playing poker. I know this from experience cos I was in a card school once where the cards were marked and I ended up losing a fortune. Of course, I was the one that marked them, but then I never was very good at cards. Anyway, there's no stopping Del when his pride is at stake, so I did the next best thing and gave him my lucky double-headed coin. A Scotch bloke gave it to me during the war. I remember it like it was yesterday: his hands were trembling and his voice was just a whisper. "I want you to have something to remember me by, Trotter" he said, "Take my lucky coin." And with that he... well... he went. He didn't die, he just deserted, but it was still very emotional. And you couldn't blame him really. The way those Germans were carrying on, someone was gonna get hurt.

Grandad

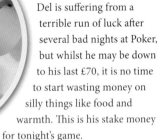

Del is suffering from a terrible run of luck after several bad nights at Poker, but whilst he may be down to his last £70, it is no time to start wasting money on silly things like food and warmth. This is his stake money for tonight's game.

The inspiration for *A Losing Streak* came straight from John Sullivan's memories of his father's gambling. "As a little kid I would sometimes come down on a Monday morning to go to school and walk into a room full of smoke, with men still sitting around gambling – they'd obviously been playing right through the night. These card games just became part of my life, so I knew all about the cheating and the accusations. There was always one guy who had much more money than the others and was much more successful."

If there was going to be one guy who was much more successful, it had to be Boycie. In March 1982 John Challis had a special delivery in the post. "It was another script from Ray Butt, with a note attached 'would I come back to do another episode' and I opened it, I read it, and thought oh lovely, this time I'm much more heavily featured. It's this Boycie bloke again, very dramatic and very funny."

A Losing Streak is where we first really get to *know* Boycie. Under the studio lights of his first scene in the Nags Head, Challis really gets to explore the car salesman's snobbish indifference. When Trigger is thrown in to the mix, the Peckham family is really starting to come together.

Making the first of five appearances in the series as the tall red-headed Nags Head barmaid, was actress Julie La

Rousse, whose Christian name was also used for character. A well-travelled background artist, La Rousse can be spotted in a host of TV classics from *The Avengers* to *Are You Being Served?*

A game of cards isn't the easiest thing to make look dramatic on screen, but Ray Butt makes up for the lack of visual comedy opportunities with a suitably atmospheric set, brought to life with some great lighting, beer cans and drifting smoke. Piles of quickly discarded pound notes also add to the proceedings, crunched up on the table under menacing glares from Jason and Challis.

As the game reaches its conclusion, it seems that all hope is lost as Del goes "all in", putting at risk everything in the Trotters' flat: the tellies, the furniture, his jewellery and van. Sullivan cleverly keeps the story alive right up until the moment Del shows Boycie his hand, a moment which, still decades (and dozens of repeat viewings) later, never fails to create a real sense of relief. "Well I've got a pair of aces... and I've got *another* pair of aces".

This poker match scene would sadly be the only time Boycie and Grandad appear on screen together, a recording which John Challis has fond memories of: "I found Lennard Pearce absolutely charming. Whilst I didn't get to know him terribly well, I really liked him and thought he was a lovely character."

Opposite page: Trotters Independent Traders' latest line: hooky Yves Saint Dior!

Above left: Grandad gives Del his double-headed coin.

Above: As the rivalry heats up in the pub, the Nags Head's newest barmaid Julie (Julie La Rousse) looks on.

Left: An Irishman with unusual drinking habits (Michael G. Jones) costs Del money.

Below middle: Del plays a winning hand – "I thought Del Boy might have something up his sleeve!"

Below right: "Where d'you get those bloody aces from?" – Del and Boyce share a moment after their duel.

Above: Del attempts to convince Rodney that a Camel hair coat is just what he needs.

Right and below: Irene McKay (Gaye Brown) wins Rodney's heart – "You'd better tell me your name, it's gonna get a bit embarrassing if I keep having to call you 'thingy' all night."

Below right: Irene's son Marcus (Steve Fletcher) seems to know Del...

Opposite page above left: Irene's husband Tommy (David Daker) mistakes Del for Rodney.

Whilst going door-to-door selling skirts, peekaboo bras and nifty knickers, Rodney finds love with an older woman. Forty, to be exact... an age that would give even Grandad cause to think twice!

"I'd read about the phenomena of toy boys," remembered John Sullivan. "For years there were older men who had young girlfriends but suddenly the tables were turning. I picked up on this and let my imagination run riot. I thought it would be right up Rodney's street, and the kind of situation in which he could get himself into all sorts of trouble."

For the second time in the series, Rodney's pursuit of romance leaves Del and Grandad in a state of bemusement, but instead of the scorn displayed in *The Long Legs of the Law*, this time their reaction is laughter... at least to begin with.

Cast as Rodney's love interest, Irene McKay, was actress Gaye Brown, who had previously made two striking appearances in cult films *A Clockwork Orange* and *The Rocky Horror Picture Show*. Although they never meet on screen, Brown's screen husband, the soon-to-be-paroled Parkhurst inmate, Tommy Mackay, was played by actor David Daker who was perhaps best known for his explosive appearance in the final episode of *Porridge*. To complete the McKay family, Steve Fletcher was cast as the pointy-haired punk Marcus McKay.

NO GREATER LOVE

11 NOVEMBER 1982

In many ways it is a shame that Nicholas Lyndhurst and Gaye Brown share so little screen time in the story – if Rodney's half of the soppy phone call is anything to go by, it would have made for some great comedy moments.

Interestingly, this is the only time we see Trotters Independent Traders going door to door, flogging their wares 'on the weekly' and offering their punters credit. Filming locations used for the Trotters' house calls include Brouncker Road in Acton – used for Irene McKay's house – and Connaught Road in Ealing – used for Ahmed's house, with the nearby corner of Bedford Road as the location for Del's encounter with Tommy McKay.

Whilst Del shows very little sympathy to Rodney's face, when the violent Tommy McKay comes on the scene (under the impression that Del is Rodney) the older Trotter doesn't hesitate to take the beating and fight on behalf of his little brother, setting up Sullivan's ironic ending: "After Del gets the beating, he goes back into the pub and everything he'd told Rodney about meeting someone his own age has come true. Rodney's forgotten about Irene and he's got another girlfriend, Zoe. In the end there was no need for Del to take the hiding. But in typical Trotter style, it was too late."

Young Rodney dating a 40-year-old! I almost swallowed me dentures when he told us. And it's so out of character for the boy. Up till now most of Rodney's dates arrive at the flat on skateboards! But the difference this time is that he's in love, and love can make you do some very strange things. It reminds me of the time I first started painting and decorating for the council. There was this girl who worked at the depot. Lilly her name was. Actually, no, it was Millie. Or was it? It might have been Tilly. No, no I remember now. It was Clara. Anyway, hers was the first face I saw every morning when I arrived at work, and after a while she took quite the shine to yours truly. She never said it, you know, not in so many words, but she gave off all the signals. Every morning she'd have a cup of tea and a smile waiting for me, and she always had a compliment for my horse (this was 1924, there weren't many cars about. Not that I could afford anyway). Well, at the time I was quite shy and a total stranger to those sort of open displays of affection, but before long she'd worked her magic and I, too, was smitten. From that moment on, Clara was all I could think about. She was on my mind all day long, which is probably why I ended up wall-papering over that serving hatch and getting the sack. After a while I started flirting back with her. Nothing big, just little things, like following her home and leaving little notes outside her window. Of course, I didn't let on it was me. I'd hide in the bushes and keep it all very discreet, which ain't easy when you've got a horse standing next to you. That went on for a while, and then one morning I arrived at the depot to find she was gone. Just like that. I went to her house but she'd moved out. I never saw her ever again, but I didn't stop looking for her, even in the other women I met later in life. But none of 'em could hold a candle up to Clara. The day I did stop looking was the day I met Violet, who soon after became my wife. She weren't the woman of my dreams or nothing, although she scrubbed up alright when she made the effort, and she did a lovely steak 'n' kidney pudding. Anyway, it was years later I discovered that Clara had in fact left to start a new life abroad. Apparently some bloke had been stalking her, so it's understandable really. They never did catch the stalker, which is just as well cos I would have killed him!

Grandad

THE YELLOW PERIL

18 NOVEMBER 1982

I received phone call from a man warning me that health inspector on his way. The man told me I need to get my kitchen cleaned and decorated or I be in big trouble. He then called me John. I was very worried. The next day Derek Trotter come to my restaurant and I tell him about call. He told me to cheer up and says it is my lucky day as painting and decorating is his family business. He also say he has new consignment of paint and offers me very good deal, so I accept. He arrive next morning with young man and old man. The young man looked very white. The old man wore slippers. I did not care. I needed job done fast. The only problem is colour of paint. I tell Derek that I like blue. "I like blue," I said. But the paint is gold. Derek then explain that he choose gold because of name of my restaurant, The Golden Lotus. He then tell me that I know it make sense. Two days later, job is finished and I am happy so I pay. But as day comes to an end there is big, big problem. The kitchen walls glow with the power of a thousand suns! It is so bright it give me headache and I have to wear sunglasses. I'm very upset so I call Derek. He say not to worry as it will save on electric bill. He also do me very good deal on new pair of sunglasses. Cushty!

Mr Chin

Thanks to a friendly 'anonymous' tip-off that a visit from the health inspector is imminent, Mr Chin, proprietor of The Golden Lotus Chinese take-away, has hired Trotters Independent Traders to decorate his kitchen.

The idea for *The Yellow Peril* came from an incident in Mitcham that John Sullivan recalled: "I'd heard a story about some guys who'd broken into a paint store and stolen the stock. They drove home and parked their van in the garage, but within about ten minutes the police were knocking on their door. They were caught so quickly because one of the cans had been knocked over and there was a yellow line leading from the store straight to their garage!"

Whilst the paint stolen in the Mitcham break-in wasn't luminous, the fact that it happened at night gave Sullivan the image of a glowing painted trail, leading him to the idea of how the Trotters would make use of dodgy stock, which in the story is pinched by Trigger and Monkey Harris from a lock up at Clapham Junction.

Leaving Rodney and Grandad to paint the restaurant, Sullivan gave Del another job in the story: "Del worshipped his mother and in this episode he shows how devoted he is by painting her headstone. Where I grew up, the departed mother became almost sainted. Yet you'd hear other women talking about these mothers and giving a different view. This is exactly how I thought Del would be with the memories of Joan."

This is the first episode of the series in which Del directly discusses his and Rodney's mother, and the first appearance of her fibreglass monument, "the bestest grave in the entire cemetery" as Del puts it.

Kensal Green Cemetery in North Kensington was used as the daylight location for the cemetery scenes around Joan's grave. For the final scene of the episode, where it is revealed that Joan's grave has been painted in luminous yellow paint, the production team used Walpole Park in Ealing, just a short distance away from Oaklands Road, where the establishing shot of The Golden Lotus was filmed.

Actor Rex Wei was cast as The Golden Lotus' manager Mr Chin. Wei had previously appeared in *The Professionals* as well as the classic sitcom *Bless This House*. Wei seems to have been a late addition to the cast as rehearsal scripts mention that veteran James Bond actor Vincent Wong was to be playing Mr Chin. In an unusual move, the studio scenes for *The Yellow Peril* were recorded on the same day as those for the final episode of the series, *A Touch of Glass* – on Sunday 6 June 1982. As both stories featured a significant amount of location filming, it made sense for the production team to group both episodes studio scenes together for one evening of audience recording. Sharp-eyed viewers might notice that boxes of export spirits beneath the curtains in the Trotter flat are clearly in identical positions in both episodes.

Opposite page far right: Filming on location in Ealing outside The Golden Lotus.

Above: The cast posed for several promotional shots outside the Ealing location.

Left: Kensal Green Cemetery in Kensington was used as the main location of Joan Trotter's monument.

Below left: Mr Chin (Rex Wei) discusses Del's decorating plans.

Below: Joan's monument, now painted in luminous yellow – "our mum's grave is now going to become a beacon for every Satanist and acid-head in England!"

Above: The Trotters are stuck in the Nags Head.

Above right: David Jason and Jillianne Foot on location in Swanage.

Above right: Shots from John Jefford's photo montage of the Trotters holiday.

Right: Grandad's false teeth put an end to all hopes of romance!

Below: Del and Rodney enjoy the beach... and the crew film them.

Opposite page: Grandad's Guard Juan (Anthony Jackson) – "The charity of my choice will be very pleased."

A rain-soaked marketplace is no place for a pair of fly pitchers, so Del and Rodney are waiting for the weather to improve from the safety of the Nags Head. It is here that a chance meeting with local travel agent, Alex, sets Del's business brain into overdrive. In an effort to drum up business, Del convinces Alex to put word out that the next person who walks into his shop will receive a discount of 80 per cent on any holiday, in the hope that the rush will encourage the rest of the customers to pay full price. Alex jumps at the idea and Del and Rodney rush to be his next customers. The Trotters are going to Spain!

It was John Sullivan's goal for the second series to take the Trotters out of Peckham: "I wanted to send the Trotters abroad to Benidorm or Torremolinos. These are the kind of resorts that many people would want to steer clear of, but they're exactly the sort of place that would constitute Del's dream holiday."

Sadly, unlike the Trotters, the *Only Fools* crew weren't able to budget for a trip to Spain. As a solution, it was decided to film on the Dorset coast, which also provided the opportunity to find suitable filming locations for the final episode of the series, *A Touch of Glass*.

To set the scene of the holiday, photographer John Jefford photographed a sequence showing the Trotters swept up in the highs and lows of packaged holidays, from discos and dancing, to the view of a building site outside their hotel window. Photographed in and around the Swanage area where the crew were based, the montage was appropriately accompanied by Mungo Jerry's 1970 hit 'In the Summertime'.

IT NEVER RAINS...

25 NOVEMBER 1982

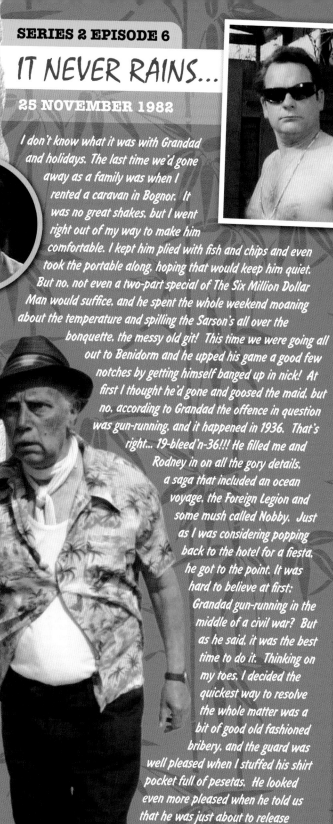

Actress Jillianne Foot was cast as the English holiday maker Jacky, who Del tries desperately to impress with a mangled and nonsensical mixture of French, Spanish and German: "My lasting memories of filming was just how cold it was, all of the sunshine you see was created by some very clever lighting." Foot's scenes were filmed at the Knoll House Hotel in Swanage, which the art department did their best to make look like Spain. The actors however had to do their best and act warm, despite it being a chilly late April on the Dorset coast.

For the cast and crew the location work would be memorable for many reasons, as Foot recalls: "It was Nick Lyndhurst's 21st birthday during the week, so we had a big party. John Sullivan was there and was such a modest but seriously funny man. We all had to struggle through the next days shooting with massive hangovers!" It was during this party that a member of the crew presented Lyndhurst with a large inflatable doll as a birthday prank, something which John Sullivan took note of for later use...

Just down the road from the hotel the crew set up on Studland Beach to film the scenes of Del, Rodney and Grandad enjoying the 'Spanish' sunshine. It is here where Grandad (looking fantastically out of place in a bright yellow Hawaiian shirt) starts to act edgy, as we realise the old timer has something on his mind.

This leads to the story's final scene in the Spanish prison cell, which John Sullivan used as an opportunity to make some interesting comments about the family history: "I recall writing a line about 'us Trotters always being bad sailors' and this eventually gave life to Uncle Albert, because I then wanted to bring in the world's worst sailor."

I don't know what it was with Grandad and holidays. The last time we'd gone away as a family was when I rented a caravan in Bognor. It was no great shakes, but I went right out of my way to make him comfortable. I kept him plied with fish and chips and even took the portable along, hoping that would keep him quiet. But no, not even a two-part special of The Six Million Dollar Man would suffice, and he spent the whole weekend moaning about the temperature and spilling the Sarson's all over the bonquette, the messy old git! This time we were going all out to Benidorm and he upped his game a good few notches by getting himself banged up in nick! At first I thought he'd gone and goosed the maid, but no, according to Grandad the offence in question was gun-running, and it happened in 1936. That's right... 19-bleed'n-36!!! He filled me and Rodney in on all the gory details, a saga that included an ocean voyage, the Foreign Legion and some mush called Nobby. Just as I was considering popping back to the hotel for a fiesta, he got to the point. It was hard to believe at first: Grandad gun-running in the middle of a civil war? But as he said, it was the best time to do it. Thinking on my toes, I decided the quickest way to resolve the whole matter was a bit of good old fashioned bribery, and the guard was well pleased when I stuffed his shirt pocket full of pesetas. He looked even more pleased when he told us that he was just about to release Grandad anyway. The stupid old div had only been pulled in for a bit of jaywalking!

Del

A TOUCH OF GLASS

2 DECEMBER 1982

Typical Del Boy. He'd spent three hours in a stately home and suddenly thought he was the Earl of Sandwich. You should have seen him. He just couldn't wait to get a shotgun and a receiver and go marching across the grouse moors all done up like a ploughman's lunch. But the really worrying thing was that he was very serious about the offer to renovate Lord and Lady Ridgemeres' chandeliers. Louis the 14th crystal they were, two of 'em, hanging very delicately from the ceiling in their main hall. Worth an absolute fortune! Come the day of the renovation, I was so nervous I felt ill, but Del kept reassuring me that he knew what he was doing. I won't go into detail about the actual job we did, but suffice it to say, Grandad gave that second chandelier the kind of treatment he usually reserves for Christmas turkeys. The only upside was that the Ridgemeres weren't there to see the results and the Butler was too old and slow to catch us when we bundled into the van and did a three-wheel-spin out of the driveway!

Rodney

"My father had a job as an apprentice laying central heating at a manor and, as a safety precaution, this team had to take down a chandelier," John Sullivan remembered. "So while one bloke went upstairs to undo the bolts, the others, including my dad, were on the ladders getting ready to catch it. But the guy loosened the bolts to the wrong chandelier, and it came crashing down. I thought the story was hilarious but my father didn't see the humour, as seven men had lost their jobs."

In spite of his father's concerns, Sullivan decided to use the idea for *Only Fools.* Writing the episode's final scenes first, as the chandelier falls to the ground and the Trotters scarper, he then had to work out how the Trotters got there.

To double as the fictional Ridgemere Hall, Claycsmore School in the Dorset village of Iwerne Minster was used. The boarding school was actually in term time when the shoot took place, so the cast and crew had to plan their shoot carefully to capture everything within a limited timeframe.

Special effects and props firm Trading Post were tasked with building a duplicate chandelier and setting up the stunt. The stunning replica they made featured specially cut parts from Woolworths plastic salad bowls, and yet still cost £6,000, meaning that the team only had one chance to do the drop and get it right.

As Jason and Lyndhurst climbed their ladders, holding a tarpaulin between them, a gathered crew nervously looked on. Director Ray Butt carefully positioned cameras to capture various angles, with the idea in mind to keep the viewers attention

focused on the foreground, so as not to telegraph the big reveal when the second chandelier comes crashing down in the background.

For the climatic crashing chandelier sequence, John Sullivan kept away: "I wasn't on set, which was probably a good job because I'm a real laugher. This scene could only be shot once and Ray Butt said he'd fire anyone who laughed, but Ray was the first one to crack up and he had to shove a handkerchief in his mouth!"

Cast as Lord Ridgemere was distinguished screen actor Geoffrey Toone, most famous for starring in the 1956 musical *The King and I* before embarking on an impressive small-screen career. Lady Ridgemere was played by actress Elizabeth Benson, who

would shortly be cast by Ray Butt again as Mrs Beecham in *Just Good Friends*. Sitcom regular Donald Bisset would complete *A Touch of Glass*' guest cast line up as the Ridgemere's dependable butler, Wallace.

After the episode's transmission a slightly nervous Sullivan awaited his father's views on seeing his past exploits brought to life: "I didn't tell him I was going to use the idea and when the episode aired he rang me straight away and admitted 'Yes, it was funny.'"

As one of Ridgemere Hall's priceless Louis XIV chandeliers crashed to the ground, one of television's most defining moments was taking place, sending *Only Fools* into the comedy history books.

Screened on consecutive Thursday evenings at 8.30pm on BBC 1 from 21 October 1982, the second series of *Only Fools* would pull in an average of 8.85 million viewers for each episode.

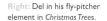

Christmas 1982 was to be a bonus festive year for the *Only Fools* team, as in addition to another full-length Christmas edition, the series was invited to appear as part of *The Funny Side of Christmas*, a television special presented by comedian Frank Muir. Comprising of ten sketches from a crop of other current BBC comedy series, the special was inspired by the long running *Christmas Night with the Stars* variety show which featured similar sketches from the likes of *Dad's Army* and *Steptoe and Son* in the sixties and seventies.

Written by John Sullivan and directed by Ray Butt, the eight minute *Only Fools* segment *Christmas Trees* was the fourth of the evening, in a show which also included short sketches from Roy Clarke's *Open All Hours* and Carla Lane's *Butterflies*, allowing viewers to see David Jason and Nicholas Lyndhurst play two very different characters.

The plot of the *Only Fools* sketch sees Del Boy attempting to sell 149 telescopic Christmas trees. With sales not forthcoming, Del convinces Rodney to offer one to a nearby church where the Vicar is all too pleased to accept. As Rodney returns to the market it is revealed that Del is now promoting the trees as having full endorsement from the Church of England!

Filmed at the opposite end of Islington's Chapel Market, from where the opening credits were photographed, the sketch makes use of St Silas Church on nearby Penton Street. Alongside the main trio, the sketch also features a returning Roy Heather in his second appearance as Sid, this time selling from a van. Cast as the kindly vicar was actor John Pennington, making his first appearance in the series; the next time we see him would be under very different circumstances in 1985's *Strained Relations*.

Transmitted three days before *Only Fools'* Christmas special proper, the sketch has seldom been seen since, which is a shame as it makes a perfect 'ducking and diving' counterpart to the sentimental romance shown a few days later. In many ways this episode features the greatest Del Boy fly pitcher scene as David Jason

seems to have the crowd eating out of his hands: "Excuse me madam, don't you know it's rude to walk away when someone is talking to you?... Go on then if you must, but hurry back."

To close *Only Fools'* second year, a second Christmas special was commissioned, one that would feature Del Boy in a decidedly reflective mood. "One of Del's ambitions, that he doesn't often speak about, is his wish to be a family man," John Sullivan remembered. "With all his many engagements, you realise that he's always been desperate to get back the family life that was taken away from him when his mum died."

The story opens with the Trotters at a Spanish night at the Nags Head, but far from getting caught up in the festivities with Rodney and Grandad, Del is feeling down after getting the 'heave-ho' from his latest girlfriend. To echo his mood he requests that the evening's singer, Enrico, sing the mournful ballad 'Old Shep', which duly clears out most of the pub. Just then Del notices a woman at the bar, Heather, who also liked the song, so Del gets up to talk to her.

Cast as Heather was London born actress Rosalind Lloyd, who was called to read before Ray

Butt and John Sullivan at Television Centre: "They were excited at the idea of a different kind of Christmas special," Lloyd remembers from her first meeting with the director and writer. "An episode without the usual razzamatazz and forced jollity of the season. They asked me to read some of Heather's lines and seemed pleased that I could produce a London accent which wasn't too strong!"

At the time, the idea of a serious *Only Fools* romance was a bit of a departure for the series and its crew, but Lloyd found herself in safe hands: "Ray Butt was a lovely, gentle man and my favourite kind of director, not aggressive or hot tempered. He placed complete trust in David and stepped back subtly to allow the relationship between Del and Heather to develop."

Butt cleverly suggested that Lloyd and David Jason met up before rehearsals to get to know each other and start developing their rapport: "I give full credit to David for helping me play Heather to the best of

Above: A 1982 promotional shot of the cast taken on location during the filming of *Diamond are for Heather.*

Above left: The Vicar (John Pennington) as seen in the *Christmas Trees* sketch.

Below: Spanish night in the Nags Head sees Del meet Heather (Rosalind Lloyd).

my ability. His generosity of spirit was second to none and rehearsals in a church hall in Chiswick were a joy."

It is in this story that we get the first real idea that there is more to Del Boy than the life of a wheeler-dealer. We also see a Del prepared to step in and be a father to someone else's child, revealing a positive aspect to his character which takes Heather by surprise.

Unlike the hastily produced studio-bound 1981 special, *Diamonds are for Heather* was allocated a full budget to take in some pretty extravagant location filming, carried out over a week from 30 November. The crew would film Lloyd, Jason and child actor Daniel Jones (cast as Heather's son, Darren) outside an Ealing newsagents, at London Zoo, The London Planetarium and on board *HMS Belfast*. Lloyd remembers that despite the short schedule, things were quite relaxed: "It was really good fun, more like a works outing. The little boy who played Darren was so sweet."

To soundtrack the romantic montage, Sullivan chose the recent chart hit 'Zoom' released by Philadelphian group Fat Larry's Band the month before

production of the episode commenced. With its gentle synth melody and rousing chorus, it perfectly captures the sentiment and echoes Del Boy's wide-eyed view of love.

Additional location filming saw the crew return to the Three Johns pub on White Lion Street in Islington to stand in as the Nags Head once more (after first appearing in *It Never Rains*), as well as a visit to the north Acton estate again for Del's kick about with Darren, whilst Grandad and Rodney have a chuckle at his expense.

Interestingly, although airing just four weeks after *A Touch of Glass* was shown, this special was produced some five months after the end of the second series' production.

With Christmas approaching, studio time was tight for *Diamonds are for Heather*, requiring an unusual Monday evening audience recording on 20 December. For studio scenes, popular sitcom actor Roger Brierley joined the cast as Heather's mature student babysitter, Brian, and John Moreno was cast as the cockney singing Spaniard, Enrico.

DIAMONDS ARE FOR HEATHER

30 DECEMBER 1982

For Lloyd, the audience raised the performance of all the cast for the studio scenes: "Having a live studio audience was fantastic because the enthusiasm and excitement made the show even better, I thought. The scene in Heather's flat with the marvellous Roger - who was so tall! – is especially memorable because of the audience's reaction to my line 'Mind the step!'"

Another unofficial casting was that of Heather's absent husband Vic, seen only via a photo on Heather's mantelpiece. As a joke and surprise to David Jason, the production team borrowed a photo of *Only Fools'* original director Martin Shardlow from his wife Jill, which Jason enjoyed thoroughly.

If there was any doubt that John Sullivan could pen an effective romance, *Diamonds are for Heather* cast them aside with its heartbreaking closing scenes. As Lloyd remembers: "The final scene with Del was so sad. You could have heard a pin drop and the atmosphere was very emotional, though there were laughs too. When the show ended and we had taken our bows, we had the opportunity to meet some of the audience and someone said, 'I wasn't expecting that. You both made me cry!'"

Although Del and Heather were never meant to be, the character foreshadowed Del eventually finding a lasting romance many years later in the series. Reflecting on her role as Heather, Lloyd always felt part of the *Only Fools* family and was there watching when Del's dream of having a family were finally made a reality in 1991's *Three Men, a Woman and a Baby*: "My turn to cry was when Del held baby Damien up to the night sky and spoke to his Mum, to the beautiful sound of Vivaldi's *Lute Concerto*."

You never know when love will strike. There I was in the Nags Head, drowning my sorrows over a love lost. Her name was Sheryl (I think) and she really was something special. I mean, fair enough, she had a bit of a nose on her, but most of the time I could see past that. At the time I thought she was the one. Unlike most of my previous loves, Sheryl came from a money background. Her dad had owned a string of laundrettes and had made himself a tidy penny before kicking the bucket and leaving Sheryl the business. I don't know what I did wrong. I'd taken her out for the obligatory steak meal and got her the biggest bunch of geraniums money could buy. I'd even offered her an unbeatable, once-in-a-lifetime, deal on a consignment of hooky Persil, but all to no avail. Anyway, that night in the pub was when I met Heather, and from the moment we began chatting I knew that she really was the one. I didn't even mind that she already had a little sprog, and invited them both to a day out to the zoo. We had a brilliant time, and for a moment there it almost felt like I had a proper family of my own. Of course, I proposed to her. I knew she liked solitaire diamonds, so I got my mate Abdul to find me a ring with a great big cluster of solitaires. She liked the ring but turned down the proposal. I dunno, maybe I hadn't been open enough with my feelings. The thing with me is that I just can't do all that lovey-dovey stuff. I do feel things, but when I try to say 'em they always come out sounding wallyish. She treated the whole thing with great sensitivity, though, explaining that she felt for me the way most people feel for a gerbil or a goldfish, and that made me feel a lot better. At the end of the day, it was a classic case of Poubelles a la mode, as they say in the Pompidou.

Del

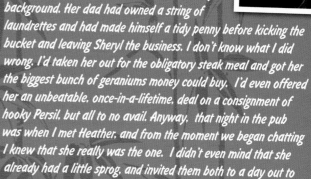

SERIES THREE ★★★

★ ★

The whole balancing-business-with-family lark was starting to give my arse an 'eadache! It had been bad enough what with Grandad talking to urns and getting himself banged up in foreign nicks, but then there was Rodney! I just don't know what it was with that boy. One minute he was inviting the old bill round for gin and tonics, the next he was falling in love with the 40-year-old missus of a soon-to-be-released Parkhurst inmate! It was almost making me miss the days he just stayed in his bedroom, popping zits and practicing the old one-gun salute. I knew I couldn't be too harsh with him, though, it weren't entirely his fault. He was just at that awkward age where his hormones were all over the shop. I s'pose he was a bit like a trifle, you know, thick and fruity. Anyway, these things were sent to try us, and, despite everything, I had high hopes that the year ahead was gonna be different. Yeah, this was the year we were finally gonna move up in the world and make our first million!

★ ★

HOMESICK

10 NOVEMBER 1983

It surprised a lot of people when Rodney became chairman of the Tenant's Association, but not me. Being the honest, caring and principled lad that he was, there was no one better for the job as far as I was concerned. It was a very proud moment in the history of the Trotters. It was also the perfect opportunity to get us out of Nelson Mandela House and into a nice little bungalow in Herrington Road. Lovely Jubbly! Of course, it was for the same reason that Rodney was perfect for the job that Grandad and I couldn't let him in on our little plan. And while you could argue that it was uncharacteristically underhanded of me, I felt it was justified. I mean, we'd been living in Nelson Mandela House since 1962. In that time the lifts had worked twice and the local crime rate had quadrupled annually. So we did what needed to be done. All it took was for Grandad to stay in bed and act weak and frail, which was really no great stretch. For my part, I simply applied a bit of gentle pressure on Rodney, like calling him a traitor and threatening to disown him if he didn't do right by his ailing Grandfather. And when he finally got his arse into gear and invited the head of the housing and welfare committee – the surprisingly lovely, Miss Mackenzie – round to see the sorry state Grandad was in, she signed the paperwork there and then. I even very nearly swung a date with her as I was bidding her a fair bonjour at the front door. Close, but no cigar. Talking of cigars, when she returned five minutes later, having changed her mind about the date, and caught Grandad bounding about with one hanging out of his gob, she wasn't best pleased. Yes, it was safe to say that not only was the cat out of the bag, it had caught a taxi to the airport, picked up some duty free, boarded a flight and was at that very moment lounging on a beach in the Bahamas writing its postcards. Margaret revised her decision and tore the paperwork up. She even changed her mind about the date, again! Oh well, you win some you lose some.

Del

Three minutes into the third series of *Only Fools and Horses* something very special happens. When Rodney racks his brains for details of recent crimes on the estate, Del tells him about poor Rita Alldridge. According to Del, Rita was indecently assaulted the previous Friday (over by the adventure playground) and has just been down to the police station to report it. "Hang on a minute," a thoughtful Rodney enquires, "if this happened on Friday night, how come it's taken her till Wednesday to report it?"

"Because," Del continues, "she didn't know she'd been indecently assaulted until this morning when the bloke's cheque bounced."

John Sullivan's brilliant gag earns an instant laugh. But gradually this laughter grows ever louder as more and more of the live audience work out *precisely* what Del is implying. As the scene cuts to the next, the audience's laughter is still growing, threatening to overpower the filmed insert and requiring videotape editor Mike Taylor to audibly fade the live soundtrack. Just 16 episodes in, and it is already becoming a battle to squeeze a plot within 30 minutes of screen time in the face of such powerful humour.

Under the original working title of 'Homesick Blues', Sullivan wrote the opening episode of his third set of *Only Fools* stories to explore how the Trotters would deal with the housing system: "Years ago, my wife and I applied for a council place and we were put at the bottom of a very long list. You had to have so many qualifications, one of which could be concerned with illness. I wondered how Del would approach this because, of course, he'd love a better place than Nelson Mandela House."

Homesick sees Rodney take the mantle as chairman of the tenants' association where he finds the perfect outlet for giving something back to the community; an opportunity which Del is certainly not going to let slip through his fingers, especially with Grandad, who is happy to play along...

Just before Rodney is voted in as chairman, we witness the only time in the series where he questions Trigger as to why he refers to him as 'Dave'. Rodney brings the bemused road sweeper up to speed and we're treated to the only time Roger Lloyd Pack utters the name 'Rodney' on screen. But after a hilarious brief exchange, Trigger straight away goes back to calling Rodney 'Dave'. Clearly resigned to this being a battle he'll never win, the younger Trotter never challenges the road sweep again on the subject.

The tenants' association meeting would take place at St Nicholas Church Hall in Chiswick, which doubled as the rehearsal space used to prepare nearly every episode of *Only Fools* for its first six years. Location filming for *Homesick,* and the whole of series three, was carried out from 2–23 September 1983, with studio recordings for all eight episodes carried out over eight consecutive Sundays from 2 October.

Actress Sandra Payne, in the role of Miss Margaret Mackenzie, was tasked with navigating Rodney's naivety and Del's charm. Payne would later be cast by future *Only Fools* producer Gareth Gwenlan as Marion (the daughter-in-law from hell) in the sitcom *Waiting for God.* Elsewhere in the episode, prolific south-London character actor, Ron Pember, was cast as the outgoing tenants' association chairman, 'Baz'.

Homesick would mark the only appearance of the Trotters family doctor, Doctor Becker (played by John Bryans), but his name would live on throughout the series (as well as in *Rock & Chips*).

"At the end of the episode," remembered Sullivan, "we realise that Del set up Trigger and everyone else to get Rodney into the Chairman position, knowing full well that his brother had that kind of innocence that people would trust. Through Rodney, Del tries to con the council and almost pulls it off!"

Whilst Miss Mackenzie left Nelson Mandela House disappointed, eagle-eyed viewers might have spotted a new addition adorning a wall of the Trotter flat in *Homesick*: a small thick-framed landscape painting which would be vital to a future episode...

Above: "You're a good boy, Rodney. You've always looked after your old Grandad..."

Above left: Rodney is voted in as the new chairman of the tenants' association... as the outgoing chair Baz (Ron Pember) goes down the pub with Trigger.

Below left: Dr Becker (John Bryans) discusses Grandad's health with Del and Rodney.

Below: Miss Margaret Mackenzie (Sandra Payne) is disappointed in Rodney.

Below: Del has not completely lost hope for his date with Margaret – "We still on for that drink?"

Above: Del nearly gets his collar felt when Rodney fails to spot an approaching policeman.

Right: Del's suitcase full of battery-operated toy dogs are left on the floor.

Below: Back at the flat, Del is fuming with Rodney – "You should have been with me in that alley Rodney, it was like *Call of the Wild.* Why didn't you warn me that copper was coming?!"

Below right: At the Auction House, Rodney and Mickey Pearce are looking for a great seller to kick start their new venture... as the auctioneer (Glynn Sweet) takes the bids.

Opposite page below: Lyndhurst, Jason and Patrick Murray on location in Dorset.

Whilst Del is attempting to sell a suitcase full of battery-operated toy dogs, Trotters Independent Traders' executive look-out, Rodney, is absently daydreaming and hasn't noticed an approaching policeman. Fearing he is about to get nicked, Del makes a mad dash through a department store and various London back streets, as the old bill gives chase. Thanks to a pack of very real dogs and the timely arrival of a three-wheeled van, Del finally manages to make his escape.

This blistering opening sequence sees David Jason as every bit the action man, as he runs for his life clutching a suitcase full of hooky gear. For a suitable department store, the crew went outside central London to take over Uxbridge's Randalls store for a day. The second section of the chase through streets and alleyways was filmed around Ealing. The beginning of this sequence was originally soundtracked by the theme from *Jaws*, and for home video releases a similar piece of stock music is used instead.

Furious with his brother's short-sightedness, Del explodes and a frustrated Rodney reveals that he has had enough and wants to go it alone... with Mickey Pearce.

After being mentioned twice previously, this is the first time John Sullivan decided to bring Mickey Pearce into a story: "Mickey Pearce was based on a few people I've met. They're the kind of guys who pretend to be your lifelong friend to your face, but the moment your back's turned, they're trying to get money from you. When I was writing the series, I thought the community wouldn't be complete without a weaselly guy who would be willing to hurt his friends."

When considering the actor for Mickey Pearce, Sullivan and director Ray Butt looked no further than their TV sets and saw the young and talented Patrick Murray. "At time, I was king of the adverts," recalls Murray. "I was in just about everything and I liked to bring a lot of comedy into the adverts. Ray Butt saw an advert I did for Pizza Hut, where I played a wide-boy, and he invited me to audition. He said to me: 'Bloody hell, we've been looking for Mickey Pearce for years and when I saw this ad I thought; I've got him.'"

HEALTHY COMPETITION

17 NOVEMBER 1983

There are times in life when you have to sit down and ask yourself some serious questions, like 'Who am I?' and 'What am I and where am I going?' That's what I'd been doing, and let me tell you, the answers weren't pretty. I mean, there I was, twenty-four years old, with two GCEs, thirteen years of schooling and three terms at an adult education centre under my belt, and with all that, I was a gopher! That is to say that I worked for Del Boy and the extent of my occupational remit more or less ended at lugging his dirty old crates around the market and shouting out "Leg it!" when he was about to get his collar felt. I wouldn't have minded too much if he'd at least have giving me a challenge every now and then, and by challenge I don't mean sending me out to sell Italian sun hats during a monsoon! Well, that all changed when I announced to Del that I was liquidating the partnership and going it alone. I new it would hurt his feelings, but he needed to hear it and I gave it to him straight. For a while at least, I felt a new lease of life. Yeah, the time had come to prove to him once and for all that I had business acumen of my own. I couldn't wait to get down that auction house!

Rodney

There were times when I felt as though I really knew Rodney, and, despite all the ups and downs we'd had over the years, I couldn't help but feel very, very proud of the way he'd turned out. Then there were times like this one, when I suddenly realised what a one-hundred per cent, twenty-four carat plonker he really is! I mean, I didn't ask much of him. Just stand there and be a look-out, that was all! But he couldn't even get that simple thing right.

"Maybe it's because my heart's not really in it" he said.

"I'm not asking you to put your heart in it." I said. "Just your eyes'll do!"

And then he went and told me that he was 'liquidating' the partnership.

"What partnership?" I said. But this is the thanks I got, after all that time spent keeping him safe and warm beneath my wing, all those years of being not just a big brother but also a mentor to him, he chucked it back in my face. But probably the biggest and worstest insult of all was his choice of new partner: Mickey bleed'n Pearce! I mean, you only had to take one look at him to see he weren't working with a full deck. The boy was about as bright as a power cut! Still, Rodney insisted on learning the hard way, so that was how it would have to be.

Del

Aside from his advertising credentials, Murray was particularly suited for the role having grown up in New Cross and gone to school in Peckham. He knew a few 'Del Boys' and 'Rodneys' at the time.

With Ray Butt and John Sullivan convinced that they had found their Mickey, Murray was given a script on a Friday afternoon and told to prepare to start the following week: "When Monday came and I read the first script at read-through, I knew what they were talking about. It was fantastic and we filmed the auction scene out in the sticks. The day's filming went great and we all got on like a house on fire, that was the start of my journey into *Only Fools*."

Murray's first scenes as Mickey were filmed at Tarrant Hinton village hall in Dorset, which was used for all of the auction scenes in *Healthy Competition* (just five miles away from Iwerne Minster where the previous year's *A Touch of Glass* location scenes were filmed).

Also present at the auction house location was *Radio Times* photographer, Brian Moody. He was on set to snap the episode's location filming and capture portraits of the Trotters in a suitably 'rough and ready' setting comprising

of fence panels and written-off cars. Lennard Pearce was also invited to the location for this shoot, even though he wasn't called for any of the scenes. The resulting photos would become the most iconic of the early years of the series, with Del Boy's red jumper and sheepskin jacket becoming a trademark of the character. For the accompanying text in the *Radio Times* feature, writer Guy Bellamy joined the crew for the filming of the next episode, *Friday the 14th*, in nearby Iwerne Minster.

Lumbered with their broken lawn mower engines, Rodney and Mickey's venture seems doomed to fail – a perfect time for the company's financial director (Mickey) to scarper to Benidorm, leaving Rodney – and the flapping soles of his shoes – in the lurch. Despite Del's bravado, for Sullivan it was important to reinforce how much he cares for his little brother:

"I included the story where Del tries to help Rodney out by secretly buying his load of broken lawn mower motors, to show that underneath it all – and even though he was winning – Del would rather give his brother the victory to bring him back into the partnership with some pride."

To give his brother that little victory, Del pays another trader 'Young' Towser (played by actor Mike Carnell) to step in and buy the broken lawn mower engines from Rodney for £200... a plan which back fires in more ways than one when Rodney reveals that Towser gave him just £165 for the engines – money which Rodney (convinced he is now on to a hot new line) spends on buying even more broken lawn mower engines (ones which are *remarkably* similar to those he sold!)

Opposite page: A selection of the many promotional photos taken on location at Tarrant Hinton... and the *Radio Times* feature from November 1983 promoting the third series of *Only Fools*.

Above and left: Del enjoys a laugh at Rodney and Mickey's expense as they realise just what they have bought at the auction.

Below left: Del gets Young Towser (Mike Carnell) to buy the broken engines off of Rodney.

Below: "Put that round yer Gucci, it will stop the sole coming off!"

SERIES 3 EPISODE 3

FRIDAY THE 14th

24 NOVEMBER 1983

Talk about the hunter becoming the hunted! We'd only gone to Cornwall to see if we could catch a few salmon and earn ourselves a nice bit of bunce – we ended up becoming the prey of an escaped axe murderer! We first became aware of the potential danger we were putting ourselves in when we came to a road block and a very cheerful copper filled us in on all the gory details. I had to weigh it all up and make a snap decision: on the one hand there was a mad axeman on the loose, no doubt not in the best of moods at having spent the last ten years in incarceration, and probably looking to vent his pent up frustrations on the first Herberts he could get his hands on. On the other hand, we stood to earn 300 sovs with that salmon. So we pushed on. By the time we reached the cottage, Rodney's and Grandad's old Aprils were doing a synchronised Mexican wave, especially when we discovered that the power was out. I'd just about managed to calm the situation when Rodney saw a bloke's face at the window.

"It was 'orrible," he said. "He had these evil eyes, and this grotesque, evil face!"

"Maybe it was a reflection," I said.

Just as he was about to start sucking his thumb and throwing a paddy, there was a knock on the front door. To our huge relief, it turned out to be a mush named Robson who was the Chief of Security at the asylum. He showed us his ID, we let him in, and all was right again. Well, it was up to the moment we discovered that the real Chief Robson was at that moment laid up in hospital. The escaped man had hit him over the head and stolen his uniform and identity papers. The things I put up with just to earn an honest crust.

Del

With the keys to Boycie's weekend cottage and an expectant larder at Mario's fish restaurant, the Trotters are going poaching – what's the worst that could happen?

In *Friday the 14th* John Sullivan takes the Trotter family on their first on-screen road trip. It is a welcome change of pace from the usual concrete tower blocks and market streets: "I was constantly trying to create different scenarios. I didn't like the comedies of the time that, even though it was a new script and a new episode, you kind of knew what you were going to see. With *Only Fools* I got the chance to paint a broad canvas, so the audience wouldn't quite know what they were going to see when they switched on the TV. Of course, they knew they were going to see the Trotters, but they didn't know what situation the characters were going to be in."

For the Trotters' ill-fated fishing excursion to the fictional Cornish village of Tregower, the production team decided once again to visit the familiar climbs of Dorset's Iwerne Minster, which is where all of *Friday the 14th*'s rural exterior shots were filmed.

One notable location scene, filmed but edited out before transmission, took place between the shot of the Trotter van driving towards the M4 and being stopped by the police roadblock. In this exterior scene we would have seen the Trotter van parked outside a country pub, with Grandad and Del sat at an outside table, having sent Rodney inside to fetch a round of drinks. On another table sits a yokel ("an old rustic type puffing on a pipe"). Here Del bemoans the lack of Pina Coladas and pizzas available out in the sticks. The Trotters then discuss the weather with the yokel,

who predicts that a storm is coming. This leads Rodney to believe that this information is courtesy of some 'country intuition'... until it is revealed that the yokel is in fact listening to Radio 4 via his radio earphone! Actor Michael Bilton, fresh from playing another 'rustic type', Ned in *To the Manor Born,* was cast as the yokel in the scene.

The simple poaching premise of the story is disrupted as we learn that an escaped axe murderer is on the loose in the vicinity of Boycie's weekend cottage, where the Trotters are staying.

Scottish actor Christopher Malcolm was cast as Chief Robson (later to be revealed as the *real* mad axeman). He had previously appeared as a pilot in the *Star Wars* sequel *The Empire Strikes Back,* and would later play Justin in *Absolutely Fabulous.*

A highlight of the story features just David Jason and Christopher Malcolm on set. During the scene, in which it is revealed that Chief Robson is in fact the escaped lunatic, Del is challenged to an imaginary game of snooker.

John Sullivan was in the studio for this priceless scene: "During the imaginary snooker game, David Jason makes a motion like he's chalking the end of his cue. And you hear the sound of the chalk. David actually made this wonderful, realistic sound! That final scene is a great piece of physical comedy. Del still insists on holding onto the cue, even though it's an axe murderer he's fighting with. It shows Del's pride perfectly, making him hold onto the cue, despite the fact that it's not real!"

With its atmospheric setting and magnificent gag-packed script, *Friday the 14th* might just be the best half-hour Trotter episode ever made. A true situation comedy master-class, it is a joy to see the cast on such great form, sparring with each other in such a claustrophobic setting.

Opposite page top right: Boycie's weekend cottage in Cornwall...

Above left: 'Chief Robson' (Christopher Malcolm) taking notes...

Above: Inside the cottage.

Left: Michael Bilton as rustic yokel Ned in *To the Manor Born.*

Below middle: The Police Sergeant (Michael Stainton) is shocked to see what is in the back of the van.

Below: "Which cue would you like?"

Del has found what he believes to be a genuine 19th-century Queen Anne cabinet. On inspecting the cabinet and finding it riddled with tiny little holes (a sure sign of woodworm), Rodney isn't so confident. Reassuring Rodney that Queen Anne played darts, Del hopes to turn the tatty old bit of furniture into profit. He places an advertisement in the newspaper and waits for the stampede.

"I always tried to create interesting episode titles," remembered John Sullivan. "In this script, Del buys a worthless antique and he's wasted his money – he hasn't got a piece of yesterday after all. It's a play on the phrase 'tomorrow never comes.'"

Straight away the cabinet catches the interest of sophisticated antique dealer, Miranda Davenport. Arriving at the Trotter flat, she instantly dismisses the cabinet as rubbish, before finding herself rather taken by the (genuine) 19th-century landscape oil painting hanging on the living room wall. At the same time, Del finds himself rather taken by Miss Davenport.

Cast as Miranda Davenport was actress Juliet Hammond, who had previously starred in the popular BBC drama *Secret Army*. Hammond plays Miranda's palpable distaste for the Trotters' way of life brilliantly, getting every last ounce of disapproval from her dialogue as her character begrudgingly goes along with Del's romantic overtures.

Inspired by Del's direct and, apparently, successful approach at pulling a "posh tart", Rodney attempts to do something similar, only to be rewarded with a smack in the face. This sequence was filmed on location outside Spy's restaurant on Castellain Road in Maida Vale. The other main exterior location visited in the story

Above and left: The set of Nelson Mandela House's entrance hall was built for *Yesterday Never Comes*.

Below: Miranda Davenport (Juliet Hammond) walks into the flat just as Rodney is having some fun with some stock.

Bottom right: Del parks the van just outside Miranda's antique shop.

Opposite page top left: At the auction house, Miranda sells the Joshua Blythe landscape (below).

Opposite page far right: Rodney's chat up line backfires spectacularly!

was Miranda's Antique Shop, which was filmed on Ledbury Road in Notting Hill.

The painting that Miranda instantly hones in on is the work of the fictional 19th century artist, Joshua Blythe. Miranda works her magic and a weakened Del gifts her the painting, only for her to discover that the painting was actually stolen by Del's gran, Violet Trotter, who once worked as charlady for an art dealer. Whilst 'out of shot' during the first two series of *Only Fools*, we would see the painting for the first time in series three's *Homesick*.

"There's a clear clash of the classes between Del and Miranda," John Sullivan remembered. "She's well-bred, while Del thinks a Berni Inn dinner and a tequila sunrise are classy! There are lots of twists and turns in this episode. First Miranda fools Del into giving her the masterpiece – believing that he hasn't a clue what it's worth. Then she sells it, claiming that it has been in the family for years. Of course, Del knew all along that his gran stole it in the first place, so he gets the last laugh."

After watching the sickly posh Miranda work her charms, it is a satisfying moment when Del gets one over on her. The episode closes with it looking like the antique dealer will soon have to answer some pressing questions from the authorities.

It's not often that Del got beaten at his own game, but that Miranda sort played him like a fiddle. The moment she turned up at the flat to check out the 'Queen Anne' cabinet Del had advertised in the paper, you could see it ending badly from a mile off. There he was, sniffing round her, trying to sound all suave and sophisticated. But when she mentioned that she owned her own antique shop in Chelsea and offered to spruce his cabinet up for a share of the profits, well, she had him hook, line and sinker. He even asked for my advice. I tried to let him down gently. "You and Miranda?" I said. "Leave it out, Del, she's an intelligent woman." But he was far too gone to listen. It never used to take Del long to fall in 'love', usually about thirty seconds or so and then all he could see were boxes of Milk Tray, candlelit steak dinners and engagement rings. That's the thing with Del, he likes to give it all the big 'I am', but deep down he's soppier than an Andrex puppy in a field of buttercups. Anyway, he spent the next couple of days reeking of Blue Stratos and skipping merrily up Miranda's garden path. On this occasion, though, I think we were all taught a tough lesson. I mean, for all her troubles, Miranda ended up with nothing more than official ownership of a hooky painting and a bad case of woodworm; Del ended up with egg on his face and a bad dose of Ghandi's revenge; and I ended up with a sore cheek and a bad headache. Take it from me, it's never a good idea to smack a woman on the bum and ask her if she fancies a curry.

Rodney

MAY THE FORCE BE WITH YOU

8 DECEMBER 1983

In his time, Rodney has brought quite a few horrible things home with him: chickenpox, nits, that skinny bird from the dry cleaners etc. But all of them combined had nothing on what he brought home this time: Roy bleed'n Slater! Or, to give him his full title, Detective Inspector Roy bleed'n Slater! We'd been at school together and he was a right snide even back then. He was one of them types that never fit in, so he took to lurking about in the background, watching and waiting for any opportunity to snitch. It was no surprise to any of us when he eventually joined the police force. Within a month of receiving his badge and big pointy hat, he unleashed himself on to the streets of Peckham. His first big success came when he nicked some poor old sod for driving with a defective rear light. It wouldn't have been so bad if it weren't that the bloke was his dad (he'd only borrowed the bike to nip down to the chippy). When he got transferred to a station in West London we all gave a sigh of relief. I thought we'd seen the last of him. Then, right out of the blue, he walks straight into the flat and starts sniffing around our new microwave oven. Two minutes later we were all under arrest and being dragged down to the station. Of course, I knew the name of the bloke who half-inched the microwave, but when it comes to tyrants like Roy Slater, you don't give them an inch. I might be many things, but I ain't a grass! Roy, being the vicious and corrupt bastard that he is, then threatened to plant drugs on Rodney and put him away, and that was the final straw. Do what you like to me, but you don't threaten my little brother (I'm the only one who has that right). That's when I decided to give Slater exactly what he wanted without giving him exactly what he wanted. First off, I agreed to give him a name, under the condition that Rodney and Grandad were released and kept out of it. He agreed. Condition numero two was the clincher: not only would all charges against me be dropped, but I'd be granted immunity from prosecution. He complained, but his eyes told a different story, and I knew then that I had him. As soon as I received the officially signed document of immunity, I gave him the name of the mush who nicked the microwave. You should have seen his face when I told him it was moi. I just wish I'd had my Polaroid with me.

Del

He's a bit of a legend around these parts is Del Trotter. A bit like a modern day Robin Hood. Everyone you meet has got a story about him. Rumour has it that he once fell into a vipers pit and emerged five minutes later wearing snakeskin boots. That was always my favourite one. Anyway, if Del was Robin Hood, then my boss, Roy Slater, was definitely the Sheriff of Nottingham. And when Slater nicked all three of the Trotters on the charge of receiving a stolen microwave oven, I really couldn't see Del finding a way out. I mean, Slater had the stolen property, discovered in Trotter HQ and covered in Trotter fingerprints. All he needed was the name of the bloke who pinched it. Del tried everything, but no amount of playing dumb or bribery would wash. Slater had him banged to rights. I didn't enjoy watching him turning the screw on Del, trying to get him to turn grass, but then again Del would insist on getting involved with hooky gear. I couldn't be too hard on him, though, not since he helped my mum out with a new gas fire. She was well chuffed!

PC Terry Hoskins

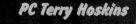

There's a bad apple in every parish, and for the Trotters of Peckham that apple was Roy Slater. "I knew kids at school who were 'snides', but Slater is the ultimate," John Sullivan recalled. "He joined the police and actually nicked his old friends. He felt he'd been rejected and he wanted to seek revenge on these people. So obviously he must have had an unhappy childhood."

To play Slater, director Ray Butt approached the actor who two years previously had turned down *Only Fools'* leading role. Whilst a long-term commitment to a character and a series was not appealing to Jim Broadbent, he had no issue with guest staring in the series. To secure Broadbent for the role, *May the Force be with You* was recorded out of sequence, right at the end of the third series, in order to accommodate the actor's theatre commitments.

From his performance as Slater, it is clear that the versatile actor was much better suited to playing the bent policeman role. Broadbent's Slater brilliantly intimidates the cast and makes the case of the stolen microwave oven sound like a matter of life or death.

Joining Slater at the police station is PC Terence Hoskins, played by *It Ain't Half Hot Mum* regular, Christopher Mitchell. A great part, Mitchell gets some wonderful little asides in the script, which suggest that Slater and Hoskins could have been a very entertaining double act.

May the Force be with You would also mark the first appearances of Michele Winstanley who was cast as the Nags Head latest barmaid, Karen. Winstanley was just feet away from Broadbent during his scene in the Nags Head, and was in a unique position to absorb the special energy with the watching audience: "I wasn't nervous about the concept of recording live when I accepted the job, or during rehearsals, but there was a definite atmosphere of excitement which built throughout the day of filming. We had a fantastic warm-up man, Felix Bowness, to tell jokes to the audience and get them in a jovial mood, prior to recording and during pauses while a scene had to be re-staged. No one wanted the audience to get bored or to stop laughing, so all the artists were being funny or silently hamming it up for the audience during down times. I was pretty nervous, but my scenes were really short. I just had to remember my lines, which I managed ok!"

Caught red handed after Rodney brings Slater back to the Trotter flat, it seems that Del Boy has been backed into an inescapable corner, right up to the magnificent moment of truth when it is revealed that Del has managed to play Slater, admitting to him that *he* stole the microwave. With his immunity from prosecution already secured, there is nothing Slater can do.

After the episode's original broadcast, John Sullivan remembered that some newspaper critics were missing the point of the outcome: "I wanted Del to come out of the situation with some decency. But the day after the episode was aired, a newspaper critic said he was disappointed to realise that Derek Trotter was a common thief. Clearly he didn't get it. Del said he was the thief because it was his only chance to get everyone off the hook. I think it's one of the cleverest things he's ever done."

Above: Rodney and Mickey try their luck with the ladies in the Nags Head.

Above right: John Challis, Roger Lloyd Pack and David Jason enjoy a moment between recording on set.

Below: Rodney comes to the aid of Blossom (Toni Palmer) – "I'll have the police on you! You touched me!"

Opposite page: Rodney runs away and hides... in Nelson Mandela House's tank room.

Rodney sits at the bar of the Nags Head with Mickey Pearce, trying to pluck up the courage to chat up a set of identical twins. After some poor attempts to catch the twins' attention, and a brief interjection from a passing Del ("Hey, girls, seen much of Cinderella since the wedding?"), Rodney and Mickey decide to call it a night.

For his second appearance in the series, Patrick Murray made his debut in the studio where he discovered that an incredible gag from his first episode had become a unit of measurement: "In *Healthy Competition*, when Grandad says 'What have you got, a Wendy house?' the audience just burst into laughter and would not stop laughing for ages. It was pure Lennard Pearce, with absolutely brilliant timing. From then on, whenever we did a read through on a Monday, if there was a particularly funny line, someone would say 'that was a bit of a Wendy' and so we'd be ready for that, and you would sort out your timing because you knew the audience would go off again."

On his walk home from the pub, Rodney comes across a woman sitting on a brick wall waiting for a bus service which was cut in 1973. Concerned for her safety, he offers to call her a cab. As the dazed and confused woman attempts to stand, she stumbles backwards and Rodney puts his hand out to steady her, an action that leads her to cry out hysterically: "I'll have the police on you! You touched me. Help!" A bemused and panicking Rodney legs it home.

The following morning, a worried Rodney tells Del and Grandad all about what happened on his walk home, desperately pleading his innocence in the matter. Del instantly recognises that Rodney is talking about Blossom, a local lady who is well known for such strange behaviour. Not telling Rodney this, Del instead decides to have a bit of "a laugh" at his younger brother's expense, spinning a yarn about how the police are now on the hunt for a man they are calling the "Peckham Pouncer!" Believing he is a wanted man, Rodney goes into hiding...

The spark which set off the story of Blossom came from a friend of John Sullivan's: "He got into his car one morning and noticed that the windows were misted up. He thought nothing of it and drove off. But when he looked into his rear-view mirror, he saw this woman looking back at him. He hadn't locked the car the night before and she'd got into the back seat and slept there. My friend got quite a fright because it was early in the morning, and suddenly there was this vision behind him. It turned out this poor old dear was mentally disturbed and her nickname was Blossom."

Actress Toni Palmer was cast to play the larger than life Blossom, joining the cast for one brief location scene filmed on Fraser Road in Perivale. A versatile face on stage and screen, Palmer would once again terrorise Nicholas Lyndhurst as Mrs Greig in the 1998 *Goodnight Sweetheart* episode, *London Pride*.

From his years working in the plumbing world, John Sullivan knew all about the vast hidden tank rooms in tower blocks and had memories of the kind of things people would put into the tanks, and so the tank room located at the very top of Nelson Mandela House became the perfect hideout for Rodney.

For this, production designer Bryan Ellis designed an incredibly effective set, complete with a rusting riveted tank and slanted wall sections through which light filtered. With the added sound effects of gusts of wind, suddenly TC3 actually feels like it is on top of the Acton tower block seen in the title sequence.

WANTED

15 DECEMBER 1983

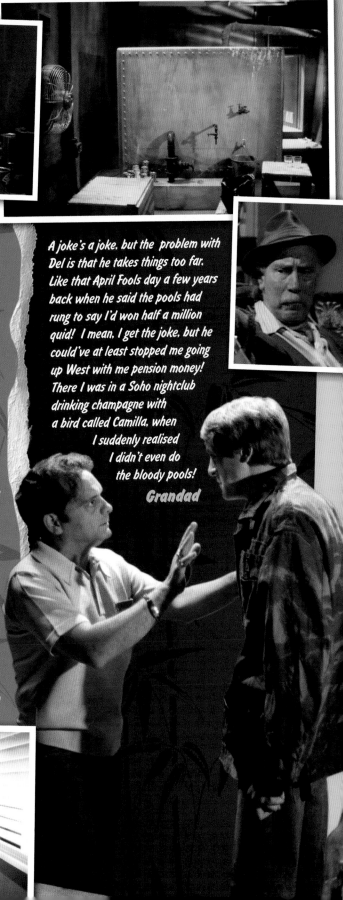

Sometimes the world can be a gutty and unfair place. I was walking back from the pub, not a care in the world, when I saw this woman staggering about, talking gibberish. I'm not sure what was wrong with her, but she stunk of booze. At one point she stumbled, so I put my hands out to steady her. That was all. The next thing I know she was outright accusing me of molestation! In a moment of panic I attempted to offer some reassurance by telling her I was a doctor, but this seemed to wind her up even more and she started screaming. I sprinted home so fast I must have broken some kind of record. And that's how I came to be holed up in the tank room at the top of Nelson Mandela House. Actually, that wasn't the only reason. It was the morning after the incident when Del happened to mention that he'd seen lynch mobs roaming the streets, police helicopters and packs of sniffer dogs, all hunting for a man they were calling "The Peckham Pouncer". I'd been staring out across Peckham through the ventilation slats, looking for them. I hadn't seen nothing, but I knew they were out there waiting for me, and it was just a matter of time. Part of me thought I should hand myself in and face the music, but there was no way I'd survive prison, not with my boyish good looks. So I decided to stay up in the tank room for a while longer, just until I figured something out. Anyway, thanks to some quick thinking and a bit of shrewd last-minute preparation, it wasn't that bad up there. I had a blanket, a couple of magazines, some fags, and enough tinned food to last me at least a week. I just wish I hadn't forgotten the bloody tin opener.

Rodney

A joke's a joke, but the problem with Del is that he takes things too far. Like that April Fools day a few years back when he said the pools had rung to say I'd won half a million quid! I mean, I get the joke, but he could've at least stopped me going up West with me pension money! There I was in a Soho nightclub drinking champagne with a bird called Camilla, when I suddenly realised I didn't even do the bloody pools!

Grandad

WHO'S A PRETTY BOY?

21 FEBRUARY 1985

I go round to my sister's to see how she is after having the stitches out, and I return home to find Del Boy and Rodney Trotter in my front room! After all the warnings I gave Denzil, there he is having a beer with them, jollying it up as though nothing ever happened. He expects me to forget about it, but how can I when it was our wedding day?! And it was Denzil who wanted the Trotters to handle the catering. "How can you trust Derek Trotter?" I said to him. "Every time you see him you end up drunk or out of pocket!"

"I know," he said. "But he's a mate."

I personally and very carefully chose every item on that wedding menu. We were going to have lobster vol-au-vents, kidney with saffron rice, beef and anchovy savouries and Philadelphia truffles. We ended up with pie 'n' chips all round! And now Denzil wants them to decorate our flat! Well, I'll let him have his way, but if one thing, just one, goes wrong, I'm gonna make him wish his mother'd had a headache the night he was conceived!

Corrine

The instructions Corrine left for us were very clear: 'Leave the TV alone, don't eat the fruit and stay out of the kitchen.' At the end of the day I don't think it was just the demise of her beloved pet canary that upset her. I think it was more when she went to make a cup of tea and flooded the kitchen.

She weren't too pleased either when she noticed the great big hole Grandad had made in her Jaffa Cakes. I'm just glad I weren't there when her next telephone bill arrived.

Rodney

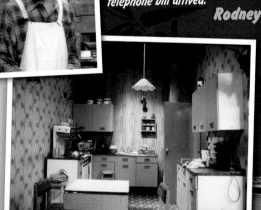

The germ of the idea for *Who's a Pretty Boy* came to John Sullivan after hearing a story from a decorator about a dead budgie: "It involved him accidentally killing a client's bird and propping the poor thing up on a matchstick. Of course, the budgie fell off its perch and the owner found it dead at the bottom of the cage with a matchstick up its bum. I thought this was really funny and that I could probably change the details slightly and make it a bit better."

To help set a scene which would require the services of the Trotters as interior decorators, Sullivan created the couple Denzil and Corinne, two people with very different opinions of the Trotter family. Whilst Denzil is faultlessly loyal to Del, his wife, Corinne, is still fuming after the disastrous catering the Trotters organised for their wedding.

Although the characters were only ever intended for the one appearance, John Sullivan soon saw their potential: "Denzil gave me opportunities in the storylines, because he's got the lorry and the transport contacts. He's more naive than the rest of the boys, but he can also be trusted. Corinne was a smashing character

as Denzil was such a nice guy, it was important to have a really strong woman behind him. And she was onto Del's antics from the start."

Against Corinne's better judgement, Del, Rodney and Grandad are given the job to decorate her and Denzil's flat… a job that soon turns to disaster when a forgotten kettle on a hob smokes out the kitchen. To make matters worse, the Trotters then discover Denzil and Corrine's beloved pet canary dead at the bottom of its cage, apparently overcome by the smoke. Del quickly mobilises and orders Grandad off to the nearest pet shop to buy a replacement canary before Corinne comes home.

A pet shop on Devonshire Road in Chiswick was used as the location of Louis Lombardi's pet shop. This location was just a short distance away from the Bolton Hotel on Duke Road which was used for the brief exterior shot of the Nags Head earlier in the story.

With the new canary installed, the Trotters think they're out of the woods, right up until a returning Corinne reveals that the canary died earlier that morning, before the Trotters even arrived!

Cast as Corinne was actress Eva Mottley who was starting to become a recognisable face on TV thanks to her starring role in the new ITV series,

Widows. Mottley was simply brilliant as Corinne and celebrated her 30th birthday during rehearsals of *Who's a Pretty Boy*. Her debut performance in the series should have been the first of many, but sadly the actress died in 1985.

For Sullivan, re-casting the role was not an option, and, out of respect for Mottley, he decided to keep the character of Corinne alive in the series through the ups and downs of her marriage to Paul Barber's Denzil.

Barber's first performance in the series was equally impressive, building on roles in several other BBC sitcoms after an early appearance in *To The Manor Born* in 1979. Thankfully the actor would bring his welcome Liverpudlian charm to *Only Fools* on a permanently recurring footing.

At the end of the story, the Trotters finally meet (and do a nice bit of business with) the Nags Head's new landlord, Mike Fisher. Director Ray Butt cast Ken MacDonald, an actor he knew from *It Ain't Half Hot Mum,* to take on the reins of the series' public house. Sullivan was instantly impressed by the atmosphere MacDonald created and decided to develop Mike further.

Opposite top right: Grandad goes to Lombardi's pet shop to buy another canary.

Above left: The set of Denzil and Corinne's flat.

Above: Corinne (Eva Mottley) keeps an eye on what the Trotters are up to.

Left: Denzil (Paul Barber) defends Del to Corinne – "Yeah I know, but he's a mate!"

Below left: The Nags Head's new landlord, Mike (Ken MacDonald), makes a deal with Del about decorating the pub… and getting Brendan O'Shaughnessy (David Jackson) to do the work!

Below: Eva Mottley – with the main cast and director Ray Butt – was presented with a Reliant Regal shaped cake for her birthday during the making of the episode.

Above: The wanderer returns, Reg Trotter (Peter Woodthope) comes back to the Trotter flat for the first time in 18 years.

Above right: The Trotter flat got a full Christmas make over for *Thicker than Water.*

Below: "I don't believe you two! Can't you see what he's doing? He's playing on your sympathy and yer family loyalty! He is evil! That is the devil standing there!"

Below right: David Jason poses with one of the flat's decorations between scenes.

To close the third series of *Only Fools*, John Sullivan decided it was the right time for a family reunion.

It is Christmas night and with Del out entertaining his latest squeeze, Rodney and Grandad are watching an old film. The doorbell suddenly rings and a dishevelled man stands outside. It is Reg Trotter. Grandad's long lost son. Del and Rodney's hitherto absent father!

After carefully establishing the Trotter family, John Sullivan took his time introducing the often mentioned and vilified Reg. When creating the character, the writer took inspiration from people he saw growing up: "Reg Trotter was based on so many men from the streets where I lived.

Hard-drinking, lazy, conniving, womanising... a complete and total let-down to his wife and his children. And there were many of them around. To be honest, my own Grandad was a man like that, a bit of a rough-house, he left the family eventually."

The reappearance of Reg in the life of the Trotters was always going to be a family hand grenade. Del's first scene in *Thicker than Water* really feels like he is being held back from ripping the man who abandoned them to shreds.

To bring the good-for-nothing Reg Trotter to life, Peter Woodthope was cast. In 1984 Woodthope could be seen with Lennard Pearce in the *Minder*

THICKER THAN WATER

25 DECEMBER 1983

There I was in the Nags Head, the shock of Grandad's Christmas lunch just about worn off, a Singapore Sling in one hand, a sort named Glenda in the other, when Rodney came racing in, sweating like a politician on a polygraph. For a moment I thought Grandad had got trapped in the airing cupboard again. Well, I almost had a connery when he told me that our so called 'Father', Reg, had returned. Praying to God that it was all just some sort of sick wind up, we rushed back to the flat and, sure enough, there was Reg, sitting in my armchair, wearing one of my shirts and smoking one of my cigars. Happy as a sand boy! He said he was only intending to stay for a couple of days. I told him to sling his hook and offered him the balcony door. He then went on to give us all a big sob story about how he was suffering with some mysterious 'blood disorder'. And Rodney and Grandad fell for it! Alright, he had me going too for a bit, especially when he said the disease was hereditary! Of course, this then meant that me and Rodney had to go and get blood tests. But by far the worstest thing of all was how he deliberately manipulated the test results, all so that he could sow doubt and cast 'orrible excursions about Mum. I've said it before and I'll say it again: that man is the devil!

Del

I always had felt like the odd one out. Ever since I was as a kid I'd just had this constant niggling feeling that there was something... different about me. When you're 12 years old and already six inches taller than your 25-year-old brother, it's hard not to notice. And right then, it looked as though my doubts were spot on! I was a whodunnit! All we'd managed to ascertain was that just before Mum became pregnant with me, she'd become very friendly with a trumpet player from the Locarno. According to Grandad there was also a saxophone player. So it looked as though my real dad was... a band. Well, the horn section at least. I just couldn't wait to fill in my next passport application form. Mother's name: Joan Mavis Trotter. Father's name: Herb Alpert and the Tijuana Brass!

Rodney

For Sullivan, it was the perfect opportunity to stir up the issue of paternity. "Right from the start of the series, I wanted the physical difference between the two brothers to be so striking that they would be the only two who truly believed they came from the same man. This episode was the first really strong hint that they have different dads."

Eventually it is revealed that Reg had engineered the whole affair, having recently fled a job as porter in a hospital in Newcastle (taking the chief gynaecologist's Lambretta in the process). Doctoring the blood tests was his opportunity to isolate Del from the rest of the family and work his way back in. Thanks to a visit to see Dr Becker, Del confirms Rodney's assertion that different blood groups do not necessarily mean different parentage.

Perhaps one of the most revealing moments in the episode is saved until the very last scene when Del silently gives his disgraced father a few quid to tide him over. This was a major character point for Sullivan: "We see all the buried resentment in Del, who's obviously very angry about how his father treated him and his mother. Despite this, Del still won't see his father go without any money. He helps him on his way, which is more than Reg ever did for Del."

Above: Grandad and Rodney have to hold Del back.

Below: The Nags Head was fully decked out for Christmas.

Below right: "I've burnt your pizza Del Boy" – things have at last gone back to normal for the Trotters.

episode *The Balance of Power* – Pearce's final screen role. Woodthope's performance as Reg is levelled absolutely perfectly, echoing a distorted version of David Jason's Del Boy but with all the warmth and charm removed.

Reg tells his family that he is there for genuine and well intentioned reasons, before explaining that he is suffering with a recently discovered and *hereditary* blood disorder. Del and Rodney have blood tests which, to their huge relief, come back negative. However, on closer inspection of the test results Grandad notices that Del has a different blood group to the rest of the family, a 'fact' that very quickly leads to Reg labelling Del as the 'Lone Ranger'.

Broadcast on consecutive Thursday evenings at 8.30pm from 10 November 1983, the third series of *Only Fools* would pull in an average of 10.5 million viewers per episode. Autumn 1983 became a bit of a John Sullivan season on BBC 1, since in the seven weeks leading up to series three of *Only Fools* being screened, the first series of *Just Good Friends* was broadcast, albeit on the other side of the news at 9.25pm.

Four days before *Thicker than Water* broadcast, the Trotters made an in-character appearance on Russell Harty's popular TV chat show. In the six-minute John Sullivan penned sketch, Del comes up with a ruse in order for the Trotters to arrive at Harty's party and take full advantage of the free food on offer. After the scripted segment ends, the trio of actors brilliantly remain in character for a brief interview with Harty, and it is a joy to see Lennard Pearce effortlessly 'be' Grandad in a live setting.

Above left: A suitably seasonal shot used to promote *Thicker than Water* in the Christmas 1983 edition of *Radio Times.*

Below and above right: Shots from a festive BBC promotional photo shoot.

SERIES FOUR

★★★★★★★★★★★★★★★★★★★★★★★★★★★★★★

Stone me what a year that was. If I weren't being chased down an alleyway by a pack of rabid dogs, I was receiving lectures about fish from an axe wielding maniac, and that's not even to mention getting it in the lughole whilst trying to explain away a resurrected canary! And talk about the past coming back to haunt yer! I was seriously thinking of getting one of those signs for the front door: 'No junk mail, no Jehovahs Witnesses, no bent coppers and no diseased wallies! Thank you.' I'd never been one for making New Year's resolutions, but after all that I got straight on it:

- *Ease off with the decorating jobs*

- *Book Rodney in at the opticians*

- *Stop drinking with Alfie Flowers*

- *Stop doing deals with Trigger*

- *Use the word deindustrialisation more often. Especially with the birds.*

- *Become a millionaire.*

The one silver-lining was that I reckoned we were finally on track with that last one. I don't know why, I just had this funny feeling that the big opportunity was waiting right round the next corner...

★★★★★★★★★★★★★★★★★★★★★★★★★★★

PHILLIPS PETROLEUM FILM LIBRARY
15 Beaconsfield Road
London NW10 2LE

LICENSED TO DRILL!

Copy no. _____

This film is protected by copyright and must not be broadcast, copied, re-sold, hired or edited without prior permission.

Above: In *Licensed to Drill*, Del has taken an interest in oil.

Above: The VHS tape label for the episode, seen on the cassettes when it was sent to schools.

Above right: The cast are joined by Iain Blair as the Oil Man (middle) and director Malcolm Taylor (far right).

Below: Filming the opening location scene for *Hole in One* in Kensington.

Opposite page above: Filming outside Kingston upon Thames' County Court for *Hole in One's* closing scenes.

Opposite page below: On the 17th December, the *Daily Express* (top) and *Daily Mirror* (below) reported the death of Lennard Pearce.

No series of *Only Fools* was planned for 1984. It was instead decided to hold off production on a fourth run until December for a January broadcast. In the meantime, John Sullivan and Ray Butt were hard at work preparing the second series of *Just Good Friends*, which would be recorded in late summer and transmitted in the autumn.

Earlier that year however, Sullivan was asked by the Maureen Oilfield Consortium to write an instalment of *Only Fools* especially for schools to promote careers in the oil and gas industry. On the surface, the Trotters' hapless adventures don't seem the obvious vehicle for an educational venture, but given the series' rising popularly, it must have seemed like a good way to promote the subject.

The resulting story is set within the Trotter flat and sees David Jason, Nicholas Lyndhurst and Lennard Pearce reprise their roles as their characters discuss the importance of oil and all its by-products. After meeting "Paddy" the Oil Man in 'Dirty Doug's café', Del has realised the potential of oil and come up with a way for the Trotters to earn from it... by buying an oil rig! The centrepiece of the episode features a clip from an educational documentary,

inter-cut with comments from the Trotters as they're watching the documentary on TV.

Licensed to Drill was made by Edinburgh based Grange Films on 16mm film. All of the props and costumes appear to have been sourced especially for this production with a recreation of the flat made by Grange Films. The film doesn't feature any of the usual *Only Fools* logos or title sequences; perhaps to make up for this, Sullivan wrote and sang a special end credit song 'Licensed to Drill', reuniting with Ronnie Hazlehurst for some very *Only Fools*-ish instrumentation. Produced and directed by veteran British TV director, Malcolm Taylor, the episodes only additional character, "Paddy" the Oil Man, is played by *Citizen Smith* guest actor Iain Blair.

The episode features roughly 20 minutes of Trotter material in total, and despite the educational premise, the clip is generally a funny piece of classic *Only Fools*.

The finished special would never be shown on television, but distributed on VHS cassette and shown within schools over the next decade.

Unbeknownst to all involved in the production however, was that *Licensed to Drill* would be the last time the original three stars of the series would be seen performing on screen together.

With winter approaching, it was time for the *Only Fools* machine to get up and running once more with seven completed John Sullivan scripts ready to be made. After steering the second and third series, Ray Butt decided that both producing and directing was becoming too demanding, so for series four he passed on directing duties to Susan Belbin.

A long time BBC production manager, one of Belbin's first jobs at the corporation was as assistant floor manager on the final series of *Dad's Army* in 1977: "Ray was lovely, really lovely. He came up to me in the BBC bar one day and we chatted away, and then he suddenly came out with, 'Oh by the way, you are directing the next series of *Only Fools and Horses*!' He had to pick me up off the floor. I hadn't directed before – only the odd canteen scene for David Croft. Thank you, Ray Butt, for my career!"

Belbin's stint on *Only Fools* would eventfully lead the director to award winning success with the sitcom *One Foot in the Grave* and comedy drama *Jonathan Creek*.

Meanwhile, the cast were getting back into the spirit of things, with David Jason, Nicholas Lyndhurst and Lennard Pearce reuniting for an animated chat with Terry Wogan for the BBC's *Children in Need* appeal on 23 November.

Location filming for series four was planned to take place from 9–23 December 1984, for a broadcast early in 1985. The first location sequence planned was for the opening episode *Hole in One*, where a pub in Kensington was found to stand in as the Nags Head. A second days filming for the same

episode was planned on the street outside Kingston upon Thames' County Court.

For two days the cast braved a chilly December to film the two sequences. One scene featured Pearce sharing his first dialogue with Ken MacDonald as Mike the pub land lord. Another scene would have seen Grandad revealing that he had long enjoyed a secret compensation scam via some surprising means.

On 12 December, Lennard Pearce suffered a heart attack at home in Archway. Rushed to Whittington Hospital in Islington, Pearce's condition improved. A few days later John Sullivan visited the actor and assured him that his role in the series would remain open to him for when he recovered. Following his release from hospital on 15 December, Pearce suffered a second heart attack and died. He was 69.

Over the next couple of days, the shocking news filtered out into the national press with an outpouring of affection for a wonderful actor who had found fame so late in life. The *Daily Mirror* reported the news on 17 December with the simple headline: "Del Boy's Grandad is Dead." *Only Fools* was only just starting to gain some real popularity in terms of viewing figures and Pearce's performance was a massive part of that.

An obviously devastated cast and crew were left stunned, including the series' new director Belbin: "I remember we were filming *Hole in One* with Lennard in a wheel chair being pushed along. And then days later we found out the news – it was unreal and very sad – it was a shock to everyone."

TV's Grandad Lennard dies

By GARTH PEARCE

ACTOR Lennard Pearce, who played Grandad in the BBC TV comedy series Only Fools and Horses, has died aged 69.

He collapsed at the weekend, only two weeks after starting filming on a new series of the top-rated show.

The BBC has postponed the series, which also stars David Jason and Nicholas Lyndhurst.

Last night Nicholas, 22, said : "Lennard could bring the house down by just raising an eyebrow. He was a great actor."

Lennard had been taking pills for the last six years after doctors diagnosed critically high blood pressure.

LENNARD: Blood presure

Del Boy's Grandad is dead

ACTOR Lennard Pearce, —Grandad in TV's Only Fools and Horses—died suddenly at the weekend. He was 69.

He had started work on a new series of the hit comedy show just twelve days ago.

Filming of programmes which also star David "Del Boy" Jason and Nicholas Lyndhurst as his grandsons, has now been postponed.

Lennard was close to death six years ago, when his blood pressure was critically high.

Gareth Gwenlan, head of BBC/TV Comedy, said last night: "He was a wonderful actor and made an enormous contribution to the series."

SERIES 4 EPISODE 1

HAPPY RETURNS

21 FEBRUARY 1985

June and I went way back. In fact I started dating her back in the sixties, not long after Mum died. She always was a big and bouncy girl (June, not Mum), but she had a nice personality to make up for it. Back then it was me and June and my mate Albie Littlewood and his bird Deidre. We went everywhere together, sort of like a little team. Everything had been going smoothly. I'd got a ring for June and was actually thinking about settling down. Then Albie died and that changed everything. The night he died he'd been on his way to see me at the Nags Head when he decided to take a shortcut across the railway lines. The dipstick got his bike stuck on the live rail. Then, just a few days after his funeral, June gave me the elbow and moved away. No explanation or nothing. So it was a right bolt out of the blue when, 19 years later, I discovered she'd recently moved in over at Zimbabwe House. I was even more surprised when I discovered that she had a 19-year-old daughter, Debby. Nineteen years?! All of a sudden June's giving me the abrupt heave-ho started to make perfect sense. I worked it out on the calculator just to be certain, but no matter which way I looked at it, the hard, cold truth was staring me right in the face: Debby was my daughter! Well, I didn't even get the chance to let it properly sink in, when I then remembered that at that exact moment Rodney was with Debby and trying to get his end away! Of course, I stormed in a bit sharpish and put a stop to it, before explaining the situation to Rodders. Naturally, he weren't happy, but he understood that this whole incense business just ain't allowed. When I finally confronted June, she revealed the actual truth and I got an even bigger shock. I wasn't Debby's dad. Albie Littlewood was! I couldn't believe it. Albie Littlewood, my bestest friend in all the world, the greatest pal a bloke could have. And all that time he'd been doinking my bird! Still, in a way it made me feel a lot better, cos I was doinking his.

Del

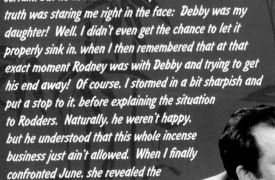

The shock of Lennard Pearce's death pulled the rug out from the making of *Only Fools'* fourth series. A wonderful actor and central component to the magic of the series was gone. In similar circumstances many other series would follow the acceptable practice of simply re-casting the part. This wasn't ever an option for John Sullivan:

"I decided that out of respect for Lennard, I would give Grandad a funeral. Of course, it should have been the first episode of the new series, but I didn't want to open with a funeral. So I pushed that back and created a brand new opening episode without Grandad in, although he is mentioned by Del when he says 'the old man's unwell in hospital', so it was an overture to the funeral episode."

Following Lennard's passing, John Sullivan had just three weeks over Christmas to write two new scripts, change the other five scripts and create a new character.

"I wasn't sure what to write for the opening episode, but I thought Del's old flames are always a good source of

comedy. So, I introduced Junie; she was someone who Del used to date years ago, so I was able to reveal some of his history. The casting was very clever because when you stood Oona Kirsch next to David Jason, there's a close resemblance, so it was believable that the two could be related."

Cast as Del's old flame June Snell was actress Diane Langton, who had recently appeared in an episode of *Minder*. Langton would later become a regular face on screens as Nana McQueen in *Hollyoaks*. Actress Oona Kirsch was cast as June's daughter, Debby. Also joining the cast in *Happy Returns* would be Nula Conwell as the Nags Head's latest barmaid, Maureen.

A trip into Del's romantic past does indeed make for an incredibly funny episode. David Jason and Nicholas Lyndhurst seem to relish the farcical situation, as we see the cogs go round in the characters' heads. Perhaps the key moment is when Del tells Rodney what would happen if he does marry Debbie: "Yer mother-in-law would have been yer aunt, yer wife would have been yer second cousin – Gawd knows what that would have made Grandad – the fairy godmother I should think."

The rescheduled location filming for series four took place from 2–17 January 1985. Studio recordings for the seven episodes were carried out on consecutive Sundays from 20 January, with the exception of a *Hole in One*, which was recorded on Tuesday 12 February.

The exterior scenes of Del and Rodney meeting June's youngest son, Jason (and his 'brother'), would be the final major scenes filmed on location at the north Acton estate. As the series had grown in reputation, filming around the tower blocks was starting to become problematic for the crew.

For the set of June's flat, designer Eric Walmsley simply redressed the Trotters' flat, seeing as both properties were in the same estate.

Despite the circumstances of its production, the fourth series opens with a truly cracking episode, a view that the British Academy also shared as John Sullivan remembered: "*Happy Returns* was the first *Fools* episode to receive a BAFTA. This was especially great because I wrote it in just a week; sometimes you find when you're under immense pressure you do your best work."

Opposite page below: Debbie Snell (Oona Kirsch) and her mother June (Diane Langton) with Del in the Nags Head.

Above left: A rare view of the entire set for the episode, showing the Nags Head, a Zimbabwe House corridor and June's flat.

Above: The cast rehearse the episode's closing scene, with Patrick Murray reprising his role as Mickey Pearce.

Left: A concerned lady in the newsagents (Lala Lloyd) asks after Grandad.

Below left: Del and Jason (Ben Davis) outside Zimbabwe House.

Above and right: Filming Grandad's funeral in Hammersmith.

Below: The flat and outside corridor as seen in *Strained Relations*.

Below inset: "Has anyone seen my hat?" – The Vicar (John Pennington) at the church.

Opposite page above left: Del and Rodney invite their Uncle Albert (Buster Merryfield) to live with them.

Opposite page middle: Del remembers Grandad.

Opposite page bottom right: Albert, Stan (Mike Kemp), Jean (Maureen Sweeney) and Del at Grandad's wake.

"This episode was very hard for everyone involved," remembered John Sullivan. "But I thought it was important to bury our grandfather in the show. It was a very strange time because we attended Lennard's funeral and a week later we were shooting Grandad's funeral."

Susan Belbin had the unenviable task of directing the episode: "John took the decision to say that Grandad had passed away and we all met up for the funeral and, oh my god, there really wasn't a dry eye in the house. Ray Butt knew his onions and was a proper Londoner, but even he was in tears. During the studio recording he had to leave the gallery and on location he had to walk away when we were lowering the coffin and all that. It was hard."

The cast were called to Margravine Cemetery in Hammersmith as the location for Grandad's funeral. Among them in costume as Boycie, was John Challis: "It was a very strange day. It was one of these slightly public burial grounds and I remember everyone being slightly hesitant, not quite knowing

what to say, the banter wasn't quite there and everyone was thinking about Lennard. Everyone was a bit reflective and the location meant there was a lot of sadness about."

Originally it was planned to also feature Joan Trotter's monument in the graveyard scene (last seen in series two's *The Yellow Peril*), since the original prop was destroyed, it was rebuilt especially for *Strained Relations* and assembled on location in Margravine Cemetery. However, the idea was decided against on the day of filming.

"It was tough for me because I loved Lennard. He was a smashing man," remembered Sullivan. "But it was especially hard for the actors, I don't know how they handled that. It was very emotional as we know the character who's died, but I was determined to somehow or other create a whopping laugh at the end of the scene. I felt it was important to move on from the sadness of the funeral and get back to the laughter. I came up with the idea of the hat, which was Lennard's symbol. And the laugh came because it *wasn't*

STRAINED RELATIONS

28 FEBRUARY 1985

At the time of the funeral I was living with my nephew Stan and his wife Jean, the North London branch of the family. Can't say I liked them much, but I had a roof over me head and that was the main thing. When you've spent as much time out on the high seas as I have, any old bit of dry land is a God send. Anyway, after the ceremony we all headed back to Del and Rodney's flat for a drink and a few sausage rolls, and I ended up overdoing it with the cognac and conking out in one of the bedrooms. When I finally came to it was almost midnight and all the mourners had left. It was just me, Del Boy and young Rodney. The next morning Del took me back to Stan and Jean's but they'd moved. Just like that. All they'd left behind was me duffel bag, you know, some clothes and a few personal belongings. Well, Del and Rodney couldn't believe it, but it was no real surprise to me. Only a few years earlier I'd been living with my niece Audrey and her husband Kevin. One day they sent me down to Sainsbury's with a shopping list. When I got back they'd emigrated. Not a dicky bird to me. Then there was Patsy's girl, Gillian. I went over there to give her a bit of company cos her husband was on nights. Six months later she set fire to the house. I can remember thinking as I stood on the ledge and jumped into the fireman's net, 'that's gratitude for yer!' But that's the problem with the younger generations. No staying power. It wouldn't have done during the war, I can tell you that for nothing.

Albert

Grandad's hat that was thrown into the grave, it was the vicar's."

The line which allows the audience to laugh some of the sadness away, was said by actor John Pennington, reprising his role as the Vicar from the 1982 mini-episode *Christmas Trees*.

Also seen at the church was actress Lala Lloyd as the old lady who had appeared enquiring about Grandad's welfare in *Happy Returns*.

To play the north London branch of the Trotter family, cousins Stan and Jean, Mike Kemp and Maureen Sweeney were cast. With Stan and Jean was Grandad's brother, Albert, who had been staying with them...

One of the finest scenes in the entire series' history is the argument between Del and Rodney after Grandad's wake in the flat. Rodney can't understand how Del 'got over it' so quickly, managing to be the life and soul of the gathering, which leads Del to explode: "Get over it? What a plonker you really are Rodney. I ain't even started yet, ain't even started bruv, and d'you know why? Because I don't know how to."

"There was never a question in my mind of recasting Grandad," remembered Sullivan, "it would have been an insult to Lennard. I wanted to keep the three generations of men. The balance wouldn't have been right if it was just Del and Rodney. The only option was to bring in a new character. I thought a funeral would be the best opportunity to introduce a new member of the family. Of course, when Albert appears after everyone else has gone home, you knew he was there to stay!"

Above: New cast title sequence photography which would be used in every regular *Only Fools* episode up till 1996's *Time on Our Hands*.

Below: An alternate 'camel hair coat' sequence of Del was photographed but not used.

Opposite page above: Promotional full length shots from 1985.

Opposite page below right: The new trio, back at the Kingston location for *Hole in One*.

To fill the hole left in the Trotter household, John Sullivan created a new character with a completely different look and energy to Grandad. Albert Gladstone Trotter, Grandad's estranged brother, was introduced.

"I made Albert an old sailor, which explained why we hadn't seen him before," Sullivan remembered. "Ray Butt told me he'd received a letter and a photo from a guy who looked like an old sailor – he had this great white beard. We got Buster in and he just looked right and sounded right."

Upon hearing of the death of Lennard Pearce in 1984, the then 65-year-old Buster Merryfield politely wrote in to the BBC putting forward his services for consideration if any thought was being given to replacing the late senior Trotter with another actor.

Merryfield had only started acting professionally a few years previously at the age of 57, after spending nearly forty years working for Nat West bank, rising in the ranks to manager. However, acting had been a part of his life since his time in the army, where he would juggle his personal training duties with those of entertainments officer. During his banking career Merryfield had also built up a long list of credits and awards in amateur theatre.

One of Merryfield's few professional roles before being cast in *Only Fools* was as Sir Miles Honeyman in 1984's PD James mini-series *Shroud for a Nightingale*, which starred future Driscoll brother Roy Marsden and, coincidentally, had also featured Lennard Pearce in a minor role.

"It was a master-stroke bringing in someone from another part of the family, so he could be completely different, but inhabit the same space," recalls John Challis. "I remember Buster saying to me 'I hope I don't bugger it up' cos he knew what it meant to people and what Lennard meant to people. He was understandably pretty nervous about how to behave."

Whilst the gently-cutting subtlety of Lennard Pearce was never going to fit Merryfield's style, in the space of just a few episodes, we would see Albert

unite half of the Nags Head in a sing-a-long of 'I'm in the Mood for Love' as he plays the piano in *Watching the Girls Go By*. An entirely new Trotter with a completely different style.

To further cement the old man of the sea's place in the series, John Sullivan accidentally created a soon to be memorable catchphrase: "I knew a lot of older people who used to tell old stories that would start off with 'During the war...' so I gave this line to Albert a few times. After a while I started to realise how repetitive it was getting, so I began to make the other characters react to it."

With another Trotter now resident in Nelson Mandela House, it was time to update *Only Fools*' titles, a job given to Peter Clayton, the designer who created the original sequence. Digging out the original artwork, Clayton arranged for new character photography to be added to the original masks and animation slides. Once completed, this final title sequence would remain in use on the series till 1996.

HOLE IN ONE

7 MARCH 1985

The hatch was definitely open, but I was down in the cellar taking in a delivery from the brewery at the time, so it had to be. There I was, emptying the last crate, when all of a sudden Albert Trotter came plummeting towards me, screaming "land ahoy!" The next thing I know, I've staggered back, tripped over a crate and twisted my neck something awful. As I slumped against the wall in agony, I'll never forget the sight of Albert hitting a plank and bouncing through the air like a geriatric springboard diver. For a split second it almost looked like he was enjoying it. Luckily, for him, a few dozen bottles of Guinness broke his fall. As for me, my neck was well and truly knackered. I dunno, it'd just been one of those weeks. First the deep-fryer threatened to explode, then I was wearing a neck brace and having to attend court. To this day I'll never know what convinced Del that he could sue the brewery and win. Oddly enough, there weren't even anything wrong with Albert. According to Del, he was suffering with amnesia, but when asked to confirm this in court, he forgot.

Mike

I was just tryin' to help, that's all. I didn't mean to get anyone in any trouble. You see, during the war I was seconded to a special Marine parachute unit and I had to undergo some basic parachute training. Part of that training was learning how to land without injuring yourself. After the war, I fell down the cellar of the Victory Inn in Portsmouth and I received £100 compensation. I can't remember why I fell, I was pissed as a newt at the time, but I still remembered my training and so I didn't actually hurt myself in the fall. Well, from then on, whenever I was hard up for a few bob I'd go and fall down a hole. I didn't wanna do it this time, I'm well past all that stuntman malarkey, but Del and Rodney had been good to me and I wanted to repay them. I also wanted to get their grandad his headstone. He was my older brother. When we was kids he used to look after me. I'd never had the chance to do anything for him, until now.

Albert

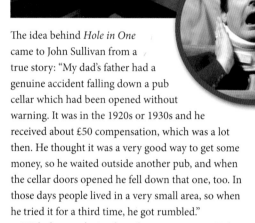

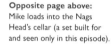

The idea behind *Hole in One* came to John Sullivan from a true story: "My dad's father had a genuine accident falling down a pub cellar which had been opened without warning. It was in the 1920s or 1930s and he received about £50 compensation, which was a lot then. He thought it was a very good way to get some money, so he waited outside another pub, and when the cellar doors opened he fell down that one, too. In those days people lived in a very small area, so when he tried it for a third time, he got rumbled."

With the story's simple and strong premise, *Hole in One* clearly would have made a fine opening instalment to the series, but it was not to be. None of the original location footage featuring Lennard Pearce could be used, and so, in what must have been an unsettling experience for the cast and crew, they retraced their steps and returned to the locations they had previously filmed at, now with Buster Merryfield joining the team.

"Because we had filmed most of this episode with Lennard, I had to rewrite it to include the new character," remembered Sullivan. "Albert then became the one to fall down the pub cellar. In a way it was more believable because he was obviously a more physically fit character, whereas Grandad spent most of his time in an armchair. It may have been a bit of a surprise to see Grandad acting very supple and lithe, dropping down a pub cellar."

With the old sailor lying in a heap on the floor of the Nags Head cellar, Del leaps at the idea of suing the brewery, asking Rodney to put in a call to Solly Atwell, a solicitor who Rodney describes as being "more bent than the villains!"

Cast as Solly was distinguished television actor Colin Jeavons, who makes the slippery solicitor such a memorable guest character. Mr Gerrard (the prosecution counsel) was Andrew Tourell, who Ray Butt had cast the previous year as Penny Warrender's estranged husband, Graham, in *Just*

Good Friends. Tourell would later star in *Waiting for God* alongside *Homesick*'s Sandra Payne as his screen wife.

Hole in One's court scene makes for a classic *Only Fools* sequence. Director Susan Belbin makes brilliant use of the multi-camera set-up and the cast are given some fantastic lines – punctured by some suitable groans of pain from the neck-braced Mike Fisher.

But it is Del Boy who steals the show, making Albert's case, as only he can, by building up a head of steam and fighting for justice. In 1991's *Stage Fright* Rodney jokes that Del has been to court so many times that he's been allocated his own parking place. If his performance in *Hole in One* is anything to go by, it would have been wonderful to have seen a few more of those court appearances.

Interestingly, it is during this court hearing that we hear the address of the Trotters' flat for the first time: 368 Nelson Mandela House, Dockside Estate, Peckham.

Perhaps one of the episode's most touching moments, saved right to the very end, is when Uncle Albert reveals that his main reason for 'falling' down the cellar was so that he could pay for Grandad's headstone.

Opposite page above: Mike loads into the Nags Head's cellar (a set built for and seen only in this episode).

Opposite page below right: Albert takes a fall.

Above: Mr Gerrard (Andrew Tourell).

Below middle: Solly Atwell (Colin Jeavons).

Below: Lyndhurst and Jason welcome Buster Merryfield to the cast as Uncle Albert.

Above: Filming the opening scene where Del takes on his 'Kandy Doll' stock.

Right: Albert helps himself to a drink in the flat.

Below: 'Mental' Mickey's band in full rehearsal, (L-R) Stew (David Thewlis), Rodney, Mickey (Daniel Peacock) and Charlie (Marcus Francis) – "We wanna be rich Marxist Trotskyite anarchists!"

Opposite page top left: A policeman (Geoffrey Leesley) speaking to Del and Rodney in the Trotters' garage.

Opposite middle: A Bunch of Wallies perform 'Boys will be Boys' on *Top of the Pops*!

For *Only Fools'* writer, *It's Only Rock and Roll* was a chance to revisit an unfulfilled dream: "When I was younger I always wanted to be in a band. I remember going to an audition across the other side of London in Dagenham. It was in this huge hall in front of a small group of people. But I never got the chance to prove if I was any good becauseI got three or four words out before it all started going wrong. These guys couldn't play and I was having trouble singing, then more people started coming into the hall to see where this noise was coming from. It was awful!"

While John Sullivan never got the chance to pursue his own rock and roll dreams, the potential of a comedy script focusing on a shambolic young band clearly stayed in his memory. And to weave the Trotters into the plot, it made sense to put Rodney Trotter on the drum stool and have Del Boy as the manager.

To front the band, Sullivan created Peckham's own version of Sid Vicious, a role for which the writer had actor Daniel Peacock in mind: "He was perfect playing the character of Mental Mickey, with that manic glare of his. I'd seen Daniel performing in lots of things before and didn't want to do Mickey with anyone else – and he was absolutely brilliant."

Peacock's incredible stage presence really was perfect as the wannabe 'rich Marxist, Trotskyite anarchist'. The actor had just made a memorable guest appearance in *The Young Ones* and would soon become a regular member of the *Comic Strip* cast. Joining Peacock in the band was actor Marcus Francis and soon to be Hollywood star David Thewlis, who has since gone on to feature in a host of big features, from *Harry Potter* to *Wonder Woman*.

Much like in *Homesick*, *Only Fools'* regular rehearsal space at St Nicholas Church Hall in Chiswick was used as Peckham's community hall,

where Mickey's band are seen rehearsing in *It's Only Rock and Roll*. During this scene, the sleeveless donkey jacket which Mental Mickey is wearing was a costume previously worn by actor George Sweeny, playing the role of Speed in Sullivan's *Citizen Smith*.

Del has been following Rodney's band's progress with interest, and when he hears that the Shamrock club are without a band for St Patrick's Day, he arranges for Mickey's band (who he gives the moniker 'A Bunch of Wallies') to perform, becoming the group's manager in the process. When the gig predictably turns into a riot, Rodney is forced to leave the group after sticking up for his brother in a band argument.

It's Only Rock and Roll was the second episode recorded for series four and would feature Buster Merryfield's very first studio scenes for the series, appropriately enough – behind the bar in the lounge, helping himself to a cigar and glass of cognac.

In a clever bit of scheduling, the episode was first transmitted just three days before St Patrick's day 1985.

Some time after the incident at the Shamrock club, Del returns home and catches the end of *Top of the Pops*: A Bunch of Wallies are in the charts (using the nickname he gave them). Rodney is going to kill him!

For the insert at the end of the episode, director Susan Belbin and the crew filmed Daniel Peacock and A Bunch of Wallies in front of a live audience in the *Top of the Pops*' studios. For this scene, and the rehearsals earlier, the song 'Boys will be Boys' was specially written for the episode by John Sullivan and arranged by Steve Jeffries.

"The strange thing was that the kids actually liked it," remembered Sullivan. "I joked to Daniel that we might have a hit, but nothing happened!"

SERIES 4 EPISODE 4

IT'S ONLY ROCK AND ROLL

14 MARCH 1985

The worst thing we could've done was let a Trotter become our manager. The second worst thing was letting another Trotter join the band. The problems started during our first rehearsals down at the town hall. I mean, just cos you're the one holding the drum sticks, don't mean you get to do the "one, two, three, fours", does it? And I warned Rodney right from the off.

"Rodney," I said, "I do the one, two, three, fours. Okay?"

"Yeah, alright Mick" he said. Five minutes later and he started off again with the "one, two, three, four"! I'm a reasonable man, so I gave him a calm reminder and thought that would surely be the end of it, but then off he goes again with those bloody sticks! "I'm not gonna tell you again, Rodney," I said, "I do the one, two, three, f*#%ing fours!!!" When that didn't work, I had no other option but to bite his ear off, and I would've managed it if he weren't so tall and wiry.

Mental Mickey

SLEEPING DOGS LIE

21 MARCH 1985

The arrival of Duke (1982-1992, RIP) really did fill a void in my life. Up to then it had just been me and Boycie. With Dukie around I finally had a bit of warmth and affection, someone to talk to and spoil. And I really didn't mind all the slobber, the breaking of wind and the hairs on the furniture... as I said, up to then I'd been living with Boycie so I was used to it. They say that dogs are very good judges of character, and Dukie always kept a distance when Boycie was around, so I reckon there must be something to it. Then again, it took me five years to convince my mum that Boycie wasn't a vampire, so it didn't come as too much of a surprise. Well, you can imagine how difficult it was to go on holiday and leave Dukie behind. I sobbed all the way to the Seychelles. "Don't worry, my little spider crab," Boycie reassured me. "He's with his uncles Del and Rodney." And as heartbreaking as it was to be without him, it was comforting to know that he was in safe hands.

Marlene

Ain't it bleedin' fair, eh? I fought a war, went down in smoke and flame, risking life and limb in shark infested waters, all so that Del Boy and Rodney didn't have to, and when all's said and done, they care more about a Great Dane than they do their Great Uncle. Everything was fine till that dog turned up. In fact the last week or so I've never felt so young and vibrant. At one point I was even considering going for a jog in the park. There I was in the flat, enjoying a nice bit of left-over roast pork and wondering why the dog had suddenly been taken comatose, when Del phones from the vets to tell me that not only have I got Sam and Ella poisoning, but I also need an operation. The next thing I know I'm in hospital! They had me on me back, on me belly, upside down, every which way but loose! I'll never forget the look on the head quack's face, telling me it was all for my own good as he shoved an industrial sized thermometer up.... well, up a place an industrial sized thermometer shouldn't be shoved! He's lucky I didn't knock his block off there and then. I used to box for the navy.

Albert

With Boycie and Marlene off for a couple of weeks in the Seychelles, the Trotters are tasked with looking after Marlene's beloved 'puppy'... which turns out to be a steak-eating, vitamin pill-guzzling Great Dane called Duke!

With five appearances behind him, John Challis was now settled into the role of Boycie, but despite being mentioned all the way back in *Go West Young Man*, there was uncertainty about meeting his on-screen wife: "I think there was a bit of discussion about whether she should appear or not as she was a bit of a 'her indoors' character. Eventually it was decided that Boycie's wife should be introduced and I remember thinking, 'I hope we're going to get on alright'."

When it came to casting Marlene, both producer Ray Butt and director Susan Belbin had been watching ITV's sketch show *End of Part One*, and, more specifically, one of the regular performers, Sue Holderness:

"In *End of Part One* I had done a range of accents, so they didn't know if I was posh, middle or working-class. Once they met me, I think they initially thought 'she isn't actually right for this' but that was great for me because I was then only known for playing 'Joanna Barrington-Smythe type' class and suddenly I got the chance to play a proper flirty tart with a heart."

Awarded the part, Holderness wasted no time in requesting tapes of the previous series to fill in the gaps in her viewing. After discussions with Butt, she was also tasked with buying a suitable costume, as well as preparing a fitting hairstyle for Marlene. Arriving on a frosty morning at the Harrow on the Hill address doubling as Boycie and Marlene's home, Holderness entered the world of *Only Fools*:

"I pitched up and Ray Butt bounced over to meet me and said 'did you meet the boys' and I said 'no, I don't know any of them', and I got that awful sort of tongue-tied nervous thing, because they all looked like stars to me. For some reason they were short on time so I didn't really get to talk to any of them.

Ray said, 'we'll do the talking afterwards, let's go straight into shooting the scene'. We went through the lines once, and almost immediately I was snogged by David Jason; he pinched me on the bottom and I thought 'there's no other situation in the world where this could happen!'"

During the location shoot, John Sullivan remembered that the dog cast as Duke grew very fond of one of his fellow cast mates: "While we were filming one of the scenes with the dog, it started getting a bit fruity with Nick Lyndhurst. The clip is still there but it was very cleverly edited. Nick was in the garden and 'Duke' was jumping all over him, but all of a sudden we began to realise that there was a misunderstanding, and this dog was getting a bit carried away!"

Later in the episode, Rodney attempts to take a lethargic Duke for a walk whilst Del attempts to chat up a posh dog walker. These scenes were filmed on Horsenden Hill in Ealing.

A visit to the vet reveals that an increasingly poorly Duke may be suffering with salmonella poisoning, a suspicion born out of the fact that he was fed reheated pork – the same pork that Albert had finished off. Albert is rushed to hospital for a series of very invasive tests, before it is then revealed that Rodney has simply been mixing up Albert's sleeping pills with Duke's vitamin pills!

Actor John D. Collins was cast as the vet who treats Duke. Best known for playing one of the British airmen in *'Allo 'Allo!,* Collins previously appeared as the riverboat policeman in series two's *Ashes to Ashes*.

Reflecting on meeting his screen wife for the first time, John Challis is grateful with how it all turned out: "Sue and I got on straight away and we've been friends ever since. She sailed through the scene and had clearly done her homework."

"I was three months pregnant at the time," remembers Sue Holderness. "I thought it was just a jolly morning's work and got on with my baby and didn't really think anymore about it, until I got the wonderful call from John Sullivan saying he loved Marlene and she'd be back."

Opposite page far left: Marlene (Sue Holderness) brings out her 'baby', the Great Dane, Duke.

Opposite page right: The Doctor (Brian Jameson) discusses Albert's case with Del and Rodney.

Above top right: The vet (John D. Collins) questions the Trotters on what they have been feeding Duke, as the receptionist (Debbie Blyth) works in the background.

Below: "Take him for walkies first thing in the morning, once in the evening and then again last thing at night. When it's his bedtime you put a blanket over him and then you talk to him for a while."

Mike is selling tickets for an upcoming party. Mickey Pearce, on his way out to the Pizza Palace, is convinced Rodney won't be needing two tickets, as he hasn't got a bird to bring. His pride wounded, Rodney tells Mickey that not only will he bring a date, but that the date in question is "a big noise in show business". Mickey bets that he is lying, Del encourages Rodney to up the ante, and they finally agree on the nice round number of 'fifty'... the only problem being that the poor little plonker doesn't actually have anyone to bring.

John Sullivan based this episode on things he'd experienced as a youngster: "In those days, if you were invited to a party your card would say, 'Bring a bottle and a bird'. You could easily get the bottle but you couldn't get the bird, and I remembered all the embarrassment involved."

One of Mickey Pearce's female friends in the Nags Head is played by actress Catherine Clarke, who would later appear as checkout girl, Sheila, in series five's *The Longest Night*... Perhaps this *is* Sheila, enjoying a night off from the Top-Buys till?

Del, Boycie and Trigger are also in the Nags Head playing cards, albeit on a slightly friendlier footing than the last time we saw them in *Losing Streak*. In a brilliantly understated scene, Del puts the brakes on some accelerated betting stakes after a standing Trigger shakes his head when he catches a glimpse at Boycie's hand.

Desperate to find a date at short notice, Rodney goes all out, dressing up like a "Liquorice Allsort" to hit the dance halls of London.

At this point in the story, Buster Merryfield comes into his own as he gets to spin a tender meandering yarn. Aside from the opening two instalments, series four was already written before Lennard Pearce passed away, with Grandad's dialogue tweaked to fit the new character. This tale of lost love in foreign climbs however could only have been written with Uncle Albert in mind. Having an old sea dog in the flat was giving Sullivan fertile new grounds of humour to plough.

After hearing Albert's tale of woe, Rodney is almost ready to throw the towel in, until Del decides to perk his brother up by buying the bet off him and joining him on a night out.

Above: A BBC technician makes an adjustment to the studio lighting above the Nags Head set... with the pubs Space Invaders arcade machine in view.

Above right: Mike sells tickets for a party to Mickey and Rodney.

Right: With his hands full carrying drinks, Del asks Maureen (Nula Conwell) to take the money from his jacket pockets herself!

Below: Rodney and Del hit the night clubs... and Del asks his old flame Yvonne (Carolyn Allen) to chat up Rodney.

Opposite page top left: "Uncle, stand very still! There is a snake in the hood of your duffle coat!"

WATCHING THE GIRLS GO BY

28 MARCH 1985

At this point in *Watching the Girls Go By*, it seems like we have stepped into *Go West Young Man* as we see the Trotters enter into another studio-set night club scene and recount their disappointing night out so far. This would be the last time in the series that we see a night club set like this, as in later episodes all similar club scenes would be shot on location in real venues.

At the club, Del recognises an old friend, Yvonne (played by actress Carolyn Allen), a stripper-turned-exotic dancer whose specialty is a double-act with a live a snake. Del tells Yvonne about the situation with Rodney and bungs her a few quid to go and chat him up. Rodney, unaware of the set up, can't believe his luck. He now has a date for the Nags Head party!

Viewers who have only ever seen this episode on home video will have missed the original version of this scene in which Yvonne serenades Del with an intentionally shocking rendition of Billy Joel's 'Just the Way You Are'.

The following evening back at the flat, a mortified Rodney returns from the party and gives a blow-by-blow account of events that we never see; events which include Rodney's date having one too many drinks and stripping off her clothes before treating the Nags Head regulars to a full routine of her act, live snake and all!

Of course, in three years' time we will get to see another version of this scene, but on that occasion it is Del who will be mortified, and it will carry a lot more meaning.

Begrudgingly, Rodney coughs up the winnings from the bet which Del bought off him: *'fifty' pence,* not pounds! When Albert laughs at them both, the two brothers instantly join forces again and turn their attention to convincing their uncle that there is a snake in the hood of his duffle coat!

Young Rodney's got himself into a right old predicament with this one. But that's the trouble with Rodney, he's never had much luck when it comes to the fairer sex. It's not so much that he can't get dates, it's more that after the dates are over they don't wanna see him again. Del and I thought he might have finally cracked it the time he got a date with the tubby girl who lives down by the community hall (lovely girl she is, teeth like a harbour wall), but no joy. Rodney puts it all down to his tendency to get too serious too soon. It's a family trait with us Trotters. We wear our hearts on our sleeves. It reminds me of the time just after the war when we'd sailed into Hamburg to pick up some prisoners. Whilst there I met this German girl named Helga who worked in a bar down by the docks. I fell in love with her the moment I saw her. The poor cow lost the little finger on her right hand when her home was bombed. I didn't mind, though. In my eyes it just added character, plus it was always a good conversation starter. I ended up asking her to marry me but she said no. The thing is, I'd mistaken her gestures of friendship as tokens of love. In hindsight I can see that it was all for the best. The authorities didn't like us fraternising with the Germans, and I was still married to my wife, Ada, at the time, and she wouldn't have let me hear the last of it. Still, to this day I think Helga loved me too in her own way. She never used to charge me as much as the other lads.

Uncle Albert

AS ONE DOOR CLOSES

4 APRIL 1985

"When the going gets tough, the tough get going." I'll never forget Mum saying that to me on her deathbed. I just wish I'd whacked a copyright on it as years later I heard the exact same line in a song (I forget its name but you know it, the one with Michael Douglas and that little bloke from Taxi). Anyway, when we suddenly got lumbered with a two-thousand pound debt, the going got very tough. Being the optimistic, never-say-die, man of action that I am, I began wracking the old filbert for a solution. Meanwhile, Rodney was using the time to catch up on some research into butterflies. I couldn't believe it! There we were, two grand in the red and with a gang of very big and very irate Rastafarians after our blood, and that little plonker was giving me the scientifical rundown of some poxy bleed'n butterfly! Alright, to be fair, the butterfly in question was very rare and some private collector mush was willing to cough up a small fortune for a live sample. But what did Rodney really expect? There was no way I was gonna be seen running up and down Peckham High Road chasing Mars Bar wrappers with a giant net! No way Pedro! I had a reputation to uphold.

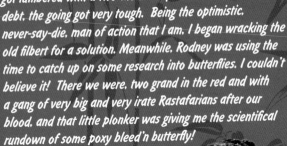

Del

Brendan O'Shaughnessy (seen in series three's *Who's a Pretty Boy?*) has a contract to fit out a new housing estate with 166 Louvre doors. Del's mate at the joinery works, Teddy Cummings, can provide the Trotters with said doors on the condition that they are sold in bulk, a stipulation that will cost the Trotters a hefty two grand!

"The idea of the doors came from a carpenter mate of mine who was fitting Louvre doors on a housing estate," remembered John Sullivan. "He actually called them 'lovvvery' doors and I added this to the script because I just wanted to hear Del say 'lovvery' instead of Louvre."

Deflated at the prospect of missing out on a deal that could see them double their money, Del and Rodney go back to the market and try to shift a load of DIY hair cutting kits. There they run into Denzil, on his way to the job centre having recently being made redundant. It is then that Del has an epiphany: "Hold on, if he was made redundant, that means he's got redundancy money!"

"You're not having any!" screams Denzil.

Having finally convinced Denzil to lend them the money, Del and Rodney buy the doors from Teddy Cummings, only to then find out from Brendan that plans have suddenly changed – the architect now wants Victorian panel doors! Lumbered with the Louvre doors and now owing Denzil £2,000, the Trotters retreat to the cemetery and pray for an answer to their woes. And that's when Rodney spots the incredibly rare butterfly he recently read about in a colour supplement... an incredibly rare butterfly that, if captured alive, is worth £3,000!

Sullivan was inspired to write this episode because of an article he had read about

a rare butterfly: "Because of the climate change, this butterfly had surfaced in the UK and collectors were desperate to get their hands on it. I thought that if it was worth some money, Del would try to get a piece of it."

To depict the Jamaican Swallowtail butterfly, a specially built prop was made and 'flown' via a fishing rod handled by a member of the production team. Whilst not the most advanced of techniques, thanks to some carefully chosen camera angles it works remarkably well.

For shots of the butterfly flying around Joan Trotter's monument, the crew went to London's Highgate cemetery and rebuilt her elaborate grave at a new location. For budgetary reasons these scenes in Highgate were recorded on video, as the series had already used up its allocation of film stock from the initial batch of unused location work filmed with Lennard Pearce.

The final stages of the butterfly chase were filmed in and around the pond at Ravenscourt Park in Hammersmith. As it was early January, artificial water lilies had to be sourced and carefully positioned for the butterfly to land on. Here is where Rodney (with a little, and *literal,* nudge from Del) takes to the water and wades out to scoop up the butterfly. In reality, Nicholas Lyndhurst wore a wet suit under his costume to keep

him warm in the freezing temperatures.

Amazingly it seems that the Trotters have actually prevailed for once. To dry the butterfly out, Del opens his hands in front of him, just as Denzil skates by.

"Denzil!" cries Del, "I've got your money!" "Great! I'll see you down the pub later!" Denzil replies, before slamming his hands down into Del's in an inverted 'high five'.

As One Door Closes brought to a close an incredibly difficult year for *Only Fools,* but the series managed to end on a suitably calmer and cheerier note. The series would never be the same again, but by welcoming Uncle Albert to drop anchor at Nelson Mandela House, it would be able to continue to thrive, surely the very best kind of tribute to the memory of Lennard Pearce.

Broadcast on consecutive Thursday evenings (now at an earlier time of 8.00 pm) on BBC 1 from 21 February 1985, the fourth series of *Only Fools* would pull in an average of 14.91 million viewers for each episode.

Opposite page below right: Looking over the balcony, the Trotters spot Denzil and his five brothers.

Above: Director Susan Belbin blocks out the cemetery scenes... as Joan's monument is rebuilt in a new home.

Above left: Denzil has his redundancy money!

Left: The original butterfly prop.

Below: Filming the final sequence at Hammersmith's Ravenscourt Park.

TO HULL AND BACK

★ ★

Just when you thought you'd seen the last of Roy Slater, he popped up again, like a stubborn haemorrhoid, only twice as painful. And on this occasion his timing couldn't have been more perfect. I'd just sealed a very big and very 'hush-hush' deal with Boycie and Abdul, that, if all went to plan, would see us Trotters net a cool fifteen grand. It was all very simple on the face of it: go to Amsterdam, pick up a few diamonds and bring them back to London. Then we bumped into Roy 'Bullshit of the Yard' Slater. He'd been promoted to 'Chief' inspector and couldn't wait to let everyone and their cousin know about it. Worse luck, he knew about the diamond deal. Well, my old April was gurning like a good'un when he told us, but as it turned out he was none the wiser as to who the couriers were. Boycie, Abdul and I held a top-secret, last-minute meeting in the back of Denzil's lorry. I let Boycie and Abdul leave first and then waited for the all clear. I was just about to step out when Slater and his merry men turned up and started sniffing around. I was certain I was a goner, but I managed to give them the slip by concealing myself under a bit of tarpaulin. Thinking it was panic over, I then discovered that not only had I been locked in, but that Denzil had jumped into the cabin and was driving away with me. Thankfully Rodney followed and, just as I was about to give up all hope, came to my rescue. That's how we ended up in Hull, all the way up in bleed'n Yorkshire! There I found myself, standing by the docks, surrounded by boats of all different shapes and sizes, when it suddenly dawned on me that there was a way to bring the diamonds back and avoid airports and customs altogether. After a bit of legwork, I hired us the bestest engine-powered trawler in all of Hull. All we needed then was a safe pair of hands to steer it over to Holland...

★ ★

Above: Abdul (Tony Anholt), Del and Boycie talk business.

Above middle: Slater is on the case, questioning Del and Rodney in Sid's cafe.

Above right: "The back of Denzil's bleeding lorry, I mean what a place to hold a meeting!"

Below: The cast pose in front of one of Hull's distinctive white telephone boxes and the Humber Bridge.

After a difficult production, the fourth series of *Only Fools* managed to emerge triumphant. Seven incredibly strong episodes which took in both heartbreak and hilarity. Viewers had voted with their remote controls and the message was clear. They wanted more.

The Christmas before that series of *Only Fools*, John Sullivan and Ray Butt produced a 90-minute instalment of *Just Good Friends*, Sullivan's popular sitcom about a couple, Vince Pinner and Penny Warrender, who meet again five years after Vince jilted Penny at the altar.

For this ambitious Christmas film, Sullivan cleverly connected the ending of the second series with the first meeting of the series' main characters. The plot comes full circle as Penny and Vince meet again at the beginning of the first series. Made on film with no laughter track, the episode earned impressive viewing figures at peak time on Christmas day, a success that

encouraged Sullivan to push for a similarly lavish instalment of *Only Fools*.

"This was the first episode of *Only Fools* that I decided to do without an audience," remembered John Sullivan. "This meant I had to write quite differently to studio-based episodes. It would have been tricky to have had to constantly return to the Nags Head or the Trotter flat. There was a lot more drama and I didn't have to create so many gags. When you have an audience, you feel obliged to make them laugh constantly."

In Sullivan's script for the proposed special, Boycie and business associate, Abdul, have arranged a diamond smuggling deal with a merchant from Amsterdam. Agreeing to act as their courier (for the right price, of course) Del Boy has to take a briefcase full of cash to Amsterdam and bring back the stones. Already a risky enough venture, the Trotters then discover that the police (namely Peckham's very own Roy Slater) are already onto the deal and have all the airports covered. This leads (via an unplanned trip to Hull in the back of Denzil's lorry) to some pretty creative thinking on Del's part: the Trotters will avoid the airports altogether and instead sail to Holland and back!

With such a well-established group of characters at his disposal, Sullivan had an idea how they would fit into his story: "Boycie is always looking for a way to make a fast buck, but never has the guts for it. Instead, he would have to find a patsy. He would never go for someone like Trigger or Rodney, but Boycie knows Del is streetwise enough to pull it off."

With such an ambitious script, one way of cutting costs was to relocate the entire production of the film to Hull. The city and its port were vital to the plot and there was a direct ferry link to Holland. Equally, Hull's city streets could double as south London

market streets, enabling those scenes to be filmed there too.

Located near the docks, the former Imperial Typewriters factory on Hedon Road was identified as the perfect place to use as a studio and production base. The factory had plenty of warehouses, ideal for rebuilding the flat and Nags Head sets (once the various set pieces were driven up from London). There was also room to build new sets required just for the film, such as Boycie's car showroom and Van Kleefe's office.

With everything prepared, filming was arranged to take place over six weeks between 2 June and 13 July 1985.

The Peckham market scenes for *To Hull and Back* were filmed on Hull's Charles Street, with a cafe on nearby John Street used as the location of Sid's cafe and the Whittington and Cat pub on Commercial road used as the exterior of the Nags Head.

Tony Anholt was cast as the often mentioned Abdul. A well-known actor and star of popular seventies series *The Protectors* and *Space:1999*, by the time *To Hull and Back* aired, he would be starring in BBC 1's *Howards' Way*.

"It was terribly exciting," John Challis remembers, "it was like doing a movie. We were in Hull – I'm pretty sure no one had been to Hull before! I knew Tony Anholt, he was a friend of a friend and he took his acting very seriously but he was still a very funny guy. The other thing was that there was no audience, and we were used to going to the studio and playing to the live laughter. But we all knew it was funny and there was a great situation."

The Transport Café and Lorry Park, where Boycie, Abdul and Del hold a secret meeting in the back of Denzil's lorry, was filmed in the storage area and car park behind the crew's ad-hoc studios on Hedon Road. Here, Jim Broadbent and Christopher Mitchell would reform their duo from series three's *May the Force Be With You* as Slater and Hoskins. The interior of their police office was also filmed inside the Hedon Road factory.

Joining the cast as Lil (the Dockside cafe proprietor) was actress Rachel Bell, who had recently been cast for John Sullivan's sitcom *Dear John*: "I had just started work on *Dear John* and someone said, 'You used to live in Hull didn't you? Would you

Above left: "I know the money is good lovey, but you'll get no overtime in the mortuary" – the Dockside cafe's Lil (Rachel Bell) warns Denzil.

Left: "Schooner with an engine? Follow me shipmate, I might have just the thing for you" – the boatman (Joe Belcher).

Below: The cast get to grips with their floating location, the *Inge*.

TO HULL AND BACK

25 DECEMBER 1985

The moment I saw Albert getting off the train, my heart froze. Watching him shuffle up the platform towards us was like watching the approach of impending doom itself... impending doom with a duffle bag! I mean, it was bad enough that Del would even suggest that we rent a boat and sail to Holland and back (let alone his choosing one that looked like it'd already gone ten rounds with Jaws), but to elect Albert as skipper! This was the man who'd been torpedoed five times! On the last ship he sailed the crew shot an albatross for luck! We didn't even make it out of the dock without getting into a fender-bender! And once we were out at sea proper, Dear God! I was physically ill, not so much from the waves, but more from the sight of Albert's head bobbing about up in the wheelhouse window!

Rodney

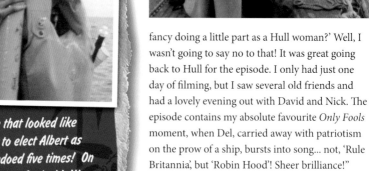

fancy doing a little part as a Hull woman?' Well, I wasn't going to say no to that! It was great going back to Hull for the episode. I only had just one day of filming, but I saw several old friends and had a lovely evening out with David and Nick. The episode contains my absolute favourite *Only Fools* moment, when Del, carried away with patriotism on the prow of a ship, bursts into song... not, 'Rule Britannia', but 'Robin Hood'! Sheer brilliance!"

Bell's scene was filmed at a redressed cafe on Neptune Street, a few minutes away from St Andrews Docks where Del meets the boatman (played by actor Joe Belcher) and the Trotters eventually sail to open sea.

The boat found to take the Trotters on their journey was the *Inge* (a Scandinavian female name), a former 'anchor seiner' netting boat built in the early 1960s. At the time of filming she was owned by Humber Divers Ltd and used for survey work. Reportedly the *Inge* was not a particularity smooth boat to sail on and both cast and crew suffered with seasickness during filming. For some night scenes set on the boat, a recreation of the *Inge*'s forecastle was built at the Hedon Road studio.

For the scene of Denzil taking a brisk walk on the beach to clear his head (before having his maddening paranoia confirmed when he spots

the Trotters on the *Inge*!), actor Paul Barber and a small crew travelled just out of Hull to Yorkshire's very own Lands' End, Spurn Point. One of the narrow peninsula's disused lighthouses can be seen behind Barber, a journey which would have been almost impossible in Denzil's Leyland DAF 2800 lorry!

By 1985, after several years of working on *Only Fools* in the role of assistant floor manager, Tony Dow had been promoted to production manager. Together with Sue Longstaff, Dow helped to manage all the location work, especially the complex sequences filmed at sea.

Whilst Ray Butt supervised the filming in Hull, Dow was left responsible for directing the sequences in Amsterdam. Dow was also on the *Inge* during the six-hour trip out to the North Sea gas rig, where he shot the scene of the rigger (David Fleesham) answering Del's request for directions to Holland. Ray Butt took the much quicker route and went by helicopter.

Arriving in Holland, Albert tells Rodney they are sailing the North Sea canal "which takes us in to the heart of Amsterdam". In reality the crew decided to film this scene along the much more picturesque banks of Kinderdijk (just outside Rotterdam), making use of the distinctive row of windmills. Since taking a well-aged fishing boat all the way to Holland for just one shot wasn't practical, a locally hired boat was used for Del and Rodney's end of the conversation. With some clever framing and editing, viewers don't actually realise that the *Inge* didn't ever go to Holland in the story.

In Amsterdam, Tony Dow and his unit filmed the opening of their sequence in the Binnenstad neighbourhood, taking in the Dam Square Street Organ and, appropriately enough, the Amsterdam Diamond Center. An address in Lauriergracht was used for Van Kleefe's office. The 'police chase' was filmed from the corner of Prinsengracht to Kloveniersburgwal, skipping across to the Walter Suskind Bridge for one shot.

Opposite page: With the *Inge* taken to sea, Del salutes Robin Hood.

Above: The cast and crew got to go on board the North Sea rig used in the episode.

Left: David Fleeshman as the Gas Rigger – "Holland? – It's over there."

Below: "Ajax!" – The Trotters arrive in Amsterdam and meet diamond merchant Mr Van Kleefe (Philip Bond).

Above: The Diamond gang turn to the door and are greeted by the sight of Slater in a sombrero!

Above top right: For the first time we see the fourth wall of the Trotter flat.

Right: £15,000 falls to the ground...

Below: The cast appeared in an advert and on the cover of the Christmas 1985 *Radio Times* to promote *To Hull and Back*... where they were also photographed with a sleigh.

Opposite page left: Denzil thinks he is going out of his mind when he sees Del on board the *Inge* from the beach of Spurn Point.

Opposite page right: Terry Hoskins is on to Slater's scam...

Whilst Hull provided the team with all of the London Market streets and lorry park locations they needed, the crew returned to the north Acton estate and Harlech Tower for a brief shot of £15,000 in bank notes being thrown out of a window. The only other major sequence of the episode filmed in London was just south of the Acton estate on Stanley Road, where the crew found a suitable suburban street for staging the police roadblock where Slater is arrested.

Back in the Hedon Road studios, *Only Fools'* regular sets came alive for their 'filmic' debut in *To Hull and Back*. Both sets now feature a fourth wall. The Nags Head becomes a cosy smoky boozer and, after all these years, seeing the other side of the Trotters' flat is a bit of a revelation. Interestingly, after being modified for filming in Hull, the next time we see these sets in series five they've both had bold make-overs.

Reflecting on the special, John Challis rates it very highly: "It was such a great story, the longevity of the show has a lot to do with the fact that the stories were so good, and the fact you could take that story from Peckham to Hull to Amsterdam, then onto a boat in the middle of the ocean, it was fantastic. It felt like we were in the movies."

To Hull and Back genuinely feels like a feature film. After being confined to 30-minute doses, it is such a treat to see the Trotters and co swept up in a bigger story told over a broad canvas.

To help promote *To Hull and Back* the *Radio Times* ran the series on the cover with a special photoshoot, and filmed an advert. The day before *To Hull and Back* was broadcast Del Boy also made a three minute appearance on BBC's *Breakfast Time* in a spoof investigation with BBC's consumer expert, Lynn Faulds about the sale of white mice.

"When we received the transmission slots," John Sullivan remembered, "we realised *Only Fools* was lined up to go out at the same time as *Minder*, which was a massive show then. They did a lot of promotional stuff, and there were *Minder* adverts and billboards everywhere you went. I thought we were going to get mullered. But when the viewing figures came back, we'd actually beaten them by quite a lot. That was when I realised how popular *Only Fools* had become – in those days, if you could beat *Minder*, then you were a very, successful show."

Broadcast on Christmas Day 1985 at 7.30pm, *To Hull and Back* pulled in an incredible 16.9 million viewers.

Corrine and I had just got back together, under the strict condition that I promise to steer clear of Del Boy. But that's easier said than done when he's on the phone to you, at your front door, in the betting shops and the pubs... he even pops up when you're stuck in a sodding traffic jam! It sounds mental, I know, but I'd been getting this feeling that he was haunting me! I'd even started to hear his voice when I was driving my lorry. Then I had to go and collect a load all the way up in Hull, and as I arrived I could've sworn I saw him at a zebra crossing. I tried to stay calm and rational, thinking that maybe I'd just been overworking myself, so I took a break and went up a hill overlooking the docks. There I sat, breathing the fresh salt air, feeling the calm slowly return, when I noticed, off in the distance, a little fishing trawler heading out to sea, and there was Del Boy standing at its bow, clear as day! As soon I returned to Peckham I booked an appointment with the first psychiatrist I could find!

Denzil

Slater was on the warpath again. He'd been promoted to Chief Inspector and was looking for one big nick before he retired. Actually, retirement wasn't his choice, he'd had orders from the top. You see, Slater had persuaded this young black fella to sign a full confession to being a peeping tom. When the case got to court it turned out he was a registered blind person. The police don't need that kind of publicity, do they? I felt sorry for the blind fella, but then again he did get a record contract out of it, so it didn't turn out too badly for him. As for Slater, he had a surprise coming too, courtesy of the Internal Affairs department.

Terry Hoskins

SERIES FIVE

Another grotty year was behind us, thank God. The old place just wouldn't be the same without Grandad around. Deep down Rodney and I had known it was coming, but you can never truly prepare for these things, you've just gotta do what you can to keep moving forward after it's happened. Of course, we did our best by him and gave him a decent send off, and apart from some git nicking the vicar's hat, it was a lovely ceremony. But the world really does work in mysterious ways. One minute you lose a Grandfather, the next you gain a Great Uncle, in this case, Grandad's estranged younger brother, Albert. And he was a strange one. He reckoned he spent half his life at sea, but when you listened to him talk you realised that he actually spent most of that time under it. He'd been sunk more times than a plunger, the poor sod. Still, he did manage to get us to Holland and back (just about) and, thanks to a bit of very shrewd manoeuvring by yours truly, we did end up with a nice little drink for our efforts. All things considered, I was certain our luck was about to change for the better. Yeah, from that moment forward the Trotter star would be on the rise!

FROM PRUSSIA WITH LOVE

31 AUGUST 1986

When Del Boy turned up to offer Marlene and I a brand new baby at a discount, I made the schoolboy error of listening to him. But what else could I have done? Marlene's hormones were so up the wall she could think of nothing else but babies! Being the loving and understanding husband that I've always been, I'd done everything in my power to get her to shut up, alas my best efforts had failed. Then in waltzed Del with what seemed to be the answer to all our problems. He went on to explain that Rodney had met some pregnant German girl named Anna. Apparently the baby's father, who hadn't gone a bundle on the whole pregnancy thing, had disowned the poor girl. Just when you'd have thought the world couldn't be a more crueller place, she ended up bumping into Rodney Trotter, who then brought her back to stay at Nelson Mandela House (now there's a losing streak if ever I've seen one!) Anyway, Anna had decided that once the baby – which Del promised me was a boy - was born she was gonna put it up for adoption. By this point, Marlene was already reaching for the Mothercare catalogue, but there were still some snags that needed undoing before the deal could be sealed, the biggest of which was that we'd already tried the adoption route but, owing to the fact that I'd once done a little stretch at Her Majesty's pleasure, we'd been blacklisted. Del then came up with the idea that we could simply say the baby was ours. This, too, came with its own set of problems, since the last report we'd received from the gynaecologist said there was more chance of Trigger winning Mastermind than there was of Marlene being up the duff! After a brief chat with Marlene, I reached a decision. "Alright, Del," I said. "We'll take it."

When the goods finally did arrive we discovered that not only was the baby a girl, it was also brown!

"It don't bother me, Boycie" Marlene said, missing the point entirely.

"For Gawd's sake, Marlene," I said. "How are we going to pass this baby off as our own?! I might be able to con people into buying my cars, I might be able to convince them that you conceived and gave birth in seven days flat, but how the hell am I gonna persuade them that my grandad was Louis Armstrong?!" Now let this be a lesson for you. If Derek Trotter ever offers to make your dreams come true, keep a tight hold of your wallet and run for the hills!

Boycie

The fifth series of *Only Fools* would perhaps feature the most distinctive collection of episodes John Sullivan would ever write, with a trilogy of rich location-heavy stories threaded in-between three very different studio-bound scripts. For Sullivan and producer Ray Butt, this would be their busiest year at the BBC. In February 1986 Sullivan's fourth sitcom *Dear John* debuted, starring Ralph Bates as the recently single John Lacey. Later in the year the team would make the third and final series of *Just Good Friends*, simultaneously with the second feature-length *Only Fools* special.

For series five, Ray Butt continued as the series producer, but passed the bulk of directing duties to *Only Fools*' former Assistant Floor Manager Mandie Fletcher:

"Ray was originally down to do my series, but I don't think he was very well. I was called in by the head of comedy who said 'Right, can you do four episodes?' and I said, 'Can I hell, I'll be there!' I think I was doing the Post Production on *Blackadder II* at the time. But I was absolutely terrified! On *Only Fools* they'd only known me as an assistant floor manager and now suddenly I was directing them. It was like going back to school, but they were very kind to me, they were very sweet. I think Ray got better and was able to come back for the last two. But I have to say wasn't I lucky, I think I got some pretty classic episodes."

The series opens with *From Prussia with Love*, a script written for the previous series but passed over to make space for Grandad's farewell in *Strained Relations*. Expertly executed, the story revolves around Del's attempt to home the baby of German au pair, Anna, with Boycie and Marlene.

The story's clear Dickensian undertones are neatly highlighted in a line by Rodney ("It's like something out of Dickens!") as the morality of the situation is suitably reacted to by each character. Reassuringly, the good nature of Del wins through.

Whilst John Challis delivers perhaps the greatest ever Boycie speech in the series, the most affecting performance of the episode is delivered by Sue Holderness, in only her second appearance in the series as Marlene.

For the actress some of the themes in the episode brought home a very different meaning. At the time Holderness had only just given birth herself: "I had two babies very close together so I was very much a pregnant producing woman and I was terribly moved by the genuine heartfelt letters from people saying how they understood the pain of my not being able to have this little brown baby that I had fallen in love with, it was very moving and it made me realise how incredibly lucky I was that this wasn't actually a problem for me."

Cast as German au pair, Anna, was actress Erika Hoffman, who Fletcher would soon cast in *Brush Strokes as* the second Lesley Bainbridge. As Anna, Hoffman gives a masterclass of comic misunderstanding whilst modelling a baby bump.

The episode's final guest actor would require a very unusual casting call for Fletcher: "The thing I remember most about *From Prussia with Love* was going to choose the baby! We went to the maternity ward at Hammersmith Hospital and I remember thinking this is really weird."

Elsewhere, this episode would mark the fifth and final appearance of Nula Conwell's barmaid, Maureen. The actress was also starring in *The Bill* on ITV at the time, where the producers were uncomfortable with her appearing on a rival channel, forcing Maureen to leave the Nags Head for good.

This episode would be the only time we see the lounge of Boycie and Marlene's original house. A lavishly detailed set was built, complete with garden and patio which would barely be seen on screen. For the one exterior scene of the episode where we see an establishing shot of Boyce and Marlene's house (and Rodney enjoy Great Dane Duke's company once more!) the crew returned to the Harrow on the Hill location used previously in series four's *Sleeping Dogs Lie*.

Above left: Del makes his Dickensian proposal to Boycie and Marlene.

Above: A look at the fully lit and dressed set of Boycie and Marlene's lounge, designed by Mark Sevant.

Below left: An audience ticket used for the 1986 and 1987 episodes of *Only Fools and Horses*.

Left: Maureen (Nula Conwell)'s last shift in the Nags Head.

Below: The Trotters mobilise as Anna (Erika Hoffman) is about to go into labour.

★ONLY FOOLS AND HORSES...★

★★ WRITTEN BY JOHN SULLIVAN ★★
Starring DAVID JASON, NICHOLAS LYNDHURST, BUSTER MERRYFIELD

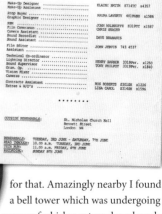

Above and below left: "I'm putting it in, I'm putting it in!" The cast pose for publicity shots in Southwark's St Alphege church.

Above top right: The rehearsal script for the episode.

Right: The leaking bell tower, with a little help from BBC Visual Effects.

Below right: The crying statue placed in the Southwark church by the art department.

Opposite page top left: Del and Father O'Keith (P.G. Stephens) see a miracle.

Opposite page far right: A trumpet-seeking Biffo (John Pierce Jones) about to mangle Rodney's head!

Opposite page top right and below: Rodney with Biffo's trumpet.

The Miracle of Peckham was a very different beast to the usual Trotter tale as it was written in part as a way for John Sullivan to explore Del's attitudes towards religion: "I think that Del is a God-fearing man. Though he doesn't know where he was christened or what his religion is, he is one of those people who are the first on their knees praying when a problem arises. Del was brought up on religion and I think it frightens him."

Way back in the first series, in *The Second Time Around*, Grandad mentions in passing that Del recently came to the aid of a church roof fund, a reference clearly worth revisiting.

"The important point in this episode is that Del didn't steal the lead from the church roof himself,'" Sullivan explained. "He bought it from Sunglasses Ron and Paddy the Greek, but he didn't know where it came from. Of course, when he realises he tries to make amends."

The amends which Sullivan described comes in the form of a 'miracle' which our tender-hearted wide-boy uses to manipulate the media for a very good cause.

Assistant Floor Manager Adrian Pegg recalls the search to find a suitable central location for the script: "I was dispatched to find the church for the miracle and had to do a fair bit of research to find a deconsecrated site we could use for filming. I eventually found the perfect location in Southwark but it didn't have the required bell tower so I then went out looking

for that. Amazingly nearby I found a bell tower which was undergoing some refurbishment work and made all the filming arrangements."

The church Pegg found for the main shoot was St Alphege in Southwark (which would be demolished in 1991). A neighbouring block of flats with a waste disposal chute was used for Rodney's trumpet search (since a trip back to the Acton flats for one scene would not have been practical).

The nearby bell tower location did prove to be problematic for Pegg however: "It would certainly have been easier to have built a set in the studio, as it was the Visual Effects team who needed to find a way to make it look as if the rain was pouring in. When we returned to film it several weeks after my recce I was horrified to find that much of the refurbishment had already been done!"

For Mandie Fletcher, the episode was a chance to direct on a larger scale: "*The Miracle of Peckham* was so wonderful, as normally as a sitcom director you had to do multi-camera in the studio and I suddenly found myself making a little movie – it was fantastic. These lovely location scripts allowed for a lot more to do than just getting everybody in shot."

Location filming for *The Miracle of Peckham* and the whole of series five was carried out between 30 April and 19 May 1986, with studio recordings for all six episodes carried out over five consecutive Sundays from 1 June and a week's pause before the recording of the series' final episode on 13 July.

Despite airing second, *The Miracle of Peckham* was the first in the series to be

recorded, and with just under nine minutes of studio footage, it would feature the shortest amount of studio recording used in an episode with an audience.

Cast as Father O'Keith was Irish actor P.G. Stephens, who brings the stern yet warm character to life. Stephens had just recently played an unnamed priest in a similar vein to O'Keith alongside Timothy Dalton in the 1985 film *The Doctor and the Devils*.

The episode's sub plot of Rodney piecing together the unseen trumpet-stealing events of the night before, make for an unusual addition to an *Only Fools* episode, but they also add some much needed belly laughs to an otherwise more reflective than usual main story. This Biffo (named by John Sullivan after *The Beano* comic character) plot however does lend itself to a perfect coda to the episode after the main story is resolved.

Distinctive Welsh actor John Pierce Jones was cast as Biffo and he fondly recalls the filming: "I had been working with director Mandie Fletcher a few months previously on *Blackadder II*, when my agent called to say I had been offered Biffo in *The Miracle of Peckham*. I was filming on the remote coast of the Isle of Anglesey in North Wales. Mandie arranged that I filmed on the weekend, so I took the sleeper train from Holyhead to Euston where I was picked up and taken to the location. We filmed all day, then I got the sleeper train back to Holyhead that evening. It was really worth the effort just to say that I was in *Only Fools*. The Saturday we filmed I had an amazing welcome from the cast and crew, and 'Where's my trumpet?' has become one of my all-time signature lines!"

SERIES 5 EPISODE 2

THE MIRACLE OF PECKHAM

7 SEPTEMBER 1986

What a night! Biffo the Bear and his band were playing at the Nag's Head and everyone was having a right laugh. That's when I got chatting to this bird named Helen – at least I think that was her name. Biffo's trumpet was so loud it wasn't easy to be sure of anything. You should have seen her. She was tall and elegant and really classy (like something out of that TV show, Dynasty) and she was all over yours truly like a dose of impetigo! She couldn't 'alf put the booze away, though, and I had to really push myself to keep up. So much so that my final memory of the evening was telling Mickey Pearce to shove it and then getting lost in the bogs. Of course, I woke up the next morning with the headache to end all headaches. To make matters worse, Albert was on the wind up, sitting there with his kipper breakfast, banging on about being woken up by a trumpet blast. I just put it down to age and thought nothing more of it. I was still buzzing about Helen. That was when Del came in and gave me the full SP. Apparently I'd got so drunk that during Biffo's final set I'd got up on stage, took his trumpet and stuck two fingers up at him. I'd then stumbled home and blew the trumpet in Albert's ear'ole. At that moment it all started to come back to me with a dreadful chill. I wouldn't have minded too much if it hadn't been for the fact that Biffo was often mistaken for Geoff Capes. Not that I was scared or nothing, but still, he was the sort of bloke who had 15 Weetabix for breakfast. I immediately set about making things right. I'd simply return the trumpet and apologise, and maybe, just maybe, he'd let me live. That's when I discovered that Albert had chucked the trumpet down the rubbish chute. Resisting the very strong urge to chuck the garrity old git in after it, I rushed down to the bins to retrieve the instrument. Bloody hell! It was so bent out of shape it looked like Uri Gellar had had a go on it. Just when I thought things couldn't possibly get any worse, I heard a rumbling sound from the chute above me and before I could even work out what was happening, the remains of Albert's kipper breakfast landed on my head.

Rodney

THE LONGEST NIGHT

14 SEPTEMBER 1986

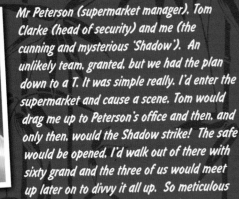

Mr Peterson (supermarket manager), Tom Clarke (head of security) and me (the cunning and mysterious 'Shadow'). An unlikely team, granted, but we had the plan down to a T. It was simple really. I'd enter the supermarket and cause a scene. Tom would drag me up to Peterson's office and then, and only then, would the Shadow strike! The safe would be opened, I'd walk out of there with sixty grand and the three of us would meet up later on to divvy it all up. So meticulous was our planning that we'd even roped in some random members of the public on a jumped up shoplifting charge. That way we'd have independent witnesses to the robbery and the whole thing would be more believable when the police turned up. There were three of 'em: a young, anaemic-looking bloke, a short older bloke whose face I was sure I'd seen before, and an old geezer who looked like a bit like a down-and-out Father Christmas. Anyway, the plan was going like clockwork, we stuck to the script and none of the witnesses noticed that the gun I was pointing at them was actually plastic and made in Taiwan. What none of us could have counted on though was the crappy wristwatch my mum had recently got for me from some shyster down the market – I missed the automatic time-lock on the safe by 15 minutes. Bloody watch! If that weren't bad enough, Peterson then said the safe wouldn't open again for another 14 hours! Bloody, bloody watch! Quickly weighing up the options, I asked myself what the Shadow would do, before deciding to lock the office door and wait it out. This caused a bit of moaning and groaning from the three witnesses, but it didn't bother me. When you'd stood in as many dole queues as I had, 14 hours was nothing!

Lennox 'The Shadow' Gilbey

Placed at the heart of the fifth series, *The Longest Night* could very much have been John Sullivan's standalone 1986 comedy heist movie. With a perfectly paced and self-contained plot, the story boasts a sublime cast and neat premise. In some respects, if you skip the opening titles, Del, Rodney and Uncle Albert could be guest starring in another comedy series! For one time only, it is a joy to see these characters out of their familiar environments (no Trotter flat or Nags Head) and away from the usual company they keep.

The supermarket used for the location of *The Longest Night*'s fictional store "Top-Buys" was a recently opened Co-op LEO's on High Road in Leytonstone. The building is now occupied by a branch of clothes chain Matalan, and from the outside still stands largely unchanged from its *Only Fools* appearance.

Adrian Pegg was on location during the filming: "In those days, supermarkets were closed on Sundays, which made it much easier to film in, and we had to fill it with supporting artists to make it look busy."

Frustratingly for Adrian and the rest of the crew, the shots outside the supermarket made it a tiresome shoot: "It was becoming very clear at this time that the series' popularity was beginning to make location filming very difficult. We were attracting attention wherever we went, and as a result it was the last series to use London locations."

Despite the problems with curious fans and onlookers, in-between set-ups David Jason, Nicholas Lyndhurst and Buster Merryfield found time to pose for dozens of publicity photos during the location filming. Making use of the car park, trolleys and iron railings, these shots would be used on a host of book covers and calendars for many years to come.

Inside the supermarket, filming was carefully blocked to avoid any of the 'Co-op LEO' branding, although the chain's "The Big 100 Price

Winners Every Week!" slogan can be seen in several shots. Properties buyer Maura Laverty successfully plastered the location with Andrew Smee's Top-Buys "Millionth Customer" poster to foreshadow (in *every* aspect) the plot.

Cast in John Sullivan's Top-Buys conspiracy were a trio of excellent guest stars, each perfectly inhabiting a different tier of social class.

To play Lennox Gilbey, 26 year-old Vas Blackwood was selected to help define the lovable master of disguise:

"I was invited down to Television Centre to meet Ray Butt who was a pacy short guy in a flat cap, a little bit like Del Boy. He put me in an office and left me to read the script. I got an impression straight away and I was laughing. Ray came back and said: 'What do you think, it's good init?', and I said, 'Yeah, it's really funny!' Without missing a beat, he

asks me to follow him. We've not even sat down together and he is walking me out the building – he has been on the move the whole time! As we're walking out, Ray says, 'I tell you what to do, I'll call your agent and you can start learning lines'. They don't make them like Ray anymore. He was like a Hollywood producer."

With the script in hand, Vas next met the production team on location in Leytonstone, which suggested some memorable ad-libs: "I remember we shot at the supermarket location before any of the rehearsals. I worked with Mandie and the crew and it was really good. The bit with the can of drink wasn't in the script, I just said to Mandie, 'Lowenbrau is a good drink, I'll drink that in one go!' I also suggested the bit with the frozen peas."

Above: The Leytonstone location was perfect, but the popularity of the series was starting to make filming tricky.

Left: Lennox Gilbey (Vas Blackwood), aka The Shadow.

Opposite page below left: Albert catches up on his sleep in a Top-Buys trolley.

Below left: Just some of the many publicity shots taken during the location filming in Leytonstone.

Below right: Designer Andrew Smee's Top-Buys "Millionth Customer" poster.

Later during rehearsal Vas further developed Lennox, with a notable addition to the rhyme which John Sullivan had written for The Shadow: "It was Nicholas Lyndhurst who gave me the line 'Sh-a-dow!' – I had been acting the speech for Mandie, but in between scenes, Nick said to me, 'Why don't you say it broken up as Sh-a-dow?' and that was it! The next time we ran it that's what I did and Nick winked at me as I said my bit."

After playing Lennox, the talented Blackwood would go straight into *The Lenny Henry Show*, before moving on to a film career, which would include a standout role in 1998's *Lock, Stock and Two Smoking Barrels*.

The Longest Night's store manager, Mr Patterson, was played by Max Harvey, another actor who director Maddie Fletcher had recently used in *Blackadder II*. Harvey brilliantly plays the put-upon manager driven to crime by his greedy wife.

Future *Eastenders* star John Bardon was cast as head security officer Tom Clark, a character not a million miles away from

Dot Cotton's future husband Jim Branning. Bardon was no stranger to sitcom, having appeared in the *Dad's Army* episode *Ring Dem Bells* in 1975, he would also guest star in *A Sharp Intake of Breath* alongside David Jason in the 1978 episode *Somewhere in the Sun*.

One of the strengths of *The Longest Night* is that it features the perfect combination of filmed location work carefully used to set-up a brilliantly staged (and claustrophobic) studio segment.

Vas Blackwood remembers this part of the episode fondly: "Come the studio, because it was all in one set, it was like an intense theatre performance, live and facing the audience."

Perhaps thanks to the theatrical energy, expert direction, and a truly magnificent script, the proceedings unfold effortlessly, making *The Longest Night* a truly unforgettable 30 minutes.

Above: The first page of the script's 'story order' page.

Above right: "Entrecote Rioja…Yes, my favourite!" Now in the studio, the cast are joined by Max Harvey as Mr Patterson and John Bardon as Tom Clark.

Below: The Trotters, armed and ready.

Far right: Del finally works out what has been going on.

The bustling Nags Head talent night opens up *Tea for Three* and we join Del, Rodney and Trigger (Lloyd Pack's first appearance in the fifth series).

It is surprising that we had to wait 35 episodes before we see the Trotter brothers involved in a love triangle, but in the crowded bar as we are introduced to Trigger's niece, Lisa, the comic interplay between Del and Rodney makes the wait worthwhile.

With the plot set and sunbed timers duly tampered with, *Only Fools* stars Jason and Lyndhurst illustrate just why their chemistry is so strong with some of the series' most engaging stage craft. This culminates in both actors holding each other's hands whilst thumbing for the hand of their character's affections.

Buster Merryfield enjoys a highlight also, singing a lament to his estranged and ailing wife, Ada. Here he sings a reworking of the classic show tune 'Hey There' (sung in this case as "Ada") from the musical *The Pajama Game*. For musical copyright reasons this scene has always been edited out of home video releases.

A memorable tea with a red-faced Rodney sees Del attempting to impress Lisa by pretending that he was once a paratrooper, leading us brilliantly to Rodney and Lisa hatching a surprise hang-gliding session for Del the following day.

Buster Hill, south of Petersfield in Hampshire, was chosen as the location for the hang-gliding

meet-up, where the production crew were joined by the team from Action Cars to help mobilise the Trotter Van for a three-wheeled hill-top jaunt.

Exposed to the elements on the Spring afternoon, Adrian Pegg remembers: "We had a great day filming the hang gliding, but it was a pretty windy day and the stunt man who was due to stand in for David Jason (and do the actual flying) was less than keen to get up in the air."

The stuntman in question, Ken Barker, was no stranger to daredevil action having arranged stunts on big films such as *Superman III* and *Labyrinth,* but the experienced performer was put off by the unpredictable weather.

Calls from star David Jason (who was a qualified pilot and keen glider) to perform some stunts himself were dismissed well before filming for insurance reasons.

On the ground Adrian Pegg recalls more traditional film making trickery was employed in order to show Del taking to the air: "For the scenes showing David flying we rigged the hang glider under a crane in a car park. With David hanging safely underneath we could get the shots we needed."

Above: The crew rigged David Jason's hang glider under a crane for filming.

Above and above right: On top of Buster Hill in Hampshire the crew get to work, as Nicholas Lyndhurst looks on.

Below and right: David Jason all strapped-in for filming.

Far right: Back in the flat, Del and Rodney are reunited after Del's ordeal in the air...

Opposite page below: Joining the cast, Mark Colleano as Andy and Gerry Cowper as Lisa.

John Sullivan was on the location shoot to ensure that his character was suitably consistent with his attitude: "I was very insistent that David keep his overcoat on for the gliding scenes, because I thought it would be such a great comedy image, anyone else would have taken their coat off, but not Derek Trotter."

Joining the cast as Lisa was actress Gerry Cowper, previously seen as Jim Hacker's daughter in *Yes Minister*, she would go on to become a long-running *Eastenders* star. Andy Williams, who we later discover is Lisa's fiancé, was played by Mark Colleano,

a popular child actor who left the profession soon after his time on *Only Fools*.

After the beautifully filmed location work we return to the studio for the story's closing scene in the Trotter flat, where a temporarily wheelchair-bound Del recounts his vivid adventures in the sky via an acting tour de force from David Jason.

Several sections of John Sullivan's monologue of these airborne adventures would be lost at the rehearsal stage, whilst others were recorded and edited out before transmission – all to fit *Tea for Three* to the required half hour. The frustration felt by both writer and actor would lead them to pressure BBC bosses into giving the series a greater running time.

Tea for Three would represent director Mandie Fletcher's final contribution to the series. After her stint on *Only Fools*, Fletcher would enjoy a hugely successful career, most notably directing *Absolutely Fabulous* and its spin off feature film.

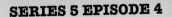

TEA FOR THREE

21 SEPTEMBER 1986

Hang-gliding must be a doddle. I mean, all you've gotta do is strap yourself on and wait for a gust of wind. A cinch! At least that's what I was thinking when the instructor, Andy, was counting me down to take off. I weren't scared or nothing. I was wearing the right thermals and all the gear and I couldn't wait to get up there in the clouds. But the moment the wind picked up and my Goochis lost contact with the old terra cotta, I immediately knew that something weren't right, and so I calmly called out a signal to make Andy and the rest of the team aware: "Oh bloody hell, help me! Please God get me down from here!" (which I'm told is the standard distress signal in hang-gliding circles). Watching the ground whizzing by five hundred feet below, I quickly weighed up the situation and came to the conclusion that I was in a bit of a pickle. From there on out the only thing I could do was hold on for dear life and pray that I landed on something soft. All told I was up there for three hours! I did a barrel-roll over Bournemouth Pier and at one point was adopted by a squadron of seagulls. After a quick loop-the-loop over Dymchurch, I managed to gain some control of the glider and thought the worst of it was over. It was then I noticed I was on a direct flight path with the giant cooling towers of Dungeness's nuclear power plant. I had this sudden and terrifying thought that even if I did somehow manage to survive all this, I'd be walking away looking like the Ready Brek man. Well, the steam from the tower must have done something to my thermals coz the next thing I new I was up in the clouds. An hour or so later, when I'd just about given up hope, I slammed into a television transmitter and landed on a Ford Sierra – it weren't that soft, but thankfully the roof, and the two occupants underneath it, did manage to break my fall somewhat. I was rushed to hospital but fortunately I only had a few cuts and bruises and a minor percussion. All in all, I blame Andy.

Del

Del was an old friend of my fiancé, Lisa. He turned up with his younger brother, Rodney, who I'll never forget had a very sore looking face. I must admit, after everything Lisa had told me about Del's exploits serving in the special forces, he wasn't what I expected. Still, with his being a seasoned paratrooper, I assumed a bit of gentle hang-gliding would be no problem. And he was very eager to get going. I set him up in the glider and, following procedure as I always do, checked everything twice. But as soon as he was airborne he started screaming and it was clear that there was a major problem. I couldn't understand it. I'd told him several times to stick close to the ridge, but he just kept going and going, and, by my calculations, was heading out to sea. Naturally we were all very worried, although strangely enough as the panic ensued I remember turning to Rodney and noticing that he had a big smile on his face. I suppose everyone reacts differently to shock.

Andy

VIDEO NASTY

28 SEPTEMBER 1986

Rodney Trotter producing a film?! Yours truly directing it?! Yeah. I had to pinch myself too. But when the council gave Rodney's art group a £10,000 grant to make a local community film, that's what happened! Rodney was also put in charge of writing the script, which surprised a lot of people, but not me. I've known Rodney since the playground and he's always fancied himself a bit of a wordsmith. My passion is for the visual arts, especially when it comes to all things cameras. I think I might have got it from my Mum cos she used to work the photographic counter at Boots. Anyway, at the time Boycie was doing a little sideline in producing videos of the blue variety, and when he saw me practicing on the camera the council had given us, he asked if I wanted in, and I thought why not? On Del Boy's advice I also did my bit for the tourist trade and made the most of the local area, which was reflected in some of my film's titles: Emmanuelle in East Dulwich, Last Tango in Peckham Rye, Debbie Does Deptford, that sort of thing. As for my directing style, I preferred to keep things loose and spontaneous, so that sometimes right in the middle of the action you'd hear a telephone ringing or a next door neighbour hoovering. A lot of people found this to be a bit of a mood killer, but I think it added atmosphere. I really wanted to capture that gritty, downmarket feel, which is why I shot my final film, Night Nurse, in Del and Rodney's flat. Of course I wanted the audience to enjoy the experience, but at the same time to think, 'Christ, I'm glad I don't live in that dump!'

Mickey Pearce

Say what you like about Rodney, but the lad's always had an artistic streak. Even as a sprog he was fascinated with paint brushes, so much so that I came home one day to find he'd got one stuck up his nostril. Naturally, I encouraged it (his interest in art, not sticking things up his hooter), and I even promised him that one day I'd get him some paint. But the fact is that liking something and being good at something are two very different things. I mean, I've always been a big fan of Jayne Torvill, but you won't catch me doing a pirouette in a pair of tights and a frilly skirt. So when Rodney wrote his first, and only, novel, The Indictment, I had to find a way of letting the air out very gently. And don't get me wrong, I had high hopes for the book, right up to the moment he explained the plot to me (something about the indictment of a failing political system. Real edge of your seat stuff!). There were no murders in it or nothing, not even a car chase or an explosion. And there he was talking about how he was gonna become the next Forsyth!

"But Rodney," I said, "You're no good at tap dancing." He just buried his head in his hands and said "Dear God!" (which I think was the moment the reality really sunk in). Realising that it was a delicate situation that required the utmost sensitivity, I decided to use a bit of good old fashioned subterfusion: I sent him off to the chippy and chucked The Indictment down the rubbish chute. He got into a right sulk when he found out and I was then forced to tell him what Mum had said to me on her deathbed: "Del Boy," she said, "Whatever you do, don't fill Rodney's head with unrealistic pipe dreams. He's not as strong or as intelligent as you are, and I don't want him getting his hopes high only to have them crushed."

"What do you mean, Mum?" I asked, "Can you be more pacific?"

"Well" she said, "Like if he ever writes a dopey book, for example."

"Right, gotcha." I can't repeat what Rodney said, but it consisted of two words and it was quite hurtful.

Del

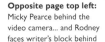

After the location excesses of the opening episodes, Ray Butt returned to the director's chair for the final two studio-bound scripts of the fifth series.

The subject of college and youth club council loans for artisan projects had caught the interest of writer John Sullivan, who wondered how the creative Trotter brother might cope with such a prospect. It was also an opportunity for the busy writer to use some of his own experiences of battling behind the typewriter: "The whole scene where Rodney tries to write a script comes from my past. He's suffering from writer's block which most writers experience at some point."

True to form, Del thinks he can solves Rodney's creative block, as Sullivan recalled: "I'd experienced these sorts of things before where people try to offer their ideas which they're so enthusiastic about but often they're not great. Del would be one of those people, because he thinks he can turn his head to anything at the drop of a hat."

Gradually, Rodney's creative dreams begin to unravel as he is obliged to include in his script a cast made-up of our familiar Peckham gang. Here we are treated to Ken MacDonald's Mike doing Humphrey Bogart ("Of all the bars in all the world…") and Roger Lloyd Pack's Trigger doing James Cagney ("You dirty rat!").

Aside from Del, one of the other architects of Rodney's screenwriting headache is Mickey Pearce. *Video Nasty* features some of Patrick Murray's finest contributions to the series, partly because Murray seems to enjoy playing a Mickey who has at last succeeded at something, albeit at Rodney's expense.

Micky's video venture *Night Nurse* featured the punkish Amanda, brought to life by actress Dawn Perlman.

Recalling the making of the story, Perlman enjoyed the rehearsals the most: "It was simply a gift of a part to play, just to be at rehearsals as the episode took shape was a joy. I can still remember watching David and Buster acting with Nick in front of a typewriter as they got their Rhino story out – just to watch the three of them work that scene, it was genius and so funny".

Guest staring in the episode as the fifth series' second man of the cloth is Rex Robinson, who previously played Harry, an auction bidder in the third series episode *Healthy Competition*. Here Robinson plays the vicar who married Boycie and Marlene 20 years previously.

Sadly, Robinson's vicar can't be seen to be amongst the crowd for the couple's anniversary party in 2003's *Sleepless in Peckham*. In *The Green Green Grass*' 2009 episode *For Richer For Poorer* however, we discover that the registrar who oversaw Boycie and Marlene's original wedding was unlicensed. So perhaps there is more than meets the eye to the gentle vicar we meet in *Video Nasty*?

During the closing moments of the episode Del makes the first ever reference to the mysterious and dreaded Driscoll Brothers, Peckham's answer to the Kray twins. The shady figures would be name-checked again in 1987's *The Frogs Legacy*, but viewers would have to wait until 1989 to meet the menacing duo in the flesh.

Opposite page top left: Micky Pearce behind the video camera… and Rodney faces writer's block behind the typewriter.

Opposite Below left: Mickey Pearce in his element filming Anna (Dawn Perlman) for his film *Night Nurse*.

Above top: Mark Sevant's Chinese takeaway set before and during recording.

Above middle: "I heard that Boycie was a Jaffa." Rex Robinson as the vicar.

Below left: The guest pose for a video shot at Boycie and Marlene's anniversary do in the Nags Head.

Below: After the anniversary party the chaps retire to the back room of the Nags Head for the British premiere of "the Boyce video and leisure arts company production of *Night Nurse!*"

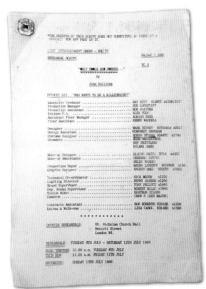

Mr Jumbo Mills
IMPORT/EXPORT

27 ALTON ST
WOOLHARA
SYDNEY 2001
NSW AUSTRALIA
TEL(010 61)576 1582

Above left: Actor Nick Stringer's script for *Who Wants To Be A Millionaire?*

Above right: Del Boy considers a future on the other side of the world without Rodney.

Right inset: The original prop of Jumbo Mills' business card, used by Del in the story and rescued after the studio recording by actor Ken MacDonald's wife.

Below: "Where's the loud mouth Aussie gone?"– Mike serves the grub in the Nags Head.

Opposite page top left: Del gets the news his emigration visa has been accepted.

Opposite page top right: Nick Stringer guest stars as Jumbo Mills.

Opposite page Below: Del has to make a decision...

Who Wants To Be A Millionaire? has a unique place in the history of *Only Fools and Horses*. For a brief time it was not just the end of the fifth series, it was the swan-song for the programme completely. On the eve of completing the first drafts of his scripts for what was to become series five, writer John Sullivan was thrown a curve-ball: "One Saturday evening I was having dinner with David Jason and I got the impression that he didn't want to do any more *Only Fools*."

To his credit the writer took the news from his star with philosophical grace. After all, how many TV sitcoms run longer than five years? Perhaps foremost in John Sullivan's mind was that *Just Good Friends* and *Dear John* had proven that there was a screen life beyond Peckham.

The following Monday, Sullivan went to the then head of comedy at the BBC, Gareth Gwenlan, explaining that the show had come to an end.

"I went away and wrote the Australian saga, with Del emigrating, and Rodney left alone at Heathrow airport, but suddenly enthused that he was in charge. I was going to write a series called *Hot Rod* where Rodney would carry on Trotters Independent Traders with Mickey Pearce as his business partner."

Fortunately, circumstances changed when news came in from Gareth Gwenlan that David Jason's agent was enquiring about a sixth series. David wasn't ready to hang up his camel-hair coat, cigar and keys to the three-wheeled van just yet.

Even stripped of all the behind the scenes rumblings, *Who Wants To Be A Millionaire?* is a cracking 30 minutes and in some ways works as a companion to *Strained Relations*, with a similar outpouring of emotion brilliantly acted out by Jason and Lyndhurst.

Guest starring in the episode as Del's former business partner, Jumbo Mills, was a returning Nick Stringer, last seen as the Cortina-buying Australian in *Go West Young Man*. Remembering his second role in the series, Nick didn't experience any issues with his re-casting, but relished the chance to act in the studio scenes this time: "Five years between appearances didn't cause a problem, the public had watched a lot of telly in five years. Some of the cast and crew had a vague memory but it wasn't an issue, but in front of a live audience... Nothing like it! Camera shots and sound booms and all the

WHO WANTS TO BE A MILLIONAIRE?

5 OCTOBER 1986

paraphernalia of a studio – you had to incorporate that into your performance."

While Del Boy remained in Peckham and the business of Trotters Independent Traders would continue, in many ways *Who Wants To Be A Millionaire?* was to be the curtain call of the series as it was originally created. The episode was to be the final half-hour *Only Fools* instalment and the last non-seasonal episode crafted by its original producer Ray Butt.

Broadcast over six consecutive Sunday evenings at 8.35pm, audience figures for the Trotter family's fifth outing would grow over its run, starting with 12.1 million viewers watching *From Prussia with Love* and ending with 18.8 million viewers tuning in to see Del turn down Jumbo's offer of a fresh start down under.

There was no doubt that the new Trotter dynamic was working, and the series had been taken to the hearts of viewers, more eager than ever to watch the hilarious heartfelt exploits of Hooky Street.

Whilst John Sullivan's *Hot Rod* would remain a road never taken, just three weeks after *Who Wants to be a Millionaire?* aired, viewers would in fact get to see Nicholas Lyndhurst go it alone in the first of four series of Alex Shearer's *The Two of Us*. This likeable ITV comedy would see Lyndhurst play middle class Londoner Ashley Phillips who was a much more cynical soul in contrast to the slightly doe-eyed Rodney Trotter of the time.

For *Only Fools* fans however, it would only be a three month wait for the now traditional festive special...

Ask anyone round Peckham if they remember the homemade fish-fingers Del and I used to flog from our stall outside the Nags Head, and you'll quickly realise the great and lasting impact of our combined business acumen. This was back in the 1960s, but even then we'd go on and on to each other about how one day we'd become millionaires. That day came for me years later after I emigrated to Australia and set up my own fast food chain. The day I left for Oz I was potless, but Del gave me his last two hundred pounds. As the business grew and the readies rolled in, I'd lay awake at night promising myself that one day I'd pay Del back, and over a decade later, when I hit upon the idea of importing prestige European automobiles, I knew it was time to cut my old mate in and reform the partnership. I returned to Peckham, did a very nice deal with Boycie and then told Del the good news. He was a bit unsure at first, worrying about how he'd be received down under.

"They'd love you there, Del," I reassured him. "They've got no class."

I even told him he could bring his younger brother, Rodney, along. "Well, he has got two GCEs," he said.

"That doesn't matter," I said. "We'll find something for him to do." We shook on it and that was that. I flew back to Oz to make some last minute preparations while Del and Rodney waited for their visas to arrive. A fortnight later, I was just about to sit down on the dunny (in the ensuite of my architect designed penthouse, the one overlooking Sydney harbour) when he phoned to tell me the whole deal was off. Some crap about 'loyalty' and 'family ties'. I did the only thing I could do in the circumstances: I called him a drongo and told him to take care. Don't get me wrong, I understand loyalty, but strewth, can you really call that a family? Then again maybe it was for the best. We did used to fight a lot and he always enjoyed embarrassing me every chance he got. Also, that Rodney clearly had some issues. As for their uncle, if his piano playing was anything to go by he needed all the support he could get!

Jumbo Mills

A ROYAL FLUSH

★ ★

Another year of ups and downs (literally!) And I got so close this time. So close I could almost smell that million. I could hear it calling to me, "Del Boy, Del Boy... I'm all yours, Del Boy". Just my luck it was calling from sodding Australia! Well, what could I do, eh? I couldn't have left Rodney in charge of the firm, it would have been like leaving Hannibal Lecter in charge of your liver. Given a week the flat would have been overrun with broken lawnmower engines and crates of Ambre Solaire! That was the problem with Rodney, he might have had two GCEs and a penchant for adult education centres, but when it came to business he was about as useful as a pork chop at a Bar mitzvah. It was all epidemic anyway; I'd made a promise to Mum, and that's what mattered. And at the end of the day what did I really lose? A golden opportunity to realise my life's dream, yes, but then again I never was keen on Australia. It's full of Australians. No, it was obvious that my work here in Peckham was far from done. Rodney still needed my guidance and, whether he liked it or not, he was gonna get it.

★ ★ ★ ★ ★ ★ ★ ★ ★ ★ ★ ★ ★ ★ ★ ★ ★ ★ ★

Following the success of *To Hull and Back* and the fifth series, it was a simple decision for the BBC to commission another feature length *Only Fools* special for Christmas 1986. This time John Sullivan had some very different ideas in mind to explore with the Trotters: "This episode was inspired by two things. One was the way the younger nobility was becoming closer, apparently, to the working class. Princess Margaret's son, for example, set himself up in business as a carpenter. There were also stories in the newspapers about Special Branch being employed to protect some of the younger royals from possible kidnapping. I put these two things about the nobility together when I was writing this episode."

Sullivan decided to take Rodney and put him in this situation, where he strikes up a sweet friendship with a young woman, Victoria, who we discover is the only daughter of the 14th Duke of Maylebury, a second cousin of the Queen.

To play Vicky, the relatively unknown actress Sarah Duncan was cast.

"It was the most extraordinary experience" remembers Duncan of her casting in *A Royal Flush*. "I had gone to the wrong place as I'd previously been to BBC castings at Shepherds Bush and this was at the TV Centre. Not too far away, but enough to make me half an hour late. Luckily the casting session was running very late too. I sat in the reception area and suddenly I just knew I was going to get the part; it's the only time I've ever had a premonition like that. Then the casting went well, and John Sullivan said 'We've found our Vicky'. Obviously, I was thrilled and just floated home. Later I discovered that Tony Dow (who was then the production manager, but went on to direct *Only Fools*) had ticked John off because they still had another day of seeing actresses and someone else might have been better. Tony told me that in fact another actress had come on the second day

Above: Del bringing the market alive as he sells his cutlery sets – "I mean, that's the Titmus test innit, the quality? These are hand-made from Indonesian steel. They've got ivory-effect handles and they come in a genuine synthetic-leather case."

Above right: A rehearsal script for *A Royal Flush*.

Right: Vicky (Sarah Duncan) on her market stall.

Below: The crew transformed a street in Salisbury into a London market. These photos were taken by art director Alison Rickman to document the teams work.

who they liked a lot, before deciding that I would be better because she was 'too beautiful' for Rodney!"

John Sullivan's script for the special was not quite as globe-trotting as *To Hull and Back*, but it did require some interesting locations, namely the grounds and the interior of a stately home and a trip to the Opera.

With filming arranged to take place over six weeks between 1st November and 13th December 1986, production managers Tony Dow and Olivia Bazalgette went about finding the required locations. For the fictional Covington House of Berkshire, a suitable stately home was found in the 18th-century house at Clarendon Park, just east of Salisbury.

"I remember we were looking for a place to do a London Market," remembers Tony Dow, "because we were filming at this massive house in Salisbury, the schedule said we need to find a market in Salisbury as well. I went around the whole of the city – which is the most middle-class area in the world – but around the back of the station I found a really good street which looked a lot

more working-class. So I went to the design team and said 'We'll put the market up here, that'll work, we'll bring stuff down, stick some bits in'. I then went back to the office and said to Ray, 'Don't worry mate, I've found a place to do the market, it's all worked out' and I showed him the plan and he said: 'Where's the pub?' 'I said 'It's only just a short walk away', and he said 'What brewery is it?'!"

The Gentleman's Outfitters, which Rodney visits in the story, was also in Salisbury, in a shop on New Canal street. Nearby, just east from Blakey Road, was the working-class street Tony Dow transformed into a London Market.

Above left: Production Manager Tony Dow (far right) walks around the location.

Above: One of the many promotional stills of the cast taken at the Salisbury market location.

Left: "Don't get many tourists round this way, eh officer?" – Trigger is questioned by a policeman (Andrew Readman).

Below: Sid behind the counter of his cafe 'The Fatty Thumb' – "You won't like it Victoria! I don't like it and I'm a regular!"

A ROYAL FLUSH

25 DECEMBER 1986

When Rodney got us tickets to see the latest production of Carmen, I was really looking forward to it. It's one of my favourite operas and it was delightfully sweet of Rodney. We were at the bar getting some light refreshment before the performance began, when his older brother, Derek, and a female companion joined us. I didn't mind at first, the more the merrier and all that, but it did take Rodney and I a little by surprise. Sadly, the surprises continued after we'd taken our seats and the performance began. To say that Derek and his guest lacked a certain decorum would be a big understatement. They talked and ate packets of crisps, liquorice allsorts and ice cream. At one point Derek started whistling along to the Habanera. The worst part was when the woman threw up over the back of the gentleman in front of her. I mean, I'm no prude, and the artist in me actually appreciates the gritty, rough and raw aspects of the real world, but... well, it's just not something you'd normally see at the Theatre Royal Drury Lane.

Vicky

The only other locations required were for the Opera sequences of the episode. In the original script this scene was meant to take place at the Royal Opera House, but it was decided it would be easier to use the exterior and foyer of the nearby Theatre Royal on Drury Lane. The filming script was altered accordingly. For the auditorium of the Opera sequence, the crew spent two days at the Buxton Opera House in Derbyshire for the filming.

"The first time I met the cast was on location in Salisbury," remembers Sarah Duncan. "I didn't know anything about the series at all, so Nick Lyndhurst had to explain some of the running jokes to me. We just got along from the start and didn't need to think too much about it. The very first scene I filmed was the one in the cafe. We filmed in Salisbury first, then Buxton, then London." With her gently enquiring demeanour, Duncan was perfect for the role and had great chemistry with Nicholas Lyndhurst. "I was quite close to Vicky in personality," remembers the actress. "That's what John had seen. Ray was lovely, very

a shotgun he's borrowed off his mate. The only person he knows with a shotgun happens to be a bloke who robs banks, but as it's a Saturday he doesn't need it!"

Sent 'downstairs' at Covington House, Albert is in his element, being made a fuss of by the kitchen staff, namely Mrs. Miles, played by *Love Thy Neighbour* and *Eastenders* actress Kate Williams.

After the shooting party scene, the special's evening dinner scene opens with a knowing shot of a stunning chandelier, a nod to 1982's *Touch of Glass*. As Del and Rodney take their seats, things gradually start to unravel when Del's attempts to earn favour with the upper-set get progressively worse.

For Sullivan, Del's actions in *A Royal Flush* were the character's way of protecting his brother: "When Del finds out Rodney's met this posh young artist, his first fear is that once they find out who Rodney Trotter is they'll get rid of him. Del decides that rather than have any harm come to his brother, he'll get him out of the situation himself, plus make a few bob on it!"

As the evening goes on, Jack Hedley's Duke of Maylebury grows more and more annoyed with Del and reveals his true views on his daughter's friendships.

warm and relaxed. They were under a lot of time pressures when we were filming but you'd never have guessed from Ray's manner."

After Del helps out by getting tickets from Limpy Lionel the ticket tout, Rodney takes Victoria to see the Gala performance of Carmen. Much to Rodney's shock and embarrassment, Del has also got tickets for himself and June Snell (last seen in *Happy Returns*). As they take their seats it soon becomes apparent that Del and June are not the most cultured of audience members and, unintentionally, they end up causing quite a disturbance. For these scenes the Kent Opera Company were hired to perform, as well as nearly 200 extras.

One of the episode's highlights is the clay pigeon shooting sequence (Sullivan purposely didn't want to feature any blood sports in the story) where Rodney is dressed up in full hunting gear and looks completely out of place.

Here we first meet Vicky's father, the Duke of Maylebury, played by actor Jack Hedley, perhaps best known for his appearance in the 1981 James Bond movie *For Your Eyes Only*.

At this point in the story Del decides to appear with Albert in tow, driving across the grounds in the Trotter van, and fully equipped to join in with the shooting. Sullivan remembered, "Of course, when Del decides to go out there, he brings along

Opposite page right: Sarah Duncan was photographed in costume as Victoria to be superimposed into the *Country Life* magazine Rodney reads.

Above: Del causes a stir at the Opera... These scenes were filmed at the Buxton Opera House in Derbyshire.

Top left: "Don't give me all that Tony Benn cobblers! Think of all the advantages! You'll be a member of the House of Lords!"

Left: June Snell (Diane Langton) – Del's date for the Opera.

Below: Rodney with his programme for the Gala performance of Carmen.

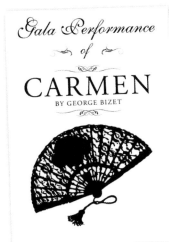

Gala Performance of

CARMEN

BY GEORGE BIZET

"Rodney has given Vicky his heart," Sullivan explained, "he's kind of fallen in love. But the Duke doesn't see it like this – at the dinner table he says to a friend 'This is what Victoria does – she brings these characters home.' To her it's just a bit of fun. On both sides, you've got people not being very nice and Rodney's in the middle. Although Del comes across as rather cruel in the episode, his heart's in the right place."

Confirming all of Del's suspicions, the Duke's patience reaches an end point as his temper envelops the grand dining room, leaving a mortified Vicky to suggest that Rodney better go home.

"It was so sad!" remembers Sarah Duncan of the episode's ending. "I wish things had worked out a bit better for Rodney and Vicky. I really felt for both of them."

The only studio portions of this episode were the two brief scenes set in the flat and corridor outside. For this, the familiar set was rebuilt and shot at Elstree Studios in the days leading up to Christmas.

For Tony Dow, *A Royal Flush* would be his first taste of spending Christmas Eve in the editing suite completing an episode of *Only Fools*, something which would become a regular event over the next 10 years. "It was great for me as Ray didn't like edit dubbing suites. He found it boring so he used to send me and I got to learn things very quickly."

Since broadcast, the special has incurred some criticism and, in some cases, has been unfairly dismissed. One aspect which doesn't seem to work for many viewers is Del's behaviour towards the very end of the story. Instead of being his usual jolly drunken self, David Jason's performance misses the subtlety called for in the script. This isn't helped by the lavish location setting and its imposing echo. Ironically if this scene had been filmed in the studio with audience laughter to guide the actor, the scene would most likely have landed perfectly. Usually John Sullivan would be on set to offer notes to make sure things unfolded as intended, however during the Salisbury filming Sullivan was in Paris on location for the third series of *Just Good Friends*.

But there is so much to enjoy in its 76 minutes. The cracking market scene with Del selling cutlery, followed by a hasty retreat from the Police and Trigger's inspired performance dealing with a multi-lingual 'tourist'. We have a fourth appearance from Sid with Roy Heather at his disgusting best and the ultimate embarrassment at the Opera, with a wonderful reappearance of Diane Langton as Junie.

The evening of 25 December 1986 really was a John Sullivan Christmas, with the final episode of *Just Good Friends* on at 6pm and *A Royal Flush* on just after 7pm, continuing the series' run of impressive ratings with 18.8 million viewers.

In 2004, John Sullivan would supervise a new cut of *A Royal Flush*, trimming the story down to 58 minutes and tightening up the plot. This new version also includes a laughter track (taken from a special screening at that year's *Only Fools* convention) for the release, which makes such a difference to the scenes around the dinner table.

During the making of *A Royal Flush*, David Jason, Nicholas Lyndhurst and Buster Merryfield were invited to perform as part of 1986's *The Royal Variety Show* with a short *Only Fools* sketch written by John Sullivan. Recorded live on 24 November and transmitted on BBC 1 five days later, the short sketch saw the Trotter trio mistakenly arrive (coincidently enough) at The Theatre Royal, Drury Lane. Thinking they are at Chunky Lewis's nightclub, 'Delaney's' in the West End, they walk on stage in front of the audience. With some excellent knowing humour at the playful expense of the royals in the audience, the Trotters make a quick exit at the thought of the papers getting hold of news that the Queen was enjoying a night out at Delaney's nightclub!

Rodney becoming a member of the Royal Family? I just couldn't see it myself. He ain't got the ears for it. But when he got hooked up with some posh bird who's old man happened to be the Duke of Maylebury, Del Boy was very keen that he make a good impression. Well, it were none of my business and I promised Del I'd keep my nose out, but not before telling him exactly what I thought about the whole situation. Of course, he dragged me into it and we ended up going to the girl's family home, a great big stately gaff out in the countryside. I wouldn't have minded, but it was all the way over in bleed'n Berkshire! I chose not to attend the banquet, preferring to stay downstairs with the help. Lovely people they were, and once they saw the medals I was wearing they didn't stop with the questions. Normally I don't like to talk about what happened during the war, but they'd been kind enough to give me a nice plate of stew and dumplings and I wanted to return the favour. I also warned them not to give Del any peas. They didn't listen, and from what I heard most of 'em ended up being squished into the Duke's 17th century oriental rug. Not surprisingly, the Duke weren't too pleased about it, and from what I heard he was even less pleased when Del offered him a deal on a job lot of fire-damaged Shake 'n' Vac.

Albert

THE FROG'S LEGACY

★ ★

I'd decided it was time for TITCo to diversify. If there was one thing I'd learned over the years it was that you had to keep your finger on the pulse in this game; changes came thick and fast. And right then, technology was king! Forget your pocket calculators, microwave ovens and home solariums, this was the age of the home computer, and I was gonna make sure we got in right at the top. Maybe not the very top, a couple of floors down from Macintosh would have done (at least close enough so that Mac and I could pop our heads out the window and have a decent chinwag when the going got slow). Yes, the future lie in all things buttons, flashing lights, joysticks and... things. But the real beauty of it was that my mate Ronnie Nelson had got a very important contact in Mauritius – the world leaders in all things gigabytes – and he'd agreed to give me an exclusive option on his latest range. Oh yes my son! I know I'd said it before, but I really did believe that this time the following year we'd be millionaires!

★ ★

THE FROG'S LEGACY

25 DECEMBER 1987

Managing an undertakers is a serious business which, thankfully, never sees a shortage in demand. So when Derek Trotter suggested that I invest in one of his computers in order to help streamline my business, I saw the sense in it.

"Having a computer is like having a second manager," he said. "One that will happily take care of all the most stressful tasks while you put your feet up and have a Kit-Kat."

Three weeks later and all his computer had managed to do was destroy my accounts, wipe out my entire annual stock records and set fire to my curtains. I chased Derek down and, after offering me a once in a lifetime deal on a set of new curtains, he told me not to worry and to give the computer a chance to get settled in its new environment.

"This computer is outer-limits-hi-tech stuff!" he said. "It's extremely sensitive."

He must have known what he was talking about because three days later it exploded.

Mr Jahan

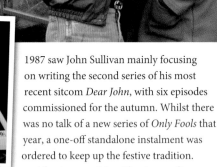

1987 saw John Sullivan mainly focusing on writing the second series of his most recent sitcom *Dear John*, with six episodes commissioned for the autumn. Whilst there was no talk of a new series of *Only Fools* that year, a one-off standalone instalment was ordered to keep up the festive tradition.

After two specials without an audience, it was decided for 1987's Christmas special to be a mixture of filmed location footage and recorded studio scenes with a live audience, much like a regular episode of the sitcom.

For *Only Fools'* producer and most frequent director, Ray Butt, this would be his final episode of the series. After ten years of working with John Sullivan across some 104 episodes, Butt had decided to accept a new challenge as head of comedy at the Midlands-based ITV franchise Central Television.

John Sullivan decided to use this special to answer some long-running questions about the history of Del and Rodney's

mother, Joan. The episode would also see the series' first reference to Freddy 'the Frog' Robdal, a close 'friend' of Joan's who had, among other things, a great interest in art.

"Del and Rodney's mum Joan is very significant – the most important person who never appears in the series. She's absolutely vital to it all," remembered Sullivan. "She was always portrayed as a tart, but then you realise that she may have loved Freddy Robdal. I had already painted Reg as a scrounger and wife-beater, so when she met this suave, rather charming man she fell for him. I tried to show her as human – to get away from her being just a slapper."

As he was leaving the series, Ray Butt decided to take his last opportunity to base the location filming for an episode of *Only Fools* in his home county of Suffolk. With filming taking place across four locations from 17–30 November, the episode would then be completed with a studio recording on Wednesday 9 December 1987.

The episode opens in the Nags Head with Del trying to shift one of the RAJAH computers he has been lumbered with. In a nice bit of continuity, the flat has had RAJAH computer boxes in it since the beginning of series five, probably to set up Rodney's joke about having "24 computers which don't compute" in *Who Wants to Be A Millionaire*.

In the pub, Del is immediately wrapped up in business with the local funeral director, Mr Jahan, who mentions that his firm is looking to hire an extra pair of hands. Thankfully, Del knows just the brother for the job. Meanwhile Rodney and Albert hear

from Trigger that they are all invited to Hampshire for the wedding of *Tea for Three*'s Andy and Lisa.

For Andy and Lisa's wedding reception the crew filmed inside one of the function rooms of the 16th century moated manor house, Helmingham Hall in Suffolk. For many of the cast it was their first real location outing for the series, and the first time that Sue Holderness had any scenes in the series with Roger Lloyd Pack and Ken MacDonald.

"When you go away for filming," Holderness recalls, "you get to know each other a bit more because you stay in hotels and you meet afterwards."

Originally the wedding reception was to feature a lovely scene where Boycie goes on an extended tirade on class, reminding Marlene to be on her best behaviour as "the groom's family are rather large in the car-hire business". Marlene just wishes they could have brought their Great Dane, Duke, with them.

Sue Holderness remembers this well: "We had a very funny scene which was regrettably cut. It was too long, and that was the problem with a lot of the episodes that John wrote; you lost such a lot of good

stuff, not because it wasn't funny but because there was either too much or that it wasn't fundamentally part of the plot, and quite often Boycie and Marlene's stuff wasn't plot-based."

Elsewhere at the reception, Mark Colleano and Gerry Cowper return as Andy and Lisa (this time without a hang-glider in sight), and cast as the easily-shocked Vicar who married them is actor Angus MacKay.

It is at the wedding that we're introduced to Reeny Turpin (both Joan Trotter's best friend and Trigger's 'Aunt') played by *Carry On* favourite Joan Sims.

"Joan Sims was such fun, a great laugh," remembered John Sullivan. "She didn't take anything seriously – everything was just a laugh with her. I thought she made a great Aunt Reeny."

In a revealing scene we learn

that Reen moved away from Peckham after Joan died in 1964. Reunited at the wedding with Del, she absentmindedly mentions the £250,000 in gold bullion that the Peckham-based gentleman thief, Freddy 'The Frog', left to Joan in his will. Freddy and Joan were 'friends' at the time Rodney was born and Joan left everything she owned to Del and Rodney. The only problem being that no one knows where Freddy hid the gold. Naturally, Del is very curious to find out more...

Back in Peckham, Del is in fly pitcher mode again, this time as 'healing hands Trotter' selling some Inframax Massager sets. This street market scene was filmed on Seymour Road in Ipswich, using the same market stall setup used for the previous years special *A Royal Flush*. The scene ends when a funeral procession led by Rodney – now working as Mr Jahan's new chief mourner – passes by the market. In true dipstick fashion, Rodney leads his procession the wrong way down a one-way street! The scene was filmed on the adjoining road to the market set up on Rectory Road.

"I got the inspiration for the funeral procession scene by looking back at my nan's funeral," remembered John Sullivan. "The chief mourner was usually a younger person and there was always something extremely Dickensian about the way they looked and held themselves. The joke that Boycie cracks about the hearse being Uncle Albert's taxi came from a joke that Ray Butt and I heard. We were in the pub when a funeral procession went by. A guy in the pub shouted to one of the old fellas, "There's your taxi!" Ray and I burst out laughing and decided we had to use it in the show at the first opportunity we got. So that one came straight out of real life."

To play Rodney's boss at the undertakers, Mr Jahan, actor Adam Hussein was cast: "I remember the first day for me was the hearse scene which we shot in Ipswich. I remember the weather wasn't very favourable, as it was nippy! The other actors were more than eager to approach me to offer any help they could provide, especially Nicholas Lyndhurst and Roger Lloyd Pack."

Eventually, via Rodney's delving into some of Mr Jahan's old paperwork and Del having a chat with the Hampshire vicar, the Trotters work out what happened to Freddy the Frog's gold. It was buried at sea! Freddy, who they discover was a frogman in the navy, hence his nickname, had been planning to dive down and retrieve the gold but had died suddenly in a freak accident before he could get the chance.

For the final shots of the Trotters standing behind the church and looking out at sea, some neat editing and seaside sound effects were employed to marry up two different locations. St Mary's in Framsden was used for the church (conveniently enough, just north from Helmingham Hall) and for the beach the crew visited Thorpeness some twenty miles away. While filming at the church at Framsden, the cast posed for several publicity shots by a red telephone box to promote the episode.

Above left: Ray Butt directs Jason and Merryfield at the Ipswich market location.

Left and below left: Rodney (as pallbearer) has led a funeral procession into a one way street!

Below: Albert, Trigger, Del and Boycie react to the traffic jam Rodney's misdirection has caused – "I know the bloke in the Cortina, I sold it to him last week!"

All those years spent captaining the good ship Trotter through the fiscal currents, scouring the horizon for our fortune, and it'd been right bloody underneath us the whole time... literally!!! And I'm not talking a little golden nugget or two here, no, I'm talking a million quid's worth of gold bullion! A burial at sea! It was beautiful. Freddy had planned it all out, he had all the kosher paperwork, an authentic ceremony with a pukka Vicar, and he even got two off-duty policemen to help carry the coffin to the boat. All he had to do was bide his time, wait for the dust to settle and then come back with his frogman gear and dive down and get it. Our legacy is still out there now, sitting on the ocean bed, waiting for us. Well, there was no way I was just gonna say bonjour to it. No. In the words of General MacArthur: "I shall be back soon!" That's what I said at the time anyway.

Del

Albert insists it's all just rumours, but I dunno, it could explain a lot. Either way, there's not much I can do about it now. Even if he is my Dad, the last anyone saw of him was on a radar screen. Freddy 'The Frog' Robdal. Killed himself by sitting on someone else's detonator. What a plonker!

Rodney

When the crew returned to the studio after the location filming, Adam Hussein was a little taken aback by one element of the production that he wasn't expecting: "The ice was broken in Ipswich, but when we came to London it was a different story. For the life of me I don't remember anyone saying anything about shooting in front of a live audience, and it did throw me out of concentration. Once again I remember Roger Lloyd Pack came over with his daughter Emily and gave much moral support."

The completed episode was duly edited and prepared for broadcast. If rooting around in the Trotters' history book was meant to suggest some kind of closure to the series, the sweeping plot seems to have had the opposite effect on the cast, who all appear energised to be back in Peckham again after a year away. Running to a leaner 60-minute running time, compared to the previous two specials, *The Frog's Legacy* has a brisk energy. It is also a welcome comfort to hear the audience again, which brings the studio scenes alive.

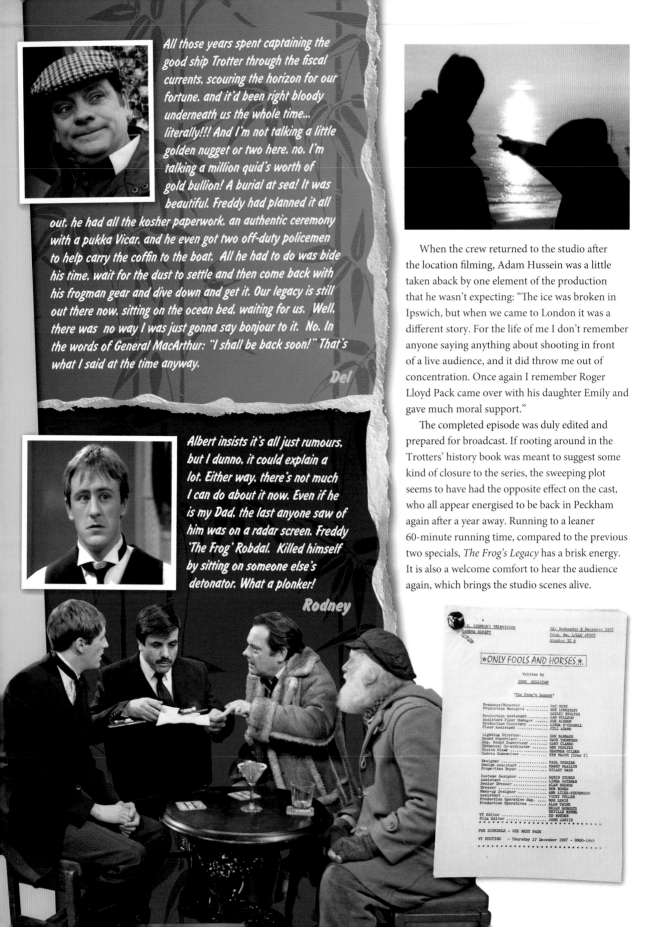

By revealing *just enough* about the history of the Trotters' mother, Sullivan manages to reinforce the mystery of the south London saga. In later years the story of *The Frog's Legacy* would resurface, forming the framework of 2003's *Sleepless in Peckham...!* and the spin-off prequel series *Rock & Chips*.

"The story was a work of genius," remembers Adam Hussein, "John Sullivan was a real showman and with *The Frog's Legacy* I felt he was putting one over those Hollywood writers."

In 1987 however, the future for *Only Fools* was a little uncertain. After the studio recording was completed, Ray Butt signed off as director by posing for a rare photo in the flat with the studio cast of the story. Interestingly, this would turn out to be the last time we see Grandad's blue

patterned armchair in the flat, which had been a feature of the flat since 1981's *Big Brother*.

Despite the evidence captured on screen showing a series still in its prime, the departure of Butt even caused the series' lead actor to speak out about the fate of his adventures on Hooky Street. In a rare interview to the *Daily Express* the day before *The Frog's Legacy* was broadcast, David Jason is described as making a desperate plea to John Sullivan: 'Please don't kill off Del Boy', with the actor convinced that the writer had no plans to write another series after six years at the top – "I hope Del Boy can live on, even if it's only every Christmas," he told a journalist.

Broadcast on Christmas Day 1985 at 6.25pm, *The Frog's Legacy* pulled in 14.5 million viewers.

As the worried Jason and millions of viewers would see, the best was yet to come.

Opposite page above right: The Trotters look out to sea where their birthright lies, sunken in the depths.

Opposite page below right: A camera script for the studio scenes of *The Frog's Legacy*.

Above: Director Ray Butt joins the studio cast of the episode in the Trotter flat.

Below left: "I'm not as technically minded as you, Mr Trotter." – Del discusses with the Vicar the workings of the RAJAH computer.

Below: "There's gotta be a way! He who dares wins! There's a million quid's worth of gold out there – our gold! We can't just say Bonjour to it!"

DATES ★★★

★ ★

In spite of its many perks, there was no doubt that
life at the top could get quite lonely. When you're
out there walking the yuppie tightrope, sizing
up the mega-deals, keeping one eye on the stock
market and the other on your competitors,
it's very easy to lose sight of... well,
personal needs, shall we say. And
I was starting to worry that that's
what was happening
on the bird front.
Don't get me wrong,
I was still oozing
animal magnetism
and knocking knees
bandy left, right and
centre. I was just beginning to long for
something a bit more permanent. Not that
I've ever had a shortage of opportunities. I've
been engaged more times than a switchboard.
The thing was that all the birds I'd known
wanted to get married, but they didn't want
to raise Rodney. Not that I completely
blamed them. He was a weird kid. And of
course, they didn't exactly go a bundle on
the prospect of living with Grandad either,
not with the way he used to leave his teeth
hanging about. That said, I still hadn't given
up hope that one day I'd find a love – a true
love, that I could call my own. Amen.

★ ★

Above: From *Dates* onwards, the Nags Head set was rotated 90 degrees so the studio audience and cameras had a view across the bar.

Above right: "I'm taking a lady out to lunch." – Trigger is dressed to impress as he stops off for some Dutch courage before meeting his date.

Right: Mickey Pearce, Jevon (Steven Woodcock) and Chris (Tony Marshall) have a laugh at the thought of Rodney playing the hard man for 'Nervous' Nerys.

Below: "Oh yes, you can't whack it. And you can tell the lucky lady she is guaranteed a steak meal." – Del visits the Technomatch Friendship and Matrimonial Agency and is interviewed by the agent (Chris Stanton).

In the early months of 1988 much discussion into the future of *Only Fools* was taking place between John Sullivan, BBC Head of Comedy Gareth Gwenlan and BBC One's controller Michael Grade. Before he would commit to writing another series, Sullivan wanted each episode of *Only Fools* to have a longer running time. Eventually it was agreed that an additional ten minutes could be added to each episode of the sixth series. A schedule was put in place for six episodes to be transmitted in early 1989, trailed by a feature length special for the festive season.

Whilst Gwenlan was happy to take on the reins of series producer, a new director was required. As Sullivan wanted these new episodes to explore more dramatic territory for the Trotters, it was important that any incoming director had experience beyond simply staging gags for the camera. It would also be preferable if they could hit the ground running and knew the series inside out. The team knew just who they wanted for the job.

"I knew that Ray Butt was off to Central," remembers Tony Dow. "But, unbeknown to me, John and David had been in talks with Gareth Gwenlan to say they wanted me to direct, and Gareth said 'What?! He's not done anything or been anywhere yet!' They said, 'no, he's absolutely right, he knows us and has done plenty of filming on the series, and we feel like we need completely new blood, and we need more substance'. Anyway, eventually Gareth agreed."

Gwenlan wasted no time in ensuring Dow was fully prepared.

"The first I knew about it I was being sent on a drama director's course in Elstree for a month," Dow explains. "I then had to put all that information to the test by going straight into several studio shows such as *Blankety Blank* and *Top of the Pops,* trailing each, then directing one in the gallery, so I got plenty of gallery experience. It was pretty terrifying really."

Dow had more than earned his stripes as a guiding presence with the *Only Fools* team on the studio floor as stage manager, not to mention taking on some of the directing strain on location. Nonetheless it was still a giant leap of faith to hand the keys for an 80 minute Christmas special to a first time director.

For the feature length special and the series beyond, John Sullivan had strong ideas of where he wanted to

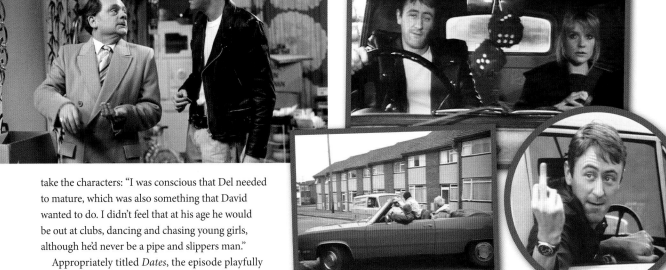

take the characters: "I was conscious that Del needed to mature, which was also something that David wanted to do. I didn't feel that at his age he would be out at clubs, dancing and chasing young girls, although he'd never be a pipe and slippers man."

Appropriately titled *Dates*, the episode playfully weaves together two distinct plots as both Del and Rodney take a woman out with two very different outcomes. Taking a nod from the latest fad of high street computer dating firms, Sullivan decided this would be the perfect place for Del to meet someone from a different world to the pubs, curry houses and markets he inhabits. Whilst at the same time, Rodney (following some deliberate misinformation from his mates) briefly forgoes his usual sensitivity for something more brash and daring as he goes all out to impress the Nags Head's newest (and shiest) barmaid.

For the Rodney plot of the story, Sullivan wanted to give the younger Trotter one last romantic embarrassment before the sixth series sent the character on an entirely different course. Setting up an unforgettable cruise in a three-wheeled van, Rodney and his date are pursued by a gang of rowdy youths in a sports car, complete with a painstakingly planned gravity defying leap.

Location filming for *Dates* and most of series six (referred to on production paperwork as Series F) was carried out between 6 November – 2 December 1988, with the studio recordings for the Christmas special taking place from 9–11 December.

As production manager on most of the recent specials, Tony Dow knew it was possible to successfully transform parts of nearly any town in the country into London, and this was a practice he wanted to continue: "It was a nightmare to film in London," he remembers, "so I said let's just get out of London as there are other areas. Our location

managers went down to Bristol to check it out as we needed dock areas for one of the upcoming episodes, but we found everything else we needed."

In Bristol, nearly all the locations for *Dates* were found, including two high street pubs to double as the exterior of the Nags Head. First chosen was the Bristol Flyer on Gloucester Road, as it faced an Italian restaurant. Later in the story the Waggon and Horses on Stapleton Road was used because of its suitable car park.

Apart from a dual carriageway shot in London and the sequence where the van makes the leap (shot on Talbot Road in Isleworth), Rodney's chase scene was filmed in Bristol.

In his first draft of *Dates* John Sullivan had intended Del to meet his 'Datadate' (changed to 'Technomatch' in the final script) by the clock in Victoria Station,

Above left: The Trotter brothers get ready for their respective dates.

Above: Rodney takes 'Nervous' Nerys Sansom (Andrée Bernard) out for a cruise in the van...

Left: Nerys is left distraught after her ordeal.

Below: Filming the chase sequence and jump required a lot of planning.

DATES

25 DECEMBER 1988

What a lovely, lovely day it was. I felt a bit silly afterwards for being so nervous about it. I mean, I knew it was going to be a lunch date, but I wasn't expecting The Hilton, Park Lane! I hadn't been spoiled like that since... well, ever! Then again, I'd also never had a date with a successful managing director before, let alone one who drove a Ferrari and received telephone calls from New York half way through lunch. But it was mostly just so refreshing to meet a man who shared an interest in the arts, and who actually listened. We talked about our passions and our hopes and dreams. It all just felt so right and comfortable and, above all, honest. For the first time in a long, long time, I felt as though I might just make it. I might just be someone!

— Raquel

It's safe to say that meeting Raquel was the happiest moment of my life since... well, since my Mum died. As soon as I saw her I thought blimey, this ain't no two halves of lager, a packet of pork scratchings and Bob's yer uncle type. No, this is a lady! An actress and a singer to be precise, and well up on her culture, which was just as well cos I've always been a bit cultivated myself. On that first date we ate the finest food and talked about the finest things in life, like art and literature, the works of Shaw and Chekov.

"I don't know about you," she said, "But I just love Cyrano de Bergerac."

"Oh definitely" I said, "You can never go far wrong with John Nettles."

At the end of the day, it was obvious that we'd made a deep impression on each other. It was just a shame she couldn't make Albert's birthday do the following Friday. But, as she explained, Friday evenings were when she taught drama class. I remember wondering what it was she was teaching, most likely something deep and meaningful that nobody could make head nor tail of. Oh yes, Pure class that Raquel!

— Del

just a short stroll from the Hilton Park Lane where a lunch table awaits. During planning stages of the production however, it was decided to move this scene south of the river to Waterloo Station. Not only did that location offer a grander clock and concourse, the station also had a direct train service to Bristol. This allowed the team to seamlessly arrange for cast and crew to board the train to the next stage of filming once shooting at Waterloo was complete.

Production Manager Adrian Pegg remembers that the clock itself posed some challenges for the crew: "We were not allowed to change the time on Waterloo Station's clock, so we had to carefully arrange the wide shots around the actual time of day!"

To play Del's date, Tony Dow spent weeks searching for the right actress. Raquel Turner was a complex creation of Sullivan's; open and slightly naive, but with layers of depth. The actress chosen would then have to quite literally strip away those qualities for a memorable scene in the Nags Head.

"My agent sent me the script," recalls Tessa Peake-Jones. "I didn't know the series, but I remember reading it and thinking this is an interesting character that I really liked. Raquel seemed very well rounded, very well written. The script had heart and it was moving at points and also really, really funny. So I went up for it thinking that there were at least five or ten people going up with me, and then I think I just met

Tony and they phoned my agent and said would I go back."

Returning to Television Centre for a read through, Peake-Jones met David Jason and John Sullivan for the first time, before getting the opportunity to work with Dow and sketch out the scene.

"I just came out thinking wow, I'd quite like this job, they're all really lovely. It just seems like an interesting project. I can't remember how soon after that they phoned, but I thought 'oh wow that's great'. When I started to tell people about the job, their reactions were 'you are kidding, you're going into that!?'"

Peake-Jones was perfectly cast as Raquel, a wonderful contrast to the established cast and a welcoming presence. The actress's time spent working on a host of BBC drama projects prepared her well for the leap straight into filming just a few weeks later.

"The first time I ever met anyone was at Waterloo Station early on a Sunday morning. I remember meeting David again and he was very lovely. I just remember him holding the hugest bunch of flowers in the world and finding it really funny as they were as big as him. It was hilarious acting with him that day, and I remember thinking that we were going to get on fine."

Opposite page below: Del meets his date Raquel Turner (Tessa Peake-Jones) underneath the clock at Waterloo Station.

Opposite page right inset: "You realise that will be extra." – Before Raquel arrives, Del is approached by 'Sonia' (Jean Warren).

Above: Director Tony Dow supervises the location shoot at Waterloo Station.

Left: Del slipped the Savoy's butler Charles (Nicholas Courtney) a few quid to interrupt him with a fabricated transatlantic call.

Below: For a second date, Raquel invites Del over to her flat for dinner.

Above and right: Despite Mike's efforts to curb the old sea dogs antics, Albert's birthday party was a great do... until Del's stripper-gram arrives...

Below: Tony Dow directs Buster Merryfield.

Below right: "Oh Del, please listen to me. I just do this a couple of evenings a week to pay for my drama lessons." – Raquel pleads to Del in the Nags Head car park.

Opposite page top left: Del and Raquel meet up again in Sid's cafe.

Opposite page below left: An anxious Raquel looks out her window to see if Del is on his way... Meanwhile a misunderstanding with the police sees Del being taken to the station for questioning – "You don't know the code for Addis Ababa do you?"

Tony Dow will never forget the memorable shoot at Waterloo which kicked off production of the special: "My very first full day directing television comedy was on a big scaffolding rig overlooking the whole of Waterloo Station."

Suitably enough to mark the occasion, and with a nod to Alfred Hitchcock, Dow can be seen making a cameo in the background of several promotional stills of Jason and Peake-Jones in Waterloo.

For Del and Raquel's lunch at the Hilton in Park Lane, the crew were actually permitted to film in the real restaurant. Here Peake-Jones got her first experience of her co-star's genius:

"David said to me 'do you think it would be a nice idea if neither of them knew which knife or fork to use?' And I looked and thought that is a brilliant observation about these two people. That's the sort of actor David is, for a lot of comedy actors that wouldn't have occurred to them, it is such a tiny detail, but actually says everything about these two people in such a beautiful moment and I thought there and then, you really know what you're doing."

Also giving a brilliant performance was actress Andree Bernard as Rodney's date 'Nervous' Nerys. Elsewhere, actor Chris Stanton was cast as the

Technomatch Agent, Jean Warren perfectly brings to life the unsavoury Sonia, and Leslie Rogers was cast as the panda-car driving policeman. With a knowing wink to the audience, former *Doctor Who* star Nicholas Courtney was introduced as the Hilton's distinguished waiter, Charles (just as part-time actress Raquel talks about her previous bit-part role as a 'Lizard person' in the series).

To broaden the Nags Head circle, *Dates* saw Sullivan introduce Jevon, played by Steven Woodcock, and Chris, played by Tony Marshall, both making the first of several appearances. Elsewhere, a brief voice over from Nerys's mother, Mrs Sansom (heard as Rodney leaves Sid's Cafe), was delivered by Jean Challis, then wife of Boycie actor John.

As production moved into the studio, another notable change was made to the Nags Head, with the angle of the entire set rotated by 90 degrees. "I always hated the Nags Head set," remembers Dow. "It was at a ridiculous angle for filming because it was flat and you had no fourth wall, so if someone was talking to Mike behind the bar where do you put the actors so they're not looking at the audience?"

It was the job of the series' new production designer Graham Lough to dust off and modify the existing set: "Moving around the Nags Head set made it much easier to shoot scenes and we also knew that we had to arrange for a side entrance to the bar to match the pub exterior location in Bristol, so we incorporated that."

For John Sullivan, *Dates* was an important stepping stone for the character of Del and reveals much about how he handles embarrassment: "It was a chance to see Del with the kind of woman he always wanted to meet, with a showbiz background, and he thinks he's going out with a serious actress. I wanted to confront Del's pride and see how he would cope when it turns out Raquel's a strippergram."

The 80-minute running time flies by as the two parallel dating plots unfold. From the opening scene with Uncle Albert showing off his dusty tin of memories, to the closing shots of Del being arrested, the episode is an undisputed classic. Broadcast at 5.05pm on Christmas Day 1988, *Dates* pulled in 16.6 million viewers.

With such a consistent and well-made episode, it seems impossible to believe it was the work of a first time director, an experience which Dow will never forget: "*Dates* won a BAFTA, so I thought 'this is a good job, I'm going to be happy here!'"

"Tony was fantastic," Peake-Jones recalls. "Not only did he know and have the respect of the crew, you would never have known he hadn't done it before, it was like a fish to water. He had great ideas, he shot it well, he gave you notes, I thought he was great."

When the dating agency called to say they'd had a hit, I was both excited and worried at the same time. You see, they'd fed all my information into a computer and it came out with a woman who was compatible with me. The reason for my worry is that even though they'd insisted on complete honesty, I hadn't told them I was a road sweeper. Not cos I was ashamed of it, I just thought it would help my cause if I went for something a bit more glamorous. So I told them I was a bus inspector.

Anyway, I put the worry to one side and focused on preparing for the lunch date. I booked a table at an Italian restaurant, bought a nice bunch of flowers and put on my best suit. After a quick stop off at the Nags Head for a bit of Dutch courage, I went to the restaurant, and there she was. Her name was Susan and she was a nice girl: mid thirties, slim, smartly dressed and very attractive. Not my usual type at all, but she was making the effort so I couldn't complain. It was a very pleasant lunch, although I did panic half way through our mains when she suggested that I one day show her my inspector's uniform. Outside the restaurant, as we were saying goodbye, she mentioned that she fancied a coffee. I pointed her to Sid's Cafe and told her I'd better be getting home. She then started acting funny, twiddling her hair and winking and nudging me, all playful like, saying that she didn't fancy sitting in a greasy cafe on her own. Reading the signals and feeling bold, I made my move.

"Alright" I said, "I'll come with you."

I don't know what happened but she then changed her tune completely and the last I saw of her she was getting into a taxi. Why do women have to be so bloody complicated? Still, it could have been worse. She could have come back to mine and asked to see my bus inspector's uniform.

Trigger

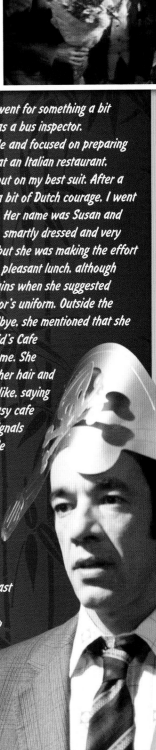

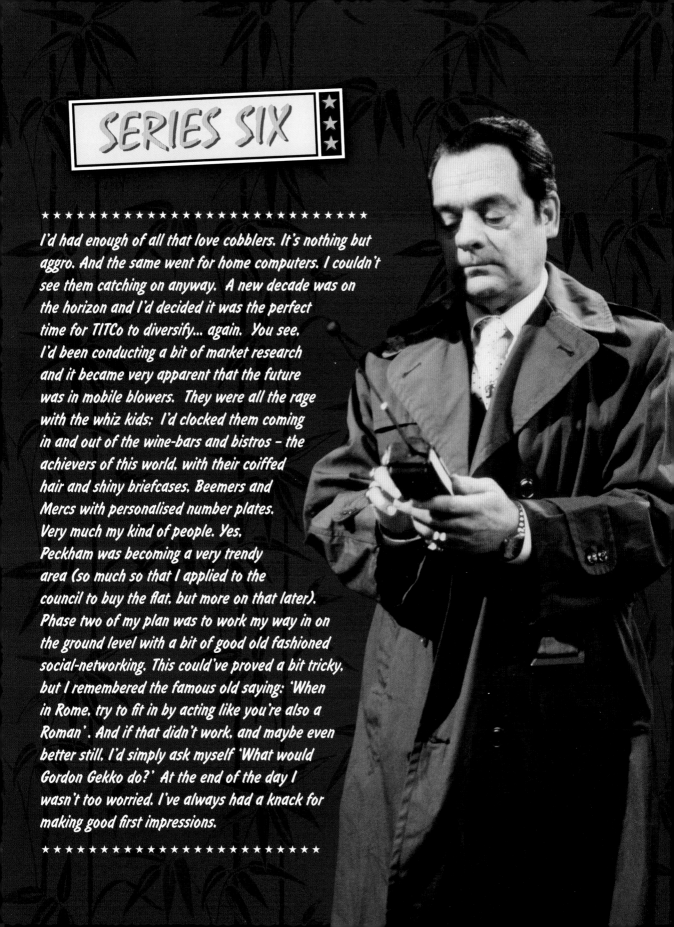

SERIES SIX

★ ★

I'd had enough of all that love cobblers. It's nothing but aggro. And the same went for home computers. I couldn't see them catching on anyway. A new decade was on the horizon and I'd decided it was the perfect time for TITCo to diversify... again. You see, I'd been conducting a bit of market research and it became very apparent that the future was in mobile blowers. They were all the rage with the whiz kids; I'd clocked them coming in and out of the wine-bars and bistros – the achievers of this world, with their coiffed hair and shiny briefcases, Beemers and Mercs with personalised number plates. Very much my kind of people. Yes, Peckham was becoming a very trendy area (so much so that I applied to the council to buy the flat, but more on that later). Phase two of my plan was to work my way in on the ground level with a bit of good old fashioned social-networking. This could've proved a bit tricky, but I remembered the famous old saying: 'When in Rome, try to fit in by acting like you're also a Roman'. And if that didn't work, and maybe even better still, I'd simply ask myself 'What would Gordon Gekko do?' At the end of the day I wasn't too worried. I've always had a knack for making good first impressions.

★ ★

ONLY FOOLS & HORSES

SERIES 'F'

Above: The Bristol location shoot for *Dates* and series six was carefully planned out by production manager Adrian Pegg.

Above right: Embracing his new yuppy image, Del reads the news that his application to buy the flat is being considered.

Right: Del and Rodney look at Kings Avenue.

Below: "I am not 'poncing about' with anything! In case it's slipped that senile, shrapnel-cluttered brain of yours, I happen to be studying for a computer diploma course!"

The sixth series of *Only Fools* would see the series break with convention and gently follow an ongoing story arc over its six episodes. With more screen time to hand, John Sullivan was free to develop more detailed plots around the laughter and explore characters further.

"With John 'never knowingly under-written Sullivan' it was always a nightmare," Tony Dow remembers with a smile. "The BBC had said 'OK, you can have 40 minutes' but we still ended up having the same problem of John having to get rid of stuff because he couldn't get rid of the plot. We were always desperate to have more time, and, once again, we got hugely lucky and they let us go up to 50 minutes a show."

Dow soon realised he had his work cut out and the extra screen time would prove to be both a blessing and a curse as the team had to make everything work under the time constraints of the 40-minute episodes already budgeted for.

"We started the series with three location-heavy episodes, but the three after that were all completely studio-based as we ran out of time to do any filming. We suddenly had to work out how to do those last three 50-minute episodes entirely over two days in the studio."

The studio recordings for series six took place a week after those for *Dates*, on consecutive Saturday and Sundays from the 17th December 1988 (skipping the Christmas and New Year weekends).

Following on from the subtle maturity hinted at in *Dates*, Sullivan saw an opportunity to show Del getting caught up in the mood of the time, adopting a new image of Filofaxes, red braces and aluminium briefcases. Inspired by the film *Wall Street*, and its money-hungry stockbroker character, Gordon Gekko, Del would become a Yuppy.

The sixth series' ongoing story, however, would be more about Rodney's life changes and how those changes affect Del.

"Rodney grows up in series six," remembered Sullivan. "But I was always conscious that he was often forcing his maturity. You'll notice that every so often, only for ten seconds or so, he'll revert to that teenage mode – the old Rodney – then pull himself back out of it."

Building upon many references to Rodney's interest in computers and desire to better himself in a life away from lugging a suitcase around, Sullivan decided to have Rodney enrol on a computing course at the Adult Education Centre, and it would be here that he bumps into someone special.

"I thought it would be nice to see Rodney not just fall in

lust with some girl," explained Sullivan, "but to actually have something permanent for once. I wanted this to be the sort of girl who, to Rodney's way of thinking, was out of reach. But this time it's different because the girl actually responds and suddenly Rodders has a romance on his hands."

In Cassandra Parry, Sullivan created a strong-willed and clever character more than capable of holding her own with the Trotter family.

"We needed a very special actress to play that part and all credit should go to Tony Dow, who did the final casting and found Gwyneth Strong," remembered Sullivan. "I thought she was perfect. It must have been quite nerve-wracking for her to come into a series that was so well established, but Gwyneth did a great job."

"The audition for the part of Cassandra was an incredibly quick and jolly affair," Gwyneth Strong recalls. "All I remember is my agent saying 'pop along to the BBC' which of course I did. I met Tony Dow, had a laugh and a chat with him, then a couple of days later my agent was on the phone telling me I had got the job."

With the part of Rodney's new flame cast, Sullivan put in to action his plan for the six episodes of the series, writing Strong's character into each story and bringing to *Only Fools* some of the witty romantic banter which had made *Just Good Friends* work so well.

The opening scene of *Yuppy Love* sets the tone perfectly as the newly christened Gordon Gekko-esque Del debates the ethics of wealth and ownership with Rodney. Giving his brother a lift to the night school, Del first makes a stop at 'Kings Avenue', a plush street of large houses with in and out driveways. As Del dreams of guest suites, swimming pools and jacuzzis, Rodney sees only the social injustice... a view which will later come back to test him.

Whilst most of the filming for the series would be carried out in Bristol, for this scene the crew went to Winchmore Hill in London and filmed on the leafy Broad Walk, with the art department adding the 'Kings Avenue' road sign.

Arriving at the Adult Education Centre, Rodney heads to class, but not before sharing a brief exchange of smiles with a female student. Meanwhile, Del spots a group of successful and trendy looking women heading down a flight of stairs into 'Charlotte's Wine Bar'. Appropriately enough, this scene was filmed on Queen Charlotte Street in Bristol, with a building of offices modified to look like the night school.

It is in a studio recreation of this wine bar's interior that one of the defining moments of the series would take place, inspired by a true event John Sullivan had witnessed.

Above: When the Bristol location originally found for the Kings Avenue was deemed unsuitable, the crew found an address in Winchmore Hill in North London. Here the art department added a 'Kings Avenue' sign.

Left: Cassandra Parry (Gwyneth Strong) smiles at Rodney as she walks towards the Adult Education Centre.

Below left: Del drops Rodney off and spots the bar over the road.

Below: "It's OK. They're very similar; it's an easy mistake to make. This one's yours!" – Rodders is mortified to discover that Del has written 'Rodney' on the inside of his coat.

YUPPY LOVE

8 JANUARY 1989

There are times when you realise who your true mates are, and this was one of them. You see, Mike had barred me from the Nags Head for stealing one of his pork pies. He was bang out of order, and I told him as much. "You're bang out of order, Mike" I said. "I don't even like pork pies. Especially yours! I mean, what d'you take me for, a complete and utter moron?"

He didn't know how to answer that one, and instead started to defend the standard of his pub grub, going on about all the certificates he's received for it. "Yeah, and most of 'em signed by doctors" I said. And I stand by that. Just a few weeks later I had a plate of his tomatoes and I still ain't fully recovered. Anyway, he had no evidence that I stole the pork pie, it was just his word against mine, so I decided to take my business elsewhere. By that point I was seriously considering suing him for delamination of character. I was making my way to the citizens advice bureau when I happened to pass one of those swanky new wine bars, so I thought I'd duck in and see what was occurring. And that's where I bumped into Del Boy, perched at the bar drinking some fizzy wine. I told him all about the pork pie situation and he agreed that Mike had gone too far. I really appreciated his seeing my point of view and gave him the pork pie as a thank you. Truth be told, I was glad to get shot of it. It was making my pocket smell.

Trigger

"I was in a pub in Balham Hill with some mates. On one table were three or four girls, and at the bar these guys were showing off to the girls. One of the guys lent forward to light his cigarette from his mate's lighter and, as he did, the barman came out and lifted the flap up. The bloke leant back against the bar very cooly and fell through. He didn't hit the floor, but he stumbled and then grinned as if to say he'd done it on purpose. It was so funny I thought, 'I have to use that one day!'"

Sullivan realised that *Yuppy Love* was the perfect place to feature this moment. Discussing the memorable account with David Jason and Tony Dow, Sullivan didn't see Del stumbling and reaching out to stop himself: "To Del's his mind, he thought he was too cool now that he was a yuppy. David took this on board, and he said, 'I'm just going to go straight down'. This is very hard because the natural reaction when you fall is to stick your hands out to protect yourself."

At the suggestion of David Jason, Welsh actor William Thomas was cast as the barman in the famous scene (Thomas had recently starred with Jason's partner Myfanwy Talog in *The Magnificent Evans*). The gifted actor remembers the week leading up to the recording well: "In the rehearsal room the bar was just a board on top of chairs. We actually rehearsed it after everyone else in the cast had gone as it was something that was slotted in towards the end. David had been known for that slapstick and physical comedy and between John Sullivan and David, they worked it into the episode towards the end of the week."

As originally scripted and rehearsed, Trigger wasn't in the scene and Del was stood at the bar alone, but a chance free day in Roger Lloyd Pack's schedule inspired Sullivan to add him to the proceedings, giving the writer a foil for Del's observations, and resulting in a classic Trig moment of confusion.

"My wife was in the audience that night," remembers William Thomas. "It was quite something to be part of, all I can remember was David's line 'I think we're on a winner here Trig' which was my cue to lift the flap and walk out

to the back of the set. And then this huge explosion and a roar of laughter. I don't think people could believe what they had just seen. It was such a magical moment. We did it once, just one take."

Sullivan was delighted with the results: "David practised this fall so much he really had it off to a fine art. Because it was filmed in front of a live audience, we only had one chance to get it. David was brilliant and he did the fall so well. And Tony kept the cameras on him and the bar the whole time, it was wonderful."

Whilst Del limps out of the wine bar nursing a bruised shoulder (and ego), Rodney is having a very different evening at a night club with Mickey Pearce and Jevon. It is here that he is reunited with the female student from the night school.

For actress Gwyneth Strong, these scenes, filmed at the Parkside Hotel in Bristol, were her very first as Cassandra.

Thanks to Mickey Pearce, Rodney's trip home from the night club in Cassandra's car is excruciating, but the character's embarrassment was only just beginning.

"The scene where Rodney gets Cassandra to drop him off outside a posh house was based on something that actually happened to me," remembered John Sullivan. "I was seeing a girl who lived in a very middle-class area, and I just couldn't bring myself to let her drop me off at my house! I remembered from school that there was this big house up the road and I thought, 'Well, I'll use that.' I didn't go through all the pain that Rodney went through, but I did have to walk about two miles home, although it wasn't raining. I never saw her again!"

A rain-soaked walk home for Rodders and a cracking scene back at the flat round off an incredible 50 minutes of television and one of *Only Fools*' best. "This is a great episode," recalled Sullivan. "It created so many changes in Del and Rodney's lives – it was pivotal".

Above left: Production designer Graham Lough designed the wine bar set to match the exterior footage.

Above: "Could be onto a winner here, Trig. Alright, play it nice and cool, son, nice and cool, you know what I mean?" – Del falls through the bar and into comedy history.

Above inset: The wine bar's barman (William Thomas).

Below left: On a night out with Jevon and Mickey, Rodney's luck is in as he catches up with Cassandra again.

Below: When offered a lift home from Cassandra, Rodney can't bear to let her see where he lives, instead he gets her to drive to Kings Avenue – "Please, Cassandra, go!"

I wasn't proud of it, but my pride got the better of me... you know what I mean. Cassandra was everything I wasn't. She looked nice, she spoke nice, she came from a nice neighbourhood, had a nice job and drove a nice car. I had feelings for her the moment our eyes met and badly wanted to impress her, so the last thing I wanted to do was tell the truth (I'd tried that before with women and it had always backfired). So when she offered to drive me home I directed her to the King's Avenue and made her stop at a great big house with a Mercedes parked in the driveway. I got out and waved goodbye, thinking it was job done, but she just sat there in the car looking at me. I then realised that the people who lived in the house were also looking at me from an upstairs window. Cassandra waved at them and then I did the same. Bloody hell, 'awkward' wasn't the word. It was like being stuck between a rock and... another sodding rock!

Rodney

When we did the pre-recorded outdoor scenes, it was tricky to film because everyone was laughing so much. Originally there was a moment in the van where one of the dolls leans forward and Del says, 'Give it up, I've got a headache'. David had to do it five or six times because he kept corpsing."

Cast as adult shop proprietor, Dirty Barry, was British TV stalwart Walter Sparrow, who would go on to star as Duncan in the 1991 film *Robin Hood: Prince of Thieves*. Elsewhere in *Danger UXD*, Tommy Buson was cast in the minor role of Clayton Cooper, who we would meet again in a younger incarnation in 2010's *Rock & Chips*.

When it becomes clear that the dolls are extremely dangerous (the manufacturer having accidentally filled them with highly explosive propane gas), the Trotters load them into the van and drive to an area of wasteland to dispose of them. The location used for this explosive finale was the site of the former Gas Works on Anchor Road in Bristol.

In early drafts of this sequence, John Sullivan had considered for the Trotters' distinctive Reliant Regal van to share the doll's explosive fate. The writer soon reconsidered however, realising the affection the van held with viewers and its importance in the series' identity.

On his Bristol reccie for a suitable wasteland for the explosion, Adrian Pegg had also found the three blocks of flats which would make their debut in this episode. "I contacted the council and asked around. It was just lucky that I came across them and the council and residents agreed to filming. It was helpful that the show was well established by then though."

These blocks were located on Duckmoor Road, in Ashton, south Bristol, with Whitemead House used as the Trotters' home. Whilst their appearance in *Danger UXD* is fleeting and at night, these flats would serve the series till the end of its production.

Above: "Just look at me! I'm supposed to be going out in this tonight!" – Rodney's tomato delivering duties have landed him with a hefty dry cleaning bill... After the recording of *Danger UXD*, BBC scenic operator Mickey Rowley came home with a bucket loads of tomatoes bought for the episode, which his daughter Louise remembers the family were eating for days afterwards.

Above right: Del gets Denzil "out of schtuck and into the money" as he signs the driver's delivery docket.

Below: Lusty Linda comes alive! – "Whatever will our guests think?"

Opposite page: The Trotters take the dolls for a night out to visit Dirty Barry's (Walter Sparrow) shop.

This episode was inspired by some uninvited inflatable guests which had attended Nicolas Lyndhurst's 21st birthday, whilst on location with the *Only Fools* team for 1982's *It Never Rains*.

Whilst the memory of the amusing prank had stayed with John Sullivan, the writer had been unsure as to whether adult dolls might be taking things a little too far for a sitcom, until he saw it from the trader's point of view: "I decided that Del would just be interested in the financial angle, the profit which could be made from these things. When he finds out they're top-of-the-range self-inflating dolls, this is quite special for him! It was quite a dangerous episode in terms of adult content, but the subject matter was handled extremely well."

Danger UXD would mark Denzil's first appearance in the series since *To Hull and Back*. Now self-employed, and with a company name ('Transworld Express') suitably inspired by Del, it made perfect sense for him to be an unwitting originator of the Trotters' unusual stock.

"We had the dolls specially made so they'd be as inoffensive as possible," explained John Sullivan. "Obviously we couldn't put the real ones on TV!

DANGER UXD

15 JANUARY 1989

It was that half-head Denzil's fault. He'd got himself lumbered with a load of faulty stock from some plastics factory over Deptford way and was doing his pieces worrying that he would lose his job. I agreed to help by taking the problem out of his hands and into ours (that's just the sort of mate I am). It was fifty dolls to be precise, and I was certain we could knock a few out down the market or maybe over at the Arndale Centre. That way, Denzil would be in the clear, a load of sprogs would get the gift of a lifetime, and Rodney and I would be up a nicker or two, everyone's a winner, petit dejeuner, as they say in Cherbourg. We got the boxes back to the flat and Albert started opening them. There we were expecting to see Barbie and Cindy, when Albert pulled out Erotic Estelle and Lusty Linda. Gordon Bennett! These things were life-sized and self-inflating (a deluxe model for the more discerning weirdo), and we had an entire platoon of the gits! Randy Rita, Saucy Suzy, and more colours than a tube of Smarties! You name it, we had it! Rodney was all for dropping 'em off at the nearest dump, and I was too until I noticed they were retailing at £60 each. Well, a sense of decency is one thing, but business is business.

Del

We were sitting there in the living room. Rodney was getting ready for another date with that Cassandra sort, Del was catching up on the Financial Times index, and I was thinking about calling it a night, when suddenly there came a strange sound, sort of like a short, high pitched rush of air. A few moments later it happened again, only this time it didn't stop. The sound seemed to be coming from over by the drinks bar, so Rodney and Del went to investigate. Just as they reached the bar, one of the dolls shot up from behind it, fully inflated and raring to go. In my panicked state, I immediately thought of the time during the war when a vessel of mine docked in Jamaica. We weren't there long, but me and a crew-mate, Dave Dulake, decided to sneak ashore and see if we could find somewhere to quench our thirst. It was then we came across this big shack. There were loads of people going in so we thought we'd join them. No sooner had we taken a seat, some local bloke came out holding a dead cat in the air. 'Hold on a minute' I thought 'something ain't right here'. He then laid the cat on a table and began waving his hands about and speaking in tongue. I almost fell off my chair when the cat suddenly sprung to life. Well, it turned out the bloke was a witch doctor and we'd stumbled into his voodoo ceremony. Dave and I made ourselves scare a bit sharpish, especially when we noticed how he was eyeing up our beards.

Albert

Above: The One Eleven Club and casino.

Above right: Del talks to a new contact of his, the retired jeweller Arnie (Philip McGough).

Below: The consortium pool their resources to buy Arnie's suitcase of 250 gold chains.

Below right: Boycie and Del accompany Arnie to watch his meeting with Mr Stavros.

Below right: A behind the scenes look at the location work for this scene which was filmed in Ealing.

Opposite page above left "It's just we're both sitting on the same side. Sort of next to each other... it might look a bit funny."

Opposite page middle: Arnie fakes a coronary.

Opposite page below right: Del's chain consortium look on as Arnie, the cash and the chains are driven away in an ambulance.

The idea behind *Chain Gang* stemmed from John Sullivan's time in the secondhand car trade: "I was talking to someone about car auctions and I found out that old ambulances and official vehicles were regularly sold at these events. The storyline was built around the idea of these con men getting hold of an ambulance – because nobody questions an ambulance, and it can run red lights. So it's quite a vehicle to have if you're trying to pull off a con"

To con the Peckham faithful, Sullivan created the likeable yet slightly shady character of Arnie, who successfully reels Del and Trigger in after he strikes up a rapport with them in the One Eleven Club casino.

To play Arnie, actor Philip McGough was cast. As a former member of the RSC, McGough more than holds his own amongst the established cast and keeps the audience guessing his motives.

The exterior of the One Eleven Club was

filmed at the Parkside Hotel in Bristol (the interior of which was used as the night club in *Yuppy Love*), with the art department modifying the rear steps and door for the scene.

The rest of the episode's locations were found in west London, with an address on The Grove in Ealing modified to appear as 'Giovanni's' restaurant. Arnie's next con was seen in Kensington with the final 'heart attack' filmed outside the Tandoori Nights restaurant in Hammersmith.

All other scenes were recorded in the studio, with production designer Graham Lough transforming TC 3 into the interior of the One Eleven Club, complete with roulette tables and bar. "The set for the One Eleven Club was loosely based on a gambling club in Russell Square in London, so it wasn't that difficult

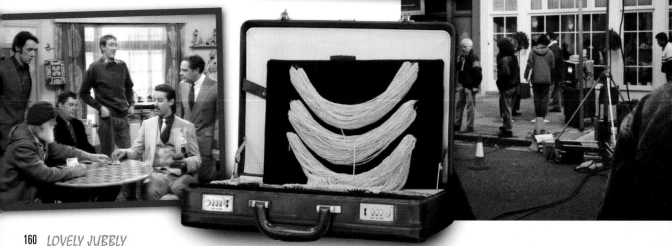

CHAIN GANG

22 JANUARY 1989

As sharp and on the ball as I undoubtedly was, there were a few occasions when I was had. This was one of 'em. Arnie and his boys had the operation down to a fine art, right down to the fake heart attack and the fake ambulance that turned up at just the right time. Well, me and my little consortium were devastated. Not only had we lost 250 eighteen carat gold chains, we'd also said bonjour to twelve and a half grand! Trigger had pawned his aunt's ring, Albert had done all his savings, Boycie's nose was broken and Mike's motor was clamped. As gutted as I was, I was also quietly confident that Arnie would soon slip up, and that's exactly what he did when he attempted the exact same scam on Denzil and his brothers. This time we had our own mission and were ready and waiting for his fake heart attack with our own fake ambulance. It was sort of like being in an episode of The A-Team, just with less explosions and more cockney. You should have seen Arnie's face when he 'regained consciousness' and realised what was happening. I really did pity the fool.

Del

a set to design," remembers Lough. "We had to hire the gambling tables from a supplier who provided tables for professional gambling venues, and I think we even had professional croupiers as extras. The gaming tables took up most of the set!"

As the plot ramps up, the characters in Del's consortium all take the bait as Arnie gives the performance of his life into the telephone at Nelson Mandela House: his former business partner, the unforgiving piece of work 'Mr Stavros' is back in town, and he wants his chains. Arnie's con is on.

The highlight of *Chain Gang* is seeing the Nags Head crew all together, wrapped up in the situation and debating their next step. Boycie is suspicious, Mike is pragmatic, Trigger as gullible as ever, and Del attempts to work out a deal.

The location filming around the Italian restaurant is handled so well; the crew utilising a real interior, with Mike's car visible on one side and the Trotter Van on the other.

When Boycie pretends to be a doctor in an attempt to remove the briefcase chained to the 'unconscious' Arnie's wrist, Tony Dow pulls the action out of the restaurant and suddenly we're watching things unfold as a silent movie, with Rodney and Albert looking on in confusion – just magic.

"When we went to the 50-minute episodes," remembered John Sullivan, "all of a

Above and left: The consortium plan their next move – "Rodney, follow that ambulance!"

Right: Del and the gang get the call they had been dreading – "Did you know the deceased very well?"

Below: The consortium finally get their own back as they beat Arnie at his own game in the closing moments of the story.

sudden characters like Boycie, Marlene and Trigger could start to stretch their wings and breathe a little. *Chain Gang* is a great ensemble piece – there's the consortium, so all the gang have something to gain and a lot to lose. And then there's one stranger, Arnie. He's a really good con man and persuades Del to suggest the scam himself – so there's no suspicion about Arnie."

Parallel with the chain plot, Sullivan keeps the momentum of Rodney and Cassandra's romance going, namely Rodney's insecurities over the training course she's on. When Del takes up Albert's suggestion to use his new phone's call-back feature, only to get through to the "Highcliffe ruddy Hotel, Guernsey!", it is a moment of brilliance.

Chain Gang would see Gwyneth Strong's very first studio scenes in the series, in the One Eleven Club as Rodney introduces her to Del for the first time, and in the Nags Head as Rodney abandons her with Denzil. Having been a keen viewer of the series, this was an incredible experience for the young actress: "My first memories of wandering around the studio sets of the pub and the Trotters' flat were very special. It was such a strange feeling to be on a job that I had watched and loved with my family over the years".

The climax of the story sees the Nags Head consortium (now extended to include Denzil and his brothers) working out what is really going on and getting some well deserved payback. The final shot of the episode, inside the ambulance with Del and Boycie clad in full uniforms, is an unusual and hilarious end to a great episode.

For the fourth episode of the series, John Sullivan was inspired by a friend who, along with his wife, entered every competition going, from supermarket flyers and tin wrappers to cereal packets. This was something that Sullivan could easily see Del getting involved in, especially if there were big prizes involved. By exploiting Nicholas Lyndhurst's boyish looks and Rodney's well established artistic leanings, Sullivan hit upon an inspired way to draw Cassandra into the flat for her first Trotter caper.

Without saying anything to his brother, Del enters Rodney's painting 'Marble Arch at Dawn' into the Mega Flakes cornflakes painting competition. Amazingly the painting wins a prize: *three* tickets for a holiday in Mallorca!

"I was aware that the audience would know that there was something wrong, why are there three tickets, not two?" explained John Sullivan. "I wondered when I should reveal the answer. I thought it would be funny to have it in the airport. When Del says 'Hang on a minute' the audience doesn't know what's coming – but they know it's something bad. Del could have told Rodney on the coach, or on the plane, but no, he leaves it till the very last minute!"

Arriving at the departure lounge, Del explains to Rodney and Cassandra the small catch in their free

holiday – Rodney has won the prize in the *under 15s* category! To make matters worse the cornflake people have laid on a full week of events via the resident kids club, the Groovy Gang. Led by the charming holiday rep Alan Perkins, played by actor Michael Fenton Stevens, Rodney is swiftly conscripted into becoming the Groovy Gang's latest member.

"I was basically offered the part," remembers Fenton Stevens. "I shared an agent with David Jason, and Tony and Gareth knew me from *Radio Active* and *KYTV* and they were happy to have me involved. I remember the first Monday morning table read, everyone was incredibly welcoming and we had brilliant fun."

During rehearsals, Fenton Stevens remembers that some elements of the script were still taking shape: "John Sullivan was there all the time and was changing things or putting things in. Or if you said something in rehearsals which made you laugh, John would take it and adapt it and put it into the script. As it went through the week, I realised it was going to be a great episode."

Above: Rodney shows Cassandra some of his works of art from his portfolio, including a water colour of a bottle of wine and 'Marble Arch at Dawn'.

Far left: A box of Mega Flakes, originally created by the art department for the episode.

Below: In the Nags Head, Del delivers the happy news that Rodney has won a holiday for *three* to Mallorca...

THE UNLUCKY WINNER IS...

29 JANUARY 1989

MEGA FLAKES **MEGA FLAKES**

Painting Competition

WINNERS ASSEMBLE HERE

THE GROOVY GANG

Having Rodney Trotter as your other half may sometimes be frustrating, but there's never any shortage of surprises. On this occasion Rodney had entered a painting competition. Actually, Del had entered on Rodney's behalf and not bothered to tell him (he tends to do things like that from time to time). That was the first surprise. The second came when he won first prize: an all expenses paid week's holiday in Mallorca. It was so exciting and just what we needed. Our relationship was blossoming and it felt like the right time to take things to the next level, so to speak. The third surprise came when Del announced that it was a holiday for three and that he was coming with us. Well, even Del Boy's tagging along wasn't enough to dampen my spirits. Rodney and I would still get plenty of time to ourselves. But no sooner had we stepped off the plane, Del dropped the fourth and final surprise. Actually it was more of a bombshell. You see, Rodney's painting had actually won first prize in an under-15-year-old category. It was funny at first and I couldn't help but laugh, but that was before I realised the full implications. Poor Rodney didn't even have a chance to absorb the news before the competition reps had conscripted him into the 'Groovy Gang' along with all the other kids. For the following week I had to pretend to be his stepmother!

Cassandra

It's not my place to pry or judge, but that Rodney is a strange boy. It clearly states on his passport that he's fourteen years old, but I've never seen another one like him. It's not just the height – at least six foot by my estimation – but lots of other little things. Just this morning we were taking the Groovy Gang out for a fun day at the local Splash and Slide, and as we were getting on the coach I could've sworn I saw a packet of Rizlas poking out of his back pocket. Then there's that step-mother of his. She's a pleasant enough woman, but last Wednesday I saw her down by the pool sitting on Rodney's lap twiddling his chest hairs. As for the father, he went out on his own on Friday night and arrived back at the hotel at four in the morning with a love-bite on his neck and lipstick smears all over his shirt. Maybe this explains why Rodney always looks so depressed, the poor lad.

Alan Perkins

Joining Fenton Stevens as fellow holiday rep, Carmen, was New Zealand-born actress Gina Bellman, right at the start of an impressive career in British drama. Elsewhere in the cast, a young Lusha Kellgren plays Trudy, a 13-year-old Bros fan who has the hots for Rodney.

By this point in the series, the allocated window (and budget) for location filming had already closed, meaning the whole episode had to be recorded in the studio.

"It's a brilliantly funny episode," remembers director Tony Dow, "but we were forced to have a horrible set, and a hotel room with the sound of the sea in the background. There was nothing we could do about that."

Whilst production designer Graham Lough did the best he could given the circumstances, he shared Dow's view: "I had an argument with Gareth Gwenlan because I needed more money than allocated to build the set for the arrivals hall, but Gareth maintained that the sets for situation comedy weren't that important anyway!"

The episode did however give Lough the opportunity to go on a research recce abroad: "I was allowed to go to Mallorca for a couple of days to do some research and buy some authentic lottery tickets which featured in the episode. I even bought a bullfighting poster titled 'EL DEL' which I thought Del would have bought if he had gone there. It was on the flat set for quite a few episodes, but I had to remove it because the anti-bullfighting lobby thought that it was inappropriate!"

For Fenton Stevens, the majority of his contributions to the episode were pre-recorded as it wasn't possible for the studio to house the expansive arrivals hall and hotel foyer as well as everything else. The other sets recorded on that night were the Nags Head and the Trotter flat. "I can remember that the laughter in the pub was so strong that they had to do a complete second take," remembers Stevens, "not because of mistakes, but because almost every line got a round of applause and the scene went on five minutes too long!"

Despite the studio bound limitations and a relentless turnaround to make a 50-minute episode in a week, *The Unlucky Winner Is...* is simply one of John Sullivan's greatest.

Opposite page top right: Alan Perkins (Michael Fenton Stevens) greets Rodney as he is conscripted into the Groovy Gang.

Above left: Alan and his fellow holiday rep Carmen (Gina Bellman) question the Trotters regarding Rodney's age.

Above left inset: Rodney meets fellow Groovy Gang member Trudy (Lusha Kellgren).

Below left and Above right: Del attempts to convince both Rodney and Cassandra to look like they're having a great time for the other's sake.

Below: The Trotters have won the lottery, but as Alan points out they can't claim any of the money – "It is the winning ticket, alright. The problem is it's got Rodney's name on it. You see, under Spanish law nobody under the age of 18 is allowed to gamble."

SICKNESS AND WEALTH

5 FEBRUARY 1989

I'd seen Del get a nasty bellyache plenty of times (the last being when he ordered the mixed-grill special at Sid's cafe), but this weren't no ordinary belly ache. Rodney and I pleaded with him to go and see a doctor, but would he? Would he ever! Still, he'd never listened to anything me or Rodney had ever said before, so it didn't come as too much of a surprise. No, the only person he had ever really listened to was his mum, Joan (God rest her soul).

Anyway, at the time he just so happened to be doing a bit of business with my friend, Elsie Partridge, and it gave me an idea. You see, Elsie had a third eye. Not literally, of course, she just had the standard two like everybody else. I just mean that she had the gift of being able to communicate with the other side. When I say the "other side" I don't mean the other side of the room or the garden fence, I mean that place the departed go. And when I say "departed" I mean brown bread. She could talk to the dead, that's what I'm getting at!

Where was I? Oh yeah. I couldn't stand seeing Del in pain any longer, so when he set up a dummy-run seance in the room above the Nags Head, I conspired with Elsie in an attempt to get him to finally see some sense. Most of the lads were there for the séance: Del and Rodney, Boycie, Trigger and Mike. Well, Elsie kicked things off by going into a trance. This panicked Mike a bit as she'd only ten minutes earlier finished off one of his pork pies. After the spirit of Boycie's old man paid a visit and had a pop at him, a woman crossed the veil, a woman who had long blonde hair and was covered in jewellery. Del recognised Joan straight away.

Elsie then passed on the urgent message telling Del that he needed to pull himself together and get down to the quacks! Neither Elsie nor I liked telling lies like that, but we only did it for Del. And it worked! After a stay in hospital and a load of tests, it turned out that all he was suffering from was an 'irritable bowel', which back in my day was known as the two-bob-bits. And there was me putting money on green parrot disease! It wouldn't have done during the war, you know. I remember one time a crew mate of mine lost both his legs to a depth-charge. Not so much as a "Blimey, that stung!" left his lips. I took some grapes over to the infirmary the morning after and he was up and about like nothing had happened. Different calibre of people back then. Tough as old boots they were.

Uncle Albert

For the sixth series' penultimate episode, John Sullivan wanted to peel back some of the bravado of Derek Trotter: "Everyone reaches an age when they become aware of their own mortality, and I wanted Del to be in that position. Also, I'd always made it clear throughout the series that Del was terrified of doctors and dentists – or, indeed, any member of the medical profession. I also wanted to see the reaction of Rodney and the rest of the family to the possibility of losing their leader – the top dog in the household."

When an ailing Del discovers that Albert's friend Elsie Partridge is a spiritual medium, he begins to see pound signs. *Sickness and Wealth* marks the only appearance in the series of Elsie Partridge, played by noted screen actress Constance Chapman. Elsie was first mentioned in the previous episode *The Unlucky Winner Is...* as an expectant Albert is preparing for a cosy night in the flat with her. It is also from Elsie's home that Albert phones Del at the end of *Little Problems,* and in 2001's *If They Could See Us Now...!*, it is revealed that Albert had been living with Elsie and her family in Weston-Super-Mare for several years. 2002's *Strangers on the Shore...!* further adds to their tale as we learn that Albert and Elsie fell in love before the war only to lose touch and meet again years later; a classic case, according to Del, of "Captain Pirelli's mandarin".

To host Elsie's dummy run séance, Del hires out the room above the Nags

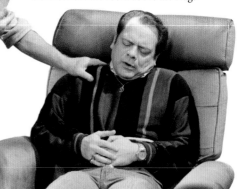

Head and invites his mates. Here the full gang are on fine form, with Roger Lloyd Pack and John Challis getting some wonderful lines and a welcome reappearance from barmaid 'Nervous' Nerys, last seen in *Dates*.

After Albert asks Elsie to conjure up a foreboding message from Joan Trotter (the only person Del would ever take notice of), Del finally decides to see a doctor about his mysterious stomach pains.

Actress Josephine Welcome was cast as the no-nonsense Peckham GP, Doctor Shaheed, in the story.

"I had been a big fan of the series from the start," Welcome remembers. "I had worked with Tony Dow before and he got in touch about the part, saying that he saw this doctor as being dressed in a traditional sari but having a 'posh' English accent! John Sullivan's dialogue is perfectly written, so it was pure joy to act it out with David Jason."

Welcome found the process of recording in front of the Television Centre audience an enjoyable aspect of the job: "There's a great atmosphere of excitement and anticipation when a studio audience is in to watch such a well-loved series like *Only Fools*. In a way it's like being on stage in theatre. Things can go wrong, sometimes hilariously, which studio audiences enjoy, but unlike in theatre you can do another take!"

When Doctor Shaheed refers an increasingly worried Del to hospital, he is eventually put under the care of Doctor Robbie Meadows, played by Scottish actor Ewan Stewart. Stewart would go on to memorably appear as First Officer Murdoch in James Cameron's 1997 blockbuster *Titanic*.

Perhaps *Sickness and Wealth*'s most powerful moments fall at the end of the story, after Doctor Meadows gives Del the news that he's basically OK (a straightforward case of irritable bowel syndrome) and hands him a prescription. As Meadows exits, the camera stays on Del and we see all the bravado completely slip away in a beautifully played and powerful moment from David Jason.

"With someone like David acting in a scene like that," recalled Sullivan, "you know you've got gold dust, because David is so good. The moment when he cries as he realises there's nothing wrong with him – to pull that off is absolutely brilliant. He opens up and admits he's terrified."

The closing moments of the episode see Del back in the flat attempting to take to a new healthy diet. It is then that he receives some news that *really* irritates his bowel: Rodney and Cassandra have got engaged!

THE SÉANCE

MAKE CONTACT OR MONEY BACK

TUESDAY 31 JAN 7.30 ADMISSION £2.50

Opposite page top: "Is there anybody there? If anybody is there, talk to us. Say something" – Elsie Partridge (Constance Chapman).

Above left: The newly made set of the Nags Head's function room.

Above right: "Larger's off!" – Nerys is given another fright!

Above: The poster Del has run off to promote Elsie's séance.

Left: Dr Shaheed (Josephine Welcome).

Below middle: Dr Robbie Meadows (Ewan Stewart) and the set of Del's hospital ward.

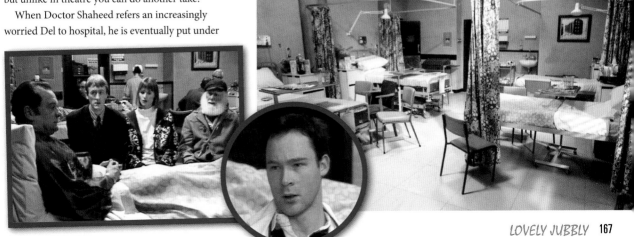

This'll let them know we're around

General Lectric Company
See we've even got a list of directors.

They'll see our high profile coming
a mile off.

Above: Del aims to impress with his new letterhead stationery – "Del, thanks to your high profile we now have a company called TIT and a director with DIC after his name."

Above right: The original prop of the letterhead expanded the final joke by giving Del the initials L.A.R.D.Y. after his name. The prop also featured three prompt lines for David Jason.

Above right: Del demonstrates to Mike the wonders of his mobile phone...

Below: Rodney finally gets his diploma, with a little help from Del and a bung of 150 quid!

Below: The heads of two great households meeting for the first time. Del and Cassandra's dad, Alan Parry (Denis Lill).

To close *Only Fools'* sixth series, John Sullivan had been gradually building up towards Rodney's wedding, but the title of the episode was an intentional misdirection:

"The phrase 'Little Problem' is sometimes used to mean that someone's pregnant – so it's supposed to fool you into thinking that Rodney and Cassandra are getting married because she's having a baby," remembered Sullivan. "But the little problems were actually to do with Del trying to handle a pair of gangsters and keeping his promise to Rodney by taking a beating rather than paying his debt."

To set up this menacing plot, Sullivan decided to finally introduce the mysterious Driscoll Brothers:

"The Driscolls were based on a family of criminals called the Richardsons. When I was growing up, the Richardsons ruled South London. We offered the role of the older Driscoll brother to Anthony Hopkins. He wanted to play the part but was filming something called *The*

Silence of the Lambs! I wrote to him and said 'You should have stuck with me, Anthony – I would have made you rich.'"

To eventually play the elder Driscoll, the celebrated actor Roy Marsden was cast, then best known for his appearance as Adam Dalgliesh in ITVs P. D. James adaptations. "Roy Marsden was brilliant," Sullivan remembered. "I thought he was very good as Danny Driscoll." Joining Marsden as Tony Driscoll was actor Christopher Ryan, remembered for his role as Mike in *The Young Ones*.

Together the duo make a formidable pair with great visual humour coming from their height differences and menacing stance.

In a nice touch of continuity, Sullivan

had already established in *Sickness and Wealth* that Mickey Pearce and Jevon had started trading together, which pre-empts their now dealing with troublesome mobile phones and the Driscolls.

"I had to rewrite the scene where Mickey and Jevon are seen to have been badly beaten up by the Driscoll brothers, as Patrick Murray had a fall and split his arm open," remembered Sullivan. "He had been in hospital and had his arm in a sling. So I decided to write his injury into the script to make it look as if the Driscolls had hurt him. Patrick was lucky, because otherwise he would have had to miss an episode."

"I'd been in the hospital over the weekend and on the Monday I got a cab to the rehearsal rooms for 8am, and no one was there," Pat Murray recalls. "Then a couple of minutes later everyone started turning up and they were all wearing false broken arm and broken leg injuries and they were all hobbling about. To make me feel at home they had all been to the special effects department and got dressed up as if they were also injured, which was a really lovely thing!"

Before the Driscoll brothers are introduced however, Sullivan uses a brilliant piece of creative

misdirection, as another mysterious and stern figure comes across to Del in the Nags Head... only it turns out to be Alan Parry, Rodney's soon to be father-in-law. A familiar BBC comedy face, New Zealand actor Dennis Lill was cast as Alan. Later in the story we meet Cassandra's mother, played by cult TV favourite Wanda Ventham.

After a game of 'hide and seek' in the room above the Nags Head (in which Del gets the aerial of one his dodgy mobile phones lodged up his nose) the Driscolls finally confront Del, warning him that if he doesn't pay up for the mobile phones, they will have no choice but to pay him with violence. Del, who has already promised to give Rodney the money as a wedding present, has a very difficult decision to make.

The story then moves on to Rodney's stag do, complete with a stand-up comic. For this, John Sullivan decided to invite one of *Only Fools'* very own studio warm up artist for the part, comedian, Jeff Stevenson.

Above: "You still haven't got the hang of those revolving doors, have you?"

Above: In the upstairs room of the Nags Head, Danny Driscoll (Roy Marsden) and Tony Driscoll (Christopher Ryan) catch up with Del, Mickey and Jevon.

Left: Rodney's stag do comic (Jeff Stevenson) – "So remember, Rodney, marriage is like a self-service restaurant – you get what you want, you see what your mates got and you want some of that!"

Below: A drunken Rodney proudly tells Denzil that Del is giving him the deposit for his new home...

LITTLE PROBLEMS

12 FEBRUARY 1989

I took no personal pleasure in doing what had to be done to Del. I've never had a problem with him. He even did Tony and I a favour once. Back when we did our first stint in borstal, it was Del who kept an eye on our Mum, making sure she had enough groceries and a few hooky bags of coal to see her through the winter. What a lovely and thoughtful gesture. I returned the favour of course, and as soon as I was released I popped straight down to Woolworths and got him a box of Quality Street. That said, the simple fact of the matter is that what we did had to be done. He owed us money, and if we'd let it slide with him, others would get the impression that we'd gone soft. It's also important to let Tony off his leash to get a bit of practice in from time to time. If I don't he starts to pine and chew on the furniture. And while it's true that many do frown upon this particular aspect of our profession, you can't deny that we are very, very good at it. Even at school it was the same. You could say that we were blessed with a natural gift for inflicting pain and misery on people. We were at one point considering going into the social services sector, but we always preferred a more hands on approach. At the end of the day you have to play to your strengths.

Danny Driscoll

"In 1977 I was working on a sitcom pilot for Denis Main Wilson when he introduced me to a scene-shifter called John 'who was going to be a great comedy writer'," remembers Stevenson. "John remembered me from this meeting, and he recommended me to Ray Butt." Shortly afterwards Stevenson was cast in the *Citizen Smith* episode *The Glorious Day* and later as PC Parker in *To Hull and Back*, before being invited to take on the job of audience warm-up for *Only Fools*.

For Stevenson, being on the other side of the camera didn't feel particularly unusual as the cast always made him feel like one of them when he was on warm-up duties.

"I loved being a cast member. I was at rehearsals right from the start and it was one of the best weeks of my career," remembers Stevenson. While Sullivan had carefully scripted the dialogue for his scene, the faded-down background material was actually from Stevenson's act, with some lines ad-libbed in rehearsals and then kept in.

On the night of the recording Stevenson had some fun with the audience: "I actually did the warm-up that night and when it came to my scene I told the audience I was just off to earn a bit of overtime – or something like that – and we did my scene in one take."

The stag do segment gave Paul Barber a wonderfully sensitive scene to act with Nicholas Lyndhurst, a moment that only the kind-hearted Denzil could deliver. Here, Lyndhurst plays the drunken Rodney brilliantly.

For production designer Graham Lough, the final episodes of the series

required him to build an upstairs back room for the now TARDIS-like Nags Head. This set was introduced in *Sickness and Wealth* as the setting for the séance. In *Little Problems* it would be used for the Driscolls' confrontation with Del and the wedding reception. The same set would also be dusted down and used again in series seven's *Class of '62*.

Lough also had the distinction of designing the Trotter flat's bathroom, as well as the registry office where Rodney and Cassandra marry: "I based the wedding venue on the Registry Office of Acton Town Hall, which I passed every day on my way to work," remembers Lough. "We generally didn't get the script until the start of the week so there was no time to come up with fancy concepts for the new sets and present them to the director. As long as the sets were shootable and conformed with the style of the show, nobody worried that much."

To bridge the wedding ceremony with the reception scene, Sullivan decided to use the recently released Mica Paris and Will Downing version of the soul classic 'Where is the Love' which fits the moment perfectly as Rod and Cass sign their wedding certificate. On this certificate the eagle-eyed viewer will notice that Reg Trotter's occupation is listed as 'porter', a subtle nod to 1983's *Thicker than Water*.

Opposite page top right: Tony Driscoll looks on as Danny gives Del an ultimatum: "If you don't come up with the two grand I'm gonna take his collar and lead off and let him loose on you."

Above left: Sat in the Trotter flat's bathroom, Del is in a bad way after taking the hiding from the Driscolls.

Above right: The set of the Trotters' bathroom.

Left: Rodney with a learner sign super-glued to his pants.

Left: The cast and crew of *Little Problems* pose for a celebratory photo on the registry office set. From left to right, Adrian Pegg, David Jason, production assistant Amita Lochab, Nicholas Lyndhurst, Gareth Gwenlan, Tony Dow (seated), Gwyneth Strong, Buster Merryfield and assistant floor manager Kerry Waddel.

Below middle: The proud mother of the bride, Pamela Parry (Wanda Ventham).

Below: The packed registry office set for Rodney and Cassandra's wedding.

Below right: The Registrar (Derek Benfield) conducts the service.

Opposite page top: The wedding reception, held in the Nags Head's function room. Here the brothers say farewell and Del and Marlene share a passionate kiss under the wrathful eyes of Boyce and Duke. Eventually Del is left alone with his thoughts, holding the 'groom' wedding cake decoration and wondering where all the years have gone.

Opposite page below right: "It's just that, well, how can I put it? You don't live here no more!"

The biggest musical contribution to the story, however, was the use of Simply Red's 1985 hit 'Holding Back the Years'. The haunting melody and lyrics perfectly sum up where Del finds himself at the end of *Little Problems,* as well as the gradual mood of change across the series as a whole.

"I remember in the rehearsal room John playing 'Holding Back the Years' on his cassette recorder when we got to the reception scene," remembers Jeff Stevenson. "I had never seen cast and crew getting emotional at a read through."

The warm-hearted mood of the reception turns to melancholy as Del is left alone and the tune takes hold. This follows a tender moment with Marlene which allows the character to put Sullivan's heartbreaking words to his feelings. Del, who gave the money to Rodney and took 'payment' from the Driscolls, reminds us of his duty of care to his kid brother, and the promise he made to their late mother.

"I loved every moment of drama, maybe because we didn't have enough of it," recalls Tony Dow. "If we had film, I would have certainly found an amazing wedding location and put him out under a night sky somewhere. But as we were stuck in the studio the thing I got was a crane, so I was able take the camera and pull further and further out."

Despite Dow's frustrations with the budget, the closing moments of the wedding reception make for an incredibly powerful scene that ranks amongst the most moving in the series' history.

As the last notes of 'Holding back the Years' fade into the final scene in the flat, it is almost a relief to see Del back in the suit of armour of his duffle coat as he rushes in to answer the phone. Sullivan decided not to offer viewers a quick fix here as it seems that even Albert has moved on. Del is truly alone for the first time.

"I had two or three letters from mothers asking me to write to their kids and reassure them that Del was alright," remembered Sullivan. "They were worried about him being all on his own. I had to write to them and describe Del's wonderful, busy social life with Trigger and Boycie and the boys!"

Just as the episode ends, we are rewarded with a familiar muffled sound of the flat's front door opening, and then in comes Rodney, cruising on auto pilot and temporarily oblivious to the fact that he doesn't live there anymore! A perfect way to close an impeccable series of *Only Fools*.

Broadcast on six consecutive Sunday evenings at 7.15pm from 8 January 1989, audience figures for *Only Fools*' first 50-minute series steadily grew from 13.9 million viewers watching *Yuppy Love* to 18.9 million viewers tuning in to see Rodney tie the knot in *Little Problems*.

During the making of the sixth series of *Only Fools*, transmission was a week behind recording, so as the cast prepared to go before cameras for *Little Problems*, *Sickness and Wealth* was airing on BBC 1 that same evening.

"They were coming back with amazing viewing figures," remembers Tony Dow, "and everyone was talking about it. But by the end of the series, I can remember us all being completely and utterly drained."

You might have noticed that I have a slight tendency to moan about Rodney every now and then, but he moans about me too. That's what brothers do. But when he stepped up and tied the knot with Cassandra, I really couldn't have been any prouder. The boy had grown up and was ready to face the world on his own. He had a new wife, a new flat and, thanks to his new father-in-law, Alan, a cushty new job. The time had come for me to pull back my protective wing and let him go. I'm not ashamed to admit that I did shed a tear or two (I shed even more when he came back, but we'll get to that in a minute) and a part of me envied him. That said, I knew deep down that if I could just hold on for a bit longer, my time would come.

Del

THE JOLLY BOYS' OUTING

★ ★

As much as I enjoyed the high pressure, dog-eat-dog, seat-of-your-y-fronts world of free enterprise, it was very important to pencil in the occasional bit of 'downtime' (or 'Are and Are' as they say on Wall Street). As I'd discovered during a chat with Cassandra's boss, Stephen, baseball was all the rage with the yuppies. A few rounds of badminton didn't go a miss either. Oh yes, there was nothing us upwardly mobile mob liked more than whacking things around with a bat. I made a note of it in my Filofax and dug for more info, and that's when Stephen spoke very highly of weekend breaks in the Serengeti. Apparently sunrise over the Kilimanjaro is a real mind-blower. That's all well and good, I thought, but why give yourself the jet-lag when you and your mates can just as easily jump on a coach and head off for a good old fashioned beano to Margate? There might not be as many wildebeests involved, but with roller-coasters, pina colada on tap, scampi in a basket and as much jellied eels as your guts can handle, what's not to like?

★ ★ ★ ★ ★ ★ ★ ★ ★ ★ ★ ★ ★ ★

THE JOLLY BOYS' OUTING

25 DECEMBER 1989

What a beano that turned out to be. I'd always wondered what an exploding coach would look like, and now I know. Some of the lads were quick to blame the Musta F80 in-car radio that I'd had fitted to the dashboard (free of charge, I might add), but there was nothing wrong with the Musta, and just because that's where the flames originated, don't mean it was the cause. Anyway, if it hadn't been for that, we wouldn't have ended up at the Villa Bella, and if we hadn't ended up at the Villa Bella we wouldn't have snuck out to grab a bit of scampi and take in a show. Cos that's where fate stepped in. The singer had just finished mangling Billy Joel, when on came a magic act: the 'Great Ramondo' and his lovely assistant, Raquel. I weren't paying too much attention at first as I still hadn't quite got over the lobster vindaloo and fourteen pina coladas I'd had for lunch, but suffice it to say that Ramondo was doing something very magical with a pigeon. It was then I noticed his assistant, Raquel... MY RAQUEL!!! I very discreetly caught her attention by whistling and shouting out "Raquel, over here!" and the rest... well the rest was history. All in all it was very much a case of Le gant de la vie, as they've been known to say in the Latin Quarter.

Del

Less than two months after the sixth series completed its run, the *Only Fools* team were back in action, preparing to film the 1989 Christmas special.

The idea of taking the Trotters out of Peckham on a coastal outing had been something writer John Sullivan had been considering since 1983. In a handwritten document ('ideas for third series') the writer made note of "The Jolly Boys' Outing to ~~Marg~~ (the beginning of 'Margate' crossed out) Southend". Giving the title as 'The Outing', it would be another six years before the writer would revisit the premise.

"The idea behind this episode came from a story told to me by my sister-in-law, Penny, about her father's annual company beano," remembered Sullivan. "They used to go on a 'Jolly Boys' Outing' to Margate, which I thought was such a lovely title. In the past, beanos were the kind of thing everyone did. I've been on a few myself to Southend and Margate, so the episode was also based on my own experiences."

"I can remember going on the reccie," director Tony Dow recollects. "Southend just didn't work so we went to Margate. All the local council people were there and basically said 'we'll do anything you want, just make sure you don't make Margate look horrible'. The day of this reccie was terrible, wet and over-cast, and I was looking around and said – 'bloody hell, I'm a director, not a miracle worker!'"

Location filming for *The Jolly Boys' Outing* was arranged to take place between 1–22 May, with three days in the studio from the 2 June. With the decision made to set the beano in Margate, it was decided to base the majority of the location filming for the episode in the Thanet area with cast and crew staying in Ramsgate Harbour's Marina Resort hotel.

The story opens with Del working his market pitch to a bustling crowd, flogging his latest, groundbreaking line in audio electronics: the Musta F80 In-Car Radio (with a free Kylie Minogue LP thrown in for good measure). This market scene was filmed in the car park/market of Ramsgate's Greyhound Stadium.

The story soon comes back to a studio segment in a brand-new set for the series, Rodney and Cassandra's flat. Here the Trotter and Parry families are joined by Cassandra's yuppy boss at the bank, Stephen (brilliantly played by Daniel Hill) and his wife Joanne (played by *Emmerdale* actress Gail Harrison) for a dinner party and a spot of *Trivial Pursuit*. In this scene, Del's embarrassing answer ("It's a Bic!") cuts across Rodney and Cassandra's dinner party guests to the opening bars of Banarama's 'Help', as the action goes straight to the Jolly Boys' coach.

With the vehicle in constant motion and the view from the windows constantly changing, the crew found that continuity was a massive problem, but the results were well worth the effort as the regular cast and some 20 extras bring the proceedings to life.

"Shooting all that stuff on the coach was always a nightmare, but it was a great piece," remembers Tony Dow.

Later in this scene we see the Peckham crew stop off at the 'halfway house', in reality the Roman Galley pub, located on the Thanet Way, just ten miles from Margate.

Opposite page top right: Shots taken on the original reccie for the episode.

Opposite far left: Del selling the Musta F80 In-Car Radio.

Opposite page middle: Cassandra's boss from the bank, Stephen (Daniel Hill), joins the Trotter and Parry families in Rodney and Cassandra's new flat.

Above: Filming on the coach, director Tony Dow can be seen behind Nicholas Lyndhurst.

Below left: The cast and crew pose outside the 'halfway house'. The regular cast are joined by (left to right), production assistant Amita Lochab, lighting cameraman Alec Curtis, Tony Dow, Gareth Gwenlan, John Sullivan, sound recordist John Parry, Adrian Pegg, locations manager Duncan Cooper and assistant floor manager Angie de Chastelai Smith.

Above: Arriving in Margate the Jolly Boys enjoy the delights of a day out by the seaside and at the Dreamland amusement park, where Trigger adopts an inflatable dolphin.

Below right: The cast got to enjoy the golden beaches that were drenched in sunshine for the entirety of the spring location shoot.

Below: The gang from Peckham board Margate's historic scenic railway. The shots below show the cast in the boarding section of the ride, which is still open today.

After Rodney's brief detention at a police station (due to some misplaced football skills in the car park of the halfway house), the beano is back on, and we are treated to a wonderful montage showing the characters enjoying the day. All played out under Harry Nilsson's classic recording of 'Everybody's Talkin', it perfectly summed up a blissful day spent on both the beach and at Margate's Dreamland Amusement park.

For this sequence, production manager Adrian Pegg had the unenviable task of making sure the sizeable cast were where they should be and that filming at each location went smoothly, including factoring in a helicopter shot following the Jolly Boys'

coach and taking in the whole of Margate seafront. Also adding to Pegg's complications was getting the series' three lead actors back to London for an award ceremony, requiring some careful planning.

"I knew about the award, and I knew that getting David and Nick back to London was going to impact the schedule. But I also knew that we needed a helicopter shot, so I simply scheduled the helicopter shot on the day of the awards, so David and Nick could use that very helicopter to get back to London quickly!"

"The day we arrived, the sun came out and it stayed all the time we were there," recalls Tony Dow. "It was a very happy time as we were all together, but poor old Adrian had a nightmare. Every time we went for a take he had to yell 'please shut up!' The cast and extras were just so undisciplined and having a great time!"

"For a montage, there will have been many shots that Tony knew he wanted, but much of it will have been created as opportunities presented themselves," remembers Pegg. "There is a lovely shot of Uncle Albert driving a toy boat – that definitely came about when someone noticed the character in the boat looked like him."

This scene holds special memories for Micky Pearce actor Patrick Murray, as it was his son Ricky who was in control of Albert's rival toy boat:

THE JOLLY BOYS OUTING NAGS HEAD PECKHAM 1989

"Instead of staying in a local hotel where everyone else stayed, I found this caravan site that was stuck between Margate and Ramsgate, I got all the family in, and I stayed there for the whole shoot. Filming down in Margate was fantastic, and when we got to the bit where they wanted to have Uncle Albert controlling a remote-control boat, Adrian said to me, 'I hope you don't mind Pat but we haven't cast the boy who crashes his boat into Uncle Albert's ship, you don't mind if we use your son?' And Ricky was spot on, they even used a picture of him with Uncle Albert in the end credits!"

"The shoot was brilliant, it was a great laugh," remembered Sullivan. "I enjoy it tremendously whenever I write an episode that includes all the characters, but it does

become a slightly schizophrenic experience, because you're going from one character's thoughts to another's, and trying to stay true to each of them. You end up with a bit of a migraine! But those episodes are worth the trouble when you pull them off."

"One thing that caused a lot of grief was when we were shooting the scene on the harbour wall with Del and Rodney," recalls Pegg. "You could see the theme park, especially the big wheel, and Tony wanted it to be going round. The problem was that the theme park was closed and this hadn't been thought of in advance, so one of the team had to go back to try to get it going. We were out of walkie talkie range and of course we had no mobile phones, so trying to coordinate this was very difficult, but in the end the moment we saw that it was going, we shot the scene."

Above top: The main cast of the series posed for dozens of photos in and around the rides at Dreamland.

Far left: Tony Dow and Adrian Pegg look up at Dreamland's 'Mary Rose' ride.

Above middle: Denzil actor Paul Barber wore a camera as part of his costume and captured these (and many other) shots of the cast as they filmed in Margate.

Above: The distinctive hand-drawn poster which was on the side windows of the Jolly Boys' coach.

Far left: Patrick Murray's son Ricky played Uncle Albert's radio-controlled model boat rival in this lovely scene.

Left: The beano montage ends with the Trotter brothers sat at the end of Margate's harbour arm, reflecting on the day – "I've really enjoyed meself... I'm feeling a bit cream-crackered now, though. I think I might have a touch of that yuppy-flu."

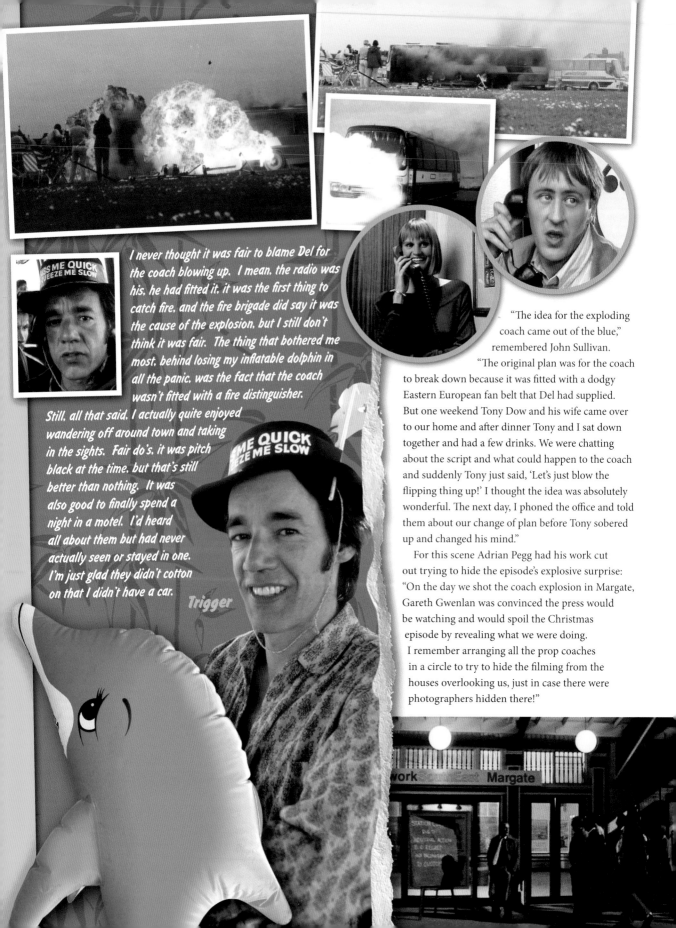

I never thought it was fair to blame Del for the coach blowing up. I mean, the radio was his, he had fitted it, it was the first thing to catch fire, and the fire brigade did say it was the cause of the explosion, but I still don't think it was fair. The thing that bothered me most, behind losing my inflatable dolphin in all the panic, was the fact that the coach wasn't fitted with a fire distinguisher.

Still, all that said, I actually quite enjoyed wandering off around town and taking in the sights. Fair do's, it was pitch black at the time, but that's still better than nothing. It was also good to finally spend a night in a motel. I'd heard all about them but had never actually seen or stayed in one. I'm just glad they didn't cotton on that I didn't have a car.

Trigger

"The idea for the exploding coach came out of the blue," remembered John Sullivan. "The original plan was for the coach to break down because it was fitted with a dodgy Eastern European fan belt that Del had supplied. But one weekend Tony Dow and his wife came over to our home and after dinner Tony and I sat down together and had a few drinks. We were chatting about the script and what could happen to the coach and suddenly Tony just said, 'Let's just blow the flipping thing up!' I thought the idea was absolutely wonderful. The next day, I phoned the office and told them about our change of plan before Tony sobered up and changed his mind."

For this scene Adrian Pegg had his work cut out trying to hide the episode's explosive surprise: "On the day we shot the coach explosion in Margate, Gareth Gwenlan was convinced the press would be watching and would spoil the Christmas episode by revealing what we were doing. I remember arranging all the prop coaches in a circle to try to hide the filming from the houses overlooking us, just in case there were photographers hidden there!"

For the explosion reaction shot, Sullivan knew it was important to get Rodney's gaze from the phone box just right. "Nick played the scene so well and it was put together brilliantly. The timing is great – Rodney's trying to convince Cassandra that Del isn't such a walking disaster, just as he turns and sees the explosion! His look of disbelief as he tells her the coach has blown up is wonderful."

To allow for a seamless sequence of film which could be edited in advance of the audience recording, a section of one of the rooms at the crew hotel in Ramsgate was dressed as Rodney and Cassandra's flat. Here Gwyneth Strong was filmed for her half of the phone conversation.

With no coach and no trains running, the Jolly Boys go their separate ways in the hope of picking up an odd room for the night. Here Del, Rodney and Albert have the worst luck. First teased by a vacancy sign at Mrs Baker's guest house (where a fluffy cat falls in love with Albert's beard), they eventually find a room at the spooky Villa Bella. To play the stern hotelier, Mrs. Creswell, Rosalind Knight was cast, with Brigid Erin Bates joining her as Inga. Sullivan named Mrs Creswell after his son Jim's teacher in class '4C' (which would later inspire Del's class name in *Class of '62*).

Both exterior guest house scenes were filmed in Margate's Dalby Square.

In a scene recorded in the studio but cut from broadcast, Del would briefly meet two more of Mrs Creswell's unfortunate guests, a northern couple named Arthur and Betty, played by Michael Bilton and Fanny Carby. Ironically, this would be unlucky Bilton's second deleted scene from *Only Fools* after he was also cut from *Friday the 14th*.

Unable to sleep, Rodney vents his jealousy over Cassandra and Stephen's relationship (as well as Uncle Albert's beard which, having been forced to share a bed with the old man of the sea, keeps tickling him). After Del works his magic in persuading Rodney to venture out, the Trotter brothers head to the Mardi Gras club and it is here that they bump into Boycie, Trigger and Mike.

Opposite page: "Alright, look, I agree that Del gets a bit out of hand, but I think it's unfair to say that everything he touches goes wrong!" – The Jolly Boys' coach explodes... and the travellers head to the railway station.

Above left: The Trotters' hopes of a nice meal and lodgings are dashed at Mrs. Bakers guesthouse...

Above: ...but they find a place to stay at the Villa Bella, with its host Mrs. Creswell (Rosalind Knight).

Left: A shot from the deleted scene where Del meets Arthur and Betty in the Villa Bella's 'Semprini Room'.

Below: The cast pose for a fun photo as David Jason squeezes into the bed Rodney and Albert are sharing.

Above: At the Mardi Gras, Trigger spots a familiar face on stage...

Right: One of the original tickets for the Mardi Gras used in the episode.

Below: Raquel and the Great Ramondo (Robin Driscoll).

Below inset: The Margate Mardi Gras' lounge singer (Lee Gibson).

Below right: Del and Raquel are reunited.

Opposite page below left right: Back at Raquel's flat, Del is surprised to find Ramondo.

Opposite page far right: "So let me run this past you, Stephen. Try and get your head round this." – Returning home, Rodney thinks Stephen is there alone with Cassandra...

Frustratingly for fans watching the episode on home video, the opening segment of this scene, in which Del and Rodney discuss scampi and the finer points of married life (as well as the results of Alan Parry's overindulgence in whelks) has been cut. This was due to musical clearances of a cover version of Billy Joel's 1977 hit 'Just the Way You Are', sung by the Mardi Gras' resident singer (played by Lee Gibson).

As no suitable interior could be found in Margate itself, the production team filmed these scenes at the Top Hat Club on Northfield Avenue in Ealing. It is here, at the the Mardi Gras club, and much to the surprise of viewers (and Del Boy himself), that Tessa Peake-Jones makes a welcome return as Raquel.

"I was working on a different series in Norfolk when my agent phoned and said 'I've got an odd request, Tony Dow would like to talk to you,'" remembers Peake-Jones. "I thought he was just calling to say 'hey, it went really well, congratulations'. Anyway, he said 'the public's reaction has been very positive about this other woman for Del. How do you feel if we were to put you into the series?'"

Weighing up the demands of taking on a role in such a popular series, it was hearing Sullivan's future plans for the character that won over the actress, and she agreed to return to the role on a permanent basis.

Peake-Jones' first scenes as a regular were as a magician's assistant on stage in Ealing, alongside actor and comedy writer Robin Driscoll who was cast as The Great Ramondo.

"Robin was terrified of birds, and I don't like them either," recalls Peake-Jones, "so it was quite odd having those birds on stage. The Great Soprendo, Victoria Wood's husband, was the magician's adviser and I remember him saying 'are neither of you that keen on birds then!?' So that was quite tricky to film."

With the couple reunited, a merry Del and a worried Rodney return to the Villa Bella only to discover that they have been locked out. After Del attempts to rouse Albert by throwing a stone up at their window (shattering the window in the process), he decides to call upon Raquel's hospitality. It is then, at Raquel's flat, that he has a marvellously comic misunderstanding with Raquel's flat mate, the Great Ramondo himself.

For the climax of this scene, Jason and Driscoll practised their brief fight at length in the rehearsal rooms, but on the night of the recording things appeared a little different: "The geography of the set had changed a tiny bit and I thought I was in danger of cracking my skull open on a doorknob," Driscoll recalls. "Luckily, a stuntman showed me a trick of the trade that saved me some pain."

Del, who believes the strictly professional and caustic Ramondo is bullying Raquel (as well as sleeping with her), ends up punching him on the nose, a rash and ill advised course of action that still wins him a kiss from Raquel. The following day, after the replacement coach brings the Jolly Boys back to Peckham, Rodney returns to his flat to discover Cassandra's boss Stephen is there, seemingly alone with Cass. Enraged and inspired by Del's actions, Rodney runs a punch past Stephen, just as the banker's wife Joanne enters, explaining that they'd only popped in to drop off some holiday brochures. We don't see the fall-out, but Rodney shortly ends up back at Nelson Mandela House with a full suitcase in tow.

The episode closes with a montage of highlights of the beano, accompanied by a special version of Chas & Dave's brilliant song *Margate*. With Jason and Lyndhurst adding a few vocals, it finally fulfilled Sullivan's original brief of getting the popular duo to provide the music for *Only Fools*.

Broadcast at 4.05pm on Christmas Day 1989, *The Jolly Boys' Outing* won *Only Fools*' highest ratings to date with some 20.12 million viewers.

In every way imaginable *The Jolly Boys' Outing* is a perfect piece of television with every second a delight. After years of seeing the Peckham gang in the studio, it is simply magic to see them all having a great time on location in such a warm and well written story. With that, it is no surprise that it ranks as many a fan's favourite and most cherished episode.

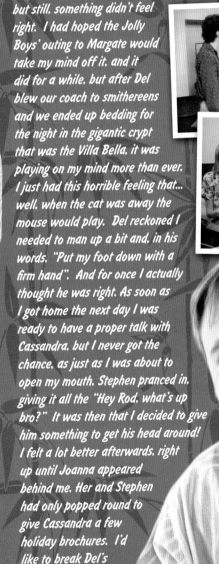

I wasn't normally the jealous type, but there was just something about that Stephen that rubbed me up the wrong way. His missus, Joanna, weren't much better, what with all the "Oh yahs" and the "Absolutely Farntarstics!" But it wasn't just how Stephen said pratty things like "Let me run this one past you" and "Try to get your head around this", it was the way he was with Cass. And alright, he was her boss at the bank and she was after promotion, but still, something didn't feel right. I had hoped the Jolly Boys' outing to Margate would take my mind off it, and it did for a while, but after Del blew our coach to smithereens and we ended up bedding for the night in the gigantic crypt that was the Villa Bella, it was playing on my mind more than ever. I just had this horrible feeling that... well, when the cat was away the mouse would play. Del reckoned I needed to man up a bit and, in his words, "Put my foot down with a firm hand". And for once I actually thought he was right. As soon as I got home the next day I was ready to have a proper talk with Cassandra, but I never got the chance, as just as I was about to open my mouth, Stephen pranced in, giving it all the "Hey Rod, what's up bro?" It was then that I decided to give him something to get his head around! I felt a lot better afterwards, right up until Joanna appeared behind me. Her and Stephen had only popped round to give Cassandra a few holiday brochures. I'd like to break Del's neck sometimes, I really would!

Rodney

RODNEY COME HOME

A new decade was upon us and things were finally looking up. Alan hadn't sacked Rodney yet and the boy was doing wonders for that computer department. Of course, it meant that Albert was now my official look-out. Having spent many the hour in crows nests, keeping watch for icebergs, pirates, giant squids and what 'av you, his mince pies were surprisingly sharp for a man of his age, but stone me he didn't 'alf moan a lot. Normally I'd have docked his wages, but I'd been in a very forgiving mood since Raquel had moved into the flat with us. We'd agreed to take it steady this time, like sensible and responsible grown ups do. I kipped in my bedroom and she kipped in Rodney's old room. You see, I'd matured a great deal over the years. The crass, brash, one-track-mind Del Boy of old was no more, and I couldn't have been happier. I was also quietly confident that with just the right ambience and a very gentle approach, she would one day soon agree to stamp my card. Yep, it was time to dust off the old Richard Clayderman LP. Lovely jubbly!

RODNEY COME HOME

25 DECEMBER 1990

Everything was going to plan. Raquel and I had just finished a very romantic dinner, the lights were low and there was just the merest hint of soft piano wafting from the stereo. I'd already laid the groundwork and was just about to reach the critical moment, when in burst Rodney! Him and Cassandra had broken up and, according to Rodney, this time it was for good! I dunno what it was with them two, they hadn't been married two years and they'd already broken up more times than J.R. and Sue Ellen! Rodney dealt with it all in a very mature fashion, seeking support from two of his oldest mates, Jim Beam and Ron Bacardi. Unfortunately, he also turned to Mickey Pearce, who advised him to make Cassandra jealous. Well, you know you've hit rock bottom when you're getting relationship advice from Mickey Pearce. The only time he ever made women jealous was the night he won the last house at bingo! Worse still, that dozy little twonk had taken the advice on board and gone and got himself a date with the receptionist at the Peckham Exhaust Center. There was only one thing for it. I had to warn Cassandra. I didn't wanna do it, but I was sure that in her heart of hearts she'd understand.

Del

Although for viewers *Only Fools* was last seen on Christmas Day 1989, when the cast and crew were reunited to start making the next series of episodes, it had been some 16 months since they were last together. In the interim, David Jason had just started what would become a 20-year association with Yorkshire Television, beginning with the leading role in the comedy-drama *A Bit of a Do*, followed swiftly by the first episodes of the hugely popular series, *The Darling Buds of May*.

For the first time, *Only Fools'* leading actor's availability set the schedule for the series, something which would be an ongoing issue.

As the 50-minute episodes had been a great success, the BBC were keen to commission more, and with Christmas approaching, thought turned to factoring in a special.

"I originally wrote *Rodney Come Home* as the first episode of series seven," recalled John Sullivan, "but the BBC said to me that if I wanted to extend it, they'd make it a Christmas special. So we used it to set the scene for the new series. It was all about Rodney and Cassandra's jealousies and problems. I wanted to start off the new series with something real – and it had to be believable so that the rest of the series made sense. It was important for the audience to understand why Rodney and Cassandra were going to be arguing for the next seven weeks!"

As well as Rodney's domestic situation, another key thread to *Rodney Come Home* was Del and Raquel taking the next step in their relationship, and for the first time in the series history we would see a permanent female resident in the flat.

With this, director Tony Dow instantly recognised a problem he might have. After successfully moving round the Nags Head set for the last series, Dow tasked incoming production designer Richard McManan-Smith to expand the series' most recognisable set: "We had to extend the Trotter flat as suddenly we had two women in the cast, and the set just wasn't big enough," remembers Dow.

By carefully extending the wall sections either side of the balcony window, McManan-Smith managed to give Dow much more space to frame shots for the expanded cast, making the set some three metres longer. Most importantly it was done in such a way that most viewers wouldn't notice. This extended set would be used from *Rodney Come Home* till 1996's *Time on our Hands*.

Location filming for *Rodney Come Home* and series seven (referred to on production paperwork as Series G) was carried out in Bristol between 7–24 October 1990, with the episodes studio recordings taking place from the 9–11 November.

After the successful location shoot in 1988, it made sense to return to Bristol once more, with the Broadwalk Shopping Centre used at the beginning of the story where we see Del and Albert attempting to sell toy dolls. For Alan Parry's printing works, the crew took over Gemini Graphics & Print Ltd, located on York Street in St Werburghs. Here, *Only Fools'* graphic designer Andrew Smee modified the Gemini logo to appear as the 'Parry Graphics & Print Ltd' logo which was seen on screen.

For the nightclub scene, production manager Adrian Pegg brought the crew back to Bristol's Parkside Hotel, where Rodney and Cassandra first danced in 1989's *Yuppy Love*: "For the night club scene we hired loads of local extras. Everything is recorded

Opposite page right: Del holds court in the Arndale Centre – "You all know me, ladies, the crusader against inflation, here to offer you yet another bargain of a lifetime!"

Above: Rodney sees Raquel walking home with bags of shopping and calls her into his office at Parry Graphics and Print.

Above: Rodney is fed up that Cassandra always seems to be wrapped up in the bank and doesn't have time for him.

Below left and below: The set of Rodney and Cassandra's flat, and a view of the corridor outside it, with the Trotter flat set visible on the other side (with Lyndhurst and Jason rehearsing).

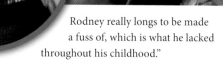

Above: Rodney leaves home (complete with his bottle of tomato sauce) and comes back to Nelson Mandela House... where he interrupts Del and Raquel's romantic dinner.

Above right: With the help of Chris and Mickey, Rodney tries to drink his way out of his marriage troubles, much to Del's disapproval.

Right: "Not now Albert!" – Del asks Albert to show his disgust at Rodney's behaviour.

Below: *Rodney Come Home* saw the introduction of the extended Trotter flat set.

Opposite page right: Del tells Cassandra what Rodney is planning... without realising that Rodney is already on his way back home to Cassandra after seeing sense.

Opposite page below left: The dramatic closing shot of the episode.

without playing the music, so the extras would be played in a basic beat track which would cut off once filming started. When you are shooting single camera it's the only way to do it, but it's weird to watch people shuffling around in silence while the dialogue is performed!"

For Rodney and Cassandra's home, Pegg found a suitably modern block of flats named Guild Court, in Redcliff Backs in Bristol.

After the happy wedding seen in *Little Problems*, Rod and Cass' struggles were alluded to in *The Jolly Boys' Outing,* and *Rodney Come Home* would bring matters to a head.

"I based Rodney and Cassandra's relationship around the fact that she was ambitious," explained Sullivan. "She was involved in the banking world – a field that Rodney believes is his strength, what with his GCE in maths. But of course, it goes too far. She's more ambitious than he wants, because

Rodney really longs to be made a fuss of, which is what he lacked throughout his childhood."

Nicholas Lyndhurst and Gwyneth Strong perfectly convey Sullivan's sensitively drawn newlyweds, with Lyndhurst stealing the show as he displays both Rodney's frustrations and sensitivity as the story reaches its conclusion.

Despite being laden with some heavy drama, *Rodney Come Home* features perhaps Uncle Albert's funniest moment in the series as he tries to follow Del's lead to appear shocked with the news

that Rodney is taking Tania (the receptionist at the Peckham Exhaust Centre) to the pictures. Buster Merryfield delivers an astoundingly good performance with magnificent comic timing as he pretends to be shocked, but always just a little *too* early – a real golden moment.

With such an emotional ending to the episode, Tony Dow decided to use an effective crane shot to pull back on Del and Rodney as they walk back to the van. In another departure, it was felt that the usual closing theme 'Hooky Street' wouldn't be appropriate for such a moment, so Sullivan chose one of his musical favourites to play over the credits: Joan Armatrading's beautiful folk tune 'Somebody Who Loves You'.

Much like *Dates*, the last feature-length special designed to open a new series, *Rodney Come Home* does a brilliant job in laying the groundwork for the six episodes to come. Broadcast at 5.10pm on Christmas Day 1990 (just five days before series seven would debut), the episode drew 18 million viewers.

Made during the production of *Rodney Come Home* was *The Robin Flies at Dawn*, a special *Only Fools* sketch written by John Sullivan for the troops serving in the Gulf War. Recorded at RAF High Wycombe and featuring Jason, Lyndhurst and Merryfield, the sketch sees the Trotters trying to sell a new secret weapon – a three-wheeled van kitted out with a machine gun! The sketch ends with an appreciative message to the troops as a group of the serving men's wives and partners join the *Only Fools* gang.

I'd made a stupid, childish threat that I never went through with. I'd had a word with myself, saw sense and was all set to make things right, completely unaware that Del Boy had already stuck his oar in! It was all thanks to him that I ended up back on the sofa at the flat, nursing a bruised shin and a perforated ear drum (Cassandra might look as though she wouldn't say boo to a goose, but get her riled up and she's like a bloody air raid siren!). I didn't know what I was gonna do. I laid there on that sofa all night trying to find an answer. At one point Albert got up for a Nelson Riddle. He did his best to cheer me up but eventually got off track and started telling me about the time a whale tried to doink his submarine. There was a moral in there somewhere, but neither I nor Albert could find it. What a life, eh?

Rodney

★ ★

Raquel and I had finally become one. A truly beautiful and tender moment that I'll never ever forget. And apart from the car alarm going off down in the precinct and the sound of Albert having a coughing fit in the bog, it was all incredibly romantic – a genuine ten-out-of-ten if ever there was one!

I was feeling perky in other ways too, since Raquel had banished the fry ups and put me on a strict regime of boiled egg and grapefruit. But whereas I was soaring high, Rodney was crashing quicker than the 1929 stock market.

Him and Cassandra still hadn't patched things up and his hormones were doing the Macarena. You could always tell when Rodney was entering the mating season, he'd get all goggly eyed and clammy and start walking like a Moby. I couldn't let it worry me too much, there were opportunities to be seized and deals to be done!

★ ★ ★ ★ ★ ★ ★ ★ ★

"There are quite a few changes at the start of series seven," recalled John Sullivan. "Raquel has moved into the flat, but not 'officially' as far as Uncle Albert's concerned. Del is quite coy about the fact that he and Raquel are now sharing a bed and he's trying to save her any embarrassment."

After extending the main flat set, production designer Richard McManan-Smith's next major task was to build Del's bedroom and outside hallway. Whilst we had seen fractions of the hallway over the years, this would be the first time it is seen in full in the series. This gave McManan-Smith a blank canvas to work out the internal geography of Trotter Towers, factoring in suitable areas for storing trading stock. Del's bedroom had never

been seen and for its debut in *The Sky's the Limit,* it doesn't disappoint. With its loud wallpaper, monstrously pink headboard and leopard print bed covers, the set oozes Del Boy.

A week after the crew had recorded the studio scenes for *Rodney Come Home,* the team reconvened to record *The Sky's the Limit* on Tuesday 19 and Wednesday 20 November 1990. With Tony Dow and the crew's attention returned to making the seventh series, the team were keen not to repeat the relentless pace of production which the first series of 50-minute episodes had endured.

"When we came back for series seven, David and Nick said 'we can't do that in a week, we've got to have ten days rehearsal'. We got our ten days, but the funny thing was, we found we didn't

THE SKY'S THE LIMIT

30 DECEMBER 1990

need ten days! We were so used to working the energy of these brilliant scripts, everyone just knew their characters. After five or six days we were all ready to go. So for those last three days I found I had to send some people home as they were going to peak too early!"

The very first scene of the series sees a bang-on trend Uncle Albert singing Kylie Minogue's 'Step Back in Time', which had only been released a few weeks before the episode was made, highlighting the attention to detail in working in contemporary references.

The episode soon sets the scene that Rodney's love life is still in the doldrums. And yet for Del, business is going very nicely, thanks to some cut-price printing, the kind of which we then see him drop off at Boycie's.

As the crew were all set on doing as much of the location work as possible in Bristol, a new location for Boycie and Marlene's

That's the last time I do any work for Boycie! God knows what my sister ever saw in the bloke. I mean, it's not like she ever had a shortage of lads after her, but she went and chose him! And he's always had it in for me, from the moment she brought him home to meet the family. There he sat in the living room, looking down his nose at me with those evil, squinty eyes. The minute he left, Mum opened all the windows and started phoning around for an exorcist. And I'll never forget their wedding day. He'd arranged for Marlene to be driven to the church in the big Rolls Royce from off his car lot, and Marlene wanted me to be the driver. I was happy to do it, but no sooner had he said "I do" and kissed the bride, he was turning to me asking for petrol money! But that's Boycie for you. As tight as they come. Apparently the one and only time he ever offered to buy a round was at an AA meeting!

Bronco Lane

Above: These photos of Tessa Peake-Jones were taken for a framed photo during the making of *The Sky's The Limit*, required for the later episode *The Class of 62*.

Above right: This establishing shot of Rodney and Del looking over the balcony was filmed on location at Whitemead House in Bristol.

Below: Del and Alan enjoy cocktails – "When your Cassandra married a Trotter you all became Trotters – maybe not in the eyes of the law, but certainly in the eyes of my heart."

house had to be found, preferably one with a suitably grand back garden, big enough for a large satellite dish to be assembled. For this, Adrian Pegg found the perfect property on Druid Stoke Avenue in Stoke Bishop. Here the production manager also arranged for his friend's son, Elliott, to appear as baby Tyler, alongside Sue Holderness and John Challis.

"For the storyline about the satellite dish to work, I had to introduce Marlene's slightly strange brother, Bronco," explained John Sullivan. "He's known for stealing the strangest things in the world. He was caught speeding in a JCB on Streatham High Street – trying to outrun a police car in a JCB!"

To play Bronco Lane actor Ron Aldridge was cast. Aldridge was a close friend of the *Dear John* star Ralph Bates who introduced him to Sullivan. "I always wanted to be in *Only Fools* because I was such a

fan. With Bronco there was a truly wonderful character breakdown in the script to help me understand a bit about him. It said, 'If Bronco played Trivial Pursuits with Trigger, he would win – but only just!'"

Thanks to Boycie's light-fingered brother-in-law, he has ended up with a television satellite dish that, unbeknown to him (or anyone else but Bronco), is actually a radar transmitter dish from one of the main runways at Gatwick airport – a transmitter dish that eventually ends up on the Trotters' balcony!

The idea behind *The Sky's the Limit*'s central premise came from a conversation Sullivan had on a family holiday to Portugal.

"We had arrived at Gatwick Airport, only to discover that we hadn't been booked on the plane. Eventually, they said they could get us on the flight, but we'd all be in different parts of the plane, and one of us had to sit in the jump seat. I thought the jump seat would be up near the cabin crew, so I said I'd sit there. But when I got on board, I found out I was actually sitting behind the pilot. We got talking and he told me about these things that guide planes in, which I'd never heard of, so that was the basis for this story."

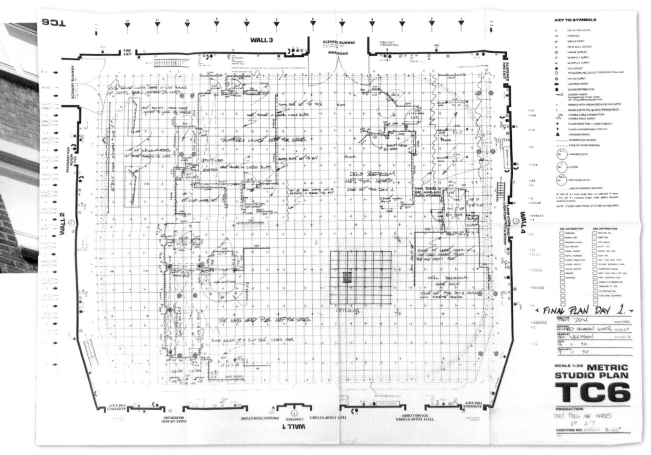

To weave the satellite dish plot in with Rodney's relationship turmoil, Sullivan had Rodney take Del up on his idea of laying on a night in a luxury hotel by the airport where Cassandra is due to land.

The hotel suite was built in the studio area in front of the flat and Nags Head sets, in the position usually occupied by the audience seating. Recorded on the non-audience day, the set was struck and replaced by seating overnight.

Cast as Henry, the slightly mocking concierge, was actor Gordon Warnecke. For the later scene at the airport enquiry desk, Nicholas Lyndhurst and a small crew went to Stansted Airport to capture Rodney's

Above: A studio floor plan for the studio pre-record day of *The Sky's The Limit*.

Left: Henry (Gordon Warnecke), the hotel concierge.

Below left: The hotel suite set as seen in the episode.

Below: The Nags Head set, lit and ready for recording.

Above: Rodney gets some bad news at the airport – "But I'm waiting for my wife! I've got a hotel suite – I've got a bottle of champagne – I've spent nigh on 200 quid waiting for this flight!"

Above right: Albert, Raquel, Del and Rod discuss the situation in the Nags Head.

Below: The Trotters watch the TV news report with interest.

Below right: Newsreader Richard Whitmore gives an urgent report – "The radar transmitter dish, similar to the one shown here, was stolen from the end of Gatwick's main runway in the early hours of yesterday morning."

disappointment at learning that, due to sudden and unexplained chaos in the skies, Cassandra's flight has been diverted to Manchester.

Back at the flat, Tony Dow stages a wonderful scene as Del tries to locate Bronco with the assistance of Raquel, Rodney and a surprisingly helpful Albert. Finally reaching Bronco at a B&B in Gatwick, Del is still none the wiser as to the true provenance of the dish, but when a sudden TV news report shows a photo of a familiar-looking (and now missing) radar transmitter dish, it all becomes clear.

"I was in the studio when we shot the scene of the miniature approaching jet and I saw the special effects, which I thought were amazing. I did worry for a while that the scene was going to look a little bit like something out of *Thunderbirds*, but it didn't,

because the special effects team did an incredible job," remembered Sullivan.

The closing scene on the balcony is both unpredictable and brilliant as Del and Rodney clutch each other in horror, looking up at the approaching jet... just as the picture freezes and the credits start to roll.

It was this laughter which was starting to have a major impact on people's social habits, as Tony Dow remembers: "*Only Fools* was given the Sunday slot for series six and seven. Because the show was doing unbelievable business and there was a massive high on it, landlords were putting televisions in pubs as they couldn't get business on a Sunday because of *Fools!*"

Above top left: The set of the flat's balcony with the satellite dish in position.

Above: For series seven the usual painted backdrop seen outside the balcony window was replaced by three models of the neighbouring flats placed in front of a distance-scaled backdrop to provide a more realistic perspective. These models were also used in the model shot where the jumbo-jet is seen approaching.

Left: "SWITCH IT OFF!"

Above: Del talks to Rodney whilst adjusting one of his national anthem playing doorbells.

Above right: Rodney and Alan head off on business.

Right: Director Adrian (Ian Redford), and set designer, Jules (Paul Opacic).

Below: An embarrassing old flame of Del's, Trudy (Helen Blizard)... who Rodney helps into a taxi...

Opposite page top: "Let me ask you two a question – how many people can you see standing there?"

Opposite middle: Raquel and Adrian outside the *As You Like It* auditions.

For the seventh series of *Only Fools*, the running thread which John Sullivan plotted was one that had been hinted at since 1982's *Diamonds are for Heather*. The return of Raquel to Del's life dared him to dream once again about finally having the things in life he had never managed to make last. This made Raquel's distant behaviour in *The Chance of a Lunchtime* all the more worrying for the character.

"I was trying to show the audience what kind of situation could possibly frighten Del," remembered John Sullivan. "It wouldn't be a big bloke coming at him with a broken bottle – Del Boy would be able to deal with it. What would make Del really frightened would be if he thought Raquel might leave him for somebody who she considered to be culturally superior."

Del's insecurities steadily grow over the course of the episode as he is drawn into Raquel's acting world.

"Del takes it upon himself to go spying on Raquel's audition. He wants to see what the director of the play's like, to actually have a look at the bloke. And, being Del Boy, he ends up making things much worse for Raquel when he tries to get involved."

Cast as Raquel's director, Adrian, was actor Ian Redford, who had just had a small role in the feature film *Three Men and a Little Lady*, which would inspire Sullivan's title for the final episode of series seven. Joining Redford was future *Emmerdale* and *Hollyoaks* actor, Paul Opacic, as the effeminate set designer, Jules. For this scene, Henry Africa's Hothouse on Whiteladies Road in Clifton was used, offering a perfect view of a petrol station across the road for Del's silent exchange with Rodney and Alan.

In the meantime, Rodney and Cassandra's ongoing issues are revisited as they meet up for dinner (thanks to one of Del's underhanded but well-intentioned interventions). For this scene, Shoots floating restaurant, moored off Canons Road in Bristol, was used, and Sullivan

THE CHANCE OF A LUNCHTIME

6 JANUARY 1991

Talk about a whirlwind of emotional ups and downs. On the up side, I'd just got my hands on a consignment of musical doorbells that played 36 different national anthems. Lovely jubbly! I'd also worked out a way in which I could get Rodney and Cassandra talking again. It meant I had to tell a little fib or two, which went right against my honest nature, but sometimes needs must. The main thing was that it worked. Now for the downsides. About half an hour after Rodney reunited with Cassandra, she caught him in a very suspect looking clinch with some old tart from the Nags Head (God knows how he managed it, but the most important thing to know is that she had nothing to do with me). Owing further to his habit of being a 42 carat wally-brain, he then kept the ball rolling by handing his resignation in to Alan. He thought he was making a point by proving to Alan just how much he needed him in his firm. Alan mulled it over for all of two seconds and accepted the resignation. I couldn't believe it! It was the best job he'd ever had, or was ever likely to have, and he willingly said bonjour to it! I couldn't worry about it too much at the time, I had my own crisis to deal with. It all started when Raquel agreed to audition for some Shakespeare play ('A Load of Ado About Nothing' or 'The Taming of King Lear', something like that). She didn't think I noticed, but I saw how different she was becoming around all her trendy and sensitive actor friends. She eventually got the part and then revealed that the play was a tour. Well, it all made sense then. It was the lure of the spotlight, applause, applause, the show must go on and all that cobblers. She then said that she'd turned the offer down, which I couldn't understand. Why would she turn down a big opportunity like that? And that's when she revealed that she was pregnant! She thought I'd be angry, but it was the most loveliest jubbliest moment in all my life. I was gonna be a daddy!!!

Del

chose the Joan Armatrading track 'Love and Affection' to set the mood.

Having finally smoothed things over, Rodney's dream of reconciliation with Cass is foiled when, in an attempt to be the Good Samaritan, he tries to help an old flame of Del's (the well and truly inebriated, Trudy) into the back of a cab. Cass drives by at just the wrong moment, completely misinterprets the sight and once again relegates Rodney to the dog house! Helen Blizard was cast as Trudy in a scene which recalls Rodney's encounter with Blossom in 1983's *Wanted*. Yet another Bristol-based Nags Head was used for the exterior shots of the Trotters' local, namely The White Horse on West Street in Bedminster.

After some hilarity with Del's new line of musical doorbells, and Rodney taking up some seriously misguided advice from Albert (resulting in him having his letter of resignation tendered and accepted), the story comes to a head as Del confronts Raquel.

Both Jason and Peake-Jones are magnificent in this scene, as Sullivan really suggests the two characters are on the verge of splitting, right up until the uplifting reveal and Del's priceless reaction.

"It was so well done by David," remembered Sullivan. "We see Del going, in the space of ten seconds, from the lowest point – the bottom's fallen out of his world and he really thinks he's going to lose Raquel – to the top of Everest!"

After all these years, Del's greatest dream is about to come true: he's going to be a daddy!

Above and left: The Trotters arrive at the Down by the Riverside Club.

Right: Eric (Trevor Byfield), the former owner and now manager of the Starlight rooms.

Below: Tony Angelino (Philip Pope) signs autographs for his fans.

Below right: The set of Tony's dressing room.

Opposite page left: The set of Raquel's dressing room at the Starlight Rooms... as Rodney the roadie talks to Raquel.

Opposite page below: Raquel and Tony bring the house down during their rendition of 'Cwying'.

Opposite page top right: "You're not alone with your pwejudice. We've got sexism, wacecism, sizeism... Well, I'm a victim of pwonunciationism!"

In the third episode of series seven, Del's attention turns to show business as the 'The Trotter International Star Agency' is formed.

"This episode was inspired by the idea of Raquel having a show-business background," remembered John Sulllivan. "It didn't matter how indistinct that background was to Del. Because Raquel had appeared in a night club as part of a duo called 'Double Cream', Del Boy sees a chance to earn some money. Of course, he ignores the fact that she's three months pregnant!"

Not wanting to leave Tessa Peak-Jones on stage alone, Sullivan came up with a musical partner for Raquel – Tony Angelino, the singing dustman, played by the multi-talented actor and musician Philip Pope.

"A script arrived in the post early Saturday morning and my wife and I read it together," recalls Pope. "Only Fools was already quite a popular and successful series at this point. As we were reading, we got to the part of the story where Tony removes his wig to reveal he doesn't have a lot of hair, then takes off his platform shoes, at which Del visibly reacts to his being short, then when we get to the final

reveal about him not being able to say his 'R's, and that's when my wife – who can't say hers – chips in with 'Is this some kind of joke?' So I said to her, "I think it's supposed to be a joke, but it's not on you and me!"

Philip's first studio scene in the episode was an intricate sequence which saw Tony gradually remove his stage costume, transforming from crooning heartthrob to down-on-his-luck dustman, and all while in conversation with Del and Rodney:

"What was interesting to me about that scene," Pope remembers, "was how David Jason took control. I'd been familiar with David's stage and radio work, and I can remember thinking I was in good hands when he started choreographing the scene with the director. David clearly knew his stagecraft and how to make the jokes work and the timing for the cameras, particularly the business with the sausage codpiece, which Tony Angelino hands to Del Boy. From memory we pre-recorded this scene to be played-in to the audience the next day, so we had to leave gaps for where the laughs would be."

Two Bristol locations were used in the episode, with The Studio Nightclub on Frogmore Street doubling as The Starlight Rooms, and Bedminster's Courage Western Social Club as the Down by the Riverside Club.

"The music and vocals were all pre-recorded in a studio just outside Henley," Pope recollects. "I think we recorded the music for the ballroom scene first. When we started filming the scene at the Ballroom in Bristol, for some reason it just seemed easier and better to do it live, so we actually sung it live to the backing track for the filming."

STAGE FRIGHT

13 JANUARY 1991

In his script, John Sullivan worked incredibly hard with Tony's early dialogue so as not to spoil the punch line later in the story, as Pope remembers: "John had impressed upon me when we were down in Bristol how difficult it had been to write for Tony, as he had to make it sound natural whilst making sure that any dialogue before the big mispronunciation reveal didn't have any words with 'R' in them."

"Normally I like to keep the audience one step ahead of the characters," explained Sullivan, "but here they were one step behind."

In the completed episode, Peake-Jones and Pope make for a curious double act as they take to the stage as Raquel and Tony. It is during their memorable rendition of the Roy Orbison classic 'Crying' that Tony's speech impediment is finally revealed.

"I think the great thing about *Only Fools* is that everyone had a great respect for each other," remembers Pope. "From Gareth Gwenlan and Tony Dow down, everyone seemed to know it was the writing which made this such a successful and happy series. Actors know when a script is good. As a writer John Sullivan had a touch of genius."

Show business can be a cwuel and unforgiving mistwess at times, but it's the only business for me... well, that and being a dustman. The fact is I've got a twiffic voice and extwaordinary tone. I've got natuwal chawisma and style. And okay, I might embellish it a bit with the sywup, the tight twousers and the jumbo chowizo, but all the big names do that, and if it's good enough for Wod Stewart and Bawwy Manillo, it's good enough for Tony Angelino. But with all my God given talent, I'm tweated diffewently from the west just because of the way I pwonounce my 'R's. This time I did evewything that was wequired of me and performed the wepertoire that Del insisted on. Normally I don't sing songs with 'R's in them. Either that or I change the lywics.

"Well why didn't you change the lyrics this time?" Del said. "How can I change the lywics to 'Cwying'?" I said, "The bloody song's called 'Cwying'!"

At the end of the day I'm just another forgotten sufferwer of another forgotten ism. And that's the weally fwustwating thing. People are outwaged by wacism, sexism, sizeism and ageism, but nobody gives a cwap about pwonunciationism!

Tony Angelino (transcribed from audio)

THE **DOWN BY THE RIVERSIDE CLUB** WELCOMES

Tony Angelino

THE SINGING DUSTMAN

SERIES 7 EPISODE 4

THE CLASS OF '62

20 JANUARY 1991

"It's like something out of an Agatha Christie film" Rodney said. "Think about it... on a cold, rainy night in Peckham, someone has arranged for you four to be in the same room, at the same time. Nobody knows who. And the most frightening aspect of the whole mystery is... nobody knows why!" He was trying to frighten us, and it worked. For a minute we thought it might have been our old headmaster, Bend-over Benson, but then Denzil remembered the judge had made a strict promise never to release him back into society. Trigger thought it was Jeremy Beadle. And then Roy Slater stepped into the room with a da-da! and we all wished it had been Jeremy Beadle! Slater gave us a great big sob story about how much prison had changed him, how he'd realised the error of his ways and that all he wanted to do was make things right with us. Probably the most surprising thing of all, though, was that we fell for it. The party ended up back at the flat, where we reminisced over our days at school. Boycie, Denzil and Trigger left and Slater passed out on the sofa. It was then that Raquel returned home and the real reason for Slater's 'reunion' was revealed. I knew she had an estranged husband who she hadn't seen for years, and I even knew he'd been a copper, but when she gave me the full story... I just couldn't take it in. It hurts even to repeat it now. Raquel and Slater?! No... no way Pedro! Only this time it was 'Sorry Pedro my old mucker, but yes... yes way!' I'm gonna go and have a shower!

Del

Thanks to a message from Mike at the Nags Head ('machine not working pro'), we discover that Del's latest line in fax-stroke-photocopying machines aren't all they're cracked up to be.

So begins an episode that was an opportunity for John Sullivan to gather the Nags Head gang and connect a part of the series' past with its present.

"It was inspired by a football team reunion that I went to," recalled Sullivan. "We all met up at a hotel for the reunion. I walked into the bar and some guy started talking to me – and I didn't have a clue who he was. It turned out that I'd played football with him for five or six years, and I was shocked by how much he'd changed. I wondered what would happen if the Trotters and their friends had a reunion. Something would go horribly wrong, of course – which made me think of Roy Slater."

Making a welcome return to the cast as Slater, Jim Broadbent slips straight back into the devious shoes of the dodgy policeman for a third and final appearance in the series.

"This episode also shows the softer side of The Nags Head lads. They're all quite tough on the outside, but it's not long before they're back at Del's having a drink with Slater," explained Sullivan. "He's out of uniform now and has almost earned his spurs by doing time in prison."

The scene where the lads are in the flat was originally broadcast with them singing Manfred Man's 1960s classic

'Mighty Quinn' (complete with Del air drumming!) Sadly, musical rights reasons necessitated its being cut from all but the very first home video release.

After the location-heavy opening episodes of the series, *The Class of 62* would be a studio-bound affair, but the strength of the cast and unfolding story make it a highlight, especially as one of the series' most brilliantly realised surprises is revealed.

"It turns out that Slater is Raquel's husband," Sullivan explained. "In an earlier episode she'd said that her husband was a policeman. That was unconnected – I think Raquel wanted to get a reaction from Del. Then, when I was bringing Slater back in, I suddenly went 'Bingo!' I hadn't planned to do this, but the opportunity arose, and I jumped at it."

A dumbfounded Del, a furious and pregnant Raquel, and a confused Albert ("Who's Rachel?") all combine to make this one of the funniest studio scenes in the series' history, as the farcical situation is brilliantly assembled and played out.

The acting chops of Broadbent draw every last ounce from Slater's wicked ways as we discover (when Del happens to find some paperwork in his arch nemesis's wallet) his real reason for coming back to the parish – to secure a divorce from Raquel so that he can keep a forthcoming 'inheritance' all for himself. In fact, according to the paperwork, this 'inheritance' is some cleverly hidden diamond loot, a holdover from his failed smuggling scam in 1985's *To Hull and Back*.

Slater's leverage over Del is the fact that if word ever got out that Raquel was once his wife, the wheeler-dealer's reputation on Hooky Street would be destroyed.

The episode's happy ending is reached via the aid of one of Del's dodgy fax machines. When Del and Rodney tell Slater they have used their machine to create several copies of his diamond deal paperwork, Slater promises to keep schtum about Raquel and leave the area for good. Just as he makes a cowed exit, Mike appears and reminds Del that the photocopier on his new fax machine doesn't work. "That's funny," Del says, "It don't on ours either!"

Opposite page top right: The Class 4C reunion in full swing... then the mysterious organiser walks in... Slater!

Above top: "Where'd you get?!" – Slater realises that Raquel, his estranged wife, is pregnant.

Above: One of the fax machines Trotters Independent Traders are selling.

Below: Slater discusses Del's predicament – "I don't think anyone would ever trust you again knowing you were living with the wife of an ex-copper. And not any ex-copper, but Slater, who is universally hated and despised!"

Below: "Michael, bring us a bottle of your finest champagne – and two glasses."

HE AIN'T HEAVY, HE'S MY UNCLE

I'd spent the evening at the Nags Head playing dominoes with my old mate Knock-Knock. I say 'mate' but he could be a right mouthy so and so at times. Still, that night I wiped the floor with him. I was walking back to the flat, counting me winnings and feeling very chipper, when from out of nowhere, they jumped me. It was dark that night, like most nights, so I couldn't make out any distinguishing features at all. The only thing I could be certain of was that there was four of 'em. Well, during the war I was the Royal Navy light middleweight champion, so I managed to hold 'em off to begin with. You could see the surprise in their eyes when my old right hand got going. 'Trotter's Trembler' they used to call it back in the navy (they also had a nickname for my left hand but I don't want to get into that). Anyway, it being five-on-one, it was only a matter of time until they got the better of me, and that they did. They then made off with all my winnings and my pocket watch. But I s'pose that's the thanks you get for being a war hero. You fight for King and Country, laying it all on the line so the younger generations don't have to, and this is how they repay you. I reckon I might've fared well had it been one-on-one, but six-on-one? No chance!

Albert

After five years in the series, Buster Merryfield had made the role as the series' elder Trotter his own. Whilst the addition of Raquel and Cassandra to the cast had perhaps seen him lose a little screen time, *He Ain't Heavy, He's My Uncle* was a welcome chance to address the balance with a very topical subject.

"This episode gave me an opportunity to show another side of Uncle Albert," John Sullivan recalled. "It was also inspired by all the stuff in the newspapers about the plight of elderly people in run-down areas of the city, where they were often the victims of crime. So I wondered how Del and Uncle Albert would handle it if inner-city crime suddenly affected the Trotters."

Unlike the much-missed Lennard Pearce, Merryfield was a very active and fit man who still kept to a regular exercise routine, a habit he had continued from his days as a boxing champion. This active streak was something the actor was always keen for Sullivan to incorporate into his scripts, making what happens to Albert in this episode all the more shocking.

One of the reasons Albert is seen to be working out early in the episode is his desire to impress Marlene's mum, Dora, played by actress Joan Geary. Geary passed away in 1994 and when we meet Dora again in the 2007 episode of *The Green Green Grass, The Lonely Herdsman,* comedy favourite June Whitfield is cast in the role.

In a later scene in the Nags Head, we see Albert and his friend 'Knock-Knock' simultaneously competing for Dora's attention whilst facing off in a heated game of dominoes. When Albert offers to buy Dora a drink and flashes a wad of fivers, a group of skinheads drinking in the corner of the pub take note.

Two hours later, just as Del and Raquel are settling in for the evening, Rodney bursts in to the flat and informs them that Albert has been mugged on his way back from the pub. In an attempt to reassure them, Rodney explains that Albert isn't too badly hurt,

"He's got a bit of double vision, that's all." "Where's this happen, Rodney?" asks Del. "Well, in his eyes," the plonker replies.

As Del seeks vengeance, a battered and bruised Albert soon lapses into a state of permanent fear, so much so that Rodney suggests they drop the softly-softly approach and adopt a tougher line. After a memorable telling of the time him and his mates came face to face with a man-eating lion whilst on safari in Africa (culminating in Albert's wetting himself – in the flat right there and then, not in Africa), Del begins his tough approach, reminding Albert that there is no room in the flat for lame ducks. The approach works so well that the next morning Albert runs away, leaving only a note promising not to bother them again.

Elsewhere in this episode, Del and Raquel become a two-car family when Del buys a clapped out Capri Ghia from Boycie. With the registration UYD 177R, this lime green 1977 model Capri would be used by Del till *Time on Our Hands*, with another vehicle sourced for the final trilogy of episodes.

The first time we see the Capri also marks the first daylight appearance of Whitemead House and its row of garages, doubling as those belonging to Nelson Mandela House. This scene, filmed in Bristol in October 1990, was topped up by an additional three-day location shoot

in London, filmed between 27–30 December, as we see Del and Rodney searching for their missing uncle. The sequence took in a host of familiar city landmarks, including Tower Bridge, the Imperial War Museum and The Prospect of Whitby pub. The search culminates at the new dockland development at Shadwell Basin in Wapping, which, we discover, was the location of Albert's old stomping ground: 'Tobacco Road'.

Suitably enough this montage also features Paul and Linda McCartney's 1971 song 'Uncle Albert/Admiral Halsey' (although only the 'Uncle Albert' part of the song is featured), which fits the moment beautifully, almost as if the ex-Beatle wrote the song specially for *Only Fools*.

Whilst Sullivan was keen not to turn Albert into an old man, *He Ain't Heavy, He's My Uncle* gives a glimpse of a deflated and retiring figure, although, as the rest of the family soon discover, his tale of being mugged on the way home from the pub wasn't strictly true...

"It was a wonderful piece of acting from Buster Merryfield," remembered Sullivan. "You really felt for him – although at the end it turns out he's been a bit economical with the truth! And Del's suddenly become a bit of a vigilante, which is classic Del Boy behaviour – despite having the best intentions, he gets it all wrong."

Opposite page top right: Boyce Autos car lot.

Opposite page below: Albert, Dora (Joan Geary) and 'Knock Knock' (Howard Goorney) play dominoes.

Above left: Del unveils his new Capri Ghia!

Left: Del and Rodney pass each other on Tower Bridge.

Below left: Cassandra visits Albert.

Below: The Trotters finally find Albert where Tobacco Road once stood, replaced now by some soulless yuppy flats.

THREE MEN, A WOMAN AND A BABY

3 FEBRUARY 1991

I despaired of that boy sometimes, I really did! There we were on the brink of welcoming a brand new Trotter into the world, and all he could do was whinge! I blamed his diet. He'd gone all 'vegan' on us again. Not that I've got anything against vegans, no, I've always said that vegans should be treated with the same equal respect as normal people, but still, you're bound to get the hump when your dinner consists of a load of stuff that's been plucked off a bush or dug up out of the ground. I mean, it's not natural is it? I tried to reason with him. I said "Oi, misog, look at Raquel, her back hurts, her knees hurt, her thighs are chafing; she's got burst blood vessels, swollen ankles, and a very sore... well, everything! But you don't hear that poor mare complaining, do yer?!" He just copped a deafen and grabbed another nut cutlet. Of course, all this on-again-off-again cobblers with Cassandra wasn't helping. Not that he wasn't trying, though. He even let me in on his plan to take her out for an afternoon at Hampton Court Palace. Well, if a day spent walking around Henry the 8th's gaff wouldn't help calm the marital turbulence, I didn't know what would!

Del

As the seventh series of *Only Fools* draws to a close, the building excitement of Del and Raquel's new arrival is contrasted by Rodney's predicament. With his marriage on the rocks and a reconciliation a far-off prospect, Rodney airs a prophecy of what The Son of Del will bring, the first in a long line of the character's satanic ramblings about his nephew.

Throughout series seven, the status of Rodney and Cassandra's marriage is an undercurrent to each episode, as we see Rodney fall from being a suited head of a computer section, all the way down to being Del's personal car-cleaner. It is a relief then that John Sullivan decided that Rodney's luck was going to change and the couple would finally patch up their differences.

In a brilliantly performed scene, Nicholas Lyndhurst and Gwyneth Strong do battle, their characters locking horns as Sullivan's dialogue takes them from the frustration of getting lost in Hampton Court maze to the potential benefits of owning a pet tin of salmon named Rex. Finally, with the help of a clip-on pony tail (taken from Del's latest line in men's wigs), Rodney's inventive bravado wins back Cass' affections.

In a way, the bigger reunion, which viewers might not have noticed, is that by the end of series seven the Trotter brothers are back together again as Trotters Independent Traders. By freeing Rodney from the computer section's computer, Sullivan got the Hooky Street partnership back, just in time to sail off into a sunset of feature length specials.

The real focus of this story, however, is the birth of Damien; from Mike's 'guess the baby name sweepstake' to Del's insistence that his iron stomach at watching an anti-natal class birthing video is down to the fact that he used to work on a jellied eel stall.

Hillingdon Hospital in Uxbridge was found as a suitable location to film the birth scenes. One of the first tasks was for the crew to find a newborn baby to appear as

Damien. When word got out that this was for *Only Fools*, several mums volunteered their newborns straight away.

As Tessa Peake-Jones recalls, in preparation, the cast were given quite an education:

"None of us had children at this point so the lovely midwife who was advising us said 'would you like to see a film of a birth?' And we all went 'yeah we would', especially me, I didn't know what noises to make or anything. So they took us into a little lecture theatre and put a projector up to play this birth scene – which was so graphic, you saw the woman screaming and grabbing things. This was very helpful for my performance, I literally copied what I'd seen. But we all soon started to feel incredibly sick as we had just had our breakfast!

"Afterwards, they took us straight to a ward which wasn't being used and it was 'right, into bed and off you go!' And that was it, we had to film it that day. But it was so beautifully written, short of being a complete dodo you couldn't really muck

CROWNING GLORY
WIGS OF DISTINCTION

Opposite page below: A heavily pregnant Raquel getting closer to the birth...

Above left: Mike is running a 'Guess The Baby Trotter's Name' sweep stake.

Above: Raquel is reading a book on baby's names for inspiration... but it is Rodney's sarcastic suggestion of 'Damien' that she takes a liking to.

Left: Del's latest line, Crowning Glory: 'Wigs of Distinction', has a problem – "I don't believe it! Me wig's going bald! This is gonna call for a bit of creative salesmanship."

I was back working for Del again and hadn't felt so depressed in all my life. I'd had this horrible realisation that if there was such a thing as reincarnation, knowing my luck I'd come back as me! All in all I just wanted to be left alone. "It's important to have people around you when you feel low." Del said. I knew what he meant, but it just ain't the same when those people are Mickey Pearce and Trigger. "Do what I do, Rodney." Mickey said. "When life gives you lemons, make lemonade!" That was all very well, but life hadn't given me lemons, life had given me a three-wheel van and a wife who couldn't stand the sight of me. Then there was Trigger, who offered me hope by telling me some dopey story about a suicidal bus driver. On top of that, Del and Raquel were about to give birth at any minute. And I just knew it was gonna be a boy. For some reason, the planets would align and decree that 'He' would be born in Peckham. What chance would I stand then, eh? I worked out that by the time I was 45, Son of Del would be 15. I could hear it then, loud as day: "I've got a good idea Uncle Rodney, I'll go and buy a load of old crap and you can go and sell it for me!" Cos-bloody-mic!

Rodney

it up, you just had to follow the instructions from John. It was so truthful. You just had to play it the way it was written, and it was there."

For the birth, John Sullivan drew upon his own experiences of fatherhood: "A lot of this came from my own experience of my wife giving birth. It was our first child and our first experience of all that. My wife was quite vociferous! Of course, once it was all over it was quite funny in hindsight.

I remembered how I cried, and I wanted to show Del – this tough South London man – bawling his eyes out over a little baby. When he went to the window with the baby and looked out at the stars, that was something my mate did, wanting to show his child to his dad who had passed away. I thought I'd use that – it's very Del, showing his baby to his beloved mum. It was a nice touch." Joining the cast on location as the wig-wearing midwife was well-known Scottish actor, Ken Drury. Assisting him as the very

understanding Sister was actress Constance Lamb.

Peake-Jones is incredible in this scene, sensitively comedic and touching in equal measure. David Jason also shines in a moving performance, fulfilling his character's dream with beautifully played delight. Whenever Sullivan writes a dramatic situation like this, the jokes seem to pack a bit more punch, probably since they're not expected.

Reflecting on the end of the episode, Sullivan was conscious of neatly ending the series: "This episode has a very upbeat ending. A lot of things are tied up. From about that time onwards, I was constantly writing endings, because we didn't know if we were coming back or if people wanted to move on".

To further suggest an air of finality, the episode features an unusual closing credits, with a freeze-frame of Del holding Damien viewed from outside the hospital, before cutting to a final shot of the Trotter family all turning to smile at the camera.

"I'd made it clear throughout the series that Del liked kids. I always

hoped he'd have one of his own – but I never knew whether the show would last that long," remembered Sullivan. "I showed in various episodes how he'd love to settle down and have kids and give them the kind of life that he never had himself. Damien was a wonderful gift for him, and he spoilt his son rotten."

Broadcast on six consecutive Sunday evenings at 7.15pm from 30 December 1990, audience figures for the Trotter family's seventh outing would grow each week from 15 million viewers watching *The Sky's the Limit* to 18.9 million viewers tuning in to see baby Damien make his debut.

Opposite page: Rodney and Cassandra manage to patch up their differences... with the help of a clip-on pony tail.

Above top: In the delivery room, Raquel goes through a memorable ordeal, with the help of the hospital sister (Constance Lamb) and midwife, Mr McCallum (Ken Drury).

Above: "They've done it! They've only bloody done it!"

Left: Del holds the new born baby Damien up to the sky – "There you are, Mum. I know you can see us. There he is, look, your first grandchild."

Left: The cast turn to the camera at the end of the episode credits.

209

MIAMI TWICE

★ ★

I'd always fancied a bit of the old transatlantic life, and when Alan handed Rodney his pension money, the chance to finally experience it was just too good to miss. Rodney copped the needle when I told him I'd cashed his cheque and spent it on a couple of tickets to Miami, but it was all very innocent on my part. I'd just happened to stumble across the cheque when I was going through his coat pockets, that's all. And I had originally intended the tickets to be for Rodney and Cassandra... it weren't my fault she had to attend a very important bank seminar the very same week as the holiday. I mean, she did say she had mentioned it to me at some point, but I dunno, I must have gone a bit mutton. Once I'd smoothed it all over with Raquel (an absolute doddle) I went to give Rodney the good news that I was coming to Miami with him.

"No you bloody ain't!" he said.

Not quite the enthusiastic response I was hoping for, but it was all a big misunderstanding. You see, he was judging me by the old Del Boy, forgetting that I was now a changed and mature man with a wife and child. Well, a child at least. I wasn't after going to Miami to live it up in the bars and nightclubs. I wanted to experience the proper culture, take in some art museums, a few nature reserves and all that game. And if we happened to stumble across the occasional all-night drinking club along the way, well, that was lovely jubbly too!

★ ★

MIAMI TWICE PART ONE: THE AMERICAN DREAM

24 DECEMBER 1991

I must say, I was quite stunned when Derek Trotter cornered me in my vestry and outlined his latest and revolutionary business idea. Trotter pre-blessed communion wine was, as he said, like a holy version of sliced bread and would save the church not only money but also plenty of "vicar-hours". It was all very commendable and, on the face of it at least, it made sense, but I hadn't even had a chance to think it through or seek advice when lorryloads of wine began lining up on the kerb waiting to be blessed. These lorries were then making deliveries to churches all over Europe. Derek was right, it was a real money saver, that much was true. The problem, which I discovered when blessing the twentieth lorry, was that the wine inside was Romanian Rheisling – white wine! Before I could say "My God!" the churches all began returning their cases and I was having to explain myself to the Archbishop of Canterbury!

Reverend Campbell

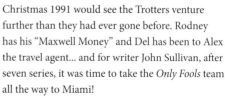

Christmas 1991 would see the Trotters venture further than they had ever gone before. Rodney has his "Maxwell Money" and Del has been to Alex the travel agent... and for writer John Sullivan, after seven series, it was time to take the *Only Fools* team all the way to Miami!

"This episode was partly inspired by David Jason's gift for accents," recalled Sullivan. "I'd heard him doing a great American accent and wondered if we could use it in *Only Fools*. At that time, holidays to Florida were becoming quite affordable for Brits and were very popular. I thought, 'What the hell would the Trotters do in Miami?'"

As Sullivan completed his final draft towards the end of September, it became clear that the story lent itself to two parts. The first instalment, titled *The American Dream*, would cover the build-up to Del and Rodney's departure and would be produced in the now standard 50-minute format. The second part, *Oh To Be In England,* would be presented as a one-off 90 minute television feature, filmed completely on 16mm film (allowing for a slightly wider aspect ratio) and without any audience laughter track.

Due to the nature and scale of the production, Tony Dow and Gareth Gwenlan would share directorial duties on the project, with Dow credited as director of the 90-minute film and Gwenlan down as director of the 50 minute opening episode.

The first part of the special picks things up from the end of series seven, as we attend the christening of baby Damien, held at Peckham's fictional 'St Mark's Church'. In reality St John's in Camden was used as a filming location for the exterior scenes and St John's, Ladbroke Road, used for the interior.

This UK portion of the location filming was actually filmed *after* the Miami shoot, from 24–29 of November 1991, explaining why some of the cast have slight sun tans.

Joining the cast for the christening was actor Treva Etienne as the vicar who gets drawn into Del's latest brain wave: 'Trotter pre-blessed wine'.

"I remember how amazing it felt to be in the Trotter family christening photo outside the church," recalls Etienne. "I also remember the small crowd of watchful fans waving to the cast on a cold and frosty morning in Camden. John Sullivan shared some precious moments with me in rehearsals, explaining his style of writing and how he always tried to keep the story funny but with honest emotional themes to keep the characters true to the situation and relatable to the audience."

After Del uses Rodney's pension payout to book a holiday for him and Cassandra to Miami, Rodney is

distraught when he finds out that Cass can't get the time off from the bank. Later, when Raquel grants his leave, Del offers to go with Rodney instead. Whilst at first unconvinced ("you seem to forget, I've been on holiday with you before!"), Del eventually wins him over.

Just before the Trotters take to the air, they end up rubbing shoulders with a famous face. "Richard Branson had a cameo appearance for this episode," remembered Sullivan. "We were using his airline, as they had offered us the best deal, so we asked him if he'd like to make a guest appearance."

Opposite page top: The Trotters' family and friends pose for Damien's christening.

Opposite page left: Reverend Campbell (Treva Etienne).

Above: Mickey Pearce and Boyce and Marlene pose for some photos at the christening.

Below far left: Parking up at the Nags Head for post-christening drinks. For *Miami Twice*, The Middlesex Arms in South Ruislip was used.

Left: Rodney chats to Trigger in Sid's cafe. This set was originally built for 1988's *Dates*.

Below: "Blimey, anybody would think he owned the plane!" – Del and Rodney are off to America!

Above: Del and Rodney take in the sights... and on a riverboat tour spot Bee Gee Barry Gibb!

Above right: When the action cuts back to Peckham, Sid and Mike share a scene in the Nags Head, the only time we see the two together in the pub.

Right: Don Occhetti (David Jason) on his exercise bike.

Below: Barry Gibb invited the cast and crew to his beautiful Miami home.

Opposite page middle: Don Occhetti cuts a suave figure in his expensive suit. This shot was taken at Television Centre to be super-imposed into the various photos seen in the Don's study.

Opposite page far right: Ricardo 'Rico' Occhetti (Antoni Corone) plots numerous ways to get rid of Del: a sniper at sea and a sabotaged jet ski.

Filming for the second part of *Miami Twice, Oh to be in England,* took place in Miami from 22 October to 20 November. Locations seen shortly after the Trotters' arrival include the wide parades of Miami Beach, Biscayne Bay (where Del gets to take a ride on a jet ski) and a night club on Lenox Avenue. Perhaps the most well-known location, however, was the house of Bee Gee Barry Gibb.

"Barry Gibb was a fan of the show and invited us to his house in Miami," Sullivan recalled. "I asked him whether he would like to appear in the episode and he was happy to do it, so that was a bit of luck, really. We didn't pay him; he was just pleased to be in it."

In the episode the Trotters only see Gibbs's luxury pad from the distance of their guided tour boat. In reality Jason and Lyndhurst joined Tony Dow and the crew as they filmed the Bee Gee star's brief scene. Here, the *Only Fools* stars posed for several publicity shots to promote the episode.

As the Trotters get drawn into the plot, we soon learn that Del has a very deadly lookalike in the mafioso kingpin, Don Occhetti (also played by Jason). When Occhetti's mobster family spot Del in a night club, it seems they have discovered the answer to all their prayers: the perfect double of the Don, who is currently on remand; if they can assassinate Del in public and pass the body off as Don Occhetti, the real Don can slip away.

"Filming *Fools and Horses* was one of the shows that I'm proudest of," remembers Antoni Corone, a former *Miami Vice* guest star who was brilliantly cast as the Don's son, Ricardo 'Rico' Occhetti. "I was asked if I'd mind keeping an ear on David's dialogue. So, unofficially, I was his 'dialogue coach'. He was brilliant to work with and glad to be invisible in Miami. No one knew who he was because the show didn't air here in the States. I remember going to have lunch with him and Nick at an outdoor café on South Beach and I was more recognized than they were."

Despite not being a well-known series State-side, the press were still keen to find out some details of the episode to sell to UK newspapers. "I was offered $500 for the script by reporters," remembers Corone. "Needless to say, I didn't entertain it. I vividly remember David being escorted to the set with a team of production grips holding up blankets to conceal him when in character as the Don."

MIAMI TWICE PART TWO: OH TO BE IN ENGLAND

25 DECEMBER 1991

What a place Miami is. Rodders and I were having a cracking time driving about in our little camper van, going on 'Star Tours' and soaking up the the old current bun. It hadn't all gone smoothly, though. Some git had nicked our camera (a real shame cos Ronnie Nelson had only let me have it on sale or return) and then the van was burgled. Fortunately we still had our passports and return tickets. Rodney had kept them safe in his pocket (what a saint!). Unfortunately the burglars had taken all our spending money. Rodney had left that in the van (what a plonker!) But that's when Rico and his mates stepped in and saved the day. Or at least that's what we thought at the time. Before we knew it we were whisked back to his pad, a great big palace of a gaff that had electric gates, a tennis court and bogs made of marble. It was very me. Rodney was the first to suspect something was off and suggested that maybe Rico and his boys might be... you know... a bit light on their loafers. I couldn't see it myself. For starters they were Italian. They were just men's men, that's all. And alright, they were snappy dressers and their house was very, very tidy, but they probably had a maid stashed away somewhere. Anyway, it was a couple of days later, after narrowly avoiding having my brains blown out whilst eating a plate of dumplings, and then surviving an ordeal on a runaway jet ski, that we discovered that Rico and co were in fact top tier mafioso and they wanted nothing more than to see Rodney and I kipping with the fishies. It did put somewhat of a downer on the overall holiday experience, but these things happen I s'pose.

Del

As per Pop's instructions, the most important thing was to make it look believable. We had to get the limey out in a public place, preferably with witnesses. When the good old fashioned bullet-between-the-eyes approach failed, we decided to get a bit more creative. Most of the time I couldn't make out what the limey was saying to me, it was all "Stone me" and "Gordon Bennet bruv", but I've always had a talent for honing in on a man's weaknesses, and with the limey that weakness was pride. We had the jet ski already set up with the brake wires cut. At first the limey didn't bite when I suggested he take it for a whirl, but one little pinch to his ego and he was straddling that baby and going at it like he was at a Rodeo. He went, and went and just kept on going, straight as an arrow (Tony had also disabled the steering) until he disappeared over the horizon. So you can imagine my shock when ten hours later I answered the front door to find that no good, limey sonofabitch standing there wrapped in a towel, looking like an extra shrivelled E.T. The Feds had been tracking his whole journey, thinking it was Pop trying to escape. I just couldn't catch a break with this jackass!

Rico

Above: Del and Rodney on the run in the Everglades.

Above right: Don Occhetti in his study.

Below: The cast seen in the Everglades sequences pose for a group shot.

Below right: Don and Del almost meet... thanks to some nifty post-production work.

Opposite page top left: The original title card to the episode.

Opposite page right: Boycie, Marlene, Tyler and their boatman, Wayne, help the Trotters escape.

Opposite page below left: Back home in Nelson Mandela house at last, Raquel, Albert, Reverend Campbell and dozens of boxes of pre-blessed Romanian Rheisling greet Del and Rodney.

"The episode gave me the chance to introduce the Trotters to the real criminal world," remembered John Sullivan. "Del and Rodney are very much on the periphery of mild criminal activities – they're always performed by someone else, and the Trotters often end up being the victims! So to mix them up with some real heavies was very interesting."

In a case of life imitating art, the crew soon found itself falling foul of the powerful Teamsters Union of drivers. As filming was about to commence, the Teamsters went on strike, requiring some very delicately handled discussions between producer Gareth Gwenlan and the heads of the union.

By this time, John Challis and Sue Holderness had joined the cast, ready for their scenes at the end of the story. "Filming was suddenly put on hold," remembers Challis, "and we spent about eight days longer than we should have done, which of course was absolute hell, as you can imagine: in Florida, by the swimming pool, having ridiculous breakfasts and drinking buckets of Tequila... we became quite unpopular with the rest of the cast for a time."

When filming resumed, one of the final sequences shot saw the crew relocate some 50 miles south of Miami to the Everglades National Park. Here the crew was joined by an animal handler to aid in the filming of Del and Rodney's brush with a live alligator. Having finally figured out the truth about the Occhettis, Del and Rodney make their escape. With an armed Rico and co in hot pursuit, all seems lost for the Brothers Trotter, right up until a chance meeting with a holidaying Boycie and Marlene (taking a leisurely airboat tour of the

Everglades) saves the day. As Del, Rodney, Boycie and Marlene speed away, we get some hilarious lines ("We were having a lovely holiday... then they turn up! And within 15 seconds some sod's shooting at us!")

Whilst location filming was underway, the London-based band The Gutter Brothers were busy creating the incidental music for *Oh to be in England*. The more dramatic nature of this story called for music to complement what was on screen, from a reoccurring *Godfather*-like mandolin piece to several fast-moving rock instrumentals. John Sullivan had already suggested using the Lovin' Spoonful's classic 'Summer in the City' to open the film, when The Gutter Brothers singer Chris Cawte suggested that they re-record it to give a consistent sound to the film.

With the location filming complete, the final part of the production was the studio recording for the first part of the story, which took place at Television Centre from 14–15 December.

The American Dream would be presented with the usual *Only Fools* opening and closing credits, while *Oh To Be In England* would start with minimalist titles akin to a feature film (video releases would later edit both parts together, omitting these titles along with footage from the end of *The American Dream*).

Shown at 7.30pm on Christmas Eve (pulling in 17.70 million viewers) and 3.10pm on Christmas Day (14.90 million), *Only Fools* was brought to the screen on a truly hilarious and thrilling Hollywood scale.

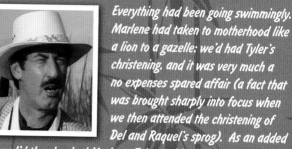

Everything had been going swimmingly. Marlene had taken to motherhood like a lion to a gazelle; we'd had Tyler's christening, and it was very much a no expenses spared affair (a fact that was brought sharply into focus when we then attended the christening of Del and Raquel's sprog). As an added bonus I'd then booked Marlene, Tyler and I a holiday in America. It was more of a tour actually, one that would see us flying to Washington, then on to Atlantic City and finally Florida. Miami to be exact. The first two legs went as well as could be expected. I'd kept the earplugs they gave me on the flight and they came in very handy during the nights when I just wanted to shut out all the noise and the drama. Tyler slept like a log too. We finally arrived in Miami and wasted no time in taking in a guided tour of the Everglades. There we were, surrounded by nothing but God's good creation, all the wondrous wildlife you could ever hope to see, when all of a sudden Del Boy and Rodney appeared from out of the reeds. For a minute I thought it must have been heatstroke, but no, there they were, screaming at us from the bank of a swamp. We picked them up and within 15 seconds of doing so some git started shooting at us! It was like the Dukes of Hazard on an airboat!

Boycie

MOTHER NATURE'S SON

Raquel had the right hump, and it wasn't just the regular pre-minstrel-tension type hump, that I could just about handle. No, this was serious. Whatever it was, you'd have thought all the taking care of Damien and all the ironing, cooking and cleaning would have taken her mind off it. Then there was Rodney, who had been taking the art of moping to a whole new level. So much so in fact that it was beginning to affect his and Cassandra's... well, you know, marital copulationship. On top of that we were potless, skint, brassic, nicht the old coin! But the real brick on top of the chimney was the letter I received from the council, confirming that I now owned the flat. I'd worked out that the mortgage repayments were two and a half times the rent, and I couldn't even afford the rent. Along with the flat, we also now owned Grandad's old allotment. I felt like a mosquito who'd caught malaria! You might have thought by now that I'd given up my dream of one day becoming a millionaire. But you'd be wrong. If anything, all the disappointment and set-backs had just made me even more determined. You see, us high-flying Richard Branston types don't know the meaning of the word 'stop'. Take that Elton Musk bloke for example: when one of his thunderbird rockets explodes on the launch pad, d'you reckon he says "Sod this for a game of soldiers, I'm packing it in and going home for a kip"? No, he knuckles down, jumps straight back on his horse and blows up another rocket. And when I happened to join Rodney on his weekly shop to one of those trendy health food centres, I discovered one hell of a rocket. One that very nearly took us to the stars!

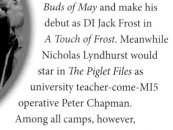

Above: The Nags Head festive party...

Right: ...but somehow, Damien doesn't have a reflection!

Above right and below: During the sequence, several portrait shots were taken.

Below right: Rodney wakes up... it was only a dream!

Opposite page top right: Raquel wants Damien to have his bedroom back again – "Three months ago you evicted Damien, moved him in with us and filled his lovely little room up with all your old junk!"

After a prolific 1991, it made sense to rest *Only Fools* for most of the following year as cast and crew moved on to other projects.

For John Sullivan, this was meant to be an opportunity to revisit his popular comedy *Dear John* for a belated third series, with former *Only Fools* director Susan Belbin set to take on directorial duties. Sadly, the tragic death of the series' star, Ralph Bates, meant this was not to be. In its place, Sullivan developed a brand-new series for BBC 1, a refreshingly female-centric comedy named *Sitting Pretty* which starred Diane Bull.

On ITV, David Jason would spend 1992 as both Pop Larkin in the second series of *The Darling*

Buds of May and make his debut as DI Jack Frost in *A Touch of Frost*. Meanwhile Nicholas Lyndhurst would star in *The Piglet Files* as university teacher-come-MI5 operative Peter Chapman.

Among all camps, however, there was a strong desire to get the family together again for an *Only Fools* Christmas special, and by November the machine was up and running for *Mother Nature's Son*, a 64-minute special for Christmas Day. "It always seemed to be the same madness for each special as no one was ever available until a few months before Christmas," remembers Tony Dow.

As the climax of the episode would see the Trotters enjoy a stay at the Grand Hotel in Brighton, it made sense to film all location material for the episode in the Brighton area. With filming scheduled between 25 November and 7 December,

MOTHER NATURE'S SON

25 DECEMBER 1992

I'd not long ago redecorated Rodney's old room, making it into a perfect little nursery for Damien. Even Del had helped out by getting a piece of carpet. It didn't fit the room, of course, but it was better than nothing. Then, right out of the blue, Del evicted Damien and started using the room as a dumping ground for all his old tat, or as he called it: 'stock'. He explained that he'd only put it there for safe keeping since someone had broken into the garage, but the implication of this still hadn't dawned on him. "Del, all we've got here is what the thieves left behind" I explained. "How do you expect to sell it when the burglars won't take it for free?!" And it was hardly surprising, considering what was on offer: 150 Bros LPs; 275 'Free Nelson Mandela' T-shirts; a crate of Charles and Di wedding plates; a 9 carat identity bracelet inscribed with the name 'Gary'; a box full of men's wigs; 50 pirated versions of The Poseidon Adventure – all on Betamax; 200 litres of Romanian Rheisling and a deep-sea divers outfit! "But who's to say I won't sell it all tomorrow?" he said. "Del" I said, "What are the chances of you bumping into a bald-headed, anti-apartheid, deep-sea-diving Bros fan who has a betamax video recorder, likes Romanian Rheisling and whose name is Gary?" He finally agreed to clear it all out.

Raquel

the episode would then be completed with two days of studio recording taking place on Saturday 19 and Sunday 20 December 1992.

"I was inspired to write this episode by a story that I'd heard. It was about some people having their water supply cut off because a dodgy substance had been dumped in a nearby reservoir," recalled John Sullivan. "At the time there was also this sort of craze about drinking bottled water. Someone told me there was a shop in Knightsbridge that sold nothing but bottles of mineral water – obviously at hugely inflated prices. I wondered what would happen if Del Boy could get on the bandwagon."

To bring viewers back to Peckham, Sullivan decided to open the episode with a scene that is shortly revealed to be Rodney's dream. Described in the script as 'the greatest party in the world', the episode opens on an overly jubilant cast acting a little out of character, with Trigger even enjoying some festive romance! In a hilarious moment, Rodney takes hold of a 22-month-old Damien and stands in front of a mirror, only to see that Damien has no reflection, causing a horrified Rodney to wake from his dream.

Originally scripted to take place in the flat, subsequent drafts relocated this opening sequence to the Nags Head to allow for a greater sense of atmosphere. Sullivan was keen to have a moment which reminded viewers about Rodney's satanic fear of his nephew.

The scene is also notable for being the last time we see Cassandra's parents, Alan and Pamela Parry, in the series. Despite not having any scripted dialogue, actors Dennis Lill and Wanda Ventham were invited to the non-audience studio day to enjoy the festivities of the brief scene.

Back in Trotter Towers, both Damien and Albert seem to be having trouble keeping their food down, and with Damien's nursery now overrun

It was the simplest of tasks: go to Grandad's old allotment, pick up the dozen or so drums filled with a mysterious, bright green sludge, transfer them to the back of the van and then drop them off at the 24-hour waste disposal depot.

The trouble was that Denzil was there (he had to be really, since we were using his van) and nothing's ever straightforward with that bloke.

"This is a bad idea, Del" he said. "Only a complete moron would go along with it."

"Well I'm game," Trigger said.

I tried to calm the situation by reminding Denzil that he was up to date with all his inoculations, but he continued to drone on about how dangerous the sludge might be. I mean, really, it was only a bit of chemical waste, when's that ever done anyone any harm? The way he was talking you'd have thought we were about to unleash a zombie plague on Peckham. That said, it's not entirely unwise to err on the side of caution in situations such as these. Of course, I'm no scientific advisor, but you couldn't deny that stuff neither looked nor smelled too clever. That being the case, I made sure to wear the deep-sea diving suit that I'd recently picked up at auction (I'd heard on the grapevine that diving was big with the yuppies, so I thought I'd have a punt). Anyway, we finally managed to get the drums into the back of Denzil's van and head off for the depot. Everything had gone without a hitch, but still Denzil whined.

"You know what, Denzil?" I said. "I'm starting to wish I hadn't asked you to help me move these drums."

"I'm just worried about our safety," he said. "I mean for all we know that stuff could be contagious!"

"Denzil," I said. "The only thing contagious round here is the pain in the arse you're giving me and Trigger, now shutup moaning!"

"But what if it is contagious, Del?" Trigger piped up. "Shouldn't we be taking some sort of medical precautions?"

"Well how should I know?" I said. "Who d'you think I am, Quincy MC or something?"

"Maybe we should try keeping two metres apart from each other," he suggested. This actually might not have been a bad idea on Trig's part, if it hadn't been for the fact that at that very moment we were wedged shoulder-to-shoulder in the front cabin of Denzil's van.

"Look" I said. "Once we get out of the van you can stay two metres apart, or two hundred metres apart, or two thousand for all I care, alright?"

"It'll be too late by then," Denzil sulked.

"Don't worry," Trigger said. "Even if whatever's in those drums is a bit contagious, it's not like we're having a bath in it. We're only going for a little drive."

"Right," I said. "Just a little drive round the corner. There's nothing dangerous about that. I mean it's not like we're going on a day trip to the Yorkshire Dales, is it?"

"Yeah" Trigger said. "We're not that stupid!"

Del

with a ridiculous array of TITCo stock, Raquel is at breaking point.

To make matters worse, it is then we discover that Del has bought the flat. "At the time, a lot of people were buying their council properties, but, true to his character, Del Boy ends up having trouble paying the mortgage!" remembered Sullivan.

As the episode unfolds we learn that Rodney and Cassandra have become Friends of the Earth and are now doing their weekly shop at Myles' 'Nature's Way' organic centre – a one stop shop for all your organic fertilisers and health food. When Del tags along with Rod on one of his trips to the centre, he is amazed by the steep prices of the organic goods and, especially, the bottles of water on offer.

Swain's Farm Shop and Garden Centre on the outskirts of Brighton was used as a location for this scene, where actor Robert Glenister joins the cast as Myles, several years before he found fame in BBC's *Spooks* and *Hustle*.

Taking its cue from a throwaway reference to Grandad's allotment in 1981's *The Russians are Coming*, we finally see the allotment in this episode. As part of Del's new responsibilities as owner of the flat, he now has a duty to take care of the allotment. And it couldn't have come at a worse time, as the site currently poses an environmental health hazard, in the form of several rusty canister drums which have been dumped there. For these scenes the crew used Moulsecoomb Estate Allotments on Brighton's Natal Road.

Roping Denzil and Trigger into helping him clean the place up, they end up disposing of the waste canisters filled with a mysterious yellow gunge. In a nice touch of continuity, a cautious Del wears an antique aquanaut helmet which was first seen in the Trotters' garage in series four's *Its Only Rock and Roll*.

With the job done, Del takes his workers for a drink at the Nags Head (the White Admiral on Taunton Road in Brighton), and we are treated to a brilliant visual gag. Out in the car park, Denzil and Trigger wave farewell and we see a strange yellow glow on their hands.

Back at the allotment, Del puts one and two together and sees a 24 carat golden opportunity. With the help of Uncle Albert, an unwitting Myles and a very carefully placed hose pipe, he puts his plan into action.

The following scene is one of the greatest cuts in the series' history, as we go from the location footage to a studio shot of a gradually revealed 'Peckham Spring' bottle production line in the Trotters' flat,

Opposite page above: Del gets Denzil and Trigger to help him dispose of the drums dumped on Grandad's old allotment.

Opposite page below right: Denzil and Trigger wave a glowing farewell.

Above left: Del amazed by the prices of bottled water.

Above: Myles (Robert Glenister) looks over Del's land.

Below: The Peckham Spring bottling plant, and a bottle used in the episode.

PECKHAM
Spring Water

Above: The Peckham Spring production line in full swing.

Right: The stress of the secret of the Peckham Spring gets to Rodney.

Above right: A night of celebration in the Nags Head.

Below: The Trotters arrive at Brighton's Grand Hotel.

Below right: Everything is well for both of the Trotter couples.

leading from the living room into the kitchen where we see Del (in full white coat and hat regalia) filling up each bottle with tap water!

The Peckham Spring is simply a brilliant plot device and makes for an incredibly funny story. The humour continues as we learn that Cassandra personally arranged for the bank loan that allowed Del to buy all the bottling equipment. Gwyneth Strong makes the character's reaction to finding out that Peckham Spring is simply tap water priceless.

The Peckham Spring is a runaway success and reverses the Trotters' fortunes, allowing them to enjoy nights out in the Nags Head again (and even earning Raquel an invitation to join Marlene's coffee mornings!) To properly celebrate, Rodney and Cassandra plan a trip away to the coast to spend some precious time alone together, until Del

decides to join in on the fun and turns the whole thing into a full family outing.

To show the Trotters arriving at the Grand Hotel, a playful montage was filmed and edited together to the Beatles' classic 'Money'. For rights reasons this song was sadly replaced for home video release with a poorly selected piece of instrumental music.

Following on from *Miami Twice*'s successful use of incidental music to undercut dramatic scenes, Sullivan and Dow were keen to make it a regular element in *Only Fools* going forward. Starting with the 1992 Christmas Special, composer Graham Jarvis joined the *Only Fools* team to add musical accompaniment as and when required, including the emotional ending to *Mother Nature's Son*.

"The episode was going out on Christmas Day which was a Friday that year," remembers Jarvis. "I didn't get a completed video till the Monday before Christmas, and the dub was Thursday afternoon! I'd spend most of Monday looking at where the cues were meant to be and trying to get a flavour of what

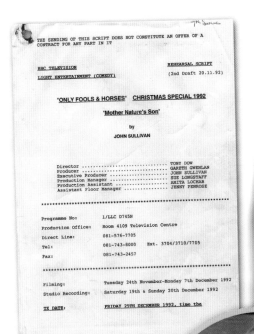

7th Issue

BBC TELEVISION

REHEARSAL SCRIPT

LIGHT ENTERTAINMENT (COMEDY)

(2nd Draft 20.11.92)

"ONLY FOOLS & HORSES" CHRISTMAS SPECIAL 1992

'Mother Nature's Son'

by

JOHN SULLIVAN

Director .... TONY DOW
Producer .... GARETH GWENLAN
Executive Producer .... JOHN SULLIVAN
Production Manager .... SUE LONGSTAFF
Production Assistant .... ANITA LOCHAB
Assistant Floor Manager .... JENNY PENROSE

Programme No: 1/LLC D745N

Production Office: Room 4109 Television Centre

Direct Line: 081-576-7705

Tel: 081-743-8000 Ext. 3704/3710/7705

Fax: 081-743-2457

Filming: Tuesday 24th November-Monday 7th December 1992

Studio Recording: Saturday 19th & Sunday 20th December 1992

TX DATE: FRIDAY 25TH DECEMBER 1992, time tba

When the Peckham Spring suddenly sprung up out of nowhere on Del's allotment, I knew he was pulling a fast one. I said to Marlene "Marlene, if this don't all end in tears then my middle name ain't Aubrey!" (and it is by the way, my parents hated me). Not that I wasn't pleased for him and the rest of the family. Say what you like about me, but I've never been one to sneer at the success of others. I mean, why would I when I've had so much success myself? No, when the Peckham Spring began to pay off it was actually quite satisfying to know that Del and Rodney were finally experiencing a tiny sip of what I'd been lapping up for years. I even managed a smile at one point (Marlene's got the Polaroid to prove it). And when the whole venture went belly up and the Trotters were forced to explain themselves to the World Health Organisation, I managed a full on, ear-to-ear grin that lasted at least a fortnight.

Boycie

was required. I then went into the studio not really knowing what I was going to do, but after a couple of coffees something came together. With such a short time frame there was no time to get any session musicians in, so that last eight minutes was just me playing my guitar part."

Graham's gentle guitar motif was a perfect ending to a festive Trotter treat as at long last Rodney and Cassandra put their differences behind them and Del and Raquel enjoy their little family.

As Del turns his bedside light out, we're treated to a hilarious final shot of a bottle of Peckham spring glowing bright yellow.

Broadcast on Christmas Day 1992 at 6.55pm, *Mother Nature's Son* pulled in an incredible 20.1 million viewers, equalling the series' record at that time and proving that the demand for the show was as high as ever.

Above left: The rehearsal script for *Mother Nature's Son*.

Above: Boycie is miffed by the success of the Peckham Spring.

Middle: News footage showing drums (like those found on Grandad's allotment) being fished out of a river...

Left: A shot of Raquel and Del in their Grand Hotel suite.

Far left: As Del turns out his bedside light, the bottle of Peckham Spring glows yellow! – "I wouldn't mind betting that this time next week my name'll be in all the papers."

FATAL EXTRACTION

The good ship Trotter had strayed off course and entered into some very dangerous waters. All my recent investments had gone down the Swannee. I was doing everything in my power to earn us a few quid and reset the balance, but the situation got so bad it was starting to tell at home. You see, I'd been spending a lot of time at the casino, hoping the roulette wheel would deliver an answer to all our prayers. Raquel then got it into her head that I was enjoying myself, but nothing could be further from the truth. If only she'd seen how much money I was losing she'd have known just how much I was trying! To make matters worse, I had a bark of a toothache, which is why I was drinking so much scotch when I was spinning that roulette wheel – it was the only thing that numbed the pain. Yep, at that moment our future was about as bright as that of a Wuhanese bat salesman. The one and only ray of hope on the horizon was the deal I'd lined up with Ronnie Nelson for a consignment of hand held camcorders. He'd already shown me a sample and I was very impressed. Big, sturdy bits of kit they were, Russian made (always a sign of quality) and virtually indestructible. Seriously, he showed me a clip of one being bombarded with Molotov cocktails. Once the flames died out there weren't a scratch on it. What with the recent spate of riots on the estate, I felt very confident we were onto a winner!

Above: The Peckham riots are in the news.

Above right: Raquel isn't happy with Del's coming home at all hours.

Right: Del makes use of the 'Relate' leaflet his uncle has given him...

Below: Del and Rodney take on the 121 Casino... and end up staying all night.

Opposite page top left: On the bus to Nelson Mandela House, Mickey Pearce is concerned about Rodney – "He look's shagged out, don't he, love?!"

Opposite page bottom right: Dental receptionist, Beverly (Mel Martin).

1993's Christmas special welcomes us back to life in Nelson Mandela House, where Del seems to have wound the clock back to his days as a single man, embracing his old ways of drinking, gambling and staying out late, and causing some frayed edges in his and Raquel's relationship.

"This episode perfectly shows the two sides of Del Boy," remembered John Sullivan. "On one hand, he's like a little boy, terrified of going to the dentist about his toothache. On the other hand, he's got all this masculine pride, which means he can't deal with Raquel telling him what to do and when he should be in at night."

Meanwhile, Rodney and Cassandra are trying for a baby, with a punishing schedule mapped out and Rodney on emergency call, ready to return to active duty at the drop of a hat.

Location filming for *Fatal Extraction* was arranged to take place in Bristol between 1–12 November 1993, after which the cast reunited to rehearse studio scenes leading up to three days in Television Centre from the 26th.

As had been the practice since the second part of *Miami Twice*, studio recording would be exclusively reserved for the regular sets only, with all other interiors filmed on location.

"That decision was really made on the basis that you could only fit so much in the studio," recalls director Tony Dow. "Once you got the lounge and the Nags Head in you had basically covered the width of the studio, and if you did have another set it would be round the back, which kind of defeated the object. We'd show all the film on the screens, so the audience would catch it all and that would give lots of room for getting laughs."

Back in Bristol, for the 121 Casino, the crew returned to the exterior location of *Yuppy Love*'s

FATAL EXTRACTION

25 DECEMBER 1993

I'd always been able to handle a woman scorned, but this woman was both scorned and an olive short of a pizza. Raquel and I had separated, so I took the opportunity to dust off the old charm laser beams and see if they still worked. They passed the MOT with flying colours when I managed to get a date with Beverley, the receptionist at the dental clinic. Of course, I weren't serious, I just wanted to prove a point. I'm still not entirely sure what that point was, but it's all epidemic now anyway. I gave Beverley a bell and left a message on her answer machine, letting her know that, whilst I was very flattered, the date was off. I thought that would be the end of it, but it was just the beginning of my woes. From that moment on, Beverley was everywhere I went. She was in the pub, in the market and even at the bloody bus stop. Rodney pointed out that she might have just been having a drink, doing a bit of shopping and waiting for a bus, but that was just too far fetched for my liking. The real panic set in when I returned to the flat one afternoon and found Beverley in the front room, chatting with Raquel. I nearly had a connery! She said she was there to buy Damien's old high-chair after seeing the ad I'd put in the local newsagents window. Yeah right, pull the other one darlin'! Well, that was enough for me to shoot down to the clinic the next morning and tell her to stop haunting me. She played the innocent and called me a moron. Well, I felt a big weight off my shoulders knowing that the whole thing had been put to bed, leaving me to enjoy a cushty Christmas with all the family. And it was all going so well up until Raquel plugged in the answering machine she'd got me and found a message was already on it. She'd got the machine from Beverley, a straight-swap for Damien's high-chair!

Del

wine bar, this time using the other corner of the same building on Welsh Back. Other locations used included Popeye's Diner on Brunel Lock Road, which became another incarnation of Sid's cafe, and York House on Bond Street, which was redressed as Peckham Rye Health Centre. Market scenes for this episode were filmed just down from Trotter Towers themselves at the Ashton Gate Stadium Car Park.

When Rodney is despatched to investigate Del's late night shifts at the casino, he gets drawn into the gambling, leading to both brothers not emerging from the smokey den till 8 o'clock in the morning!

Fed up with Del's behaviour, Raquel takes Damien and moves out of the flat to stay with Rodney and Cassandra, leaving Del to take solace with his mates in the Nags Head, and to face the dentist alone.

Sullivan was keen to reinforce that Del couldn't just simply back-pedal and apologise after Raquel leaves him. In a similar fashion to Rodney in *Rodney Come Home*, male pride gets the better of him and he asks another woman out on a date. "Del really loves Raquel to bits and is desperate for her to come home, but he's got to play Jack the lad. Of course, the real reason why he's been spending nights in the casino is because he's got a deal lined up – he really wants to be able to provide for Raquel and Damien – but it doesn't even cross his mind to tell her about his plans!"

Cast as the date that never was, the dental receptionist, Beverley, was well-known TV actress Mel Martin, who employs just the right amount of intensity to suggest she could be the 'bunny boiler' Del fears her to be. The episode's knowing title *Fatal*

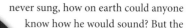

Above: Del sells Trotters Independent Trader's latest line, ski ware from Fiji!

Above right: The men of the Nags Head discuss the mystery that is womankind – "Why ask!"

Left: Del sings 'One Voice' and starts a riot!

Below: Del faces his fear as the dentist (Andrew Charleson) gives him an injection.

Below right: The Russian camcorders Del has bought have one major flaw: the cassette tapes don't fit British VHS players!

Opposite page left: Rodney falls asleep in a lift and returns home from work to report for duty.

Opposite page right: Sid serves another delicious meal.

Extraction gives a nod to the film *Fatal Attraction* and also a neat reference to Del's rotten tooth.

Fortunately, Del quickly sees sense and calls Beverley, leaving a message on her answering machine to let her know the date is off. He is soon on the phone again to Raquel and they are reunited.

Blissfully happy that Raquel is coming home, the showpiece of the episode sees Del stumble home from the pub whilst belting out a drunken rendition of the Barry Manilow number 'One Voice'. So merry is Del, he doesn't even realise that his singing has kicked off another riot on the estate.

"David had never been recorded singing so didn't want to do it," remembers composer Graham Jarvis. "We originally hired in a 'David Jason' sound-a-like to sing, as we all agreed that as David had

never sung, how on earth could anyone know how he would sound? But the impersonator sounded more like Bud Flanagan. I think eventually John, Tony and Gareth treated David to a meal and got him to agree. At the studio, everybody was on tenterhooks. David's last note had to be really long, and he did it in one take. Brilliant."

"In my original script, I was only going to mention the riot in passing, but Tony [Dow] persuaded me to show it in the episode," recalled John Sullivan." It was a tough scene to shoot – we wanted to make it look realistic, but it had to be funny rather than frightening – but everything worked out very well in the end."

"The flats were right next to Bristol City's stadium, Ashton Gate," remembers Dow. "They were run as retirement blocks, so it made it great. They looked like council flats and we were able to give them money towards their Christmas fund. And they were brilliant to work with as they'd all be in bed by 8 o'clock!"

For this sequence, producer Gareth Gwenlan, a keen horseman, doubled as a riot policeman, getting a few lines in the finished episode. Sat on the horse,

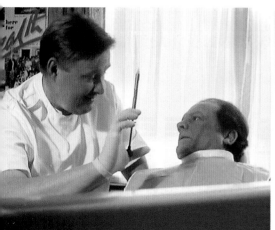

Cassandra and I had been trying for a baby... 'trying' being the operative word. I'd always thought that getting pregnant was a pretty straightforward process. I mean, once you know what goes where the rest should take care of itself. But nothing's ever straightforward in my life. We had to make use of schedules, charts, thermometers, specimens, muscle exercises, the lot! Cassandra always said she wanted it to be a special and tender moment, but this was more like boot camp! In fact the only thing that would've been more off-putting was if I'd had an actual drill sergeant screaming in my ear whilst I was... you know... doing it. I'd never been so knackered in all me life, and I became so pale at one point I had to update my passport photo. On Del's advice, we went to Sid's cafe. I was hoping a bowl of his porridge might boost my energy levels, but after seeing the hairs Denzil pulled out of his bowl,
I stuck to a cup of tea.

Rodney

Over the years many questions have been raised about the hygiene standards of my establishment, but it's all a fuss about nothing if you ask me. Normally I just point to the five-star hygiene-rating plaque that takes pride of place on the front of the counter, and that's enough to end the discussion. And fair enough, Del sold me the plaque, but as he rightly said, "What can't speak, can't lie." The thing a lot of people don't understand – health inspectors in particular – is that I've always specialised in serving a very distinct kind of clientele, the kind that want good old fashioned grub, fried in a good old fashioned dollop of lard and with a sprinkling of good old fashioned fag ash. Top that off with a good old fashioned squirt of ketchup or HP (sometimes both) and these people are more than happy to shove it down their gullets. You have to understand, that these are people who have been digesting bacteria, hairs, and other various bits of foreign debris for so long that they've built up a natural immunity to it. All I do is provide them with what they need, and I'm proud to say I'm bloody good at it too!

Sid

Above: For the riot scene, police and the fire brigade were on standby at Whitemead House in Bristol.

Above right: The set of the flat as it appeared in *Fatal Extraction*.

Right: *Only Fools'* producer, and riot policeman, Gareth Gwenlan.

Below: Both the rioters and police stop to make way for Del Boy and family.

the producer was suitably placed to oversee the incredibly large group of extras, both in front of and behind the cameras.

The riot was featured twice in the episode, the second time being the following evening when Del brings Raquel and Damien home in his Capri. Here, a blast from the Capri Ghia's horn clears a path, as both rioters and police make way for Del Boy.

With everything sewn up, it seems that the Trotters are all set for a happy Christmas, but Del is still haunted by Beverley, who he has now spotted in the market, in the pub, and even in the flat (buying a highchair from Raquel). Del finally confronts the receptionist and makes matters clear.

A few days later, with Christmas in full swing, Raquel has a surprise for Del: she swapped Damien's highchair for an answering machine.

When Rodney sets the machine up he notices that it already has a message on it, and we then hear Del's voice explaining to Beverly that their date is off. The camera pans down from the flat as we hear Raquel start a riot of her own!

Unusually for an *Only Fools* Christmas Special, *Fatal Extraction* was made under a much more comfortable production schedule throughout November 1993, which gave the production team the best part of a month to edit and complete the episode before 25 December.

Topping BBC One's 1993 festive schedule, *Fatal Extraction* drew in a whopping 19.6 million viewers. Among those viewers watching on Christmas night was Perry Aghajanoff, who, the following year, would be one of the founders of the *Only Fools and Horses* Appreciation Society:

"I had been an avid viewer since 1982 and was immediately blown away by the brilliant humour and characters," recalls Aghajanoff. "I'd grown up with Del and Rodney, and as the show went from full series' into occasional specials, it seemed that something was required to keep the fans going, which led to the magazine."

Originally home produced and photocopied, the society's magazine, *Hookie Street*, grew from strength to strength, soon evolving into a glossy publication that would keep fans up to date on all the latest news on the series and cast.

"I think the initial print run of issue one was in the hundreds and that sold out instantly. We gradually made contact with members of the cast and crew and were delighted that John Sullivan himself became a great friend of the society, generously giving us his time and introducing us to people."

The growing popularity of *Hookie Street* convinced Aghajanoff and his colleagues to turn their attention towards fan events, and soon enough the first *Only Fools* Convention was organised, with John Challis and Ken MacDonald among its very first guests. These events allowed fans to meet their screen heroes and get autographs, as well as to chat about the show with fellow fans. The series was taking on a life of its own beyond the screen.

Ironically, just as fans were getting organised to celebrate Peckham's finest, and thanks to the demand of the series' cast, *Only Fools* was heading into its first completely fallow year.

David Jason's fruitful relationship with Yorkshire Television was continuing with *A Touch of Frost,* a massive hit for the actor. Similarly, Nicholas Lyndhurst was enjoying impressive viewing figures with his third sitcom as leading man, this time on BBC 1 as the time travelling Gary Sparrow in *Goodnight Sweetheart*. Elsewhere, Tessa Peake-Jones, Roger Lloyd Pack and Paul Barber were also enjoying screen success away from their Peckham roles.

Suddenly, uniting the company for an episode of *Only Fools* had become a scheduling nightmare. Whilst John Sullivan never intended *Fatal Extraction* as a final visit to Nelson Mandela House, the realities of television soon made it feel like it might be.

Above: Del can't seem to get away from Beverly.... and expects the worst on discovering a boiling pot on the stove...

Below left: Rodney sets up the answer phone and a message starts to play – "Hello Beverly, this is Del Boy. Erm... Listen, I've got to cancel our date tonight..."

Left: Raquel hears Del's answer phone message...

Below: The sound of an argument raging on the twelfth floor of Nelson Mandela House drifts down into the precinct... as children sing 'Silent Night' and Beverly smiles.

CHRISTMAS TRILOGY

★★★★★★★★★★★★★★★★★★★★★★★★★★★★★

The sun rises and the sun sets, that's what life is all about. It's like the changes of the seasons and the tides of the sea. One minute you and your brother are legging it through a misty Peckham night dressed as Batman and Robin, the next you're receiving medals for bravery for apprehending a gang of muggers. One day you receive the most loveliest and jubbliest news ever, the sort that makes your soul shine and your heart sing, the next it's taken away in the most cruelest of manners. And one moment you're arguing with a pub landlord over a torn fiver, the next you're laying on the floor of Sotheby's having just hit the jackpot of a lifetime! I don't know how or why these things happen. All I know is that when the light starts to fade, you mustn't give up on that old sun. Because you mark my words, it will rise again, often when you least expect it and shining brighter than ever before. At the end of the day it's... well, Excusez mon visage, as they say in Picardy.

★★★★★★★★★★★★★★★★★★★★

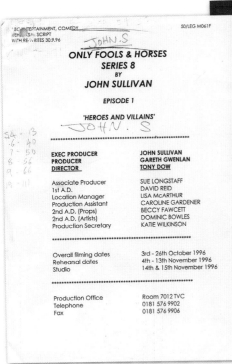

ONLY FOOLS & HORSES
SERIES 8
BY
JOHN SULLIVAN

EPISODE 1

'HEROES AND VILLAINS'

JOHN. S

EXEC PRODUCER	**JOHN SULLIVAN**
PRODUCER	**GARETH GWENLAN**
DIRECTOR	**TONY DOW**
Associate Producer	SUE LONGSTAFF
1st A.D.	DAVID REID
Location Manager	LISA McARTHUR
Production Assistant	CAROLINE GARDENER
2nd A.D. (Props)	BECCY FAWCETT
2nd A.D. (Artists)	DOMINIC BOWLES
Production Secretary	KATIE WILKINSON

Overall filming dates	3rd – 26th October 1996
Rehearsal dates	4th – 13th November 1996
Studio	14th & 15th November 1996

Production Office	Room 7012 TVC
Telephone	0181 576 9902
Fax	0181 576 9906

Above: The rehearsal script for *Heroes and Villains*.

Above right: The *Only Fools* cast rehearse the Christmas Trilogy at the Acton Rehearsal Rooms.

Below: Director Tony Dow in front of Del's 'Lord Trotter of Peckham' painting, on the set of the futuristic Trotter Towers.

Christmas 1994 would be the first year without a 25 December *Only Fools* outing for nearly a decade, leaving a hole in millions of viewers festive celebrations. 1995 rectified matters with a welcome repeat of *Mother Nature's Son,* airing before the Queen's Speech, but what viewers really wanted was a new episode.

John Sullivan was determined not to let the series end without properly bowing out. In the back of the writer's mind was an idea that would see Del and Rodney finally become millionaires. However, with David Jason and Nicholas Lyndhurst tied up on several long-running TV commitments, it seemed a distant possibility.

In the intervening years, Sullivan had been working with much of the *Only Fools* team on several projects for the BBC. Firstly, *Over Here*, a two-part film detailing the lives of US airmen in Britain during World War 2 (starring Samuel West, Jay Goede, Martin Clunes, Geraldine James and Andrew Lincoln). This was followed by a new comedy drama series, *Roger Roger* (starring Robert Daws, Phil Glenister and Keith Allen).

It was during production of *Roger Roger* that Gareth Gwenlan learned that both of *Only Fools'* lead actors had windows in their schedules for later that year. The stars it seemed had aligned. Seizing upon the moment, a deal was ironed out for a one-off special for Christmas 1996.

Delighted to be delving once more into the world of the Trotters, Sullivan soon realised that he couldn't do justice to the whole Peckham gang in one final outing. He needed more. Although time was limited, it was agreed to turn the farewell special into an eighth series of three episodes, which would eventually become known as the Christmas Trilogy. The Trotters were back!

In the intervening years, the *Only Fools* Appreciation Society had been keeping busy with their popular publications and events. In the summer of 1996, the society's president Perry Aghajanoff was interviewing Ken MacDonald when the actor received a phone call. "Ken's landline went off and it was a call from Gareth Gwenlan to say that 'it's official, the show was coming back!' Ken was punching the air and smiling. After the call, he was playing it cool and joking that 'It's not for me son, I've moved on' – but there was no hiding his utter delight to be heading back to active duty with his friends on set again."

Location filming for the trilogy returned the crew to Bristol from 3 October for three weeks, followed by some additional location work in London which took production into early November. The cast would then gather for a week of rehearsing in the Acton rehearsal rooms in advance of *Heroes and Villains'* studio recording from 14–15 November.

After two years away, for the established cast and crew it really felt like a family reunion to be back together again with a brand new script to work from.

"It was our favourite moment of the day and just the biggest joy," remembers Tony Dow. "First of all, we'd say our prayers to John Sullivan and then we'd read the script and prepare for the laughs."

For Tessa Peake-Jones, getting a new *Only Fools* script was like gold dust. "We'd sit down with John and Tony and the whole production crew and hear all the actors read it out in character and live for the first time, exactly as the audience would be hearing it on Christmas Day. It was always such a joyous moment as it always worked, you'd always pause for the laughter."

To open the trilogy of new episodes, Sullivan decided to do something a little unexpected. Knowing that after two years of anticipation fans would be climbing the walls to see the familiar Trotter flat, the writer denied viewers the comforting sight of the bar and bamboo wallpaper for just a little longer.

"I thought it would be nice to see Rodney's idea of the future," remembered Sullivan. "We get a glimpse of the horrible vision in his head that Del is Lord

Peckham, with this conglomerate that's ruling half of Europe and America. Damien's even giving the President of America advice on how to run the world!"

Taking a nod from the dream that opened *Mother Nature's Son*, *Heroes and Villains* takes things one step further with a full-on mini movie set in a nightmarish dystopian future. The scene opens with an elderly Rodney walking with the aid of a stick whilst dodging rats and throwing coins to scrambling vagrants.

Taking advantage of the generous production budget, all sorts of video tricky was employed to give this view of a Trotter tomorrow the feel of a major film. In a series of animated billboards we see an advertisement for Del's very own airline 'Trotter Air'. He has his own food range in 'Trotters Meat Fingers' (advertised with a photo of John Sullivan's daughter Amy) and even 'Trotterex family planning!' (Go Equipped).

For this scene Nicholas Lyndhurst and crew filmed on wasteland next to the mothballed Battersea Power station, which was digitally tweaked to become the giant and dimly-lit 'Trotter Towers'.

Above left: Trotter Towers, 2026.

Above right: Lord Derek and Rodney the messenger.

Above: Inside Damien's vast futuristic office complex.

Left: Lady Raquel.

Below: T.I.T. Co billboard adverts. In this nightmare future, the Trotters own everything.

Inside the Towers we learn that Rodney is a mere messenger in the 'TITCo' machine, with a demonic and warmongering Damien running the show under the proud watch of an elderly Del and Raquel. Just to rub salt in the wound, Cassandra is in maid service and an ancient Uncle Albert has been wired into the wall!

Cast as the adult Damien was actor Douglas Hodge (who was married to Tessa Peake-Jones at the time) who plays the larger-than-life role brilliantly alongside the familiar cast. These interior scenes were filmed at the suitably grand Royal Horticultural Hall in London.

Composer Graham Jarvis was tasked with creating the ominous music which set the mood for the opening, and remembers that Sullivan, Dow and Gwenlan were conscious about getting things just right. "For the dream sequence nobody really knew what they wanted at first," remembers Jarvis. "Wether it was tongue in cheek or if they wanted something realistic, as they'd never done anything like this before on *Fools*. They kept on chopping and changing bits and I think they were still a little unsure if the reanimated Uncle Albert was funny or not!"

As it turned out, this nightmare vision was the perfect way to bring *Only Fools* back. When the elderly Rodney protests "I want to go back to how it used to be", he could be speaking for all the fans watching at home.

Blissfully, as a frail Lord Derek of Peckham calls out to Rodney, we suddenly drift out of the nightmare and are back in the flat again, as a much more familiar Del Boy is yelling in his brother's lughole.

As Rodney wakes up, life in the real Trotter Towers is just as it has always been, with Del bemoaning TITCo's current stock situation: 125 Latvian radio alarm clocks that go off whenever they bloody well like; a consignment of horse-riding crash helmets (sprayed red) and some incredibly unfashionable baseball caps that even EAST 17 fans wouldn't be seen dead in.

On top of that, Del has had his home improvement grant turned down by the council, Rodney and Cassandra are *still* trying for a baby, and Raquel is preoccupied with a recently received letter. As proceedings unfold we discover that it is also Rodney's birthday and Del and Raquel have got him a chunky gold identity bracelet inscribed with his name, which, due to copper plate writing and a dyslexic engraver, reads 'Rooney'.

Above: An incredibly old Uncle Albert is plugged into the wall.

Above right: Casandra, now working as a maid.

Above right: The adult Damien (Douglas Hodge).

Below: "Wake up you dipstick!" – Back to reality.

Opposite page above left: Raquel and Del have a tender moment as it is revealed that her long lost parents have been in touch.

Opposite page below right: Del with Damien.

HEROES AND VILLAINS

25 DECEMBER 1996

When Raquel got a call from her Mum and Dad saying that they missed her and wanted her to go and visit them the following Saturday. I was as shocked as anyone. Up to that point I'd never even realised Raquel had a Mum and Dad. Of course, she begged me to go with her, and I really did want to (especially when I found out that her old man, James, was an antiques specialist. I had a Jacobean cine-camera in the garage that I was itching to get a verdict on). But as sod's law would have it, that very same Saturday I had to go to Covent Garden to pick up a van load of water-damaged aubergines. So Raquel and Damien had to go on their own. It just so happened that that very same weekend Cassandra was going to stay with her Mum and Dad in their villa in Spain, giving Rodders a much needed break from all the thermometers and what 'ave you. The boy had been at it like a rattlesnake and deserved a bit of time off. By complete and utter coincidence, that Saturday also happened to be the night of Harry Malcolm's publican ball, an annual fancy dress do with a top prize of a grand's worth of stereo system for best costume. Well, I didn't really fancy it to be honest, I just wanted a quiet night in, but Rodney insisted we get a pair of costumes and go and win the prize. Eventually I caved. He's always had a knack for wrapping me right round his little finger.

Del

This opening scene back in the flat is even more jam-packed with gags than usual, with Sullivan clearly delighted to be back writing *Only Fools* once more. There are countless 'blink and you'll miss it' moments, such as Del hiding Rodney's cards and present in the freezer and Damien's card to his uncle featuring a cartoon devil (which Rodders recoils at as soon as he realises who it's from).

For the Christmas Trilogy, child actor Jamie Smith returned to the role as Damien after being first cast in the part aged 4 in *Fatal Extraction*. Here the young actor gets some cracking little lines to chime in with, especially his requests to play 'war' with his uncle Rodney (just moments after Rod's nightmare!).

Before the Latvian radio alarm clocks all go off in unison, Del and Rodney escape to Sid's cafe. Once again, Popeye's Diner on Brunel Lock Road in Bristol was used as the cafe, where the unhygienic proprietor has now taken to serving bowls of hairy porridge.

It is in this scene that Trigger proudly displays his medal, awarded for saving the council money after having had the same broom for 20 years... albeit with 17 new heads and 14 new handles!

All was not well in Gotham city. It began when Trigger was awarded a medal for services to sweeping. I wouldn't have believed it if it hadn't been for him repeatedly showing me the thing every five sodding minutes! Old Harry Malcolm, fellow mason and landlord of the Crown and Anchor, then popped his clogs. Harry was a good man and his sudden passing affected me quite badly, especially since he'd only a week earlier promised me a very good price on a dozen bottles of the finest Courvoisier. Just my luck. Then, as ever, there was Marlene, who was still trying to get me and her Mum to see eye to eye, a futile pursuit if ever there was one. Dora hated me with a passion and the feeling was mutual, but her birthday was coming up and Marlene wanted to drag me along to the celebrations. She even accused me of being 'anti social' when I refused to go. "Marlene, my little bluebottle," I said, "I am not anti social. I just don't like being around people."

I don't know what she expected. I was still having nightmares about the previous Christmas when we went round to Dora's for dinner. I don't think I'm exaggerating in saying that genital warts get warmer welcomes than what she gave me. And alright, maybe I was being a bit overly cautious, but since the recent outbreak of Mad Cow Disease everyone was a little bit on edge. Of course, Marlene wouldn't leave it alone and I eventually folded just to shut her up. Needless to say the celebrations were just as depressing as I'd expected them to be. In fact the one and only highlight of the evening that I can recall was seeing Dora's face when she unwrapped my present to her: a nice big leg of British beef.

Boycie

In a joke which only Roger Lloyd Pack could make work, a legendary Trigger moment was born, as the road sweeper's leap of logic has viewers both laughing and scratching their heads at the same time.

Back at the flat it is revealed that Raquel's letter was from her estranged parents, who she arranges to visit over the weekend. Coincidentally, it is the same weekend that Cassandra is staying with her parents at their holiday villa.

"The other halves were the straight women, and they knew that," remembers Tony Dow. "Tessa and Gwyneth are both fantastic actresses, but I will always remember in *Heroes and Villains* when Del and Rodney were left on their own, they got into that ridiculous situation. It was them back to being prats again!"

The ridiculous situation in question was the annual publican's ball (that year, a fancy dress do hosted by Harry Malcolm from Dulwich). Convinced that he and Rodney can win the top prize, Del persuades his younger brother to join him in shopping for a pair of costumes.

"A friend told me he was going to a vicars and tarts party with his wife – but he was dressing as

the tart," John Sullivan recollected. "Later, I realised he was driving through south London's badlands and I had this dread, what if he broke down in this situation at night? It's not the kind of place you'd want to be dressed like that. Then I thought what could I do with the Trotters? I came up with Batman and Robin because although Rodney should be Batman and Del Robin, due to their size, Del would automatically take the major role. Then, of course, they break down in the middle of Peckham!"

Due to the popularity of the series and the anticipation for its return, it was always going to be a difficult task to film this sequence. "The problem was the press," remembers Tony Dow. "If they had got a shot of Batman and Robin it would have spoilt the episode. We had so much security out and we got construction to build these two big wires on all sides of the street so no one could get in."

Whilst a shot of the van passing London's Elephant and Castle roundabout opened the scene, the rest of the sequence was filmed in Bristol, starting at the row of shops in Broadmead and moving on to Bristol's Coroner's Court, also used as the Town Hall in the story.

With Jason and Lyndhurst in costume at one end of the street, time was of the essence for Dow and the team to get the shot. "They came out and ran down the street with all the dry ice and we then sent them back again to capture the shot with a different lens. It took about an hour, probably

the quickest thing I ever shot, and probably the most effective! John and Gareth said 'why have you got dry ice?' and I said 'don't worry, it will give us tremendous atmosphere'. And of course, when they saw it they thought it looked brilliant."

During their run, the caped crusaders come across a gang of youths in the process of mugging Councillor Murray (the same councillor who turned down Del's home improvement grant and awarded Trigger a medal).

In one of the most magnificent moments in television history the Trotters' sudden appearance scares the muggers away, all accompanied by Graham Jarvis' rendition of the *Batman* theme.

FANCY DRESS   **£10 TICKET**

South East London's
Publican's Ball

Hosted by: Harry Malcolm from Dulwich

Spot Prizes
Top Prize - £1000 Stereo System

Opposite page top right: Trigger buys a ticket to Harry Malcom's Publican's ball.

Opposite page below right: Trigger proudly displays his broom and medal with Councillor Murray (Angela Bruce).

Above and below: Del convinces Rodney into going to the ball in costume... but on their way the van breaks down in the middle of town.

Left: In this scene Rodney is reading a mocked-up paper with the headline "Freddie Starr stole my Trotter" - an *Only Fools* version of the famous tabloid headline.

I'd just finished an urgent and very late-in-the-day conference at the townhall, and I couldn't wait to get home and relax for the weekend. I'd just reached my car when the gang surrounded me. "Give us your money!" the ring leader hissed. Needless to say, and putting it mildly, I was shocked. Part of me knew that the safest option was to comply and give them what they wanted, but another part of me wanted to fight back. I'd only recently completed a self defence course, so I knew what areas of anatomy to strike. The muggers grabbed me, snatching at my handbag, but before I even had a chance to make a decision on the best course of action, the strangest thing that's ever happened to me, happened. There, running out of a misty alleyway, and directly towards us, was Batman and Robin. Neither I nor the muggers quite knew what to do. We just stood there, watching. A few seconds later the muggers took off and then Batman stopped to talk to me. It was already beginning to dawn on me that this wasn't actually Batman and Robin, not unless they had changed accents and really let themselves go. Still in shock, to this day I can't remember what was actually said, only that they then disappeared back into the night just as quickly as they had appeared out of it. The worst part was filing the police report. They breathalysed me four times and called in a psychiatrist for back up.

Councillor Murray

"I was a little bit concerned about putting Del and Rodney in costume," recalled John Sullivan. "I've always had this conviction that when a long-running comedy series puts characters in fancy dress it's because the writers are running out of ideas, and I didn't want to give the audience that signal. But when Tony read the script he was convinced it would work. So I wrote in the mugging scam and came up with the idea of Del and Rodney running into them. Tony filmed it brilliantly and David and Nick played it so well and with such conviction – it was wonderful."

Cast as Councillor Murray was actress Angela Bruce (well known for her roles in *Doctor Who* and *Bad Girls),* whilst the two main muggers were played by Scott Marshall and future *Emmerdale* actress Sheree Murphy.

"I remember the script was sent via a courier to my mum and dad's house," recalls Murphy. "I could have burst with excitement when it turned up! When I read the script for the first time I knew it was going to be an instant hit, and it would be everything and more any *Only Fools* fan would want from a Christmas special!"

Arriving at the ball in full costume, the Trotters are dismayed to discover that poor Harry Malcom died a couple of days earlier. Rather than being at a fancy dress party, our dipstick duo are at a wake!

The episode wraps up with the Trotters foiling the gang of muggers once more in an excellent chase sequence which was filmed in both London's Borough market as well as various parts of Bedminster in Bristol. This earns Del a medal of his own and, at last, an all-important home improvement grant. For the icing on the cake, Rod and Cass announce that they are finally expecting a little one!

"The ending of this episode is upbeat; it was a great opener for the trilogy," remembered Sullivan. "I wanted to come back on a high note."

Heroes and Villains brilliantly re-establishes the Trotters in a concise 60-minute episode that delivers all the laughs and heart the series is known for. In many ways it is *the* perfect *Only Fools* episode.

Promoted as 'the BBC's Christmas present to the nation' the trilogy opener was screened on Christmas Day at 9pm, drawing in an incredible 21.3 million viewers.

Opposite page top: Leaving the town hall after working late, Councillor Murray is attacked by a group of muggers... until a pair of mysterious figures emerge from the mist...

Opposite page bottom: After doing their duty to keep the streets safe, Del and Rodney arrive at Harry Malcom's house...

Above left: Working on the market, Rodney reads the *Peckham Echo.*

Above middle: One of the muggers (Scott Marshall).

Above top right: The proud Trotter family look on as Del receives his medal for being a 'have-a-go-hero'.

Below: Councillor Murray, Del and the Mayor (Robin Meredith).

Right: Taking a leaf from his new book, *Modern Man*, Del pays Raquel a compliment – "I tell you what, Raquel. If she can be in a James Bond film, so could you... I'm serious. I mean, look at her, she's a dog!"

Below: The full cast are joined by John Sullivan and Tony Dow... and a shot of the photo being taken during the making of *Modern Men*.

Opposite page top left: Following Del's example, Trigger has a new game to play – "I can make you turn your hands over without touching you."

Opposite page top right: Del and Rodney catch up with Doctor Singh (Bhasker Patel).

Following Rodney and Cassandra's happy news, the opening of *Modern Men* sees the Trotters in a celebratory mood. It also sees both brothers with self-improvement on their minds, with Del lapping up the contents of his new self-help book, *Modern Man*, and Rodney considering braving the job market once again.

Much like how Del decided to embrace yuppy culture in 1989, Sullivan decided that the character would now also fully embrace the mid-nineties trend of masculine sensitivity... or at least his version of it!

"Del wants to be a new man," Sullivan explained. "He's got a book all about it. He wants to show Raquel how much he loves her by changing, but he's too busy reading the book to pay attention to her! His heart's in the right place, but where's his brain?"

As the middle entry of the trilogy, *Modern Men* didn't have the pressure of making an entrance or resolving an ongoing plot. This freed Sullivan up to explore the characters and give some great moments to the series' extended cast.

"You just hoped you'd at least have a scene in the Nags Head with all the guys," remembers John Challis. "Obviously for the supporting characters it was one of the favourite bits in the show as they'd all be winding each other up, buying drinks and having a jolly. It was one of the things you'd

MODERN MEN

27 DECEMBER 1996

The really tricky part was tracking Mr Trotter down. For days I rode around on my moped following his trail through the back alleys, the markets and pubs, but he somehow always managed to give me the slip. Unfortunately for him, I am a very determined man, and with machine-like focus I pressed on until finally I caught up with him. I explained to him, in no uncertain terms, that the paint he had sold me for redecorating my surgery was now peeling off in great chunks. To my surprise he accepted this and promised that he would rectify the matter. Mission accomplished, I left him be, but not without first warning him that if he didn't keep to his word, I'd be back!

Doctor Singh (The Turbanator)

be looking forward to throughout your year. There was so much pressure on John Sullivan to try and include everybody, so that they had their little bit to do."

Modern Men would indeed give Challis a great Boycie scene, as the character holds court in the pub, offering his thoughts on the future of electric cars – very much ahead of his time in 1996!

Up at the bar, Patrick Murray's Mickey Pearce (absent from the trilogy's opening instalment) winds Rodney up about his still being Del's dogsbody after all these years.

"I was trying to show Rodney deciding to move on from Del and find a new job, what with Cassandra being pregnant," recalled Sullivan. "He doesn't want to stick with his brother, he thinks his life's being wasted. When I was writing, I remember my son was looking through the paper for work and reading the claptrap that people put in these job ads. And in the end you find out that the position is for a messenger or something!"

In a classic Trotter flat moment, Rodney finds a promising looking job in the newspaper and phones up to apply, only to reach Del, who we then discover placed

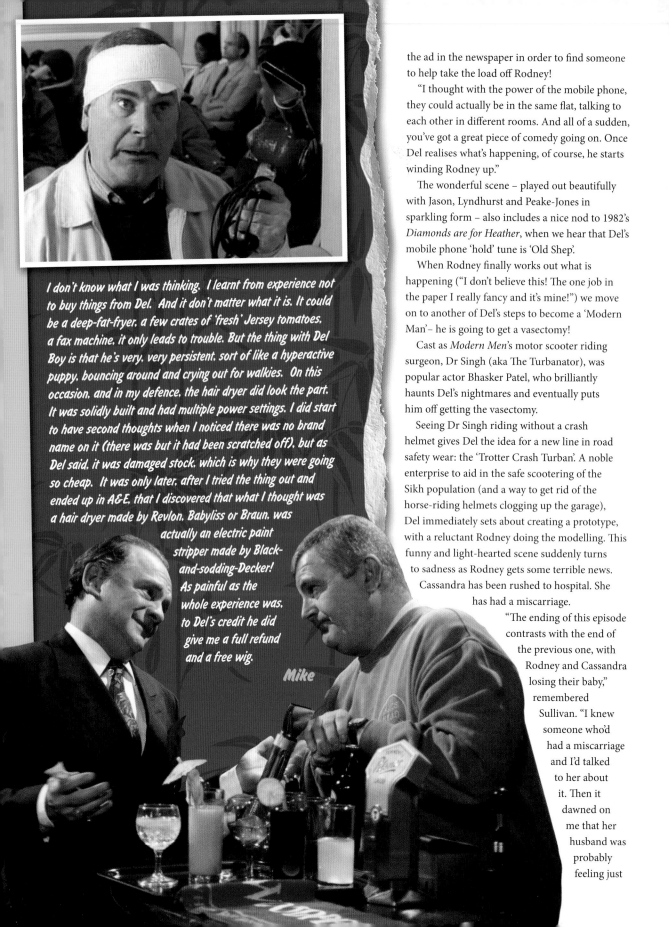

I don't know what I was thinking. I learnt from experience not to buy things from Del. And it don't matter what it is. It could be a deep-fat-fryer, a few crates of 'fresh' Jersey tomatoes, a fax machine, it only leads to trouble. But the thing with Del Boy is that he's very, very persistent, sort of like a hyperactive puppy, bouncing around and crying out for walkies. On this occasion, and in my defence, the hair dryer did look the part. It was solidly built and had multiple power settings. I did start to have second thoughts when I noticed there was no brand name on it (there was but it had been scratched off), but as Del said, it was damaged stock, which is why they were going so cheap. It was only later, after I tried the thing out and ended up in A&E, that I discovered that what I thought was a hair dryer made by Revlon, Babyliss or Braun, was actually an electric paint stripper made by Black-and-sodding-Decker! As painful as the whole experience was, to Del's credit he did give me a full refund and a free wig.

Mike

the ad in the newspaper in order to find someone to help take the load off Rodney!

"I thought with the power of the mobile phone, they could actually be in the same flat, talking to each other in different rooms. And all of a sudden, you've got a great piece of comedy going on. Once Del realises what's happening, of course, he starts winding Rodney up."

The wonderful scene – played out beautifully with Jason, Lyndhurst and Peake-Jones in sparkling form – also includes a nice nod to 1982's *Diamonds are for Heather*, when we hear that Del's mobile phone 'hold' tune is 'Old Shep'.

When Rodney finally works out what is happening ("I don't believe this! The one job in the paper I really fancy and it's mine!") we move on to another of Del's steps to become a 'Modern Man'– he is going to get a vasectomy!

Cast as *Modern Men*'s motor scooter riding surgeon, Dr Singh (aka The Turbanator), was popular actor Bhasker Patel, who brilliantly haunts Del's nightmares and eventually puts him off getting the vasectomy.

Seeing Dr Singh riding without a crash helmet gives Del the idea for a new line in road safety wear: the 'Trotter Crash Turban'. A noble enterprise to aid in the safe scootering of the Sikh population (and a way to get rid of the horse-riding helmets clogging up the garage), Del immediately sets about creating a prototype, with a reluctant Rodney doing the modelling. This funny and light-hearted scene suddenly turns to sadness as Rodney gets some terrible news.

Cassandra has been rushed to hospital. She has had a miscarriage.

"The ending of this episode contrasts with the end of the previous one, with Rodney and Cassandra losing their baby," remembered Sullivan. "I knew someone who'd had a miscarriage and I'd talked to her about it. Then it dawned on me that her husband was probably feeling just

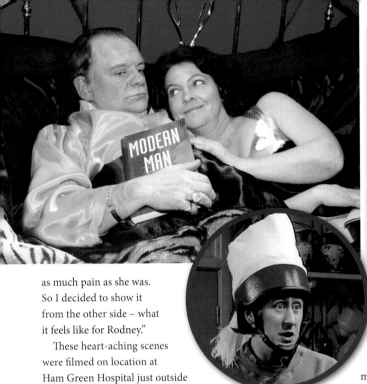

as much pain as she was. So I decided to show it from the other side – what it feels like for Rodney."

These heart-aching scenes were filmed on location at Ham Green Hospital just outside of Bristol.

Here, Del's stone-faced pep-talk to his brother ironically crumbles away when he walks in to see Cassandra and instantly balls his eyes out, neatly breaking the tension without robbing the drama. As the scene unfolds, Sullivan doesn't trivialise the situation and lets the gravity of the issue remain, with Gwyneth Strong and Nicholas Lyndhurst

handling the tender dialogue with great care.

It is up to Del Boy (still dressed in his scrubs after visiting Cassandra) to finish the episode as he notices an obnoxious man being abusive towards the nurses in A&E. In another spot of vigilantism, Del gives the lout a good smack in the mouth. As the other patients in the waiting room look on in shock, 'Doctor' Del turns to them and closes the show: "I bet you wish you went private now!"

"John was so brilliant at taking you into a character's drama and then putting something so completely and utterly bonkers in which you were not expecting," remembers Tony Dow. "With *Fools* John knew the characters' world so well and how they would react."

Transmitted on 27 December at 8pm, *Modern Men* equalled *Heroes and Villains'* viewing figure of 21.3 million.

Opposite page: Del sells Mike a special kind of 'volumizing' hair dryer...

Above left: Del discusses with Raquel his decision to have a vasectomy.

Above: Only Rodney could apply to be his own assistant.

Left: Rodney models the Trotter Crash Turban prototype.

Below left: Heartbreaking scenes in hospital for Cassandra and Rodney.

Below: Del takes care of a yob in A&E.

Above: Del attempts to be a 'counter worry' to distract Rodney.

Below inset: During a stock take in the Trotter garage, Rodney moves two Russian VCRs (from *Fatal Extraction*).

Below: Filming of Del, Rodney and James in the garage.

Opposite page top: Rodney opens up to Del – "You can't run away in a broken lift."

The BBC's trailers for the 1996 Christmas Trilogy made it clear that these would be the last ever episodes of *Only Fools*, with the continuity announcer at 8pm on 29th December declaring "One last Christmas outing for Rodney and Del Boy now on BBC 1, and it's going to be a night to remember."

Suitably enough, as the opening credits fade, *Time on our Hands* begins with an ominous view of Peckham at dawn, seen through the balcony window. Sat alone, an anxious Raquel prepares a shopping list for the dinner she'll be cooking that evening for her parents. Del and Albert offer reassurance, telling her not to worry and offering to help (Albert on coffee duty, Del on veg), and then talk turns to Rodney. Since the events of *Modern Men*, Rodney has spent the last two weeks with his head in the sand, going out of his way to avoid dealing with his and Cassandra's loss.

In a lovely moment, Albert avoids getting Del's cup of tea poured over his head by cleverly rewording his familiar catchphrase of "during the war" to "during the 1939-1945 conflict with Germany" – a gag which, given the air of finality, earns a massive laugh from the studio audience.

Albert suggests that what Rodney needs is a 'counter worry': to be distracted from his problems by a sudden concern for a close friend or relative. Del agrees to give it a go and duly feigns illness when his brother arrives, only to find that Rodney takes absolutely no notice.

Later that day, Del catches up with a despondent Rodney in their lock-up garage, where we find him shuffling about a couple of Russian-made video camcorders, a batch of Showaddywaddy LPs and a pile of old and tattered paperwork.

In an intricate scene which both brings the entire series full circle and pre-empts the end of the story, Sullivan has Rodney lamenting the last 16 years, holding in his hands the same receipts the character was taking stock of when first introduced to us in 1981's *Big Brother*. What Rodney really wants is some luck, for all of them. Del spots a box and puts his hand inside. "If this was life's lucky dip," he says, "I'd like to put my hand in and go, da daaa!" He pulls out the random object: a dirty and old-looking pocket watch. "There you are, Rodney, this is the thing which will change our lives. But life's not like that is it?" Del chucks the watch on to a pan on a nearby stove and the brothers head back up to the flat.

"I wanted to find a way of breaking down Rodney's defences and relieving the strain that losing the baby had put on him," explained Sullivan. "Del had to find a way to get Rodney in a situation where he couldn't not speak about it. So I thought I'd have them stuck somewhere together."

To record the broken down lift scene, it was decided to build a detailed set in the studio on an extra pre-record day so that Jason, Lyndhurst and Tony Dow would not be rushed. As it turned out, the sequence came together very smoothly.

I don't mind admitting that I've never been very good at coping when emotions strike a bit too close to home, if you know what I mean. When my Mum died I was too young to properly understand what was going on. I just had this vague and hazy memory of the reflection of a blonde haired person sitting in front of a mirror... one minute they were there, the next they weren't. A bit like Jedward I s'pose. But when Cassandra and I suffered a miscarriage, well, I'd never felt a pain like that in all my life. She was in pain too, of course, and I wanted nothing more than to be there for her and somehow make things okay again, but where do you even start? Instead, I tried to run away from it and blank it all out. It didn't work. It never does. Thanks to Del and a 'broken' lift, I finally managed to pull myself together and face up to things. "You've just gotta hold on, Rodders," he said. "Cos you never know what's waiting for you round the next corner." I remember thinking at the time, 'I hope it's a bit of good luck...

Rodney

"I think the audience enjoyed this scene because it really broke the mould," remembered Sullivan. "Nick and David were absolutely great in it and it was all filmed in one take. I was nervous about putting such an emotional scene in *Only Fools*, but having Nick and David do it took a lot of the nerves away."

With nowhere to go, Del gently encourages Rodney to open up in what is probably the series' most tender moment between the brothers. In a faultless performance, Lyndhurst shows his incredible acting chops as he exposes Rodney's pain. The reveal that Del deliberately sabotaged the lift in order to get Rodney to talk was an inspired touch of magic on Sullivan's part.

Despite getting the perfect take, a slight technical issue concerned Dow, who approached composer Graham Jarvis to prepare some emergency back-up music. As Jarvis recalls: "Tony said, I don't know if we need music or not, but if we can't fix this camera issue in post, we think it might be needed to help distract people from the fact that the whole scene was at a slight angle. Luckily, they could crop it down to make it level, and they didn't need the music."

Later on back at the flat, it is action stations. Denzil and Mickey Pearce have already delivered the furniture on hire from the town hall (a giant eight-seater dining table more suited to the dining room of a stately home) and Raquel is about to have a hot flush with worry, making sure that all is perfect before her parents arrive.

Cast as Raquel's father, James, was Michael Jayston, a distinguished screen actor and a recent cast mate of David Jason's on ITV's *A Bit of a Do*. To play the part of Raquel's mother, Audrey, both Sullivan and Dow wanted Ann Lynn, who had memorably played Vince's mum, Rita, in *Just Good Friends*.

Above: Recording Raquel's parents arriving at the flat.

Above right: The same scene from a different angle.

Below: Raquel's parents, Audrey (Ann Lynn) and James (Michael Jayston).

Below right: A view of the flat's fourth wall being put in position.

Bottom right: Del makes sure Albert gets lots of 'gravy'...

Opposite page above: Del and Rodney with their Victorian egg-timer!

Opposite page middle: The auctioneer (Seymour Matthews).

Opposite page bottom: The Trotters' cheque for £6.2 million, and one of the three Harrison watch props used on screen.

In a nice reference to the earlier garage scene, we can hear two Showaddywaddy songs playing during the dinner party, and, for the first time since 1985's *To Hull and Back*, a fourth wall was added to the flat in order to show James and Audrey's side of the conversation with the Trotters.

In the kitchen with Albert, Del Boy is chuffed with how well the evening is going. Everyone is getting along famously, the food has been served and the gravy is being poured. And that's when we discover that Albert has mistaken the coffee jar for the gravy granules jar! Del looks on in horror from the kitchen doorway as his dinner guests pour Maxwell House all over their lamb noisettes. "I don't believe you, Albert," says Del, "not only have you managed to sink every aircraft carrier and battleship you ever sailed on, now you've gone and knackered a gravy boat!" We don't get to see it, but you can just imagine the moment after dinner when everyone receives a steaming hot cup of Bisto granules to wash away the taste of coffee soaked lamb.

The following morning, Del drives James's car out of the garage whilst Rodney continues his stock take. James, an antique dealer by trade, spots the old pocket watch, the one Del had cast aside the previous day...

"I was looking for something to make Del a rich man, but it had to be something that he wouldn't know was valuable," Sullivan explained. "We had a wonderful historical consultant called Mona Adams, who told me about a Harrison watch. I was dubious at first, but the curator of horology at the National Maritime Museum in Greenwich told me about a missing Harrison watch that would go for anywhere between five to ten million pounds at auction. Of course, Del had it down on his list as a Victorian egg-timer!"

To keep the watch story a secret, Gareth Gwenlan saw that the press got wind of a false rumour that the Trotters were going to win the lottery.

"We had to throw them off the scent," remembers Tony Dow, "and they all fell for it, apart from the *Daily Express* who couldn't believe that a writer of the quality of John Sullivan would get them to become millionaires by simply winning the lottery!"

When setting out to write the final trilogy, Sullivan had considered several angles. At one time in *Heroes and Villains*, publican's ball organiser Harry Malcolm was to be at death's door. In his final moments he would pass on a treasure map that would send Del and Rodney on a wild goose chase throughout the trilogy. Tony Dow also recalls that Sullivan was going to have the Trotters find a rare violin.

With the Trotters stumbling upon something purchased in a house clearance that took place just prior to the very first episode of the series, the irony isn't missed in that for all their years of struggling, Del and Rodney had something of incredible value in their possession the whole time, just waiting to be found!

With the watch verified, it is off to Sotheby's. Here the crew were able to film at the actual location, hiring dozens of extras to populate the scene. To play the auctioneer, actor Seymour Matthews was cast.

The auction scene is an absolute delight and there is a wonderful sense of things finally going

When Raquel's Mum and Dad, James and Audrey, came over to the flat for a very special dinner, Raquel was doing her pieces trying to make sure everything was just right. I forget the exact name of the dish she cooked, but it was lamb noisettes... something or another. It did look very impressive, but thanks to Albert, who got confused over what was gravy granules and what was coffee granules, nobody ate it anyway (who would have thought that lamb and Maxwell House doesn't mix?). The most important thing was that I made a very good impression on my new in-laws. I could see old Jimbo testing the waters, trying to get my measure. "Are you a naval man, Derek?" he asked. "No James," I said. "I'm more of a leg man myself". It was a bit of a personal question at the best of times, let alone when the whole family are sitting around the table about to tuck into their lamb noisettes, but I let it slide. Anyway, the evening soon picked up and things went so well that James and Audrey agreed to stay over the night. The next morning, Rodders and I were down in the garage doing a stock check, when Jimbo turned up to check on his motor. It was then that he spotted an old pocket watch, sitting about amongst all the other bits and pieces we'd collected over the years. I actually remembered acquiring the thing at a house clearance some sixteen years earlier, not long before I'd made Rodney a partner in the firm. Jimbo was getting very excited about this dirty old watch, and asked if we had any proof of ownership, and, thanks to Rodney's very short lived stint as the firm's accountant (remember that?), it just so happened that we did. Before we knew it, this incredibly old and by all accounts mythical 'Lesser Watch' was up for auction at Sotheby's! There was Rodders and me, waiting for the bids to kick off, hoping that we'd at least get a decent drink out of it. Well, I'm pleased to say that we did just that, as the watch sold for a final bid of SIX POINT TWO MILLION POUNDS!!! I'd always said it, hadn't I? "This time next year, we'll be millionaires!" Well at that point right then, we were millionaires... and some!

Del

Above: The regulars of the Nags Head clap and cheer at the arrival of the Trotters.

Right: As landlord of the Nags Head, Mike greets the new millionaires – "On the house Del"

Below: The Trotters all dressed to celebrate. Boycie begrudgingly shares in the happy news, whilst a beaming Marlene gushes with pride.

right for the Trotter brothers. Then we have the moment viewers had been waiting for since 1981: the Trotters becoming millionaires. £3,100,000 each to be exact. As Del says to Rodney, "We've had worse days".

Stopping off at Boycie's Automobiles and Car Hire shop, Rodney treats Del to a brand-new Rolls Royce. Here the Miles Motor Company on Bristol's Marsh Road was given a makeover to double as Boycie's showroom.

Following the scene at the showroom, Sullivan originally intended to go straight back to the flat to see Albert, Raquel, Cassandra and Damien eagerly awaiting the return of Del and Rodney. As soon as they return, the brothers playfully make the girls and their uncle guess at the final bid before revealing the full amount. In a lovely moment which would have bookended the trilogy's opening nightmare, Rodney looks at a smiling Damien and considers that perhaps his nephew had something to

do with their good fortune. As *Time on Our Hands* was already over running, this scene was dropped at the rehearsal stage.

Arriving at a packed Nags Head, the pub falls into an uneasy silence as the new millionaires walk in. It is only when Denzil claps that the whole room follows his lead and starts to erupt with cheers. Ken MacDonald's Mike now delivers a moving line which best sums up the Nags Head spirit. Even though the Trotters are now rich and can easily afford it, the drinks are on the house.

Sound tracked to Crosby, Stills and Nash's *Our House* (although replaced for video release with a dreadfully inferior cover version), this montage shows the Trotters living their dreams. Colwood House in Haywards Heath was used as Del and Raquel's mansion, where Del (who has lovingly lined up the three-wheeler, the Capri Ghia and the Rolls in the driveway) spends most of his time playing snooker. For Rodney and Cassandra's new home, a luxury apartment in the South Bank's Red Lion Court would suffice, offering the couple a perfect view of the river and a chance to watch Uncle Albert sail by in his new motor cruiser *Princess Khadija*. True to form, he crashes it into a bridge.

As *Our House* draws to a close, we see Del getting fed up with playing snooker alone, and as the final chorus of the song kicks in, Sullivan properly brings the Trotters home. Back to Nelson Mandela House.

We are so used to seeing the flat chock-a-block with random pieces of furniture and Del's latest gear, seeing it so empty is almost a painful sight. In a scene beautifully performed by a visibly moved Jason, we hear a trio of 'ghost' voices echo through the flat (audio clips of Grandad from *Big Brother*, Reg Trotter from *Thicker than Water* and a specially recorded piece from *Time in our Hands* guest star Ann Lynn as Joan Trotter, reprising the same cockney accent she gave Rita in *Just Good Friends*).

As Rodney and then Albert join Del in the scene, the heart strings are stretched to the limit as Sullivan tinges the

moment with the melancholy moral that sometimes the climb can be better than the view. The real heart break comes when Del receives a phone call from a mate offering him a deal on a consignment of electronic carpet steamers, a deal that could potentially see him double his money. For the slightest moment the excitement returns, right up till Rodney reminds Del that they are no longer in the business, and with a heavy heart Del has to inform his caller that: "Trotters Independent Traders have ceased trading. Bonjour."

To provide a musical theme for the upbeat final shots of the Trotters walking away into the sunset (or perhaps a new dawn), Graham Jarvis composed a lightly nostalgic brassy piece that perfectly fitted the musical palette of the series. Jarvis titled the piece 'Yellow Brick Road', taking its name from the note in Sullivan's script.

"Filming the last scenes was extremely emotional. It was wonderful and awful at the same time in the studio," remembered Sullivan. "For the first time in all my years doing the series, there was a standing ovation at the end. They were all on stage and they called me out too, but I can't face that sort of thing. It was wonderful and very tearful. We had a party afterwards, but after about 15 minutes you knew it wasn't over, because everyone was talking about the future. They all wanted to come back!"

Time on our Hands was the perfect salute to 16 years of adventures on Hooky Street. The episode pulled in nearly half the population of the UK with an absolutely staggering 24.3 million viewers, becoming the highest viewing record ever for a comedy in the UK.

But as the trio walk away from us along the yellow brick road, we are offered a sense that this might not quite be the end, as the ever optimistic and tirelessly ambitious Del throws his hands up in the air and opines, "This time next year, we could be billionaires!"

Above left: Raquel and Del in their new country estate.

Above right: Rodney and Cassandra look out from their riverside penthouse.

Left: Uncle Albert takes to the waves again.

Below left: Del returns to the flat the Trotters once called home.

Below right: The Trotters decide to take a Toby to the Golden Dragon for a Chinese... then Del has a brainwave.

IF THEY COULD SEE US NOW...!

★ ★

After divvying up the dosh, and making sure Albert got a nice slice, we firs
sprucing up Mum's headstone, transforming it into what I like to think is n
Lamborghini of grave sites. Next, we did our bit for charity and donated tr
'Trotter' wing to Peckham General Hospital. It was round about this time tr
decided to move in with his 'girlfriend' Elsie Partridge down on the south co
Naturally, we did indulge in a few of the finer and more expensive things in
the way, but nothing flash. Rodney and Cassandra got themselves a Jag a
modern apartment right by the river; Raquel and I opted for a Rolls Royce a
great big estate house that had its own peacocks. We went on holiday a fe
you know, Concorde, chauffeur driven limousines and all that game. But lik
nothing flash. And of course, there was still business to attend to. The fact r
never been one to rest on my laurels, and finally having money in the bank r
that we also had money to invest in the stock exchange (oh yes, I don't care
they say, you can't whack a footsy one-hundred!) and so TITCo simply shift
one market to another. At the time the Central American market seemed the
and for a while at least it paid off handsomely. It goes without saying that o
keeping an eye on the exchange meant that we were frequently cream crack
and so regular breaks were a must. We were all enjoying a lovely break in M
Carlo when the Central American market crashed and disappeared down the
quicker than you could say "Chateau neuf du pap!" Before we knew it, our a
were frozen and we were being dragged off to bankruptcy court, where TITCo
liquidised and I was barred from running a company. Just to add a bit of icing
cake, the Inland Revenue than slapped us with a debt of £48,754 (plus inter
and gave us twelve months to pay it off. The one small saving grace was Nels
Mandela House, pretty much the only thing we had that wasn't a company as
So back to the flat we went. Now, if only we could pay off that debt before be
evicted and kicked out onto the streets, we'd be laughing!

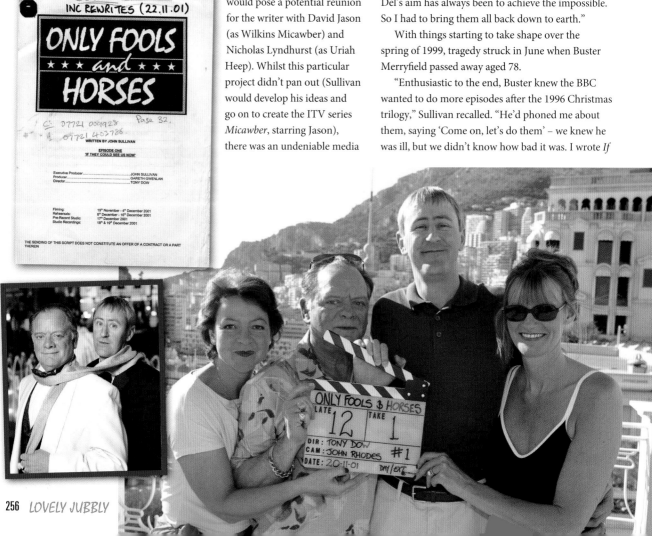

Below: John Sullivan's copy of the shooting script of *If They Could See Us Now...!*

Bottom left and right: Five years after *Time On Our Hands*, the *Only Fools* cast are united again on location in Monte Carlo.

Following the unprecedented success of the 1996 Christmas Trilogy, *Only Fools* became more popular than ever. The series would continue to be a regular fixture on BBC 1, with repeats becoming a feature of the TV schedule. Home videos of the series (which had slowly been released since 1991) had become one of BBC Worldwide's most popular releases, and numerous tie-in books would become regular stocking fillers. Everywhere they went, however, John Sullivan and the cast would be asked the same question: 'Will it ever come back?'

Immediately after the Christmas Trilogy was completed, Sullivan, Gwenlan and Dow settled back into work on *Roger Roger*, which would eventually run for three series. Concurrently, much of the same team would work on *Heartburn Hotel*, a sitcom that Sullivan had been developing with writer Steve Glover since 1994.

It was also at this time that Sullivan began work on an adaptation of the Charles Dickens novel *David Copperfield*, a project that would pose a potential reunion for the writer with David Jason (as Wilkins Micawber) and Nicholas Lyndhurst (as Uriah Heep). Whilst this particular project didn't pan out (Sullivan would develop his ideas and go on to create the ITV series *Micawber*, starring Jason), there was an undeniable media and audience frenzy surrounding even a very slight reunion of three of the key components of *Only Fools*.

As the millennium approached, Sullivan gradually became more open to the idea of bringing the Trotters back. Audience demand had never gone away, but as the years passed by even the writer was curious as to what the Trotters had been up to since becoming millionaires.

"Every so often we'd have reunions and get-togethers and you could just tell everyone wanted to do something," remembered Sullivan. "Sometimes David would phone up and say, 'Oh, we have to bring the old sod back.' Originally we were going to do a millennium special, but once I started writing, stories began to come back to me and I found that I couldn't just write one. So it ended up as another trilogy."

With a loose arc in place, Sullivan knew that the key to the new episodes would be to get the Trotters back to Peckham. "I wanted to show a glimpse of the Trotters living in luxury, but I knew that it wouldn't work for long. You've got to have a target in life and Del's aim has always been to achieve the impossible. So I had to bring them all back down to earth."

With things starting to take shape over the spring of 1999, tragedy struck in June when Buster Merryfield passed away aged 78.

"Enthusiastic to the end, Buster knew the BBC wanted to do more episodes after the 1996 Christmas trilogy," Sullivan recalled. "He'd phoned me about them, saying 'Come on, let's do them' – we knew he was ill, but we didn't know how bad it was. I wrote *If*

They Could See Us Now...! with Albert in it, and it was extremely difficult to have to go back and rewrite."

With the loss of Buster, it didn't seem right to continue plans to unite the cast for a new trilogy for the millennium, so Sullivan held off for a year. By early July 2001 the BBC had green lit the project with a budget agreed and the cast booked to reprise their roles later that autumn.

On 6 August, two days before the BBC had planned to officially announce the new episodes, Ken MacDonald died suddenly, aged just 50. The cast and crew were absolutely heartbroken to lose the life and soul of the rehearsal room in his prime.

"We couldn't replace Ken," Sullivan explained, "and I didn't want to kill Mike off, so I came up with the story of him embezzling the brewery's money. In a sense, it was a way of keeping Ken in the show."

Despite the sudden loss of MacDonald, the BBC were now committed to the new trilogy and on 8 August the press office announced the new episodes ('BBC comedy classic *Only Fools And Horses* is to return to British TV screens in three new one-off episodes') with the then Director of Entertainment, Alan Yentob, saying "It's been a long wait, but the best things are always worth waiting for".

By the time the news broke, and considering it too generous to blow three new *Only Fools* specials over one Christmas, the BBC made the decision to only confirm that one episode would be shown in December 2001.

"To begin with, this episode was part of a trilogy that was supposed to go out over one Christmas period," recalled Sullivan. "I didn't realise at the time that the BBC would show the episodes over successive Christmases."

The decision to hold back the second and third episodes was also a practical one, as cast availability leading up to Christmas would have made it impossible to make all three stories in 2001. Filming for the first episode, entitled *If They Could See Us Now...!,* was scheduled to take place in Monaco, Weston-super-Mare and Bristol between 19 November and 4 December, with studio recording set to commence on 17 December for three days.

Opening proceedings with a mystery in a taxi, Sullivan gives us a slightly agitated Del and Rodney asking questions on their way to an unknown meeting, before the story moves into a lengthy flashback sequence – a first for *Only Fools.* Meeting Justin (who we later find out is a bankruptcy barrister), Del gives a brief

Above left: Tony Dow directs Nicholas Lyndhurst and David Jason outside the Casino De Monte Carlo.

Above: The Trotters arrive in style at the Hotel De Paris... but when news reaches them that the Central American Market has crashed, they make a hasty exit.

Below centre: Justin (Kim Wall) gets to the bottom of the Trotters' situation.

Below left: When the Trotter brothers became millionaires, they donated to charity...

Below: At the bankruptcy court, Del and Rodney point out that they were slaves to detail and made certain they always got their cheques off to the Inland Revenue on time – "Fair do's they bounced, but they were *always* on time."

IF THEY COULD SEE US NOW...!

25 DECEMBER 2001

At first we were all in deep shock, but it didn't take long for us to realise that we were also in deep shit! "Don't worry, Rodders," Del said. "This time next year we'll be millionaires!" "Del" I said, "This time last WEEK we were millionaires!!!" He just brushed it off and started going on about how big his shoulders were. But what use are big shoulders when you've got a brain the size of a Ferrero Rocher?! I'd warned him right from the off that investing in the futures markets was an iffy prospect, but as ever he wouldn't listen. It was all "Oh Shut up you tart!" and "He who dares wins!". Well this time he who dared cocked it right up! Just when you thought things couldn't get more grotty, we then received the news that Uncle Albert had moved on (not moved on as in 'moved on'; he'd already moved on, I mean he died). Talk about life kicking you in the teeth when you're already down. Despite everything, though, there were still some glimmers of hope on the horizon. First off, Del had been banned from running a company, meaning that I was now the one calling the shots. Secondly, and the brightest glimmer of all, was that Cassandra was pregnant again. We were getting a second chance!

Rodney

recap of Trotters Independent Traders before they found their fortune (via clips from *A Touch of Glass*, *The Jolly Boys' Outing*, *Danger UXD* and *Heroes and Villains*). We then get a taste of their lives as millionaires, as they embark on a luxury holiday in Monte Carlo. Originally, however, Sullivan considered an even more lavish opening.

"When the original script came through they were in South Africa," remembers Tony Dow. "Del and Rodney were doing a big tour, going from bar to bar, becoming progressively more drunk as the evening progressed, before ending up in the middle of a very dangerous situation. John wrote this scene and it was amazingly funny, but it was nearly half an hour long! Just as we were about to go on a reccie to South Africa, I called John and said, 'I don't know how to say this, but I'm worried about this scene. It's just not *Fools*'. He sighed with relief and said, 'Thank God you said that! The only reason I kept going with it was because I thought everyone wanted to go to South Africa and have a great time!' And of course he came back with a great scene in Monte Carlo. The idea was to make them poor again; you see them rich, then you see the news, and they're back to square one."

The Trotters' trip back to square one was caused by the crash of the Central American market (considered one of the "futures markets" that Del talks about at the end of *Time on Our Hands*). Setting up the motivational arc of the new trilogy, the Trotters are declared bankrupt and given a year to pay off their debt (£48,754... plus interest!) before the Inland Revenue claim all assets.

To play Justin, frequent BBC comedy actor Kim Wall was cast. These office and courtroom scenes were filmed on location at the former Council Chamber in Weston-super-Mare. Here all of the UK scenes of the episode would be filmed, aside from a few shots outside Whitemead House in Bristol and the West End taxi ride which opens the episode.

As we cut to the Trotter flat for the first time in five years, we see that Del and Rodney have already started to repopulate the lounge with a mixture of stock. Since the sets used throughout the 1990s had been destroyed, newly appointed production designer David Hitchcock recreated the flat from scratch, opting to go back to a width closer to the original set from 1981.

It is here we meet the series' new Damien, played by Benjamin Smith. Written as a typical early 2000s adolescent (cheeky and mad about football and gangsta rap), Smith perfectly plays the role that would kick start an impressive acting career.

Still coming to terms with their new financial situation, and believing that things couldn't possibly get any worse, the Trotters then receive the news that Uncle Albert has passed away.

With a nostalgic instrumental of Albert's Nags Head piano favourite 'Red Sails in the Sunset', the scene cuts to a shot of the Trotters' Capri driving along the coast of Weston-super-Mare, on their way to what they believe is the home of Elsie Partridge. On arrival they are greeted by Albert's housekeeper, Marion, played by Joan Hodges (wife of Chas Hodges), who had previously starred in Sullivan's *Roger Roger*.

"I'd gone down to Weston-super-Mare to the cast hotel and I was in the bar to have my dinner on my own," remembers Hodges. "The door swung open and in walked Nick Lyndhurst, Tessa Peake-Jones, Gwyneth, Sue Holderness, there was a gang

of them! Nick saw me and said, 'What you doing out here on your own?' and I said, 'Ah, I'm just eating my dinner'. He said, 'Not on your own you're not!' And he picked my dinner up and led me into the restaurant and sat me down with them all. That evening you could feel the warmth and they made me feel so welcome."

After a heated exchange between Del and Albert's niece's husband, Roland (played by Colum Convey), it comes to light that the Trotters are actually at the wrong funeral! Outside, they spot the rest of the Peckham faithful at the other end of the street, attending *our* Albert's funeral. After the sadness of the preceding scene, and in true Sullivan style, it is a welcome relief to laugh at the mistake, and the slow reveal just makes it all the more funnier.

Back in Nelson Mandela House, Del hits on an idea to lift the family out of their financial black hole: he will become a contestant on the latest TV game show, *Goldrush*.

"The idea of the game show was going to be Del on ITV's *Who Wants to Be A Millionaire*," remembered Sullivan, "but the accountants weren't keen on the idea, so I had to invent another game show. We asked Jonathan Ross to be the host, and he was terrific."

Opposite page below left: Let the games begin. Rodney Trotter – Gladiator!

Opposite page below right: Del: "Don't worry, this time next year we'll be millionaires." Rodney: "This time *last week* we were millionaires!"

Above left: The Trotters' Capri decorated in sombre black ribbons for Albert's funeral.

Above: Rodney fetches an anchor funeral reef, as it finally dawns on the Trotters that there are two funerals taking place on the same street!

Left top: Roland (Colum Convey).

Left below: Marion (Joan Hodges).

Below left: The Trotters are at Albert 'Bunny' Warren's funeral...

Below: ... and the full Nags Head gang are at Uncle Albert's funeral.

Above: Marlene, Trigger, Mickey, Boycie and Denzil watch with disbelief as they see a familiar face take on TV's *Goldrush*.

Above right: A behind the scenes look at the new Nags Head set built for the trilogy.

Right: Cassandra and Rodney are caught by Del as they indulge in a bit of 'iconoclastic auto suggestion' (dressing up).

Below: Del meets Jonathan Ross as Raquel and Damien watch in the *Goldrush* audience.

Below right: Director Tony Dow on the *Goldrush* set with Ross and Jason.

For these scenes, the set of the BBC's popular quiz show *The Weakest Link* were used at Pinewood studios on 7 December, with a special audience largely made up of members of the *Only Fools* Appreciation Society.

With Del chasing TV game show glory, Rodney and Cassandra take full advantage of the empty flat and attempt to give their love life a much needed injection of spice...

"Rodney's had a penchant for women in uniform ever since the first series," remembered John Sullivan. "I thought it would be funny if he could persuade Cassandra to dress up as a policewoman for him... but what would he have to do in return? I was originally going to put him in an England football kit, but then I went off the idea. I thought about what I would find funny – and who Cassandra would fancy! At the time, Russell Crowe in *Gladiator* was the hot news of the year and, of course, you couldn't get two more different men than Russell and Rodney!"

Meanwhile, in the *Goldrush* studio, Del is stuck on a question. He decides the time has come to use one of his 'lifelines' and Jonathan Ross phones the flat to see if Rodney can help. Thanks to an earlier wind-up (courtesy of Boycie's mobile phone and Mickey Pearce's gift for accents), an ultra cautious and extremely frustrated Rodney tells Jonathan to piss off!

By the story's end, and despite the dire predicament hanging over them, the episode sees the Trotters installed once more in Nelson Mandela House and doing what they do best... struggling!

As one of the most anticipated TV programmes of all time, *If They Could See Us Now...!* in many ways had an impossible task to perform. Sullivan wisely brought us back to Peckham early on by cleverly stitching a story around a flashback and then weaving in the Trotters' financial turmoil, a funeral, the *Goldrush* game show plot and Rodney getting a promotion.

When stripped of the weight of expectations, the episode is pure vintage *Only Fools*. Merryfield and MacDonald are sorely missed, but having both Trotter couples living in the flat offers a great new dynamic. Laden with some brilliant one-liners (Del's comparing a dancing Rodney to "Billy Elliot with worms") and magic moments (Trigger's discovering the "karaoke version" of Bach's Opus in G Minor) there could've been no better way to set up another Hooky Street trilogy.

Broadcast on Christmas Day 2001, *If They Could See Us Now...!* drew in 21.35 million viewers.

As ecstatic as I was when Del finally came into some real money, I can't say I was at all surprised when he then lost it. And, just as I expected, it very soon became clear that nothing had changed. No sooner had he returned to Peckham he was flogging me the latest 'top of the range' mobile phone. Feeling sorry for him, I took it, only to find that it had a very strong tendency to rapid and extreme levels of overheating. Still, I had no need to worry, as just the following week he was offering me a discount on a pair of fireproof earmuffs. Yes, you can take the market trader out of Peckham, but you can't take the Peckham out of the market trader. What with his being a mate in dire straits, I didn't even ask for a refund. That's just the kind of benevolent man that I am. Since becoming a fully-paid up member of the Lewisham Lodge of Freemasons, helping the less fortunate has become second nature to me. Why, only a couple of months back I wired Trigger a score so he could get a new handle for his broom and a cheese roll. I probably won't ask for it back. The sad fact is that we can't all be successful. To quote my acceptance speech on receiving the award for Peckham's top Honda salesman, 1989: "Some people just have greatness thrust upon them."

Boycie

I really felt for Del and Rodney. You could see how much losing all that money affected them. Del was like a broken man when I saw him. He didn't even give my bum a squeeze. But it was Raquel who I felt most sorry for. For the first time in her life she'd gotten to experience the simple joys that a lot of us more upper-class ladies often take for granted. She'd finally discovered what it was like to fly in club class and how it felt to do some proper, coupon-free, shopping. She'd finally discovered what is was like to be able to hold her head up high, only to have it all cruelly snatched away. It broke my heart, and I wasted no time in offering her all the support I could give. Luckily, that very week I was treating myself to a new wardrobe. I'd intended to give all my old clothes to Oxfam, but I instead offered them to Raquel. Out of pride, she refused them, which was understandable, so I took them to Oxfam. They refused them as well. They didn't say why but it was probably because their stock room was full. As for Boycie, I'm still not sure he's got a heart to break. I've tried so many times to get him to be more thoughtful and giving, but his approach to charity has always been 'less is more' (an approach he takes in other areas too). You know, I sometimes wonder if he's one of those... what d'you call 'em... narstatistics. It's like everything revolves around him and what he wants. He's so cold and lacking in empathy, it seems he's just incapable of showing any genuine kindness. But my mum did warn me. All it took was one look at his face and she was telling me he was a wrong'un. I said to her, "Alright, so he's ugly, but he's successful". And I s'pose that is one thing you can say for Boycie: despite everything, he never let the success change him. He's still the same miserable git he was when I first met him.

Marlene

LOCAL MILLIONAIRES GO BUST

STRANGERS ON THE SHORE...!

★ ★

When Boycie offered me some part-time work being his personal chauffeur. I took no pleasure at all in accepting. But desperate times call for desperate measures. Unsurprisingly, he took every opportunity to rub it in, banging on about a multi-million pound deal he'd lined up with some Lebanese businessman. I got my own back by squirting a tube of onion purée into his hair gel, so it all evened itself out. Whilst Boycie went around smelling like a Big Mac, Rodney, under his new title of 'Director of Administration' was all set to take TITCo down the 'party planning' route. What a wally! I tried to get it through to him that this was Peckham, where the only plan required for a party was to make sure to bring a bottle of Liebfraumilch or a six pack of Strong Bow. Obviously, he was still riding high on the news of Cassandra being up the duff again, but the way things were going they were gonna end up with the bailiffs as godparents!

★ ★

STRANGERS ON THE SHORE...!

25 DECEMBER 2002

We received a letter from the Seaman's Commission. At first I thought it must have been for Rodney, but it turned out it was for Albert. An old crew mate from his days stationed on HMS Cod was arranging a reunion in Normandy. He obviously hadn't heard the sad news that Albert had said bonjour to this mortal curl. Rodders and I gave it some thought and decided that it would best if we went along as Albert's representatives, only for Raquel to question our motives (she can be a right cynical mare at times). She thought we were planning some sort of booze cruise, but that couldn't have been any further from the truth. Not only were we going there to honour Albert, we were also gonna take the chance to scatter his ashes at sea, which he would've wanted. Of course, we'd have to do it as soon as we got out of harbour cos we'd have been too pissed to do it later. It was Denzil who came up with the idea of bringing a load of cheap booze back with us that we could then flog for a tidy little profit. A brilliant idea if ever there was one. I don't know why I didn't think of it myself. Del

SEAMAN'S RECORD BOOK
AND
CERTIFICATES OF DISCHARGE

SURNAME
TROTTER

CHRISTIAN NAME(S)
ALBERT
R27866

The middle act of the second *Only Fools* trilogy sees Del and Rodney go on a sea-faring pilgrimage to salute their late uncle, with a stop-off at a wine warehouse on their return.

"The episode opens with the Trotters in dire financial straits again," remembered John Sullivan. "We see Del here as this desperate get-rich-quick businessman, who's prepared to break the law by bringing a load of booze back from France and flogging it in the Nags Head. But he also wants to honour his uncle by going to the memorial."

After the frantic rush to get the first instalment of the trilogy ready in time for Christmas, *Strangers on the Shore...!* was produced at a much more leisurely pace, with location filming in Cherbourg from 6–13 February, then Bristol from 14–20. This would be followed by rehearsal for the studio scenes leading up to the recording on 2 and 3 March.

The story opens with Del at Boycie and Marlene's house, now reduced to working as driver and general skivvy in order to earn a few bob. For this scene the crew returned to the Druid Stoke Avenue address, previously used as the Boyce residence in *The Sky's the Limit*.

When Boycie rubs salt in the wound by bragging about a soon-to-be-signed international car deal that will see him become a multi-millionaire, a resourceful Del gets his own back by mixing a generous dollop of onion puree into his new employer's hair gel, an act that will hilariously plague the car dealer for the rest of the episode.

Back at the flat, we find out that Rodney and Cassandra are at long last expecting a baby again. Also, a letter from the Seaman's Association has arrived. Completely unrelated (as Del first assumes) to Rodney's procreational duties, the letter is addressed to Albert, inviting him to a reunion of his old shipmates in the French village of St Clair La Chapelle. Discussing the matter in the Nags Head with Raquel and Cassandra, the brothers decide to represent their uncle and go in his place.

One thing missing from *If They Could See Us Now...!* was seeing the Trotters back in their local pub. Thankfully an extended scene in the Nags Head in *Strangers on the Shore* makes up for that, and it is great to see the main cast mixing with the Nags Head ensemble once more.

Also in this scene, Roy Heather's Sid gets to properly inhabit the role of landlord for the first time, looking right at home behind the bar. The moment does Ken MacDonald's memory proud as we hear once more about Sid's regular contact with Mike in Prison, Sullivan's touching tribute to the much-missed actor and friend.

On the outbound ferry to France, the Trotters scatter Albert's ashes overboard. To help set the scene, composer Graham Jarvis was called upon to provide a new nautical theme with a French twist. "Gareth said, 'We want something for when they go to France, something with accordion on it,'" remembers Jarvis. "I said, 'Please don't make me do that! People will say, "Graham Jarvis – how original, they go to France, and he gets out the accordion!"'" Despite his misgivings, Jarvis's sea shanty-like theme suits the episode perfectly.

For the fictional French village of St Clair La Chapelle, the crew filmed in the Normandy village of Place Notre Dame in Gatteville-le-Phare. As no suitable cafe could be found that faced an open area, production designer David Hitchcock turned an outbuilding into Claire a la Chappelle's Cafe de la Place for the exterior and interior cafe scenes.

It is in this cafe that we learn from Albert's HMS *Cod* ship mate, George Parker (played by former *Z-Cars* actor James Ellis), that Albert was a bit of a ladies man back in the day. According to George, he, Albert and the rest of the crew spent considerable time hiding out in the village, and Albert wasted none of it in getting to know the local women and saying 'merci beaucoup' in his own special way. Taking the info in, it suddenly dawns on Del and Rodney that the village is

Opposite page top right: Del cleans Boycie's 'GTI'... then adds an extra ingredient to the car dealer's hair gel.

Opposite below far left: Uncle Albert's urn, medals and *Seaman's Record Book*.

Above: Del and Rodney take the ferry to France and drive to St. Claire a la Chappelle, where they spot some familiar-looking men...

Below: The Mayor (Martin Friend).

Bottom right: George Parker (James Ellis).

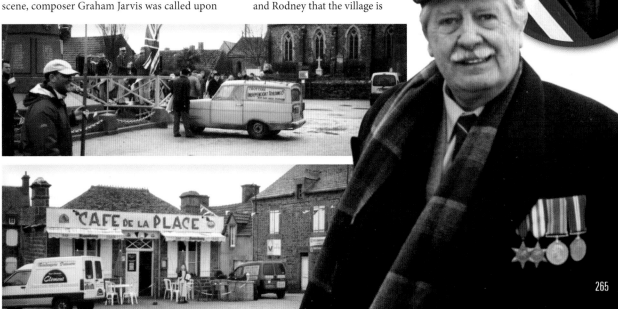

populated with dozens of men of a similar age who look very much like Uncle Albert!

Stunned by Albert's wartime antics, the brothers head back to the ferry via a stop off at the 'Ferry Superstore' wine warehouse in Cherbourg. Here (and initially unbeknownst to Rodney), Denzil and Trigger are waiting to help with the booze mission. Thanks to a misunderstanding over the different time zones, Del takes it upon himself to hastily load the palettes of beer into the back of Denzil's lorry.

Returning to the Trotters' garage, the ever-obliging Trigger and Denzil are seen unloading their contraband when they suddenly catch sight of a weary and frightened looking young man in the back of the lorry.

"When Del and Rodders find what they believe to be an illegal immigrant, the two don't just throw the guy out, they look after him," explained John Sullivan. "Del Boy is a kind person – if someone's really down on their luck and in trouble, Del will knock 'em up some egg and chips. I wanted to cover two topical issues of the day here – illegal immigrants and booze cruises."

Perfectly cast as the confused 'stowaway' (christened 'Gary' by Del) was actor Nabil Elouahabi, a few years before his debut in *EastEnders* and subsequent feature film roles.

Worried what might happen to Gary if they simply let him go, Del and Rodney bring their guest up to the flat, much to Raquel, Cassandra and Damien's suspicion. Here Elouahabi plays 'Gary' brilliantly as the increasingly bewildered character is treated to some unique Trotter hospitality.

A few days later, after a kick-about with Damien and his mates, 'Gary' makes his escape. Reporting his ordeal with the Trotters and Boycie to the police, the trio are soon nicknamed 'the Gary Gang'. The wonderful irony which closes the episode is the reveal that 'Gary' is in fact the son of Mr Mamoon, the international businessman who Boycie is arranging the massive car deal with; a fact that sees the episode end with the trio being taken away for questioning by the police!

Despite some passing references to the ticking clock of their Inland Revenue debt, *Strangers on the Shore...!* has a wonderful celebratory feel, with the characters going on an adventure and getting caught up in layers of misunderstanding. Sullivan's script is a real lattice-work of interconnecting plots with lines that thread through different scenes across the story, setting up several long-running and hilarious pay-offs.

Whilst there was some talk of airing the 75-minute special at Easter or over the August Bank Holiday, it was decided by the BBC to save *Strangers on the Shore...!* for Christmas Day 2002, where 17.4 million viewers tuned in to watch.

I never blamed Del for mine and Corrine's divorce, but I think she did (under the 'reasons' section of the divorce papers she wrote 'Del Boy'). But there are times I wished I'd listened to her more. This was one of those times. First he roped me in to helping him smuggle a load of duty-free beer and wine into the country. The really annoying thing was that I saw it coming a mile off. I knew exactly what he was gonna do and I watched him do it. Sometimes dealing with Del is like having an out of body experience. Not only did he persuade me to drive my truck to and from France, he even convinced me that the whole thing was my idea! Anyway, that wasn't the worst of it. The worst of it came back in Peckham when we were unloading the booze from the truck and discovered an illegal stowaway! God knows where he was from. He looked harmless enough but you can never be too careful. Del suggested we just release him onto the streets and let him find his own way home.

"How can you say that, Del?" I said. "For all we know he might be Al-Qaeda!'"

"Don't be stupid, Denzil," he said. "I mean, does he look like he works in a furniture store?"

But that's Derek Trotter for you. One minute you're cruising through life, minding your own business, wondering what you're gonna have for tea. The next, Del shows up and you're wondering how you're gonna explain to a judge that you're not a people trafficker!

Denzil

'The Gary Gang' consisted of five men, two women and a young boy. But it was the three main leaders of the gang that I remember most. One was short and loud, another was tall and softly spoken. The third had a moustache and smelled like onions. It began in Calais where I was working at my father's hypermarket. I was loading an order into the back of a truck when I was suddenly boxed in and driven away. Several hours later they released me from the truck and I wasn't sure where I was. I was then taken to a tower block where I was held in an apartment that had horrible curtains. From that moment on they tortured me in a variety of unique ways. First they humiliated me by making me wear lime-green pyjamas and a shiny, bright-red dressing gown. Then they made me eat extra spicy food. At one point I tried to escape, but the one with the moustache saw this and threatened me with a knife. I wasn't sure what language they spoke, although

at times I detected what sounded a bit like English. The next day, and with great relief, I managed to escape. Thankfully I wasn't seriously injured during the ordeal, but to this day I have nightmares about it. Some nights I wake up in a cold sweat screaming "Gary!!!"

Rachid Mahmoon (Gary)
Translated from Lebanese

★ ★

We'd been chipping away at the debt, trying to raise enough funds to at least bring £48,745 down to a more manageable figure. We had just a few days to sort it all out and save our bacon. I'll never forget that final board meeting in the kitchen, asking Rodney how much we'd raised so far, and the way he referred to his calculator before saying, "Fifty two pounds and twenty five pence". Gordon Bennet! I still hadn't completely given up, though. After all, I'm Del Trotter, the chairman of Wings and Prayers R Us: the man who can smell a fiver in a gale force wind. Oh yes, I could sell coffee to Brazil. It was just a pity I didn't know any Brazilians at the time. We were right out of coffee anyway. Everyone else rallied round and did their best. Raquel suggested we try Feng Shui, but I couldn't see how eating raw fish was gonna help the situation. Trigger came up with an earth-shattering invention that he was gonna patent in our name. It was a lovely gesture, but the 'invention' in question turned out to be a foldable back-scratcher made out of a couple of chopsticks. Then there was Rodney, who had given party-planning the elbow and was now embarking on a mail order screenwriting course. What a plonker! Meanwhile, there was me, and I did the only thing I could do... I went to see Mum and asked for a miracle...

★ ★ ★ ★ ★ ★ ★ ★ ★ ★ ★

SLEEPLESS IN PECKHAM...!

25 DECEMBER 2003

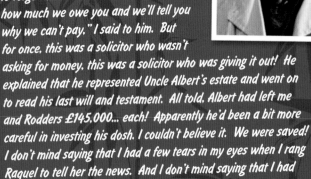

Who'd have guessed it, eh? Uncle Albert sailing in to save the day! When Rodders and I were called to the solicitors' office, all we could think was 'here we go again!' As soon as we sat down I told the mush to forgo the formalities. "Just tell us how much we owe you and we'll tell you why we can't pay," I said to him. But for once, this was a solicitor who wasn't asking for money, this was a solicitor who was giving it out! He explained that he represented Uncle Albert's estate and went on to read his last will and testament. All told, Albert had left me and Rodders £145,000... each! Apparently he'd been a bit more careful in investing his dosh. I couldn't believe it. We were saved! I don't mind saying that I had a few tears in my eyes when I rang Raquel to tell her the news. And I don't mind saying that I had a good few more when, later that very same day, Cassandra gave birth to a beautiful and healthy baby girl. My first and only niece! And when Rodney and Cassandra named her Joan, after dear old Mum, well, you couldn't have asked for a more sweeter cherry on top of your cake. You see, this is what I'm saying about holding on. If there's one thing I've learned over the years it's that as you go through life you're guaranteed to be thrown a good few surprises along the way. Sometimes they're the kind of surprises that make you wanna runaway and cry your heart out, and that's alright, we all do it at some point. But sometimes, just sometimes, they're the kind of surprises that make life worth living. I've had me ups and downs, my wins and losses, just like everyone else, but when all's said and done, things really did turn out lovely jubbly!

Del

To close the second Christmas trilogy, and once more sign off the series, a suitably emotional episode was required. It is quite fitting then that out of all of the *Only Fools* feature length specials, *Sleepless in Peckham...!* spends more time actually in Peckham than any other.

Made straight after previous episode of the trilogy, location filming for *Sleepless* took place in Bristol from 9–16 March, just a week after *Strangers* studio recording was completed. The full cast would then rehearse in London one last time, leading up to the three studio days at Television Centre, on 26, then 29–30 March.

With only a two weeks remaining for the Trotters to pay back their debt to the Inland Revenue, the story opens in the flat with Del, Raquel and Rodney summing up the desperation of the situation. Cassandra is due any day now and Del finds himself inundated with dozens of official-looking letters from a firm of solicitors named Cartwright, Cartwright & Cartwright; letters he does not dare open.

Instead, he heads off to the cemetery to tend to Joan's grave and ask for a miracle. For this scene, filmed at Bristol's Greenbank Cemetery, art director David Hitchcock designed a suitably garish and even more eye-catching monument than the original.

As Del updates his late mother on the 'help' he is receiving from his friends, the action cuts to a studio scene in the Nags Head where Trigger demonstrates an invention that he promises to patent in Del's name: a backscratcher made out of two chopsticks and a hinge (also very handy for when you want to point at things).

Back at the flat, Rodney is also doing his bit by attempting to 'write' the Trotters out of their debt (a creative interest last touched upon in 1986's *Video Nasty*). With Del's assistance the brothers start to cook up a movie idea, but their initially fruitful creative brainstorming session runs aground when they pass out drunk.

Elsewhere, Sid has dug up an old photo taken during the very first Jolly Boys' Outing in 1960; a group shot that catches Rodney's eye in particular. Borrowing the snap, he takes it to have a blown-up copy made.

One of the episode's funniest secondary plots involves the mysterious and simultaneous disappearance of both Marlene and Denzil. As speculation increases, unwholesome rumours begin to spread...

"A lot of celebrities were having cosmetic surgery, so I thought it was the kind of thing that Marlene would go for," recalled Sullivan. "Sue Holderness is such a great sport and really enjoyed playing the scene where she reveals her boob job. Of course, the storyline leading up to this scene is all about everyone thinking that Boycie has done away with Marlene. We all know that he can be a nasty piece of work, but surely he's not capable of topping his wife?"

After it is discovered that Denzil has merely been recuperating from what his haemorrhoids-specialist surgeon called 'keyhole surgery' ("He forgot to say it was the keyhole to the Tower of sodding London!"), the truth about

Opposite page below right: A very pregnant Cassandra and Rodney are shocked by Del's delivery room predictions.

Above left: Trigger has hit upon a brainwave, a foldable pocket back scratcher... made from chopsticks.

Above right: Rodney and Del start writing their movie.

Left: Del visits his mother's grave...

Below: The original design sketch of Joan Trotter's new monument, and the model on set.

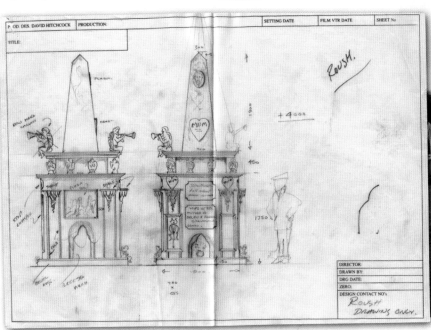

Above: The cast and crew of *Sleepless in Peckham...*'s studio recording gather on the set of the Nags Head.

Right: Marlene reveals her bold new look.

Below: A design miniature of the 2001–2002 Nags Head set, built as a reference for the production team by art director Les McCallum.

Opposite page above left: Boycie makes an entrance at the special anniversary party and faces the music in front of the regulars.

Opposite page below left: Tribute acts Ziggy Sawdust (Alan Nichol and Norman Langton) and Lordy Geordie (David Merrett and Anthony Plant) wowed the Nags Head regulars.

Marlene is finally revealed at the pub. This final Nags Head scene – an anniversary party organised by Boycie – gives us a hilarious insight into what Sid considers top notch grub and entertainment: English Tapas and a Robson & Jerome tribute band named 'Lordy Geordie'.

After the big night out, Raquel soon discovers that Del has been keeping to himself news that the flat is set to be auctioned off the following week, and that he *still* hasn't told Rodney about the solicitor's letters.

This moment leads to a dramatic scene between Del and Raquel, with a Del Boy speech that recalls a similar pivotal moment in 1985's *Strained Relations*. "I'm not a control freak, it's just that I've had no choice. Do you realise that when I was 16, my old man walked out and left me and Rodney in the care of our daft old Grandad? He tried his best, but he weren't up to it. So I had to take over. I've been doing it ever since and I can't get out of the habit."

Looking out from the flat's balcony, for the briefest of moments it seems that Del and Raquel will be going their separate ways.

The next day, in a scene filmed at a branch of the London Camera Exchange on Bristol's Baldwin Street, Rodney takes Sid's old Jolly Boys photo to be enlarged. Looking at the photo from 1960, Rodney sees what at first seems impossible: his own face staring back at him.

A few days later, the Trotters pluck up the courage to visit Cartwright, Cartwright & Cartwright's solicitors office. Expecting the worst, Del and Rodney are

taken completely by surprise when the reason for all the letters and requests to meet is revealed to be the reading of Uncle Albert's will.

"It was a nice end to the series for Uncle Albert to save Del and Rodders from eviction," remembered John Sullivan. "There was this lovely situation where nobody could see a way out of the Trotters' predicament – Del's bankrupt and he owes all this money. I wanted something to come out of the blue and save them – and Uncle Albert was the obvious answer. When they became millionaires, Uncle Albert would have got a nice bundle from Del and Rodders and, not being a big spender, would have invested it over the years. It all added up to an awful lot of money. It saves the Trotters and keeps it in the family."

Before they have a moment to celebrate, Del and Rodney receive a call: Cassandra has been rushed to hospital. With memory of the sad scene in *Modern Men* in viewers' minds, the dramatic dash into the maternity ward ends with the happy news that both mother and child are fine.

To this day Marlene still calls me tight. But she weren't saying that when I got her that boob job! Cost me an arm and a leg those boobs, even when I managed to knock the second one down to half price. I shouldn't be too hard on her, though. You see, not long ago I had an epiphany of sorts. It was during the height of the lockdowns when everyone was practising social distancing. Marlene was staying with her Mum, and I was all alone at home. Of course, I had some outlets for communication with the outside world. Marlene and I would 'Zoom' every other day. At one point - it must have been a moment of sheer desperation, either that or I was Oliver Twist - I even attempted a session with Trigger. I can't remember much of the call, only that it didn't make much sense (it was like getting caught in a crossed line with Mr Bean and Diane Abbott). But I'm not ashamed to admit that I did find it all a bit of a struggle. And it wasn't just that all the pubs and casinos were shut, it was also Marlene's not being there. It was the little things I missed: the sight of the back of her head as she sat at the dressing table doing her boat race up; the sound of Loose Women blaring from the front room and making me question the point of existence; the smell of charred spaghetti hoops wafting through the house come tea-time. I missed not having someone to ignore. And then there were the rows. I especially missed the rows. It'd all just been so... quiet and peaceful. It reached the point where I almost, but not quite, wished that Tyler was still living at home. But just as my inner turmoil was about to reach critical mass, Marlene reassured me that it would all be over soon and that things would get back to just the way they were. At that moment, I suddenly remembered why I married her.

Boycie

Talk about going through the emotional grinder. It was just one thing after another. First, I got the confirmation I needed to finally be able to say, with certainty, that Freddy 'The Frog' Robdal was my real dad. I'd suspected it for so long. I wasn't really sure how to feel about it at first. It definitely explained a lot of things. I mean, by all accounts Freddy Robdal (aka The Raffles of Peckham) was very well liked: he was a bit of charmer, a snappy dresser, and very popular with the ladies, which is me to a T. On the other hand, he was also a womaniser, a liar, a cheat and a thief. My biggest worry was that it would make things awkward between me and Del, but I soon realised that he already knew the truth, and it really didn't matter. Not after everything we'd been through. And not after the birth of Joan, the best and most cosmic thing that's ever happened to me. All I wanted to do then was break the mould and be the best dad I can be. Well, that and avoid sitting on any detonators. And with my big brother by my side.... I reckoned it'd be plain sailing from there on out. Lovely jubbly indeed!

Rodney

To accompany the magical moment when Rodney meets his daughter for the first time, composer Graham Jarvis was tasked with writing something suitable. "I wrote a theme for baby Joan and also used the same theme for the graveyard scene," recalls Jarvis. "I then changed the baby theme into the upbeat version as they drove off. It was called 'Del & Rod Walk Away' – these names were for the dub so always descriptive to help place the music. I think all involved felt it was sad that this was the definite end."

In the episode's penultimate scene, Rodney shares a lovely moment with Del at their mother's grave, in which he reveals that he has named his daughter, Joan, after her. As the brothers walk away, they finally confront the uncomfortable truth that they have been avoiding for the longest time: Rodney's father wasn't Reg Trotter, he was Freddy 'the Frog' Robdal.

"We knew that this episode really was the last one," Sullivan explained, "so I wanted to tie all the ends up. There were always doubts about Rodney's parentage – and he finally finds out. The important thing was that Del knew that they had different fathers, but never told him. He'd said

a lot of horrible things to Rodney, but he never spoke about that."

For the final parting shot of the series, the Trotters' van is seen driving away in the direction of three tower blocks. For this shot, the crew took the Reliant Regal to West Cross Route in Shepherd's Bush, just around the corner from Television Centre.

"The trilogy was originally to be shown over the Christmas 2001 period," remembers Jarvis. "When it was played over three years John joked that Cassandra's pregnancy was the longest known to mankind!"

Despite being completed by April 2002, *Sleepless in Peckham..!* was held back for over a year and a half before broadcast

(and *Strangers on the Shore...!* was ready some eight months before its broadcast), giving Tony Dow a rare opportunity to look at the episode with some distance. "I can remember going back with John to revisit them in case there was anything we needed to change, and since we had the time we tweaked quite a bit."

Broadcast on 25 December 2003 at 9.20pm, 16.37 million viewers tuned in for the final *Only Fools* adventure.

In many ways, *Sleepless in Peckham...!* gave *Only Fools* the satisfying sense of closure that was missing from *Time on Our Hands* seven years previously. Rodney both discovers who his real father is and becomes one himself, bringing the story right back to Joan Mavis Trotter and answering the mysteries of *The Frog's Legacy*.

Opposite page top right: The Jolly Boys' Outing to Margate, July 1960... With (left to right) Sid, Slater, Freddy 'the Frog' Robdal, Denzil and Del. This= photo was specially made by the art department using photos of the actors in their youth as well as a new photo of Nicholas Lyndhurst as Freddy Robdal.

Above: "A work of art": Cassandra and Rodney welcome baby Joan to the world.

Below left: "Del, can I ask you a question... other than looks, was he like me in anyway?"

Below middle: The Trotters head home in their trusty three-wheeled van.

Below: The cast clap with the audience at the emotional ending of *Sleepless in Peckham...!*'s studio recording.

THE TROTTER LEGACY

★ ★

After a ratings-smashing homecoming trilogy, the Trotters signed off at the end of 2003, this time back where they always belonged, in Nelson Mandela House, surrounded by their close-nit Peckham community.

For John Sullivan, however, drawing the screen exploits of Del and Rodney to a close didn't necessarily mean there wasn't more to explore within the rich world he had created.

Over the years, regular trips to the Nags Head had only allowed for all too brief scenes involving the extended family of Only Fools' recurring characters, often just scratching the surface of their potential. Boycie and Marlene in particular had grown to become almost as well-known as Del and Rodney, yet despite seeing them together for decades, there was still much that we didn't know about them. What would it be like to focus a series on their unique relationship?

Furthermore, the saga of the Trotter brothers was built upon a dramatic 1960s-set love story involving their mother Joan and the mysterious Freddy Robdal. Whilst snippets had been revealed in a couple of episodes of Only Fools, the full details of what really happened had yet to be explored...

There was also the possibility of taking the Trotters to the stage as a musical adaptation, an idea Sullivan had been toying with since the 1980s. Now with the bow tied neatly on Only Fools' screen life, it was time to make these things a reality.

★ ★

The possibility of making a spin-off series following the extended cast of *Only Fools* had been something John Sullivan had pondered for many years, but it wasn't until John Challis' 60th birthday party that the writer finally got an idea he wanted to explore.

Growing tired of life in London, in 1998 Challis and his wife Carol decided to move to the rural climbs of Adforton in Herefordshire, where they began the slow process of restoring an old house that needed a lot of attention. Several years later, to celebrate Challis turning 60, Carol organised a big party, inviting many of his colleagues from *Only Fools*, including his on-screen wife Sue Holderness

and John Sullivan. Upon seeing Challis play the genial host taking delight in showing guests around his new home, Sullivan couldn't help but see the actor's alter ego in the same position and started to see the premise of a new series.

"I just remember John – during the inebriated afternoon – saying something along the lines of 'I've had a bit of an idea, I'll get back to you.' Sue and I waited with bated breath for about two years," remembers Challis. "Sometime later John came to a theatre show me and Sue were doing in Brighton, and afterwards he took us out for dinner and pitched the idea of the series to us. We were at first euphoric at the opportunity, and then we thought, 'Christ, how do you follow what had gone before?'"

Sullivan knew that any spin-off from *Only Fools* had to be a completely different beast and the country setting seemed the perfect way of achieving this. Transporting two urban characters and putting them in charge of a farm would be fertile ground for lots of fish out of water humour. But there had to be a good reason for taking Boycie and Marlene out of Peckham. Fortunately, the inspiration came from a past classic.

"The BBC did a repeat of the Driscoll Brothers' *Only Fools* episode," recalled Sullivan, "and seeing Boycie terrified of these two brothers, I thought, 'That's it, the Driscolls are the key to it. Boycie is so terrified of them, that would keep them all in the country no matter what.'"

As we learn in the opening episode, which starts off in Peckham, Boycie has provided the evidence that has finally put Danny and Tony Driscoll behind bars... but in their trademark style, the two gangsters have managed to overturn the judge's verdict. What's more, they know full well that Boycie grassed.

Above: Marlene, Boycie and Tyler pose for a portrait outside of their new home, Winterdown Farm.

Below: An audience ticket to a studio recording for the first series of *The Green Green Grass*.

Below right: Denzil tells Boycie that the Driscoll brothers are on to him in *The Green Green Grass*' opening episode, *Keep On Running*.

The Green Green Grass
by John Sullivan

Starring
John Challis &
Sue Holderness

This ticket is only valid on the date shown below:

Friday 17th
June 2005

Teddington Studios,
Broom road, Teddington,
TW11 9NT
Doors open: 6.45pm
Doors close: 7.15pm

Admit One
THIS TICKET IS COMPLIMENTARY AND NOT FOR SALE

The Green Green Grass
by JOHN SULLIVAN

Sullivan wrapped this premise up in the title of his new series: "Obviously the 'Grass' is because Boycie became a super-grass, and because it was new to him, he was Green, so The Green Green Grass just seemed right!"

"It was a tremendous compliment to think the characters were strong enough to have their own series," remembers Challis, "and the fact that it had been inspired by my move to Herefordshire. It changed our lives. There we were, doing our own show."

In addition to being the inspiration for the series, Challis' home would also be used as the central filming location, which in the world of the series would become Shropshire's Winterdown Farm.

"With The Green Green Grass you knew you were going to be in every episode," remembers Holderness. "Gradually we saw a little more of the relationship between Marlene and Boycie which was just great to be able to explore."

Joining Challis and Holderness was actor Jack Doolan as their son Tyler, last seen as a toddler in Only Fools' 1991 Miami Twice specials. Doolan seamlessly carried off Tyler's teenage indifference. Straight after The Green Green Grass, Doolan was cast in the Ricky Gervais and Stephen Merchant film Cemetery Junction, and has since gone on to appear in dozens of TV and film roles.

The final member of the Boyce family in the series is their dog Earl, a nice nod to the couple's old dog, Duke, seen in Only Fools.

The setting of the series lent itself to having a large ensemble cast, with Sullivan creating a colourful group of rural types who have been working on Winterdown Farm for many years.

The trio of farmworkers are headed up by Elgin "farm manager" Sparrowhawk, brought to life by actor David Ross. Under him is the cow-loving farm hand Bryan, played by Ivan Kaye, and the farm's ploughman Jed, played by Peter Heppelthwaite. Ella Kenion was cast as Winterdown Farm's eccentric housekeeper, Mrs Cakeworthy, who dabbles in plenty of rural supernaturalism and meandering conversation, but never any actual housekeeping.

The series' antagonist (and hilarious counterpart to Boycie's shifty Londoner) was patriotic Welshman and neighbouring farmer, Llewellyn, played by actor Alan David.

Above left The picturesque Winterdown Farm.

Above: Mrs Cakeworthy (Ella Kenion), Jed (Peter Heppelthwaite), Bryan (Ivan Kaye), Elgin (David Ross), Boycie, Marlene and Tyler (Jack Doolan).

Below inset: Llewellyn (Alan David).

Below: Jed, Marlene, Boycie, Tyler and Bryan look on at their new bull Rocky...

As the series developed, Tyler's girlfriend, Beth (played by actress Lisa Diveney), became a regular element, and the teenage lad from Peckham going out with the Welsh country girl made for a perfect contrast.

Since they were so central to the arc of the series, it was no surprise that the Driscoll Brothers would eventually make several appearances in the series, with original actors Roy Marsden and Christopher Ryan effortlessly reprising their *Only Fools* roles from 1989. First seen in the series in the 2005 Christmas Special, *One Flew Over the Cuckoo Clock*, the dreaded duo finally catch up with Boycie in *Brothers and Sisters* and appeared once again in *Home Brew*.

"The filming of it was such fun in that beautiful part of the world where John lives," remembers Holderness. "I stayed in his house while everybody else stayed in London! John Sullivan loved the countryside, so the filming experience was great, and we all got to know each other so much better."

Originally Sullivan wanted to use the 1963 New Christy Minstrels' song 'Green Green' as the series' theme tune, but when the song couldn't be cleared, he decided to write and sing his own theme. This served as a nice bit of continuity with the theme music the writer wrote and sung for *Only Fools*, it was also another way to neatly explain the series' premise.

"John came down to the studio to sing the theme," remembers composer Graham Jarvis. "He had a really good voice and told me the sort of thing he wanted, and I wrote three or four different pieces and he sung the melody he liked."

After setting the series up and writing the first seven episodes, Sullivan opened the chair for a host of both brand new and established writers.

The first episode of the second series, *Testing Times*, was written by John's son, Jim, who would end up writing seven episodes of the series over its run. "After the first series, dad was looking to give new writers an opportunity to be involved," Jim remembers. "I grew up with *Only Fools* and know those scripts inside out, and I felt pretty confident that I knew the characters and their personalities well enough to make a decent go of it. I also knew how my dad approached these things and had an ear for his voice. Even so, it took me a while to build up the courage to show him my ideas. But he was very pragmatic about the whole thing. He didn't sugarcoat it at all, he just let me know what worked and what didn't and why. He told me to work on more ideas, so that's what I did. And that's how I ended up writing for the series."

"We were lucky we had Jim to write so many *Green Green Grass* episodes," remembers Holderness. "He writes exactly like his father; he understands the characters and writes with Boycie's and Marlene's voices because he understands those people."

Joining Jim Sullivan as a writer was future *Benidorm* creator Derren Litten who wrote the second series' *Bothered and Bewildered*, an episode which featured Boycie in a brilliant abstract dream sequence. Other established writers joining the series included regular *Goodnight Sweetheart* contributors, Gary Lawson and John Phelps, and *My Hero* writer Paul Alexander.

Sullivan was especially keen to offer a first rung on the ladder to new talent, with writers James Windett, Keith Lindsay, David Cantor and Robert Evans contributing to the series. This combination of new and established writers gave the series a real vibrancy with many different types of stories told.

Behind the camera, Sullivan's regular director Tony Dow was unable to work on the second series, so Dewi Humphreys was brought in to take the reins, with *Only Fools'* Gareth Gwenlan producing

Above right: Tyler asks out Beth (Lisa Diveney) in series one's *Sex and the Country.*

Below: The cast and crew pose for a shot during the location filming of the first series of *The Green Green Grass.*

and Chris Wadsworth in the editor's chair once more. Teddington Studios in Richmond was used to record the series' studio scenes.

During one memorable studio recording of *The Green Green Grass* Chris Wadsworth recalls that another former member of the *Only Fools* family returned, but this time as an audience member:

"At Gareth's invitation, Ray Butt came along to watch an episode. He was quite pleased that it was all made pretty much as he had left it, with pre-records, an audience warm-up man and five cameras. We were making those programmes in the same way he had made *Fools*. It was a lovely moment."

As far as comebacks in front of the camera, whilst Paul Barber appeared as Denzil in the series' opening episode, and Roy Heather appeared as Sid in the Nags Head (in a brief scene in the first Christmas special), no other *Only Fools* characters appeared in the series.

"A lot of people kept suggesting that Del and Rodney should come down to the farm," remembers Holderness, "but John was really quite clear that the series had to stand on its own two feet. By the time we'd got to series four I think he was of the mind that we'd established those characters, and it would be fun to bring some of the *Only Fools* characters down to the countryside, which was another reason why we were all so disappointed that series five didn't happen."

"A regime change at the BBC and the credit crunch meant they kept us hanging on for months," remembers Challis. By late 2009, the BBC had given an 'amber light' for a fifth series, but by the new year further changes in the BBC comedy department led to the series not continuing.

"They mucked us about in the schedules so not as many people saw us," continues Challis. "It wasn't the cheapest show in the world to do, it looked beautiful. I'm still living here and you remember little things

we did in locations all over the place. John loved his filming and was always ambitions and wanted to spread his wings. We're proud of it."

"I remember the times at Teddington Studio spent sitting in the viewing box that overlooks the audience, waiting for the show to begin," says Jim Sullivan. "I always felt so nervous that the jokes wouldn't land and that nobody would enjoy it. In contrast, my dad, being the seasoned pro, was always excited. He loved the live audience and got a real buzz from it. Looking back now I wish I had relaxed more because everyone was so nice and I got to learn so much. And of course, now that my dad is no longer here, I cherish the memory and experience even more. At the end of the day we had a great run and I still get letters from fans around the world saying how much they miss the show."

For any sitcom, running to 32 episodes in the early 2000s was a massive achievement, let alone one spun-off from such a well-known series. Thanks to repeat viewings *The Green Green Grass*' audience continues to grow with new fans drawn into the charming fun at Winterdown Farm.

"Since the series has been repeated on Gold, many more people have been stopping me and saying they have just discovered *The Green Green Grass*," remembers Holderness. "John and I had the great good fortune to be able to go on and keep these characters in our lives for four more years."

Above left: *Only Fools*' Sid appears in a brief cutaway shot to the Nags Head in *One Flew Over the Cuckoo Clock*.

Above: Bryan, Marlene and Mrs Cakeworthy.

Below: Christopher Ryan and Roy Marsden reprise their roles as Tony and Danny Driscoll.

considered writing the story as a novel, but by 2009, he decided to bring it to screen in a one-off film with the hope of it continuing into a series.

"I decided to return to those misty days of 1960 to meet all those characters then," Sullivan elaborated. "Joan's husband, and Del's father, Reg Trotter. Was he really as horrible as Del always described him? The younger Grandad, what was he like back then? And what part did the villain Freddy Robdal play in the Trotters' lives?"

Originally titled *Sex, Drugs & Rock 'n' Chips*, before being shortened to simply *Rock & Chips*, the series was designed to build upon snippets revealed in several *Only Fools* episodes, but more specifically *The Frog's Legacy* and the character of Freddy Robdal.

Since Robdal was to be central to the plot, it was important to secure Nicholas Lyndhurst's involvement, especially as he had already 'played' the part in the group photo seen in *Only Fools'* final episode, *Sleepless in Peckham*. With Lyndhurst on board and happy to be working with Sullivan again, the rest of the casting soon came together.

Future *EastEnders* actor Kellie Bright was tasked with bringing Joan Trotter to life. In a role that would both project the dramas of the period and foreshadow the familiar mannerisms of grown-up Del, Bright was fantastic in the role.

Above: Grandad (Phil Daniels), Del (James Buckley), Reg Trotter (Shaun Dingwall) and Joan Trotter (Kellie Bright).

Below: Freddy 'the Frog' Robdal holds his son Rodney.

Below right inset: Reenie Turpin (Emma Cooke) and Clayton Cooper (Roger Griffiths).

Below right: The Trotters move into their new home: 'Sir Walter Raleigh House'.

For many years John Sullivan had wanted to explore the back story of the Trotters in the 1960s and the circumstances that led to the incomplete family we met on the 12th floor of Nelson Mandela House in 1981's *Big Brother*.

For Sullivan, the key to unwrapping this past was the most important character who never appeared in the series, the Trotters' mother, Joan. "Throughout the series Del constantly referred to her and past events," the writer explained, "but much of his historical information was at best contradictory, and at worse outright lies. We were left with a situation where the only person who really knew what had happened was an unreliable witness."

With the working title of *Once Upon a Time in Peckham*, Sullivan had at first

To play a young Del Boy, with bucket-loads of confidence and a soppy heart to match, *The Inbetweeners* actor James Buckley was cast. *Quadrophenia* star Phil Daniels was cast as Grandad, and for his son Reg, who we only met once in *Only Fools*, actor Shaun Dingwall was brought in.

Rock & Chips also featured the rest of the Peckham gang as teenagers: Boycie, Trigger, Denzil and the already snidey Roy Slater. Alongside those familiar faces, the series introduces Del's "bestest" friend, Albie Littlewood, who we discovered in *Happy Returns* had died young after taking a short-cut across the railway line. Elsewhere, Del's former business partner Jumbo Mills – who appeared in *Who Wants to be a Millionaire* – forms part of the young Peckham Pack.

"This back-story to the Trotter saga and all its ghosts has been locked away somewhere in my mind for the last couple of decades," commented Sullivan at the time. "I thought it was about time I released them all and gave them their time in the sun."

The first episode of the series introduced the Trotters living in their terraced house on Orchard Street in 1960, with Joan holding down two jobs and Reg every bit the lazy git Del always made him out to be. Over the course of the story Joan meets and falls for recently released convict Freddy Robdal.

By the episode's end, the family have moved into their new flat and Joan has given birth to Freddy's child, Rodney, letting Reg believe that he is the father.

The spot-on 1960s production design recreates the period perfectly, showing Nelson Mandela House (known in *Rock & Chips* by its original name of Sir Walter Raleigh House) and the Trotters' flat when they were brand new. We also see the Nags Head in all its 1960s splendour, with its landlord Don (played by former *Only Fools* warm-up man Bobby Bragg) and his wife Gwen (played by Joan Hodges).

To further set the scene, each episode is brilliantly soundtracked by dozens of musical classics from the time.

After the successful opening instalment aired in January 2010, two more hour-long episodes were commissioned to continue the story in December 2010 and April 2011. Plans were afoot to complete the series with another four episodes which would explain how Freddy and his explosives expert pal "Jelly" Kelly *really* met their fate, and how

Above top left: Behind the scenes of Rock & Chips, producer Gareth Gwenlan, James Buckley, a visiting David Jason, Nicholas Lyndhurst and John Sullivan.

Above top right: Gerald 'Jelly' Kelly (Paul Putner) and Freddy.

Above: The manager of the Ritz cinema, Ernie Rayner (Robert Daws).

Below left: The Nags Head landlord Don (Bobby Bragg) and his wife Gwen (Joan Hodges).

Below: Denzil (Ashley Gerlach), Del, Trigger (Lewis Osborne), Jumbo Mills (Calum MacNab) and Boycie (Stephen Lloyd).

Right: Freddy and Joan in *Rock & Chips*.

Below: A Blue Plaque celebrating John Sullivan's career was unveiled at Teddington Studios in 2012, with (left to right), Ella Kenion, Sue Holderness, David Jason, John Challis, Jack Doolan, Nicholas Lyndhurst and Peter Heppelthwaite.

Joan coped without Freddy in her life. Tragically, these episodes were never made.

After a three-month battle with viral pneumonia, John Sullivan died on 22 April 2011, just a few days before the third episode of *Rock & Chips* aired. Tributes from across the world of television and comedy left no doubt that John was one of the greats in his field.

Gareth Gwenlan spoke about his friend and colleague: "John was a writer of immense talent, and he leaves behind him an extraordinary body of work which has entertained tens of millions of viewers and will continue to do so for many decades to come."

Although Tony Dow had stepped aside from directing Sullivan's most recent projects, the two were still close friends, having attended a Chas & Dave concert together only a few months previously. "The one thing about dying," Dow said, "is that now John is up there, I know that when I get there I'm going to have a bloody good laugh."

A special programme, *The Comedy Genius of John Sullivan,* was broadcast on 15 May, and made for a touching tribute featuring interviews with actors from across many of Sullivan's sitcoms.

In July 2012, a blue plaque was unveiled by a group consisting of cast members from both *Only Fools* and *The Green Green Grass* at Teddington Studios. David Jason and Nicholas Lyndhurst each spoke about their years of working with Sullivan.

"Nick and I have been so proud and privileged to have worked with him. John Sullivan made the ammunition and we just fired the bullets," said Jason, with Lyndhurst adding, "It was an absolute heartfelt privilege to be anywhere near the man and his work. He was a genius and must never be forgotten."

With *Rock & Chips,* Sullivan showed he was still very much at the peak of his powers as a writer, with three scripts laden with loving wit and emotional drama. Although only three specials were made, seeing Joan Trotter and her struggles brought to life enriched all of the many times Del alludes back to that period in *Only Fools.*

At the same time as developing *Rock & Chips,* Sullivan had also been considering bringing back *Only Fools* for another special, with a story revolving around Del Boy's 65th birthday and a possible retirement from Hooky Street.

"I think John would have written *Only Fools* for forever and a day," remembers Tony Dow. "I'm sure John would have found a way to do another special and David and Nick would have come back if the script was right. But they were getting of an age and it would have been slightly different. I think we had some discussion of making it, but another series, where they had all moved on and they were much older? I don't remember how far that got."

In January 2014, the BBC announced that Del Boy and Rodney would return to British TV screens for the first time in more than ten years with a short sketch in aid of Sport Relief.

Written by Jim Sullivan, and including some unused lines of his father's, *Beckham in Peckham* reunited Jason and Lynhurst with a very special guest.

"The people at Sport Relief contacted us to say that David Beckham was keen to do an *Only Fools* sketch," remembers Jim. "They already had a script written up. I can't remember who wrote it, only that it wasn't very good. I basically looked at what the Trotters do and what Beckham does and came up with the idea for the new underwear range. Of course, Del being Del, these would be personally autographed underpants and Rodney would be the one having to model them. The joke here was that on this occasion it wasn't just Del's sales spiel, he actually is in business with David Beckham."

Broadcast as part of BBC 1's Sport Relief evening on 21 March 2014, the 10 minute sketch sees Del and Rodney in the market selling the personally signed 'Golden Balls' underpants. With sales proving slow, the Trotters head to a nearby cafe for a spot of lunch, when the camera pulls back to reveal David Beckham sitting with them at the table.

Here it is revealed that David Beckham knows the Trotters and that, unlike the Viv Richards Cricket Bats mentioned in *It's Only Rock and Roll*, he did in fact sign the pants! Beckham goes on to discuss art with Rodney and to offer some modelling tips to help sell the gear.

For David Beckham, appearing in an *Only Fools* sketch was a dream come true, and to his credit the former footballer does a great job in both his scene in the cafe, and the end shot as he recreates a version of *Yuppy Love*'s unforgettable bar fall.

"We went to a hotel in London to meet Beckham and discuss the idea," recalls Jim Sullivan. "He originally wanted a scene where he and Del are legging it out of the market and diving into the back of a moving three-wheeled van, a funny image but not very practical. I suggested he parody the famous bar-fall, and he seemed very pleased with that."

Filmed at Wimbledon Studios, Tony Dow returned to the director's chair for the sketch, which also featured

John Sullivan's grandchildren Mia and Joe (who takes his football up to David Beckham to be signed, moments before the star casually leans back and falls to the ground).

"I had originally written Trigger into the cafe scene, and Roger Lloyd Pack was very kind about the script and eager to be involved," Jim remembers. "I knew he had been unwell but I had no idea how serious it was and he very sadly passed away the day before filming. After some very quick rewrites we shot the whole thing in a day and edited it all a week later. Everyone was on top form and David Beckham was a gentleman. He did the fall in one take."

In tribute, the sketch was dedicated to the memories of both Lloyd Pack as well as John Sullivan.

Naturally news of the sketch was seen by many fans as a possible entry point to a new series or another special, but this was something never considered.

"At the time I had only recently cleared up rumours of a new series being produced and promised that without my dad it would never happen. But the chance to bring Del and Rodney back to the screen for a one off with David Beckham was different. It was for a worthy cause and I could almost hear my dad saying 'Go for it!' It turned out to be a record-breaking year for Sport Relief, which just made it even more lovely jubbly!"

Above left: Del and Rodney have a new line: 'Golden Balls' pants (inset), signed by David Beckham.

Above: The Trotters are joined by David Beckham.

Below left inset: John Sullivan's grandson Joe.

Bottom left: David Beckham leans on a market stall cage...

Below right: Del and Rodney in 2014's *Beckham in Peckham*.

Above: Paul Whitehouse, Ryan Hutton, Tom Bennett and Jim Sullivan at rehearsals for the *Only Fools* musical.

Above right: The cast on set performing one of the many musical numbers in the show.

Below: The full original cast (left to right), Peter Baker (Trigger), Andy Mace (Mike), Paul Whitehouse (Grandad), Ryan Hutton (Rodney), Tom Bennett (Del), Adrian Irvine (Denzil), Chris Kiely (Mickey Pearce), Oscar Conlon-Morrey (Dating Agent), Pete Gallagher (Danny Driscoll), Dianne Pilkington (Raquel), Adam Venus (Tony Driscoll), Pippa Duffy (Cassandra), Samantha Seager (Marlene) and Jeff Nicholson (Boycie).

Ever since the 1980s, John Sulllivan had been considering the possibility of taking *Only Fools* into the setting of live theatre. Gradually the writer realised that a musical would be the perfect fit for the big emotions and even bigger laughs of the series.

"Dad had been toying with the possibility for some time and had met a few producers," recalls Jim Sullivan. "Sadly he never got to fully commit to it. He liked the idea but naturally was concerned about whether it was worth the risk."

In 2015, Jim decided the time was finally right to reignite the project. "I met with producer Phil McIntyre, who had also had a couple of meetings with my dad, and he was still keen to develop the idea," remembers Jim. "I then checked all of my dad's notes and discovered snippets of thoughts he'd scribbled down. I knew from talking with him that his focus was on his personal favourite episode *Dates*, where Del and Raquel first met, so that was my cue. Next I found a two-page opening scene and a dusty old audio cassette tape with the words 'This Time Next Year' written on it. I played the tape and there was Chas & Dave – as Del and Rodney – singing 'We're gonna be alright, the good times are on their way!' My mum recalled that back in the late 1990s Dad had gone to Chas's studio to work on a

song, and this was obviously the result. So we had the beginning of an opening scene and what I felt would make a great and uplifting final song."

To add another creative voice to the project, Jim invited comedian Paul Whitehouse to come on board and build on his initial ideas.

"I met Jim and I was very conscious of how precious the legacy was for him, and for me too as someone who loved the series," remembers Whitehouse. "But the fact that Chas Hodges and John Sullivan had already written a song together for it struck me as a positive element."

For Jim, the biggest challenge was to do justice to the story of the series which had spanned over two decades and included births, deaths and marriages. "The task was to boil that down into a single two hour story... with songs!" he recalls. "Ultimately it was very important to me that we respected the original work. I always try to think of the fans first, being one myself, and so right from the off we set out not to reinvent the series but rather to pay honest tribute to it. At its heart, *Only Fools* is all about family, loyalty and sacrifice, and this theme was perfectly summed up in the episode *Little Problems*, in which Rodney and Cassandra get married. It was a major crossroad in the life of Del

and Rodney and so I weaved that plot into the whole. It also gave us a chance to introduce the Driscoll Brothers and really up the ante for Del."

The lavish production, set design and costumes are all authentic to the world seen in the TV series, and the musical numbers are carefully considered and slotted into the staged action. In addition to the original numbers, the show also features the series' opening and closing titles and pivotal songs featured in the episodes, from Chas & Dave's 'Margate' to Simply Red's 'Holding Back the Years'.

"We had some songs that we knew we were going to include," explains Jim, "but when it came to new songs we focused on the beats of the story. For 'Bit of a Sort' I rewatched the dating agency scene and it felt only right to have a song about Del's idea of the perfect woman. It was also my attempt to write at least one song that had a 'Chas & Dave' feel to it. For Raquel's song 'The Girl' we needed something to introduce the character and a bit about her backstory. Since we were focusing on hers and Del's relationship, and since we'd already been introduced to the 'boy' (Del), I just thought 'okay, now let's introduce the girl'. 'The Tadpole Song' began when I had a vision of Boycie singing to his testicles – I'm not proud of it, but there you go. I already had the tune and then started on the lyrics. It was a lot of fun to write but I also wanted it to feel somewhat hopeful and sweet, and not just be about Boycie and Marlene tearing each other down. Paul then wrote a lovely and very poignant poem for Grandad. The first time I read it I got really choked up. As I was reading it I looked out the window just as it began to snow. I'm not sure why, but right there and then, as I read the words back, a tune began to play in my head and I scrambled to get it down. That was how, what is now, 'Raining for Grandad' came about."

"I thought that we shouldn't just revisit *Only Fools*," notes Paul Whitehouse. "It might sound a bit pretentious but I thought one of the unsung stars of the show was London itself. I came up with the idea for a song called 'Where Have All the Cockneys Gone?', a phrase I'd heard around, and it struck me as something that Grandad could empathise with and give voice to."

Opening in February 2019 to both audience and critical acclaim, *Only Fools and Horses The Musical* brings Peckham's finest to life in a lavish West End production. For its opening run Whitehouse also performed in the role of Grandad, alongside Tom Bennett as Del Boy and Ryan Hutton as Rodney.

Generations of viewers have heard the laughter of the lucky audiences present when all those classic *Only Fools* episodes were recorded, but thanks to the musical, fans now have the chance to laugh first-hand at the antics of Del Boy and co in a live performance that captures all the laughter and warmth of the original series.

"It was a big responsibility and I was very aware of the risk going into it," Jim explains. "You can never know for sure how these adaptations will translate and be received. I still feel the nerves every time I watch the show, but by the end I'm up and singing along with everyone else. I've been very fortunate to be working with such an incredible and talented team, from the amazing cast to our brilliant director, CJ Ranger, and our music arranger – the maestro – Stuart Morley. And, of course, the legend that is Paul Whitehouse. The real cherry on the cake for me is getting to see people enjoying themselves. It rarely fails to bring a tear to my eye to know that what my dad created all those years ago still brings so much joy to people."

Above: The original poster for the musical.

Below middle: Cassandra and Rodney on their honeymoon.

Below right: Del Boy reaches for the stars!

Bottom left: Grandad wonders, where have all the cockneys gone?

Bottom right: Trigger gazes into his crystal ball.

F orty years on from its creation, *Only Fools* continues to entertain millions of viewers. Generations have grown up with the Trotters as part of their lives, with families united on the sofa by the evergreen exploits of Del and Rodney.

In that sense, John Sullivan's writing does the almost impossible in breaking down the barriers between grandad and granddaughter, and everyone in-between. The truth in the characters' struggle is timeless, and the family bond is one instantly familiar to audiences, regardless of age, race or class.

Add to this a brilliant cast headed up by two of the finest comedy actors of our time, and you have a television series jam-packed with razor-sharp wit and rib-aching belly laughs, as well as pathos and genuine warmth.

In the years since the Trotters last appeared on screen, appetite for merchandise has never been greater, with fans seeking out everything from clothing to kitchenware and books. In 2021, the series even received the honour of having its own set of Royal Mail postage stamps released.

"It has become a true British phenomenon," recalls *Only Fools* Appreciation Society president Perry Aghajanoff. "Our conventions are fully booked almost instantly, and it is a joy to see fans celebrating together. Amazingly, there is also a younger generation watching the show, having been handed the magic baton from their parents."

In 1993's *Fatal Extraction*, an exasperated Raquel tells her 'significant other' that: "The only time my clothes look fashionable is when I'm watching UK Gold!" Today Gold is one of the highest rated digital channels in Britain and *Only Fools* is aired almost daily, more than holding its own alongside modern-day favourites.

Without knowing it, Sullivan future-proofed his scripts for the streaming age, with 64 richly-written episodes that actually benefit from repeat viewings, rewarding viewers who pay attention as subtle references are paid off a dozen or so episodes later, or even in a spin-off series.

"In preparation for *Rock & Chips*," Jim Sullivan remembers, "I had the task of researching every scene of every episode of *Only Fools* and compiling a history of the series, its characters and their relationships. All that was seen and mentioned; events, dates, places, family trees, the lot! It still amazes me how rich that world is, and that it all came from my old man's mind."

Perhaps the most unusual footnote to the series' success is that the Trotters really did go international, as authorised remakes of the series have seen the familiar episodes recreated by new casts in Holland, Portugal and Slovenia, to name but a few.

Much more than a situation comedy to fill the half hour before the news, *Only Fools and Horses* has grown to become a timeless parable for our age, on screen, in print, and now on the West End stage. The dysfunctional little South London family that John Sullivan created continuously reminds us of what really matters in life: family, friends, laughter, and, perhaps most important, not giving up on your dreams. After all... this time next year, eh?

Lovely Jubbly!

★ ONLY FOOLS AND HORSES....★

STARRING DAVID JASON AND NICHOLAS LYNDHURST
★★ WRITTEN BY JOHN SULLIVAN ★★

8th May. 6/13

20th May 6/9

ck.J.

OF CAR!

EXT' ELEV G-G

20' WHITE C/C DROPS

KITCHEN

DOTTED LINES SHOW
POSITION OF 8×4
SHEETS OF CHIPBOARD
(3/4") TO BE UNDER
PAINTED MR 8D
22 SHEETS OFF
CHIPBOARD

TROTTERS
CORRIDOR

TROTTER'S LOUNGE

PLAN SCALE 1:50 "TROTTERS' FLAT

"ONLY FOOLS AND HORSES ...." (4th Series)

Episode 1 - "Hole in One"

CAST LIST

Del .... DAVID JASON (Film/Studio)

Rodney .... NICHOLAS LYNDHURST (Film/Studio)

Grandad .... LENNARD PEARCE (Film/Studio)

Mike ....
(Pub Landlord)

Karen ....
(Barmaid)

Man ....
(Cockney-one speech)

Solly ....
(Solicitor)

Mr.Fraser ....
(For Trotters)

Mr.Gerrard ....
(For Brewery)

Judge ....

Clerk ....
(One Line)

FILM

Drayman N/S   Passers-by outside court N/S
Mate N/S   Court people N/S
Passers-by? N/S

STUDIO

Pub Customers N/S   Ushers N/S
Clerks N/S   Jury? N/S
Brewery Rep. N/S   Police? N/S

Audience Warm-Up ....

- c -